Bond

A STUDY OF HIS PLAYS

by

MALCOLM HAY

and

PHILIP ROBERTS

EYRE METHUEN : LONDON

First published in Great Britain in 1980 in simultaneous hardback and paperback editions by Eyre Methuen Ltd, 11 New Fetter Lane, London EC4P 4EE

ISBN 0 413 38290 7 (Hardback)
ISBN 0 413 47060 1 (Paperback)

Photoset and printed in Great Britain by
Redwood Burn Limited
Trowbridge & Esher

For John Mackendrick

Contents

Preface

To date, Edward Bond's works for the stage fall into three groups. The first begins with *The Pope's Wedding*, ends with *The Sea*, and includes his work from 1962–1973. The second is a group of three plays, *Bingo, The Fool* and *The Woman*. The third group so far comprises *The Bundle* and *The Worlds*. His plays have been premiered at the Royal Court theatre, the National, the Warehouse, the Northcott, Exeter, the Belgrade, Coventry, the University Theatre, Newcastle, the Almost Free, the Institute of Contemporary Arts and the Royal Opera House. He is widely regarded as one of the most important living dramatists. Yet his work is better known abroad than in the United Kingdom, and his plays are not as popular in this country as elsewhere. Critically, his work has invariably had a very mixed reception and opinions of his plays have tended to polarise over the last fifteen years.

This book tries to clear away some of the confusion about Bond's main preoccupations and about his theatrical methods. We have drawn on the notes and drafts of the plays and talked to many theatre artists involved in productions of his work in an attempt to make clearer those areas of his stage works which too often seem to be a source either of bafflement or of annoyance for those who see or write about them. In the Introduction, we have sought to place Bond's early writing in the context of the middle and late fifties generally and the context of the Royal Court theatre in particular by tracing his early career and the fifteen plays which precede *The Pope's Wedding*. Each chapter offers a critical evaluation of one or more of the plays, together with the details of its production history, where that is available, and some ideas about the directing, design and acting of the plays. These ideas are not meant to be prescriptive, still less definitive. They are offered as comments upon the theatrical process and upon the problems which sometimes arise if his work is played, as it is on occasions, in certain rather traditional ways. What we hope emerges is some sense of the ideas in Bond's work, and the means whereby those ideas are rendered in performance.

Given that Bond is a developing writer, this book is hardly the last word. As we write, *The Worlds* is in rehearsal for its London premiere and in March 1979, the Stutttgart Ballet Company performed Bond's *Orpheus*, with music by Hans Werner Henze. In a letter to the authors of 22 April 1979, Bond argues that 'Only what I could make work (or work enough) in a play have I believed – that is my job as a dramatist'. This book examines how Bond achieves his purpose.

Acknowledgements

This book would have been impossible in its present form without the patient and generous help of many theatre artists. We are particularly indebted to those who made themselves available for often lengthy, occasionally multiple interviews. They are:

Jonathan Bolt; Robert Brustein; David Carson; Gerald Chapman; Deirdre Clancy; Louis Criss; Ron Daniels; Howard Davies; John Dillon; William Dudley; Chris Dyer; Jack Emery; William Gaskill; David Giles; Peter Gill; Richard Gregson; Hayden Griffin; John Gunter; Mike Gwilym; Giles Havergal; Hans Werner Henze; Jane Howell; Marvin Kahan; Jonathan Marks; Christopher Martin; Bob Peck; Philip Prowse; Roland Rees; Louis W. Scheeder; Alan Schneider; Michael Sheehan; Jack Shepherd; Patrick Stewart; Henry Woolf.

We are equally obliged to the casts and production staff, who allowed us to watch rehearsals and who readily gave us their views, of the following plays:

Stone (I.C.A., June 1976); *A-A-America*! (Almost Free, October-November 1976); *The Fool* (Washington, October 1976); *Saved* (New York, October 1976); *The Bundle* (Warehouse, January 1978); *The Woman* (National Theatre, August 1978). And to the students who performed *Bingo* and *Early Morning* (University of Sheffield 1975 and 1977).

Edward Bond's agent, Margaret Ramsay, readily allowed us access to her files, as did his former American agent, Toby Cole, while his publishers, Eyre Methuen, were similarly generous.

The administrative staff of a great number of theatres, in the U.K. and abroad, supplied us with production details, the full results of which are embodied in our *Edward Bond: A Com-*

panion to the Plays (Theatre Quarterly Publications, 1978). We here acknowledge their assistance and hope they will forgive us for not being able to mention them by name. Such a list would be of great length. We must, however, mention individually those who have been of particular help in a number of important respects: Tony Coult; Harriet Cruickshank; Peter Coe; Michael Finegold; the late John Mackendrick; John Napier; Andy Phillips; Robert Ritchie; Richard Scharine; the staff of nearly all of the national centres of the International Theatre Institute; the Curator of Manuscripts, the Lilly Library, Indiana University, where the drafts of *Saved* are kept.

We are grateful to the photographers and owners of photographs who have given permission to reproduce pictures in the illustration sections between pages 128–129 and 224–225. They are: Edward Bond, Deirdre Clancy, Rosemarie Clausen, Chris Davies, Zoe Dominic, Anthony Gascoigne, Mike Henderson, Douglas H. Jeffery, Leeds Playhouse, Stefan Odry, Barbara Pflaum, Nicholas Toyne.

We are obliged to the B.B.C. for permission to quote from the transcripts of several radio programmes; and to the Research Fund of the University of Sheffield for financial assistance in the preparation of this book.

Finally, this work could not have evolved in the way it has without the help, encouragement and friendship of Edward and Elisabeth Bond over the last three years. We hope our work does his work some justice.

M.H. and P.E.R.
December 1979.

List of Abbreviations

Companion	HAY, MALCOLM and ROBERTS, PHILIP, *Edward Bond: A Companion to the Plays* (Theatre Quarterly Publications, 1978)
Coult	COULT, TONY, *The Plays of Edward Bond* (Eyre Methuen, 1977)
Gambit 17	*Gambit International Theatre Review*, no. 17 (1970)
Loney	LONEY, G., 'Edward Bond: the First Cycle'. *Performing Arts Journal*, 1,2, Fall 1976
Plays: One	*Plays: One* (*Saved, Early Morning, The Pope's Wedding*). Eyre Methuen, 1977
Plays: Two	*Plays: Two* (*Narrow Road to the Deep North, Lear, The Sea, Black Mass, Passion*). Eyre Methuen, 1978
Scharine	SCHARINE, RICHARD, *The Plays of Edward Bond* (Lewisburg: Bucknell University Press, 1976)
Stoll	STOLL, K.–H., 'Interviews with Edward Bond and Arnold Wesker'. *Twentieth Century Literature*, 22, 4, December 1976
Theatre Papers	*Dartington Theatre Papers* (Second Series) no. 1, 1978. Bond, Interview with M. Ferrand, 6 November 1973 (pp. 2–8). Howard Davies, Interview with P. Hulton, 6 January 1978 (pp. 9–17). Bond, Interview with P. Hulton, 24 April 1978 (pp. 18–27)
T.Q.	*Theatre Quarterly*

All quotations from Bond's plays are from the following editions:
The Pope's Wedding, Saved, Early Morning – Plays: One (Eyre Methuen, 1977)
Narrow Road to the Deep North, Lear, Black Mass, Passion, The Sea – Plays: Two (Eyre Methuen, 1978)
Bingo (Eyre Methuen, 1974, reprinted 1975)
The Fool and *We Come to the River* (Eyre Methuen, 1976)
A-A-America! and *Stone* (Eyre Methuen, 1976)
The Bundle (Eyre Methuen, 1978)
The Woman (Eyre Methuen, 1978)

Unattributed quotations, unless otherwise indicated, are from taped interviews. Details of all such interviews are given on pp. 308–10.

The Plays of Edward Bond

The Pope's Wedding
First performance 9 December 1962, Royal Court Theatre.

Saved
First performance 3 November 1965, Royal Court Theatre.

A Chaste Maid in Cheapside (*adaptation*)
First performance 13 January 1966, Royal Court Theatre.

Three Sisters (*translation*)
First performance 18 April 1967, Royal Court Theatre.

Early Morning
First performance 31 March 1968, Royal Court Theatre.

Narrow Road to the Deep North
First performance 24 June 1968, Belgrade Theatre, Coventry.

Black Mass
First performance 22 March 1970, Lyceum Theatre.

Passion
First performance 11 April 1971, Alexandra Park Racecourse.

Lear
First performance 29 September 1971, Royal Court Theatre.

The Sea
First performance 22 May 1973, Royal Court Theatre.

Bingo
First performance 14 November 1973, Northcott Theatre, Exeter.

Spring Awakening (*translation*)
First performance 28 May 1974, National Theatre.

The Fool
First performance 18 November 1975, Royal Court Theatre.

Stone
First performance 8 June 1976, Institute of Contemporary Arts.

We Come to the River
First performance 12 July 1976, Royal Opera House, Covent Garden.

The White Devil (*adaptation*)
First performance 12 July 1976, Old Vic Theatre.

A-A-America! (*Grandma Faust; The Swing*)
First performances 25 October 1976 and 22 November 1976 respectively, Almost Free Theatre.

The Bundle
First performance 13 January 1978, The Warehouse.

The Woman
First performance 10 August 1978, National Theatre.

The Worlds
First performance 8 March 1979, Newcastle Playhouse.

Orpheus
First performance 17 March 1979, Stuttgart Ballet Company.

Introduction

On 3 November 1965, the English Stage Company performed *Saved* by Edward Bond at the Royal Court theatre, London. The following is one eye-witness account of that first night:

> . . . it was extraordinary for two reasons. The first was the furore the play elicited in the audience that night and in the press and courts of law in the months that followed. I've always felt the stories of the opening of Ibsen's *Ghosts* and the first performance of Stravinsky's *The Rite of Spring* to be exaggerated romance justified by theatrical licence. That night at the Royal Court I came to believe in their veracity. There *was* verbal interruption and abuse in the course of the play, and there *was* the odd physical punch-up in the foyers at interval and afterwards. The cause was in particular the scene in which the baby was stoned to death . . .[1]

The author of *Saved* was a thirty-one year old writer who had been associated with the Royal Court since 1958. Edward Bond was born on 18 July 1934, one of four children, in Holloway, North London. His parents were farm labourers in Cambridgeshire. They moved to London in the thirties to find work, but their roots were rural. During the Second World War, Bond was evacuated both to Cornwall and subsequently to his grandparents' house near Ely. In 1946 he went to Crouch End Secondary Modern School, where he was not thought good enough to take the eleven-plus examination. While at school, he went to see a performance of *Macbeth*, given by Donald Wolfit at the Bedford theatre, Camden. He has described the impact that evening had upon him:

for the very first time in my life – I remember this quite distinctly – I met somebody who was actually talking about my problems, about the life I'd been living, the political society around me. Nobody else had said anything about my life to me at all, ever . . . I *knew* all these people, they were there in the street or in the newspapers – this in fact was my world.[2]

Bond lived his early years in a context which he always considered to be a political one. He recalls seeing a woman canvassing for Churchill in the 1945 General Election and knowing then that 'the class structure was dangerous and vicious'.[3] Growing up meant that 'You were always involved in questions of necessity. Politics was the way one experienced growing up'.[4] The *Macbeth* experience clearly translated this general awareness into a concentrated artistic form. It became a natural progression when Bond began to write at any length that he would write for the theatre.

After leaving school, Bond did various jobs, including that of a paint-mixer, an insurance clerk and a checker in an aircraft factory, before being called up for military service in 1953. He was stationed in Vienna with the Allied Army of Occupation and, curiously, the army did Bond a good turn:

What really started me writing seriously was being in the army because then that presented a lot of problems that I had to sort out in some way. So that was certainly why I became the sort of dramatist I became. The army's a sort of parodied version of civil society – it's without all the face-saving rituals and without all the social excuses and just the naked barbarism. It's a very corrupt form of society and a very foolish and vicious form which is an amalgam of sentimental sloppy reverence for dead idols combined with a real viciousness.[5]

It was while stationed in Vienna that Bond wrote what he calls his first serious work, a short story. On leaving the army after serving his two years, Bond began writing in earnest at a time when opportunities for unknown writers were about to become available in an unprecedented way.

While Bond was in Vienna, the newly-formed English Stage Company bought the lease of the Royal Court theatre from Alfred Esdaile, and opened on 2 April 1956 with Angus Wilson's *The Mulberry Bush*. Under the Artistic Directorship of George Devine, with Associate Director Tony Richardson, the

Company formulated a policy which centred upon the writer. Devine stated that 'Ours is not to be a producer's theatre or an actor's theatre; it is a writer's theatre'.[6] The aim was 'to find a contemporary style in dramatic work, acting, décor and production. We hope to present exciting, provocative and stimulating plays . . . And we want to attract young people'.[7] Plays were to be presented in repertoire and the writer encouraged to attend rehearsals (of any play, not merely his own). It is important to note that there never was at the Court an overall theory of production, but that the aim was to serve whatever text in whatever way best suited it, to allow the text to make its own demands and to devise a means of satisfying those demands. In 1955 the proposals of the new company were a considerable gamble, as Tony Richardson has noted. The new company 'would show a repertoire of modern plays and the possibilities of modern theatre, and . . . would also present plays which hadn't been produced in England, with the belief – and it was absolutely only a belief at that time – that this would produce a kind of renaissance of writing inside England'.[8]

As Bond returned to London, the Royal Court was proving an obvious magnet for new writers. Such was its reputation even in the early years of its existence and, more importantly, its unique position in London theatre, that it became the logical place for Bond to send his plays.

He did so in 1958, but wrote some apprentice work before that. He also for about two years up to 1958 embarked upon a systematic survey of as much theatre as he could afford and fit around a working day. Amongst other things, he saw work by Osborne, Brecht, Beckett, Ionesco, Arden, Simpson, Jellicoe, Delaney and Behan. Perhaps the most important single event was the visit of Brecht's Berliner Ensemble to London in August 1956, with productions of *Mother Courage*, *Trumpets and Drums* and *The Caucasian Chalk Circle*. Bond was, as were many theatre people of the day, massively impressed with the work of the Berliner. In one sense, that experience gelled with his responses to Wolfit's *Macbeth*, for he saw aspects of the Berliner style as resembling the style of the earlier actor-manager companies. Since he once remarked that he saw *Macbeth* in terms of music-hall (one of his sisters used to be sawn in half nightly in a music-hall act and Bond frequently stood in the wings watching the performances), there emerges something of a continuous thread in terms of how Bond saw the theatre and of those areas of theatre which stayed uppermost in his mind. More than this is the sense of theatre as a popular expression. Devine himself had insisted that his new company at the Court would not be *avant-garde* or highbrow, but a popular theatre. As Bond subjected himself to everything available in the theatre of the middle fifties, he also knew that 'what mattered and what intrigued one was what was happening at the Court. There was some relevance there that was lacking in other theatres'.[9]

One of Bond's first plays was *The Asses of Kish* which was entered for a competition announced by *The Observer* in the autumn of 1956. There were nearly two thousand entries and the results were announced in the spring of 1957. The number of entries indicates that Devine was not mistaken in supposing an enormous interest in playwriting, but *The Observer* did not pick out Bond's play as one of the more promising. Though the piece is clearly very early, there is, as always in the first plays, a suggestion of ideas, situations, phrases, which will be developed later on. The main character, Saul, thinks he killed his wife, which he did in order to rid the world of her. Finding out that she still lives, he laments that if he had killed her, he would have been better for it: 'The murder makes me innocent, not the innocence of doing nothing – most men do that and most men are fools . . .'. The phrase 'an innocent murder' resurfaces strikingly some fifteen years later in *The Sea*. At about the same time, Bond wrote five radio plays, all of which were rejected between December 1957 and September 1958, and to this period belongs a television play, *The Broken Shepherdess*, which tells of a boy forced by his circumstances (aged parents and the need to earn for the family) to relinquish hopes of further education. He eventually and bitterly resigns himself to a dead end situation, morally blackmailed into a hopeless existence, as were his parents, formerly country workers, who moved to London to find work. One more play, *The Roller Coaster*, belongs here and anticipates certain preoccupations which later are found in *Early Morning* (see Chapter Three).

While these plays were being written, an important development was taking place at the Royal Court, which was to affect Bond considerably. As the Court began to gather writers who either had had one show produced or who were thought to show promise, there arose a need for somewhere to meet. Ann Jellicoe recalls that the notion of a writers' group began to form, where Devine's wish to encourage new writers, make them feel a part of the company, might be satisfied. The first meeting of the Writers' Group was in January 1958, and, if Devine thought of it as in some way a social gathering, it quickly became a more active learning group. When Devine withdrew, largely so that the group would not feel inhibited, William Gaskill, who seven years later was to succeed Devine as Artistic Director, took over and the group comprised, amongst others, Ann Jellicoe, John Arden, Arnold Wesker, Keith Johnstone and Wole Soyinka. At that stage, Gaskill, with whom Bond was to form a long relationship from *Saved* onwards, had directed one play at the Court, N. F. Simpson's *A Resounding Tinkle* (December 1957).[10] Thus, just as the English Stage Company itself had begun work as Bond left the army, so the Writers' Group was formed at a time when Bond felt ready to submit his work, naturally, to the Royal Court.

About the middle of 1958, Bond submitted two plays to the Court. They were *Klaxon in Atreus' Place* and *The Fiery Tree*. They were read by Keith Johnstone, a member of the Writers' Group, and employed by the Court as a reader of new scripts. *Klaxon in Atreus' Place* attracted some attention, and Michael Geliot, then assistant to Devine, wrote to Bond on 22 December 1958 that he would 'very much like to meet you personally and talk about it with you. I shall only say now that it interested us very much, but that we feel that it needs some work done on it'. Bond was invited to meet Geliot shortly after Christmas. He then became a member of the Writers' Group. Though *Klaxon* was not performed, Bond worked on the play perodically (parts of it were rewritten in January 1960), and it provided the basis for what became *Early Morning* (see Chapter Three). *The Fiery Tree* is notable once more for beginning to explore the choices between opting out in despair or acting to modify an unacceptable *status quo*. Its central figure, Bill Sody, finally declares that 'while you can it's worth it to be free'.

The Writers' Group was both stimulus and practical help. It was run by directors, did not use actors, but concentrated upon offering writers a direct experience of acting techniques. There was very little analysis or discussion but, once a fortnight, writers met to improvise around a set theme, or a spontaneous idea, to act out Stanislavskian or Brechtian methods, to work through the acting process. Devine at one stage gave a series of sessions on the use of masks, which led to the writing of Arden's *The Happy Haven*. But more often than not, the aim was not to result in the writing of plays, but for writers to work towards some of the central activities involved in performance. Bond as a member of this group was the least known. He wrote three pieces for the Group, between 1959 and 1960. One was *I Don't Want to be Nice*, a ten minute sketch for a proposed group work called *Stars in Our Eyes*. It details the last ten minutes of a group of six people after a nuclear war. Another was titled *The Golden Age*, completed for the Writers' Group by October 1959, and the third was called *The Outing*, written between December 1959 and March 1960 (both of these plays are discussed in Chapter Nine). *The Golden Age* and *The Outing* found their way to Peter Gill, at that time an actor interested in directing (his directorial debut at the Court was not, however, until 1965), via Ann Jellicoe and as a consequence of both plays being seen at the Writers' Group. The proposal was that they might be put on at the amateur Questors' Theatre, Ealing. Gill wanted to do *The Outing* and though he and Bond talked about it, the idea fell through for a variety of reasons.[11] The Writers' Group itself began to fall away in 1960, mainly because it had fulfilled its function for most of its participants. Bond became a new play reader for the Court and during 1960 spent a long time on another television play on the theme of beauty and the beast. In January 1961, he began some notes for the play which was to become *The Pope's Wedding*. He was not to become a full time writer until *Saved* went into rehearsal in the Summer of 1965.

By 1965, Bond had therefore been associated with one theatre for seven years. His development as a writer is in one sense as regards these early years a paradigm of Devine's ideas to do with the encouraging of young writers, though Devine apparently did not have a high opinion of the quality of Bond's work (see Chapter One, note 3). Bond is a prime example of early Court policy, a debt which he repaid over the following years. When *Early Morning* was advertised in 1968 as celebrating the twelfth anniversary of the English Stage Company, it was perhaps with the conscious sense that his work spanned the life of the Company from just after its inception to 1968. Bond himself spoke of the theatre which gave him his opportunity in a letter of 6 January 1978:

> The Royal Court has been a very important place for me, and the theatre in general, I think . . . It was the pioneer theatre for new work when I first started to write seriously. It found and encouraged many new writers . . . Nowadays young writers get this practical training by working in the fringe . . . The Court had the resources (or at least pretended it had) of a major European theatre – it didn't have the money, but it certainly had the actors, designers and directors . . . This was a very fortunate thing for writers because it meant their work was subjected to the greatest scrutiny and pressure during production, and so they learnt to write to a certain standard . . . Young writers nowadays are in some ways less fortunate than I was because they don't always have the chance to work to those standards. Other pressures are put on them. Their plays often have to be short, quickly written, and the productions may have to be easily mobile . . . There are of course certain advantages in these things – but there are obvious dangers . . .

The distinction made by Bond is between the theatre of the sixties in England and that of the seventies, between the Royal Court as a focus for new work under the Artistic Directorship of George Devine and his successor, William Gaskill, and the emergence of a great variety of theatre groups working mainly in small experimental theatres. The work of the Court paved the way for what developed under the general umbrella title of 'the fringe' in the late sixties and seventies. As the Royal Court entered a quieter period after the early seventies, it became less of an obvious centre for new work. What had existed as a natural home for writers from Osborne onwards in part yielded its function to smaller, more categorically defined companies. Bond's own writing career reflects this process. Most of his plays up to 1975 were first presented at the Royal Court (the exceptions are *Narrow Road to the Deep North* and *Bingo*, which were both directed by Gaskill's former assistant at the Court, Jane Howell, and both of which transferred to the Royal Court; and *Black Mass* and *Passion*, his two short occasional pieces). Since 1975, his work has been seen at a variety of theatres (see the Preface). In this respect, 1976 proved an important year. He responded to three invitations to write work for, first, Gay Sweatshop (*Stone*, I.C.A., June 1976); second, a libretto for Hans Werner Henze (*We Come To The River*, Covent Garden, July 1976); and, third, a double bill for Inter-Action (*A-A-America*!, Almost Free, October and November, 1976). In the same year, Bond adapted Webster's *The White Devil* (Old Vic, July 1976) and in January 1977 wrote his first scenario for a ballet (as yet unperformed). All of these activities were part of a general broadening of range on Bond's part and he felt that 1976 had yielded a great deal.

Since 1976, Bond has become immersed in the performance of his work more than ever before. Although it was always his habit to make himself available at rehearsals, he began to move towards a more thorough analysis of the job of acting. While holding the Northern Arts Literary Fellowship at the Universities of Newcastle and Durham (1977–79), he used the opportunity not only to conduct acting workshops, but also to develop his latest play, *The Worlds*, with his students. He said at the time of directing *The Woman* at the National Theatre (August 1978), which was his directing debut in Britain, that he had reached a stage

> where I'm making new demands on actors in my writing, which may be good or may be bad. But if I'm making these demands, then it seems to me I have to interpret the making of these demands . . . in order to learn more about my own craft, I have to get more closely involved in the actor's aspect of it. You have to get as deeply involved in the realities and nature of your craft as you can.[12]

This investigation has extended, so far, to returning to the Royal Court theatre in November 1979 to direct *The Worlds* again, this time with the Activists (the youth theatre of the Court).

The seventies have also seen the development and publication with the plays of related material by Bond. The 'Author's Preface' to *Lear* began a sustained series of prose, poems and notes to do with the particular play basically not as explanation but as providing a context for the staged work. This becomes a regular feature of Bond's work unlike his plays of the sixties (the 'Author's Note' to *Saved* is basically a response to the hostility with which it was received). The poems (many of which were collected and published in 1978) represent work in progress towards the finished play. Bond, in a letter of 24 March 1977, confessed to not liking writing his prefaces and went on to explain their *raison d'être:*

> The prefaces only rarely refer directly to the plays – but this is by design. I would like the reader of the prefaces to get involved in problems about the world and then, by a sudden reference, to transfer his roused interest to the play. In this way he stops thinking of the play as a fantasy . . . and sees (I hope) that it is really about aspects of his own life . . . I don't want them to feel that my plays are a 'serious' exposition about life that can only be understood by footnotes. They can be verified by walking down the street . . . So the prefaces just give the general ideas and problems behind the play.

Bond happens to be a playwright, but he has never seen the theatre as something which exists in a way isolated from any other activity. His theatre is an expression of, and contribution towards, the means of living rationally, the means of making a sane world. His views have not changed fundamentally from the earliest days:

> I think it was because I was brought up in a war, but the moment I start sitting at my typewriter then immediately I get involved in those fundamental questions simply because I was born into a society in which you didn't know if you were going to last the day. You could have been killed. When I was very young I saw people running for their lives. So those questions come very naturally to me . . . I am concerned with important issues. That's part of my basic response. The subjects I deal with are not minute. They are full scale. They are about the future of our society. Whether I deal with them well others must judge.[13]

The plays to date reflect a continual process of analysing the nature of modern problems as carefully as possible. Their writer warns against the danger of incomplete analysis: 'One of the things about the twentieth century is that it has been full of nauseatingly simplified situations. They have been disastrous and I can't find any conviction or desire to do anything other than to try to understand the problems as completely as I can.'[14] They also reflect a consciously developing stagecraft, and a need always to go further:

> I wouldn't write *Saved* now, but I think it's a very honest account of what it felt like to be that age working in a factory and living in that sort of society. One couldn't understand what alternatives there were, one could see the pity and the misery of it all. But I could not now write in that way. That play must just stand on its own feet and be treated with whatever respect it can earn. You have to respect it for what it has to say at that time, just as I respect the plays of Shakespeare without accepting them as a final revelation of the truth.[15]

I

The Pope's Wedding

On 17 April 1962, George Devine wrote to Edward Bond about the play that was to be the author's first performed work:

> Congratulations on the new play, which I have at last read. Although I think it is not right yet, I do think you have made a considerable advance.
> The group of young people is very alive. I think the progression of the play needs more clarification. At one reading anyway it is difficult to see how the play develops dramatically from scene to scene, and although some of this could emerge during production, I think it should be clearer in the script. This refers particularly to the first half of the play.
> I have talked to Keith [Johnstone, who directed the play] about it and he has some very definite ideas, which I think are good, and to which I think you should listen, and I hope he will see you soon.

The play under discussion was *The Pope's Wedding*. Set in and around a small town in rural Essex, the play shows in sixteen short scenes the growing obsession of Scopey, one of a group of young labourers, with Alen, an old recluse. Scopey becomes fascinated with Alen's way of life and intrudes more and more into it. Finally, he kills the old man and takes his place. The point of the title (and of the original title, *The Pope's Wife*) was later explained by Bond: 'The pope's wedding is an impossible ceremony – Scopey's asking for an invitation for something that isn't going to happen, that *can't* happen'.[1] The invitation Scopey wants is to share what Alen knows. But Alen knows nothing, and the play ends in tragedy.

The Pope's Wedding was first performed at the Royal Court on

9 December 1962 as a Sunday night production without decor. Such productions had begun in 1957 as part of the Court's policy of promoting new dramatists, giving them the opportunity to see their work on the stage. Plays were rehearsed up to dress-rehearsal standard and shown with minimal set and costume, all on a very low budget.[2] As with all Sunday night performances, economy was uppermost. The set for *The Pope's Wedding* was built out of the set of Devine's production of *Happy Days*, which had finished a little before Bond's play. Winnie's heap of sand was 'turned upside down in some way', Bond recalls, 'and a door was cut into it. It made a funny sort of cone shape'. Originally, there were to have been two Sunday performances, but a member of the cast was committed elsewhere. Bond recalls that Harold Goodwin made Alen 'too small and tetchy, whereas I wanted him to appear more sombre and more as he appeared in Scopey's imagination rather than the tetchy man he was. The idea is that only towards the end should he become tetchy and before that he should be rather enigmatic. He was meant to be very tall [but] there's no doubt about it, it was a good performance'.

Goodwin himself was very pleased. He wrote to Bond on 10 December: 'So pleased about your notices in the press – but the main thing is that we all know in our hearts that we "pulled it off" last night, in spite of everything. Keith, the actors and yourself all became a whole living unit . . . thanks so much for writing me such a wonderful part'. Philip Lowrie, who played Scopey, was similarly happy about the production and wrote to Bond on the 18th December that it was 'a pleasure to work on something that could stand up to varying interpretations. I still feel that I don't know Scopey – though I had a glimmer of understanding once or twice'. The feeling generally at the Court was that the production had been effective. Devine, returning from a Brazilian tour, was unable to see the play. He apologized to Bond in a letter of 13 December: 'I am terribly sorry I missed seeing your play. It was a matter of my plane being five hours late. I hear it went very well and Keith did a very good job on it. I am asking Miss Dixon [the General Manager] to commission a new play from you, as we would like to have one and it would give you the encouragement that we feel is right'.[3] Bond received five guineas for the production and £25 for the option taken up by the Court. The play was submitted for the Charles Henry Foyle New Play Award.

Though it was not performed professionally in Great Britain again until 1973, it was nevertheless a reasonably auspicious beginning.[4]

Reviewers were generally sensitive to the play, although Tynan in the *Observer* (16 December) found it 'Too long, too portentous, too elliptical'. Reviews of later productions were more appreciative. Of the Northcott theatre's performances at the Bush, London, in July 1973, John Peter in the *Sunday Times* pondered whether Alen was 'an emotional intruder, or is the marriage already dead of boredom? The play creates a breathy, palpable sense of a small community . . .' (17 July). John Elsom in *The Listener* accurately gauged the two worlds: 'The short scenes alternate between village life, with its cricket matches and pub chatter, and the isolated hut, swinging between the extremes of togetherness and alienation' (19 July). The best description of the group came from Patti Hardy in the *West London Observer*: 'The country boys with their tight jeans, greased hair and rolled cigarettes; the giggling arm-in-arm girls, their white high-heels, the green factory overalls, and above all, that gondola wicker basket which no self-respecting female of that time was without. And the complete lack of culture amongst them . . .' (17 July). Anthony Vivis debated in *Flourish* the killing of Alen: 'Why Scopey suddenly kills Alen is not exactly clear, but it is not a game that gets out of hand like the baby-stoning in *Saved*. Perhaps the only way Scopey can get any independence of the world is by robbing another man of his . . .' (Summer 1971). The *Birmingham Post* commented on the play's pace in the production at Birmingham in 1973: it was directed 'at the unplanned snail's pace of real life. To begin with, this was eerie and faintly irritating, but gradually the action takes on an unstoppable inevitability' (23 November).

Scopey, the protagonist, is seen initially as one of a group, one of a gang whose age range is from seventeen to twenty-four and part of his curiosity is directed at a seventy-five year old man and what he knows. Bond:

> Why is it that people change very often into a sort of dramatic opposite of themselves? You see someone who is very old, and they tell you about their youth, and you think, well, how could you have done all these things and now become this? And . . . the idea . . . was to see

how something *could* go so drastically wrong. Scopey doesn't understand his situation at all, not at all, but I wanted the audience to understand the way it could happen to Scopey, who I suppose is a typical member of the audience in a sense.[5]

But to begin with, Scopey is not distinguishable in the first two scenes of the play from the rest of the group. He is as much a part of the scuffles, irritability, moaning and joking as anyone else. Both scenes show a group with nothing to do and no money. They wander from subject to subject or else someone like Bill harps on the same theme of wanting a drink. The topics are alternately important and trivial and by the time that Pat and June arrive, the scene is charged with the latent energy of a group lolling about in the close atmosphere of a summer evening. The snatching of Pat's bag is no more important than kicking a stone about earlier, except that the release of energy leads to the bag being broken, at which point, logically, the group rounds on Scopey, who started it, as a way of disassociating itself from Pat's tears. Scopey's speech, his longest in the scene, where he says he'll mend the strap, does not show 'a sensibility different from the others'.[6] It's an attempt to rejoin the group and evidence of feeling slightly guilty. The bag game is not 'the friendly harassment' of Pat[7], for it contains the charge of all the frustrations of the earlier part of the scene. It creates the context of an aggression which later on results in some of the mob attacking Alen's hut, not because they hate Alen, or Pat, but because both are convenient objects on which to vent their aimless animosity. In scene two, Scopey's identity is merged with the others. In the cricket discussion he carefully says little. It is only later (scene five) that there is the suggestion that he has been training for the match, but again, this is not evidence of Scopey's drawing apart from the group. Rather it's the careful action of someone who is only twelfth man and who would not welcome the group's reaction if it were to learn that he had been training for a match in which he was unlikely to play.

Scopey's move away begins rather with the cricket match itself (scene four), and even then he is content to bask in the admiration of his mates. What this scene does do, however, is show a Scopey alternating patience and frenzied excitement as, against all expectation ('Yoo 'ont never get thirty-two, but owd Joe's good for a dozen.'), he makes the runs. His success brings him closer to Pat (scene five) whose previous encounter with Scopey had ended in tears over the torn handbag. It is a glorious day for Scopey but he prefers to spend its aftermath with Pat and not in the pub with the rest of the team. For a brief while, Scopey is in control of his situation. He is the local hero and he has stolen Bill's girl. The cricket match offers a glimpse of an alternative. But from then on the alternative becomes increasingly sombre. For the rest of the play, Scopey looks to recapture his moment, and part of his obsession with Alen is that the old man is able to exist without such moments. For the cricket match is substituted Alen's newspapers and his recollection of the past. Scopey's life consists of episodes, of short sequences, limited to the duration of throwing a bag about, playing in a cricket match, making love to Pat. Alen appears to be able to sustain more than moments, to offer connected significance rather than spasmodic intervals. The structure of the play reflects the structure of Scopey's life: 'when I started to write I discovered I could only tell the truth in those short episodes and I felt those long scenes, those long developments aren't somehow true to my experience . . . [Life is] much more, you see, full of contrasts and short things'.[8] Though the search ends in tragedy, it is important that the audience should value Scopey's unremitting search.

Out of the scene with Pat comes Scopey's first fleeting contact with Alen, as he waits for her outside the hut while she is cleaning up for the old man (scene six). The relationship between Alen and Pat is not clarified, although Pat promised her dying mother that she would look after Alen. Scopey's attitude to Alen at this point is the same as that of any of the others: Alen is a kind of spellmaker, and also someone useful as a whipping-boy. There is nothing to suggest that Scopey has any further interest in him. Similarly in scene eight, where Scopey and Alen come face to face, Scopey's tone is derisory and threatening. The growth of Scopey's fascination is so gradually revealed that by the end of scene eight – halfway through the play – there is little to suggest how it will develop. What intervenes and precipitates the development is the stark reality of Scopey's marriage to Pat. Her vision of Scopey in scene five ('You look beautiful all in white . . . Sounds like a bride') and scene six ('I keep seein' 'im chargin' up an' down in 'is white') is diminished in scene seven to not being able to marry in white ('No money') and in scene nine, the two are presented in a domestic situation, talking *'in the clichés of argument, but they sound friendly'*. Scopey's dissatisfaction with his way of life and his distrust of romantic alternatives has been made clear in scene seven, when Pat produces a postcard from a girl friend, Betty Legs. She is married to a U.S. serviceman and the postcard shows an idyllic picture of where they live. While Pat and June look enviously at the postcard, Scopey's reaction is one of distrust. What he is looking for cannot be satisfied by that kind of illusion. From the cricket match romance, Scopey and Pat move to a bare tied cottage with the lights fused. Scopey is already looking for a way out and offers to take Alen's food to him, and to sweep out his hut (scene nine). In so doing, he is already committing himself to something which would afford the other lads endless amusement were it known. Yet he cannot master his growing interest. He lies to Alen in scene ten about why he has come instead of Pat ('For Chriss sake – she's ill!') in order to get in and then talks non-stop to the frightened old man. To start with, Scopey uses the same bullying tone as before, modified in some way by his amusement at what he is doing. He gets little but grunts and moans from Alen, but then reveals his curiosity in a string of questions:

> What yoo get up to all day? Yoo must 'ave plenty a time, yoo ent put a finger t'this place for months . . . Where yoo sleep? . . . Where yoo put it? . . . 'Ow long yoo been 'ere?

Because Alen says nothing in reply, Scopey assumes there is something to tell. By now, the audience knows that Scopey will have to return. The next time they are shown together is also the last time Alen is seen alive.

Before the climactic scene twelve, Bond interposes another, grimmer, domestic scene. It is months later; the developing relationship between Alen and Scopey is assumed, while Pat and Scopey's marriage has settled on rock bottom. Scopey is ostensibly putting in a great deal of overtime and Pat is slowly reverting to the original group. She goes round to June's house and she has been seeing Bill. Scopey by now has lost all contact with his mates. Such information emerges gradually from the scene as Pat and Scopey talk almost reluctantly to each other. Scopey's neglect of Pat is obvious. Whereas in scene nine he was still eager to go to bed with her, in this scene she tries to persuade him – but without success. He wants to talk about Alen's watch and the scene ends in a row. As Scopey's obsession develops, the marriage declines.

Scene twelve between Alen and Scopey (with Pat as an unwelcome intruder for Scopey) is both climax and anticlimax mixed. It is here that the development of the strange relationship is shown for the only time. As Pat used to, Scopey begins writing the shopping-list out. Until Pat arrives, Alen and Scopey talk more than ever before. Alen is now the one asking questions and some of them cannot help but suggest to Scopey that Alen possesses some kind of wisdom: ''Ow owd's yoor Dad? . . . What's 'e done? What's 'e got a show?'. Scopey's absolute involvement is shown by the fact that he, unknown to Alen, was outside Alen's hut the previous night. Alen's involvement with Scopey has persuaded him to give Scopey the key to the hut. The two moments of their greatest intimacy (and for Scopey, his greatest disappointment) are sparked off by Alen's old army greatcoat, and by one of the many photographs he has hoarded away. The photograph shows a different life style, a lady in a carriage with her dog, and a servant holding the horse's head. The ambiguity which characterises the following exchanges is set by Alen's saying 'I know 'er. Know 'oo she is?', when in fact 'she' is the photograph, not the lady: 'I bought she out a that owd scrap shop stood on the corner a Dunmow. She were stood out on the pavey in a box'. Though Alen breaks the ambiguity quickly ('Why'd I buy that owd junk? She could a been dead seventy, eighty year'), Scopey's imagination cannot let it go. He wants to know which shop, which town, had Alen ever actually seen the lady. And the conclusion leaves Scopey's curiosity unsatisfied at the precise point when he feels he nearly has an answer:

Ent you ever seen that lady when yoo was a boy?
ALEN. How?
SCOPEY. Walkin'? Shoppin'? Ridin'?
ALEN. When I were a boy.
SCOPEY (*after a long pause*). Cold now.
ALEN. Years turned.

'When I were a boy' might mean 'Yes'. It might mean he collected things when a boy. 'Cold now' can refer both to the old photograph and Scopey's situation and the turning of the year. The beauty of this exchange is to combine past and present as an impenetrable conundrum for Scopey and a reflection of a life passed for Alen. The two figures are for that moment united as people who have not made sense of their situation. One young, one very old. The scene gathers pace again as Alen shows Scopey the greatcoat hidden between the blankets, bought when Alen was young. The link between them is reinforced by Alen's giving Scopey this spare coat. As Scopey puts the coat on, the visual picture presented to the audience is of two figures settling close together. The coat pockets are sewn up in order to keep the coat's shape and through the scene, Scopey picks away at the thread. After the row and at the scene's end he finds that the 'Pockets're empty'. As Scopey begins to open the pockets, the relationship is shattered by the unexpected arrival of Pat who, though she moans about looking after Alen, had remarked in scene eleven, 'I miss gooin' up there'. Alen reverts to brief responses when Pat is there, picks up the dialogue as if Pat had never been away and his obvious pleasure at being given some boiled sweets by Pat enrages Scopey as he listens from behind the couch. As Pat leaves, the scene is fanned rapidly into a row as if Pat had disturbed a domestic scene and Scopey reverts to the loutish tone which characterised his first approaches to Alen. The newspapers are for standing on, the pockets are empty, and in his despair, Scopey falls back on the popular image of Alen as a wartime spy, one of the random accusations of the other villagers. Alen in turn shows a different side of himself, that of a fire and brimstone preacher: 'Tobacco an' drink are Satan's whores'. In the first version of the play, written early in 1961, Alen is presented as a kind of Old Testament prophet. He attacks Pat for not looking after him properly: 'I'll put the curse of god on you. May the lord strike you down. The lord smite ye'. In this version, the group wrecks Alen's room as he rants: 'The lord will curse you. He will strike you down between the night and the morning'. Scopey's contempt for Alen is also for himself now that the illusion is shattered and in the face of his anger, Alen quaveringly begins to sing a remembered hymn of agony, blood and sacrifice. Scopey makes one more attempt to extract something from Alen and is faced with confirmation that the image he has so carefully built out of his need is false. 'I don't believe that' means the reverse of what it says. Without resources or understanding but a driving need, Scopey kills Alen and takes his place:

> In the first play, the young man kills the old man because there's absolutely no possibility of any communication between them. Not just words, not even feelings. If you cannot convey feelings, then you're really isolated, aren't you? If you're isolated, you become violent, like people in a madhouse. And this leads to murder.[9]

If Scopey cannot convey feelings, by now to anyone, the external world is seen to be continuing without him. The scene that follows (thirteen) shows the group again. June and Joe have moved from bickering in scene one to holding hands and the rest talk in the same way as they did at the start of the play, without Scopey. Bill sees Pat home, while, in the next scene (fourteen), the rest attack Alen's place after having been in the pub. As they do, there is a variation on the much earlier scene (three) where Alen was seen for the first time – a recluse, alarmed by anything outside his hut. Now Scopey is in Alen's coat and indifferent to the noise. He has begun the process of attempting to unravel the meaningless:

> What you see in *The Pope's Wedding* is a sort of identity of opposites, I think. You see two completely separate worlds, and then, when they are brought together, they are the same world . . . The important thing is not to be intrigued or puzzled by images, but always to understand them. So that what I wanted to do was to try and get inside the image, and see what it was all about. That is what Scopey does in the play, and in the end he kills a man and wears his clothes in order to find out. And of course there's nothing there. The truth about this man's charisma, you see, is that it's based on nothing.[10]

Scopey emerges from the hut once more during the play to find himself an interloper in the scene between Pat and Bill, who are now back together again as they were in the first scene. Bill and Scopey talk to each other like the strangers they have become. As soon as Bill and Pat have gone off to the pub, all Scopey's actions reflect Alen's. He collects newspapers and returns to the shack, unable to resist the notion that there is still a truth there to be discovered. Instead, Pat discovers him, Alen's body, and a situation which none of them will ever be able to understand, still less articulate. Scopey does not reply to Pat's wanting to know why he has killed Alen, and the text shows Scopey dwelling only on how he killed the old man. In the first draft of the play, Scopey does respond but only with 'I don't know. It can't be helped. I don't know'. Even such a minimal response as this is cut out of the final version to show Scopey utterly absorbed by his preoccupations.

The development of *The Pope's Wedding* reflects Bond's assertion that 'the structure of the play actually lays down your view of the world. The thing about the structure of a play is that what is vital to human beings is their relationship to society and the sort of society in which they live . . .'.[11] *The Pope's Wedding* shows a steady intensity of focus upon Alen's hut and the consequent displacement of scenes involving the rest of the group, including Pat. Thus by scene thirteen, set exactly as scene one, the group is peripheral. By the penultimate scene (fifteen), Pat and Scopey's house is equally peripheral. The narrowing down of the location of the scenes to Alen's hut and its subsequent expansion in the play's scheme is organised to show the extent of Scopey's preoccupation with Alen. The group's last active part in the play is in scene fourteen, where it is only heard attacking Alen's hut. As the world thus represented is relegated, the hut, from being briefly seen in scene three, alternates from scene six onwards as a magnet for Scopey. The group's steady exclusion makes it assume another function which, according to Bond, emerged rather than being planned:

> well, it wasn't my conscious design but there is a sort of central character [and] almost a Greek chorus . . . people act like choruses and that I think is a very useful dramatic device, because if I'm concerned as I always am with this basic relationship, the individual and society, then . . . the chorus can represent society and one [also] has the individual.[12]

The play shows the group's preoccupations in an obvious manner throughout. They do not alter. In the first two scenes, the talk is essentially of sex, beer, money, work; Scopey is a part of a common attitude. The context is the working week. The work is on the farm for the boys and in the factory for the girls. The boys' activity is determined by the time of the year. As the play opens it is nearing harvest time. Ron in scene one has oiled 'that owd Ferguson this mornin'' and Lorry in scene two has hung the scythe 'up in owd apple tree t'take the rust out on 'er'. With the harvest comes the annual village cricket match. Scopey is still part of these concerns. By scene fifteen, the row between Scopey and Pat, with Bill an embarrassed onlooker, is about money, the cricket match (for a year has passed by), and the harvest:

BILL. When yoo start bringin' it in?
SCOPEY. Anytime, I reckon.

But now Scopey is not employed, has not brought money home for a while, Pat has reverted to Bill and the group, and Scopey has killed Alen. Bill and Pat go off to the pub for the booze up after the match. Scopey does not.

The time scheme of the play revolves around the idea of harvest and the ironic relation this has to the lives of the characters, for whom harvest is no more than a time of increased work. The sequence is planned so that the concept of harvest relates both to the social circumstances of the group and also to the completely fruitless act of murdering Alen. Bond remarked that the play is 'set in a rural background, with an emphasis on the seasons coming and going. But also with the idea of industrialism on the horizon, just beginning to invade that community'.[13] As industry (presumably indicated by the new estate at Dunmow) begins to appear, the use of time within the rural community demonstrates both timelessness and economic pressure. On the one hand the larger background is created by the cyclical sense of harvest, by the sixty years of the annual cricket match and by Tanner Lob dying of cancer; on the other, immediate time is a matter of the day's proximity to pay-day, where Thursday is the dead spot of the week. Later on in the play, it is shown that, once married, Pat and Scopey have not been out together for months. Against Alen's sense of the past in scene twelve is set the action of Scopey in scene fourteen, as he tries to prise open Alen's watch with a knife. The timeless sense of the setting, its inevitable round, is part of Scopey's inarticulate sense of being trapped. His way of attempting to disturb the pattern is to act violently. The last view of him in the play is, ironically, his sitting in Alen's place, waiting.

The setting of the play reflects this process. Bond:

In these sixteen scenes the stage is dark and bare to the wings and back. Places are indicated by a few objects and these objects are described in the text. The objects are very real, but there must be no attempt to create the illusion of a 'real scene'. In the later scenes the stage may be lighter and Scene Fifteen may be played in bright light.

The minimal settings of a railing for scenes one and thirteen, an apple for scene two, the outline of the bottom of a pub sign for scene five, a bench for scene seven and a few bits of furniture for Pat and Scopey's place in scenes nine, eleven and fifteen, obviously have a functional use. They locate the scene. They also describe the context and reflect the activity in the scene. Thus the railing is 'used for leaning against' and it is a way of showing the desultory activity of the scene. When Hayden Griffin designed the production of the play at the Northcott theatre, Exeter (which subsequently transferred to the Bush theatre, London), his aim became to work for specifics, using Brechtian models. Thus the railing was 'not green, Victorian, [but] long ones, used to wait for buses'. The function of the railing was to evoke what happens in a small rural town once the day's work is finished. The apple onstage in scene two is used for teaching purposes by Griffin as an example of why 'the simplest possible image is always the strongest. The green apple, if you place it properly, and you get the bare space right, evokes the countryside immediately. You don't need to feel the corn, the sky. He [Bond] knows that'. The inn sign is carefully described as 'the dark outline of the bottom part' and it is used as a means of indicating that Scopey is already moving away from the tightly-knit community in the pub. The image helps the scene to demonstrate the developing gap between Scopey and his former friends. Throughout the play (and in Bond's subsequent work) there is a consistent deployment of simple, expressive settings of this kind, and of objects which define social circumstances and relationships.

In contrast to such sparseness is the cluttered shack in which Alen lives. Its congestion and randomness fascinate Scopey and he misreads its significance, until scene twelve. Before Pat's entry in that scene, the newspapers and the clutter Alen has collected seem to Scopey to hold a secret, which he is on the verge of discovering. As he, enraged by Alen's welcoming Pat, articulates his anger, the setting and objects quickly acquire conventional status. They change their function because Scopey's relationship with them has changed. As Scopey redefines them (as 'functional' rather than 'expressive'), Alen's world and the world outside are seen by Scopey as the same world. There is no mystery. It is this realisation above all which drives Scopey to murder. And then it is Scopey's refusal to accept it which turns him into Alen. In the last scene he is surrounded by five hundred tins of food, which Pat has continued to buy for Alen. The tins define the determination and also the hopelessness.

Hayden Griffin in designing the Exeter production was influenced by the landscape where Bond's parents and Bond himself subsequently lived and by the necessity for a fluid transition between Alen's hut and a bare stage. When designing *Lear* for Bond's production in Vienna (January 1973), he used to drive up from Exeter to Bond's home outside Cambridge. During 1972, he saw the countryside in Spring, late Summer and Autumn

> and the landscape was extraordinary. The sky was indigo blue and the fields as far as you could see were ripe corn . . . and the green trees, that Constable green or Gainsborough green against this brooding, indigo sky. And other times I'd see it with a solid green landscape, bright, bright, pale blue sky. And then I saw it again in Autumn. When I did *The Pope's Wedding*, I couldn't think of it without that background.

Bond's note on the play's lighting are part of his instructions which insist upon there being no attempt 'to create the illusion of a "real scene"'. Generally, the stage is to be dark. The stage may be lighter in the later scenes, with the option to play scene fifteen in bright light. The note has a clear Brechtian tone to it. It stresses the use of lighting both to resist illusions (particularly romantic illusion) but also, and more importantly, to make statements about the various situations in the play. Thus the darkness of the stage for a good part of *The Pope's Wedding* is not only a rejection of naturalism, but also a way of showing the situation of the figures in the play. The limitations of the characters, the limited routine of their lives and their economic imprisonment are strongly expressed by the meagre amount of light available to most of the scenes. It spreads across both the village world and Alen's hut. It insists on the sameness of the two locations. The light may grow, according to Bond, 'In the later scenes' and this perhaps relates to the growing relationship of Scopey and Alen, that is to say, from scene ten onwards, where Scopey cooks for Alen. When Bond suggests that 'Scene Fifteen may be played in bright light', it is because by then Scopey has assumed Alen's status and is virtually an interloper into a domestic scene between Bill and Pat. It is, crucially, a scene which, a year later, repeats some of the topics of the first two scenes. It is the first meeting of Scopey and Bill (and by implication, the rest of the boys) since scene two. It is here that the worlds are interfaced, and Bill and Scopey talk as the strangers they have become. The point, according to Bond, is that 'you see his social situation in scene fifteen at its starkest, and then he goes back into that personal situation. It's highlighting the social situation'. If scene fifteen is in bright light, then logically, scene sixteen should revert to the darkness of the earlier scenes as a statement that, although Scopey's curiosity is not satisfied, his attempts to change his world have failed. Alen, after all, had no secrets.

The Pope's Wedding announces a view of theatre which Bond has developed consistently. In 1977, he wrote about the stage

> as an area that has the characteristics of society, and doesn't merely represent it . . . I make a girl tell about the loss of her child while she is preparing the cooking, or while she is working in a factory: it is necessary that she works, it's also necessary that she speaks honestly about her bereavement. Society does not regard her as an actress who can take ten minutes off for a dramatic solo. The situation must be made concrete in its social setting. I also make people argue over money while they are cutting bread: we stop listening so much to their words; instead the way the bread is cut, the knife held, the crumbs collected – analyse the words for us.[14]

Of another, unpublished early play, he remarked 'I must avoid any revelations, any explanations, any sudden "seeing the light"'.[15] The importance of these ideas cannot be exaggerated. They run through all of Bond's plays, and they account for some of the confused responses to many of the plays. The play for Bond is a dramatized analysis of a series of events; it is not the dramatization of a story: 'A dramatist shouldn't be dogmatic about people. Examine commonsensically people and their problems. This examination mustn't be prejudged by a doctrine. The examination ought to be the play . . . he must find the various truths, not *the* truth . . .'.[16]

Allied to the insistence upon the stage as an area with the *characteristics* of society is a view of character which emphasises the ordinariness and everyday quality of a character's movement, the fact that in real life a pattern is rarely clear:

> I take destiny to refer to something in oneself that doesn't involve others . . . Now I try to bring out a person's destiny in this sense: given this person and this event . . . then X is bound to happen . . . This is not a philosophical determinism. One could always say that someone would come, or something would happen, to effectively interfere with the pattern. But it is a contingent determinism, because one can say that in life such people and such events don't turn up. So one can be legitimately tragic in the grand manner.
> Using the word 'destiny' might create misunderstanding. But it is in some ways a very suitable word – because it describes the feelings of the protagonist – he feels he is destined to silence, etc. It happens to him . . . the wishes I refer to belong to a scheme of things, they are part of a man's daily life – they don't suddenly run up on him . . .[17]

Scopey, like the rest of Bond's protagonists, searches for meaning and is most strongly characterised by his curiosity and his restlessness. The movement towards understanding is directly related to the resources possessed by a particular figure. The more limited the resources, the more brutal the solutions tend to be. The nature of the solution shows how that figure relates to the society in which he finds himself. It offers a paradigm of individual (and representative) understanding of society. For Bond is at pains to deny the uniqueness of his protagonists: 'what I would like to say is you could take any member of the chorus and treat them in that same way. I just think Scopey would be typical and . . . I think you could . . . look at the lives of other people and find the same concerns and the same problems. They might not always be so clearly worked out or so graphically obvious in the consequences . . . '.[18]

It is in this sense that a play like *The Pope's Wedding* shows Scopey both as an individual and as representative. Scopey is himself and represents the other figures in the play. Scopey's solution is his own. The play unravels the process both for the individual and for his stratum of society. It mirrors the conflicts and the possibilities:

> Society's laws are obvious, its intentions reasonably clear. But a man's private wishes and conflicts and troubles are more obscure – to himself . . . It is difficult to investigate this area, but a man's actions can often be taken as symbolic of it. Actually, just indicating something of what he has in mind. But what we usually see is a compromise, distorted by conflict on the one hand, and on the other by conformity (with the social norms). Difficult to detect the pattern behind the actions. But this is what the dramatist is to get at.[19]

The Pope's Wedding attempts 'to detect the pattern behind the actions', and it is the first of a group of plays, the overall development of which occupied Bond for more than ten years:

> that was a series of plays . . . that began with *The Pope's Wedding* and ended with *The Sea*. I had an idea about all of them before I started to write . . . I had an idea of the shape . . . That I would begin with a tragedy in which the old man would not talk. This boy called Scopey keeps saying: 'Why do this?' And the old man can never say anything. He just drools. Scopey never gets an answer from him.[20]

Scopey is the first of a line of protagonists who develop, successively, their capacity to understand, articulate and take responsibility for what they say and do. Each of the central figures in the plays up to *Lear* tries to advance his ability to perceive the nature of his situation. And each exists with an opposite, a socially negative version of himself, with whom the protagonist struggles. Out of the struggle emerges the paradox of aggressor and victim becoming swappable. Much of the main circumstances of the early plays emerge from the conflict between two versions or two halves of the same character.

2

Saved

Scopey's successor as protagonist is Len in *Saved*. Like *The Pope's Wedding*, *Saved* contrives a style directed at recording experience without analysing it, a means of presenting and showing without overt comment a series of situations which are calculated to force an audience into asking who is responsible for the events shown on the stage. The question 'How did this come about?' is not answered by the play. It is left to the audience. *Saved* is obviously not about South London, though that is its location. The play is a passionate and logical account of life lived by the social stratum engineered to fit the needs of a consumer-based and technologically-fuelled society. Responses to the play cannot be based upon sympathetic judgements to do with the material poverty of the characters. The central figures do not exist in the 'poverty trap'. Harry and Mary are working (though this is used by them as a way of avoiding contact) and only rarely do the people in the play dwell on the subject of money or the lack of it.

Saved was commissioned by the Royal Court on 24 April 1964 and submitted on 18 September of the same year. Intended for a Sunday night production, the play went to Keith Johnstone and thence to Anthony Page, one of the Court's Associate Directors. William Gaskill eventually acquired a copy in April 1965 and outlined his plans for his first season as Artistic Director in a letter to Bond of 23 April:

> I have at last been given a copy of 'Saved', which I will read as soon as possible. I don't know whether Keith has explained to you but we plan to do a certain number of plays in repertory for a very limited number

of performances – say fifteen. Of course, if they are successful, we shall keep them running indefinitely but initially I cannot risk more than fifteen.
If I liked 'Saved', it could be 'Saved', if not, I would like to revive 'The Pope's Wedding'. I don't want to take up an option on both until I have made this decision. Please forgive this delay . . .

By 30 April, the choice was made and Gaskill explained his reaction later:

> *Saved* was commissioned by the Court as a result of the success of *The Pope's Wedding* and would have been scheduled for a further Sunday night had not I read it myself . . . I remember reading it straight through and being absolutely convinced that it should be done . . . I had some doubts about the extremes of violence but I knew the play had to be done.[1]

Gaskill's concern over certain aspects of the play, specifically in terms of the likely response of the Lord Chamberlain, is clear from the fact that he consulted George Devine, who, on 28 April, sent a memo to Gaskill:

> I have read this play from the point of view of the Lord Chamberlain's office.
>
> 1. The intrinsic violence will automatically disturb the reader.
> 2. I have marked with pencil all the things I could spot that are likely to meet with objections. I may have missed some. It should be checked.
> 3. My advice is to cut out all the words we *know* will not be passed – such as bugger, arse, Christ etc. *before* submission. To have them in creates immediate hostility. The problem is to *get the play on with a licence*: not to alter the L. C. I presume.
> 4. I suggest that Charles Wood's technique is a good one. Swallow pride and reinvent, even one's own swear words and phrases. Re-write scenes, if necessary, to retain intrinsic rhythms etc. rather than arguing over words or phrases which he will never yield on.
> 5. Cut out stage directions which suggest sexual situations. I have bracketted these.
> 6. I think you might get away with the stockings scene if you present it carefully, as I have indicated. Often things are *said*, which don't always need to be *said* – except in free circumstances which you don't have.
> 7. As for the baby, I don't think the scatological bits will get through

under any circumstances. Worse kinds of violence may well be passed but references to shit and piss will never pass in my opinion.

8. I suggest EB works on all this – show it to me again if you like . . .
9. The passages I've marked with a *squiggle* are dubious – finally it's give and take, but the shorter the list of dubious passages and *obvious* disallowances (piss, bugger etc.) the better chances you have.

P.S. A few less bloodies would help – esp. Act II.

Devine's memo, apart from illustrating vividly the conditions under which the theatre generally laboured at that time, proved prophetic, for when the play was submitted in June 1965, it was returned a month later with a demand for cuts, including the complete deletion of scenes six and nine. After an unproductive visit by Gaskill to the Lord Chamberlain's office, and since Bond refused to cut his play, it was decided to present the play as a club performance to members of the English Stage Society. The Society had begun life (and continues) as the supporters' group of the English Stage Company. As a club, any productions done under its auspices were not subject to the licensing control of the Lord Chamberlain and the Theatres Act of 1843. Though *Saved* was not the first play to be put on in this way[2], its production brought to a head the rumbling discontent of the profession at the means used to control it, and the determination of the Lord Chamberlain's office to do its legal duty.

The play was first performed on 3 November 1965 and, although given as a club performance, it created intense public discussion. Although a few critics spoke with some objectivity (amongst them, Penelope Gilliatt, Ronald Bryden and Alan Brien), most were hostile and many hysterical.[3] The theatre held a teach-in on 14 November, chaired by Kenneth Tynan, where the play was defended by, apart from Bond and Gaskill, Mary McCarthy and Ronald Bryden. At the same time, the Chamberlain's office moved against the play and early in 1966, the theatre was charged with presenting *Saved* without a licence. The judgement delivered against the theatre in April 1966, though on a technicality relating to the conduct of the club's organisation of *Saved*, dangerously blurred the distinction between club and public performance. The movement to relieve the Chamberlain of his control over the theatre gathered head because of *Saved* and was to continue and be intensified over Bond's next play, *Early Morning*. One practical consequence for *Saved* was that it had to wait until February 1969 for its first public, professional performance in the United Kingdom. By that time, there had been thirty-three public productions abroad.[4]

If *Saved* earned the dubious distinction of being the last play to be prosecuted by the Lord Chamberlain, it also was prevented by the sensationalism it gathered around itself from being seen with any degree of fairness, with the exceptions mentioned above. Most of the debate centred on scene six, where a baby is killed by some men in a park. The shock of one image in one scene became the focus for most of the rage directed against the whole play, and it consequently became transcribable in terms that guaranteed it notoriety and, equally, an almost total lack of analysis. Gaskill recalls that the perspective only changed when the play was given again in 1969 at the Court and on a subsequent European tour. By that stage, 'the shock value had already worn off. They all made that reassessment about the scene in which the baby cries [scene four] being the most horrifying scene in the play and that was quite a general reaction here and, I remember, in Poland'.

Saved is about the lives of a group of working class people in South London. Pam, a young woman of about twenty-three, picks up Len and brings him home to her parents' house. Len becomes a lodger in the house, but his affair with Pam is replaced by her falling for Fred, one of a group of young men who go around together. Pam has Fred's child but Fred tires of her. In an atmosphere of bickering and unhappiness, Pam attempts to win Fred back, leaves her baby for him to look after, and the child is subsequently murdered by the group of men in the park. Fred is convicted of the crime and goes to prison. Pam still tries on Fred's release to get him back. Len remains in the house and in the end he is sullenly accepted as a permanent fixture. The play ends in a stalemate. The only activity which closes the play is that of Len's mending a chair broken in an earlier quarrel.

The environment of *Saved* is urban and cramped. Eleven of its thirteen scenes are set either in a small living room (or bedroom), or in the manufactured space of the park. Bond chose to set it in South London for two reasons. It is 'slightly newer and I always get the impression . . . that it's more industrialized. I've got a feeling too that it's physically flatter – there are those miles and miles of long straight streets that always look the same. I used to call it the brick desert, and this feeling of being in a desert of bricks seemed to be absolutely right for the play. As to why it wasn't North London [where Bond was living] . . . I think that quite often one feels the need to see something at a bit of a distance, just to see its relationship to oneself better'.[5] The living room relates to compression, proximity, unavoidable collision; the park to acres, not of freedom, but frustration and boredom, being at best a brief interlude. The park and the house are intimately related, for it was in the park that Harry and Mary's son was killed during the war. Equally the pattern of noise and silence is carefully developed. There is a continual alternation of loud sound and comparative quiet, of doors banging in the house and in the prison cell, of television and radio blaring out, of a child screaming, a teapot shattering, a park bell ringing incessantly, a balloon bursting, of voices shouting offstage, quarrelling onstage, of stones thudding into the pram: and there is the silence of boredom, of regrouping before renewing a quarrel, of the drugged baby and then of the dead baby, of intimate, if infrequent, ordinary conversation. In the final scene, noise and silence change their function, for here the silence is watchful and neutral and the noise is that of Len repairing the chair. These elements establish the characters as victims of their situation and the purpose of the play is to make this unsentimentally clear. There is an extraordinary level of physical movement in the play, all to little purpose but defined to show the wasted energy involved in frustration and purposeless activity. The gang of men is characterised by its intense nervous energy, which finds release in larking about and then in killing, which begins not menacingly, but as a consequence of there being no other outlet. In the house, there is a continual movement in and out of the living-room, and a steady trekking between table and sofa. It seems impossible for anyone to be still, apart from Harry whose stillness is retreat and accusation. Even in the final, virtually silent scene, the movement is unceasing, though at the last Mary and Pam do sit and Len rests.

The overall strategy of the play is one of gradual enlargement of the focus. Bond: 'the play should open out all the while, so one has a feeling of the society outside. Not in the rather naive sense of putting factory chimneys around the basic set; I don't think that's necessary. But one should be very aware of the play opening out into a society; it shouldn't be shut up in a room on stage. One should have to ask questions about the society in which the play takes place'.[6]

The first two scenes are directly concerned with the affair between Len and Pam. Scene one is 'built on the young man's sexual insecurity – he either invents interruptions himself or is interrupted by the old man' ('Author's Note'). What the note does not say is that the first scene of the play works essentially through the comedy produced by Len's nervousness and his attempts to fit a role which he cannot maintain. He spends the scene avoiding making love to Pam and it is Pam at the end of the scene who takes the initiative. As a pair, they are defined immediately by their separateness. The only moments when they are at all close are when they tell each other dirty jokes, and when Len tries to persuade Harry who is in another room that there is an orgy going on. The scene creates accurately yet obliquely the social context of the situation. Pam has brought Len back to make love to her, but she won't take him into the bedroom because 'Bed ain' made . . . It's awful. 'Ere's nice'. Her strange fastidiousness prevents her from being seen as just a tart, and her accomplished, amused coolness at Len's jumpiness both indicates her wit and her ability to manage some situations. She needs her wit in the face of Len's incessant questioning, seen here as part of his panic and subsequently as an index to his entire character. The level at which Pam is forced to live is tellingly shown by the fact that she picks up Len but objects to his nosiness when he asks her her name. The scene derives its comic strength partially from the fact that it begins as a seduction, wavers because of Len, and finally *becomes* a seduction scene, not shown, but, as the scene ends, insisted on by Pam. The second scene is again centred on Pam and Len. Len is now a lodger in the house. Apart from scene twelve, this is the most intimate scene in the play and it isolates the couple in a boat on a bare stage. It also shows how both are already apart, Pam particularly from boredom. The dialogue proceeds in fits and starts, the pauses notating the bankruptcy of the topics they discuss. At the same time, the topics become circular and mix eventually together Len's rent, Pam's intention to knit a jumper for Len, their life together and the life led by Pam's parents. What explodes the comparative peace of the scene is Len's insistent curiosity. He cannot temperamentally keep still and as in subsequent scenes his nagging and repeated questions irritate those whose security is paper-thin. Even when Len knows he risks anger, he cannot help himself. Eventually he has to ask Pam: 'Yer wouldn't go back with any ol' sod?', just about retrieves the situation and persuades Pam out of her angry sulking, tries joking with her as in the first scene, and then destroys a precarious stability by asking about Pam's parents. The direct antithesis then emerges in the shape of Fred, who is in charge of the boats and who conducts everything on a joky level and to whom Pam is immediately attracted. As Pam and Fred spar with each other Len is automatically relegated to his role for the rest of the play – the observer who continually tries to join in. Len's role as outsider was partly developed in a filmscript written by Bond early in 1963 and called 'Workmen In'. Len here is one of a group of building-site labourers who watches one of his mates, Ron, fall helplessly in love with June. She and her husband have moved into a newly completed house on the site. As Ron despairs over his unrequited love, Len appears intermittently to tell Ron that 'A bit a fun's alright. But yer wanna keep out a trouble'.

In scene three, the world of the play and its context opens out with the group of young men minus Fred. They are not exactly boys. Colin is the only teenager, while the rest range from twenty to twenty-five. The scene is characterised by its unflagging pace as the members of the group vie with each other to assert their status in the group. Pete has been to an inquest on the death of a child in an accident involving Pete's car and a lorry. The casualness with which they discuss Pete's being part of the death of the child is not to do with their lack of feeling but with the need to make light of everything given the world they inhabit. None of them is actually unfeeling. Even in scene six, when they work up to the stoning of the baby, most of them at some point attempt to restrain one another. Yet all are driven publicly to appear unconcerned. There is a clear hierarchy to the group. Pete's status is enviable to someone like Barry, five years his junior, and Barry is frequently the object of derision from the others. Bond emphasises Pete's view of himself by giving him a pipe: 'Those ones who saw themselves as rather steadier. I wanted to get away from the idea of a yobbo being a yobbo. There's a complex range of experience and type within that and so the steady, slow puffing of the pipe I think is important for his character'. Barry tries to assert his status by arguing his familiarity with killing while doing National Service, but the group never takes him seriously. In this scene, Barry's humiliation is complete and because he is usually routed, it is inevitable that he it is who later instigates the terrible action in scene six. Into this comic scene comes Len as the outsider who by accident meets the group and is recognized by Colin as an old school mate. The rest of the scene shows the group focussing on Len as a novelty, an even greater novelty when they deliberately misconstrue his meeting the fifty-year old Mary as meaning that she is the one he is to marry.

By scene four, two things have happened. The gap between Pam and Len has grown greater and Pam's baby has been born. She maintains throughout that the father is Fred. After the comedy of scene three, comes the numbing effect of scene four. It works ironically by comparing Pam and Len with Mary and Harry. After their resolve in scene two never to be like Pam's parents, their response to one another now identifies them as moving the same way. Three of the four are involved in asserting their dislike and resentment of someone else in the room. Pam's anger is directed at Len and vice-versa. Mary, while fussing over Len, criticises her daughter. The silence between Mary and Harry speaks volumes and the scene is conducted in terms of bursts of bickering. Over all of it spreads the parallel increase in volume of the baby's cries and the television which doesn't work properly. None of them is prepared to do anything about the baby. Though Len wishes he could take the baby out of the mess, he also says that the child will 'cry itself t'sleep'. The effect of the baby's cries is appalling but it highlights the neglect felt by everyone in the room. Part of the reason that Pam refuses to attend to it is that everyone else is trying to force her to. They expect her to accept responsibility. Even Len makes no move, while Harry's first line in the play denies any concern: 'I ain' gettin' involved. Bound t'be wrong.'. The pressure on the audience is to provoke blanket condemnation. Bond means the crying to be unbearable. In his first draft, the baby begins crying from the opening of the scene, as soon as Pam has switched on the television. Bond notes there 'Too soon' and holds the effect back as in the final version. It's also in scene four that Fred is established as Pam's regular man, that his casual attitude towards Pam sets up against Len's, and that Harry demonstrates monosyllabically that he is aware of what goes on in his house. As he picks his time and talks to Len, there is the briefest of connections between them, a contact which emerges towards the end of the play.

Scene five is one which Bond had not originally envisaged as part of the play: 'the scene where the baby is on the bed was added after the play was written, and is really unnecessary – nothing happens that isn't made plain somewhere else. But somehow I felt that before the killing it was necessary to sum things up for the audience'.[7] While it is true that what happens in the scene is available elsewhere, it is also the case that the events of the scene demonstrate important ways of regarding Pam, Len, and the baby. It is this scene which stresses that Pam is hopelessly attached to Fred. Equally, Pam's nervous instability and desperate responses to pressures are calculated to show the extent to which she is a victim of her situation rather more explicitly, and that Len's well meaning attempts to persuade her to accept the baby only increase her neurotic awareness of how badly wrong everything is for her. At the same time, the sequence deepens the sense of Len's readiness to sacrifice himself. When all else fails, Len says he's bought some tickets for the football match and has thus manoeuvred Fred into coming round to see Pam. Len does what he does against his own interest. The baby throughout remains 'it'. If thematically, the scene marks time, structurally it is a means of setting out clearly the premises of the play up to that point.

Scene six, the longest in the play, sees the death of the child. No-one can ignore the horror of the child's murder, but no-one should ignore what precedes and follows it. The scene opens with Fred fishing and Len sitting on the bank. It is one of the few relaxed and peaceful episodes in the play. The atmosphere, it is true, is disrupted by Len, who is there to try to find out why Pam wants Fred so much. Since Len's characteristic habit is one of unavoidable disruption, it means that the talk alternates between Len apparently taking an interest in the fishing, talking of the rod, the bait and so on and quite unconsciously generating a tone of sexual ambiguity which creates a cleverly orchestrated comic undertone to the dialogue. Len, despite Fred's irritation, eventually battles towards what is in his mind: 'Why's she go for you? . . . No, why's she – ill over it?'. When the answer doesn't satisfy, he returns to it and tells Fred he could hear the two of them making love. Nothing illustrates Len's bewilderment and loneliness more than this admission. It was originally pointed more emphatically. In the first two drafts, Len tells Fred that he masturbated when listening to him and Pam making love and Bond notes by the side of that section: 'I might be ashamed of the blatant sexuality of this but in genuinely pleading for themselves (not grovelling) everyone gains dignity. This is true of L.'. The exchange ends inconclusively as Fred packs up his fishing gear and Mike enters. As he does, the mood changes, becomes lighter, and Len reverts to his status as outsider. Briefly, the jokiness, always part of the group's activity, holds the stage as a transition between the discussion of Pam and her arrival with the pram. She, like Len, attempts to engage Fred by asking about the fishing and Fred's mood of anticipating a 'Bit a fun' gives way to irritation at Pam's repeating many of Len's questions. Pam thus moves from simulated interest into casually feigned attempts to persuade Fred home, from there into anger and thence into pleading and desperation. She is taking pills like her mother and the baby has been drugged with aspirin as part of her last-ditch attempt to win Fred back. Finally, Pam hurls the only thing of Fred's she has, the baby, at him, rejects her responsibility again and leaves Fred to assume his. Fred resolves to take the baby back to Pam's house, but waits in case Pam returns. It is this waiting for Pam which sets the situation leading to the murder into motion. The rest of the group drift in, in high spirits for the night out. They inevitably turn their attention eventually to the only object on stage with them.

As the men begin to move the pram about, two centres of action are created on the stage. As Gaskill puts it: 'You get that wonderful, extraordinary perspective of Fred being downstage, just lying there, doing nothing, just half sitting with legs stretched out, and the whole of the other scene is behind him . . . like a film director would see it'. The restraint of the scene is organised not only by the amount of time it takes to build up to the assault of the baby, but also has to do with the number of times various members of the gang express worry or concern for the child or alarm at what others are doing to it. Only Barry of all of them never deflects from the escalation and it is Barry who initiates most of the attacks. The escalation begins when the balloon suddenly bursts and the pram is pushed over Colin. What forces the pace is nothing to do with the baby, but to do with Pete who 'touches' Barry. From then on, energy is released via the pram and only when the violent movement wakes the baby does attention focus on what is in the pram. As this begins, Fred and Mike are still downstage discussing their plans for the evening. Still the scene is held on a tight rein, as the group, and particularly Barry, becomes curious about the child. As Pete pulls the baby's hair, Mike drifts upstage to see what is happening and Fred remains down left. Throughout the mounting series of abuses, he remains sullenly where he is, having nothing to do with the baby: 'Ain' my worry. Serves 'er right'. The sequence reaches its first climax and the first pause with the baby being rubbed in its own excrement. Only then does the group realise what is happening and its attention wanders briefly from the pram to realising that Fred has taken no part. As he is dared over to see what has been done, the scene then dips carefully after all the raucous yelling to the quiet and frightening action. If before, they were larking about, now with the stones, they know and understand what they are going to do. For the first and only time, Fred begins the sequence by throwing a stone. After the deadly quiet, the men are possessed. What Bond calls the 'atavistic fury' ('Author's Note') is released and the baby killed. Beyond what the others do is Barry once more. As the others eventually respond to the park bell and leave, he is still attacking the child. After a long pause Pam returns to collect the child. For all her refusal to accept responsibility, she does return and talks to her baby in a curiously childish fashion, in a tone she has not used before. Her tragedy is nowhere more apparent than in her crooning to a child which she doesn't realise is dead. Sympathy for Pam needs to be balanced, says Bond, against the fact that what she produces is 'a purely formalised response, a conventional sign. She can perform those formalities without even noticing that her child is killed. I don't think she has any real feeling for the child. What I want to say is that all those formalities, which could be taken as signs of social responsibility are in fact purely conventional and don't have any real meaning. Her relationship to the baby is murderous'.

Gaskill testifies to the problem of maintaining the balance of the scene:

> The killing of a child in a pram when it doesn't cry – it can make no statement about the pain it feels – has already a kind of abstract, symbolic quality about it, although one tries to do it as naturalistically as

possible but there is something very strange about it because you know there's only a dummy. You are watching a kind of ritualised action. What you're watching really is the boys.

The ritualised effect is created from two elements. Firstly, the length of time taken by the games played by the group and secondly, by the fact that the baby is drugged and makes no sound. Originally, the baby was not drugged, and in the first two versions the scene is punctuated with its screams as it is hauled out of the pram, thrown up in the air, and then killed. Only in the fourth draft is the child sedated and silent. D.A.N. Jones accurately gauges the scene's intention, when he notes that 'We don't see the baby – only a hooded pram with the youths pushing it, sticking their hands or throwing stones into it. We merely hear their words, like the reporting of a Greek messenger or chorus . . .'.[8] The movement into the last sequence, that of the stoning, is one which modifies the function of the men, from that of a collection of totally limited figures to that of a representative embodiment of the worst features of modern society. They become for that moment something other than naturalistic figures. As they leave the stage, they are making '*a curious buzzing*'. Of this strange moment, Bond says:

> I like to find those moments where the known experience frays over into something which cannot be pinned down to very common usage, but is somehow suggestive of the experience. Instead of being an identifiable gang, their behaviour is so horrendous that it blurs over into something that can only be described in terms of the animal kingdom, and that's the buzzing of a swarm of bees. There's a moment of panic and escape and of realisation, but instead of coming to themselves and saying, what have we done, they don't, they come into the realisation of some animal state. I didn't want the scene to escape into classical cries of horror.

It was Laurence Olivier who pointed out that the structural device of a first half murder was comparable to the situation in *Macbeth* and *Julius Caesar*.[9] Like these two plays, *Saved* concentrates its attention on areas to do with murder and yet is not primarily about murder. Murder is inevitable, given the situation. In *Saved*, the impact and potency of the image overwhelm at first our underlying knowledge that this, or something comparable, is bound to happen. The vulnerability of the helpless child is so powerful that the degree to which it affects our instincts for that moment renders an audience uncritical in its response. It strikes absolutely at what we suppose we all agree on, the unquestioned consensus that children are to be protected. And it is precisely this consensus, this assumption which is so radically disputed by the image. This is the point of Bond's remarks on the matter in the 'Author's Note': 'Clearly the stoning to death of a baby in a London park is a typical English understatement. Compared to the "strategic" bombing of German towns it is a negligible atrocity, compared to the cultural and emotional deprivation of most of our children its consequences are insignificant'. In other words, the child in the pram is dead long before scene six. Culturally and emotionally, it is a dead thing being assaulted by other dead things. If it had survived, is it really to be thought, given its situation, that it would become something other than Fred, Mike, Colin, Barry, Pete, Pam, Mary, Harry and Liz? If some responses to the scene are that it unbalances the play's structure, or that the scene is the centre of the play, then those reactions can only be justified if scene four is ignored, and scene five, and the scene which follows the killing (seven), where Fred is in a prison cell, awaiting trial.

The shocking effect of scene seven is Fred's mouthing reactionary sentiments against 'bloody gangs like that roamin' everywhere. The bloody police don't do their job'. He is of course saying it to Pam so as to avoid her realising who has killed her baby, but his willingness to identify himself when necessary with the 'hanging's too good for them' brigade is both Bond's ironic comment on the response to the scene which duly emerged and, more seriously, on the extent to which people like Fred are ready to endorse the social structure that denies his right to live rationally. In dramatic terms, the scene demands of an audience that it begins to reduce its collective temperature by apprehending Fred's situation while at the same time wishing him to be viciously punished. The process is one of deliberately involving an audience emotionally and then insisting that it thinks as well. Bond's argument is that the audience cannot judge

> until they have been emotionally involved, but it's not the emotional involvement which is the important thing. Normally if you talk about

cause and effect, what people are concerned with is effect, and they ought to be concerned with cause and consequence of cause. They begin by asking, what is a thug, and they end by saying, that was a thug, and so their social attitude is reinforced, whereas what I want to do is not reduce the thuggery to a convention, but show it in all its horrible detail, so that the audience can't apply their immediate response to it. They might in a way apply a much more violent response to it, but then you can analyse it out.

Scene seven in many ways is the fulcrum of the play. Bond invites a natural loathing for Fred, but also invites the audience to see him as a victim. The three occasions on which a steel door bangs (the effect was introduced late on, in the seventh draft) are as confining as the basic domestic triangle. That Fred can only lie, that he is utterly indignant at being mobbed outside the courtroom, that he bitterly attacks Pam for leaving the baby and that during the scene he can find very little to help the childlike and romantic Pam (who at one point stands '*fingers at her mouth*'), all suggest the hopeless situation of Fred. The 'solution' to the problem, and one which an audience would no doubt heatedly endorse, involves putting Fred away, but when he emerges from prison he is, as far as his mates are concerned, a more glamorous figure than when he went in. Originally the scene did not contain Len. In the first two drafts, he waits outside. He is introduced in draft three with some cigarettes for Fred and chiefly in order to say that he witnessed the murder. Len legally is an accessory to the murder. Morally, he is as responsible as the others. It is important to establish his guilt, as it is important to see that Len learns from the situation in a way no-one else does. He is able eventually to pass judgement on Fred and by implication the others. It would have been quite simple to leave Len out of scene seven and out of the killing, make him a purer hero than he actually is. Yet to do that would be to give an example of what Bond in the 'Author's Note' calls 'fatuous optimism'. What is 'almost irresponsibly optimistic' is that Len, in spite of his experience *and* his culpability, nevertheless tenaciously refuses to submit, in the way that everyone else in the play does. Len is not *so* different from them. To make him so would be to distort the truth. Gaskill remarks in the programme to the 1965 production that 'when critics talk about Pam as a "slut", or of the boys as "hooligans" . . . by compressing the evil into one image – sometimes into one word – you avoid the responsibility, because if you include the rest of the social life which surrounds any act of violence, the responsibility is bound to spread to one's own life'.

After the interval, the play resumes as Fred is about to be released from prison. Scene eight is concerned, as are scenes nine and ten, with a distinction between the active fury of the gang of men in scene six and the suppressed fury of the family. What these scenes show is the oppression 'kept under painful control by other people in the play, and that partly accounts for the corruption of their lives' ('Author's Note'). In scene eight, the violence is implicit and verbalised, mainly between Pam and Len. Pam's anxiety at the imminent release of Fred centres upon the continual presence of Len. The mechanism is the argument about her Radio Times. What she is pathetically attempting to do is hold on to the belief that she and Fred can begin again. Len's intrusion into the house involves Pam's hostility, Harry's intermittent recognition of the parallels between Len and himself, and Mary's shift from maternal cossetting of Len to flirting with him in the next scene in more explicitly sexual terms. Although Mary in scene four had rebuked Pam for wandering about in her slip, she deliberately enters in a slip herself at the opening of the scene. Up until the seventh draft of the play, Mary is onstage as the scene opens, but the revision makes it clear that she deliberately enters, knowing Len is in the room. The innuendo becomes more apparent as the scene progresses, as Len tentatively tries out what for him are quite daring remarks to Mary, who in turn is quite aware of what is happening. What is extraordinary is that she still has feelings after twenty years' emotional isolation. It is one of the funniest and most erotic scenes in the play and parallels the opening scene, even to Harry's silent entrances and exits. As Mary leaves, Len's response, left alone, is to begin to masturbate. The Oedipus reference, implicit in scene three, becomes very obvious in this scene, and then is quickly distorted by the scene's last stage-direction: '*Mary goes. Len takes a handkerchief from his pocket. He switches the light off and goes to the couch*'. Up to this point, the play, as Bond says in his 'Author's Note', follows 'the tragic Oedipus pattern'. The consequence would then be Len's killing his 'father', Harry, and taking his wife to bed, as Oedipus had killed Laius and married his mother, Jocasta. The death, as it were, of Laius, is never in question, given Len's nature as demonstrated in the play up to scene nine, and given Bond's clear rejection of the conclusion of *King Oedipus*:

> Then learn that mortal man must always look to his ending,
> And none can be called happy until that day when he carries
> His happiness down to the grave in peace.[10]

What does find expression in the play is Bond's judgement that '*Oedipus Rex* isn't a play about family trouble but about the disorder in a society'.[11] Len's refusal in scene eleven to enact the Oedipal pattern ramifies the play's optimism, in the face of the crumbling figures around him. Pam's dreams are utterly routed by Fred in scene ten, where both Len and Pam try to take possession of him. By scene ten (the cafe scene), Len has developed considerably. He is still fascinated by the killing of the child and badgers Fred for an account; but he is able now to judge Fred, which he does at the end of the scene. His pity for Pam and his willingness to stay with her are a demonstration of his indestructibility.

The painful control and corruption of people's lives ('Author's Note') shows most dramatically in scene eleven, as Mary and Harry, to Pam's amazement, quarrel. The scene's violence is, in many respects, far more terrible than that of the killing of Pam's baby. Even Harry has his breaking-point and sense of decency. He knows Mary, and her invective against him proves his point and her guilt. The violence is terrible because it comes with so many years' hate behind it. It is almost metaphoric. As Mary hits Harry with the tea-pot, the action underwrites the whole family's despair. Pam summarises her tragic sense of her world, what one critic termed 'the oppressive destiny of this house'.[12] As Pam collapses in despair, she becomes a Cassandra-like figure. Bond writes in his first draft that, at this point, 'She repeats over and over again her prophecy of future calamity'. The end of this scene shows the completeness of the tragic cycle which killed both Mary and Harry's son, and Pam and Fred's son in the same park. Yet the play rescues itself from pessimism by Len's emerging in the two final scenes as the possible means whereby such fragmented lives may be mended. When Harry enters Len's bedroom (scene twelve), he is the embodiment of what the family has come to. '*He wears long white combinations and pale socks. No shoes. His head is in a skull cap of bandages.'* As Harry appears, ready for bed, with his head wound in bandages, Bond creates the first of a line of damaged, ghost-like characters, appealing for help. Bond says of this moment: 'Harry acts as the representative of the family when he comes to Len's bedroom. The members of the family need Len because he's the only human being they know – because he's the only one who's learned something from the park killing. When Len stays on it's an act of moral integrity, though it is limited to this one house: and that is its weakness'.[13] The scene between Len and Harry is intimate and revelatory. In his need to persuade Len to stay, Harry talks about his life, offers Len what little he has by way of contribution. Len never really wants to go and by the end of the scene has dropped the pretence, when he asks if Harry will come up again the following Saturday. Typically, Len takes advantage of Harry in order to ask him about his relationship with Mary and gets the answer he got from Fred in scene six about Pam. Fred says 'Depends on the bloke'; Harry, 'Up t'the man'. Harry's sense of the war is summed up eloquently in two images, the peace and quiet, and the picture of a dying man 'Like a coat fallin' off a 'anger'. Harry and Len's conversation in the bedroom has a cathartic effect after the tumult of scene eleven. If the family needs Len, then Len also needs the family, needs Harry to invite him to stay. It is in this scene, according to Bond, that there occurs the only kind of overt statement about anything in the play at the point where Harry says, 'Yer never killed yer man. Yer missed that. Gives yer a sense a perspective. I was one a the lucky ones'. Any reading of Harry must take into account that this repeats the sentiment expressed by Barry in the third scene: 'In the jungle. Shootin' up the yeller-niggers. An' cut 'em up after with the ol' pigsticker. Yeh'.

Thus Len enacts in the final scene the role he has developed throughout the play, and the family is brought from quarrels, discord and anger to 'a silent social stalemate' ('Author's Note'). Bond remarked to Gaskill that 'there was no rhetoric in the play except the last scene [which is] rhetorical by being a pattern of action'. The family in the last scene is strictly neutral as regards Len, as if they as a group tacitly accept the eventual dominance of Len as the outsider who has created his place within that group. They may not like or welcome it, but they have no resources with which to combat it. Thus there are two patterns of action in the final scene, the family's activities and Len's mending a chair. In the first version of the play, Bond had noted after writing scene eleven: 'A chair must be broken in this sc[ene]', so that Len's action is the direct result of the row in scene eleven. It is that which Len attempts to set to rights. The oppressive noises of doors banging gives way to the noises, off and on stage, of Len working. The last direction concerning Len throughout the drafts asserts Len's resilience and strength, for the statement '*His head lies sideways on the seat*' is substituted for 'His head is low' only in the seventh draft. Bond's intention is clarified: 'I saw it as resting but potential strength. The chair is broken not the mender'. The ending of the play is deliberately left unglossed. It is simply presented as logical. It has, nevertheless, produced a variety of interpretations from directors, which mirror and anticipate the argument about Bond's 'pessimism', and the ending of many of his plays. Neither William Gaskill, nor Giles Havergal (Citizens' Theatre, Glasgow) construe the ending as other than pessimistic. Gerald Chapman, when at Leicester, saw Len's last action as 'not resigned but resting, not aggressive but realistic', while David Carson at Leeds caught 'a seedling of hope'. Philip Prowse, who designed *Saved* for the Citizens' in 1972, seems to catch the intention of the ending: 'I think it's very well judged. But the optimism is so minimal. At the end of that play, that is the best he can offer and I think he offers so little on a very calculated level'. And Len stays put. He is told by Harry in scene twelve that to leave will solve nothing, or as Bond glosses it, Harry says 'if you go out of this house . . . you will open the front door, you won't find yourself in the street, you will find yourself in a house exactly like this. So that for Len, there is no escape. All he can do is preserve his integrity, preserve his humanity'.[14] The strength, endurance, wit and energy of many figures in the play are demonstrable. It is equally demonstrable that these qualities are under constant and tireless pressure. It would be naive or romantic to show a Len triumphing. It would be cynical and despairing to show a Len broken at the end. Len neither triumphs or despairs: 'his resources lead to that point . . . I agree that Len was totally unaware, but I wanted that to be obvious, I mean what could you expect of him? What other opportunities were really open to him, given the sort of life he was made to lead and the sort of future that was offered him?'.[15]

Saved formed part of William Gaskill's first season as Artistic Director of the Royal Court, a season which tried to return to George Devine's principle of playing in repertoire. Gaskill recruited John Gunter to design the play from a number of applicants for the job of resident designer. They were all set certain plays as design exercises (*The Pope's Wedding* because, said Gaskill, 'it was a particular kind of modern play', *Serjeant Musgrave's Dance* and *The Knack*) and given four weeks to design them. Gunter recalls that with both *The Pope's Wedding* and *Saved*: 'I didn't really understand what I was doing. It was a whole new teaching process when I went to the Court. We were all learning at the same time'. Another recruit as Assistant Director was Jane Howell who, watching Gaskill work, 'couldn't understand it. I wondered when he was going to start directing the play'. She also saw demonstrated one of the most important priorities of the Royal Court: 'it was an explicit thing that you were there at the service of the text and you weren't there to show off. You could start using your brain instead of thinking your soul was important. The emotion followed'. What surprised both Gaskill and Gunter was the simple but striking basic design of the play. Gaskill remembers Bond describing the first scene: 'he said it's like a bowling-alley. I'd never seen a piece of scenery like that before. It has a kind of enclosing feeling. I don't think I've ever seen it used before or since. A real, imaginative invention. And then in front of that, we just had the necessary furniture'. Essentially, therefore, eight of the play's thirteen scenes were played on a set enclosed by a triangle of flats. The three park scenes took place on a bare stage, the cafe scene had chairs and tables without the flats, and the cell scene was set with a simple door-flat. Thus the setting was of the abstract kind evident in *The Pope's Wedding*. Bond: 'I do usually want to concentrate on certain things – not just verbal things, but also on certain objects . . . I do think that that sort of abstract staging is in a way more realistic'.[16] The reduction of the elements involved means in fact that what is used assumes great importance. As Gaskill says: 'because you have so little on the stage, what you have is absolutely crucial, and we spent hours debating the exact colour a flat should be painted, and all the props and furniture became very crucial, and Edward was very insistent about certain colours for the boat and the pram'. Gunter made scale models of the two latter items, and the production was prepared with the kind of meticulous attention which recalls Brecht writing of himself and his own designer, Caspar Neher.[17]

The directing and acting of *Saved* (and Bond's later plays) require a particular clarity and scrupulousness. For a good deal of the play's power has to do with the obsessional occupation of stage space as an individual possession. All the characters, except Len, 'possess' certain areas (and certain objects). They live within a particular space and the narrowness of that space, whether sofa, bed, place by the park pool or table in a cafe, is itself a statement about the nature of their existence. It is related to possessiveness throughout: *my* Radio Times, *my* fishing rod, *my* baby, *my* teapot, *my* cigarettes, and the effect of the words on the stage finds its correlative in the particular space on the stage in which the words are spoken. The space and the object produce statements as much as anything else.

Gaskill's direction of both the 1965 and 1969 productions subscribed to the needs of precise placing and speaking:

> As a director casting [a] Bond text, the speaking of it is almost the first essential. It's got to sound right . . . I suppose you could describe the style as a kind of pared-down naturalism; the actual placing of everyone on the stage sculpturally is very important, and the actors have to have a kind of awareness of the economy of themselves, without that becoming in any sense a stylization. It has a laconic style that should feel very natural, but should look simplified . . . When you have a thing which is extremely accurately written, the text has to be extremely precisely played even in the moments of extreme violence. And the orchestration has to be exactly right. And in working like that, what comes out is bound to be very controlled . . .[18]

Bond endorses this view of the playing. The audience 'ought to feel that, for every part of the play, there is a certain purpose behind it, a certain control. That's very important. Especially if you write about sometimes unnerving or difficult things, then I feel it's very important the audience shouldn't feel this is just some sort of big emotional wallow in horror, that there is a certain discipline or control behind it'.[19] To demonstrate the difference between this approach and others, Gaskill at the teach-in on *Saved* of 14 November 1965 directed scene eleven (the quarrel between Harry and Mary) twice, once employing an emotionally-based technique and then presenting the scene as directed in the production in order to demonstrate that 'the greater the restraint, the greater the effect of violence'. As one critic conceded, 'Mr. Gaskill had made his point that the effect and degree of violence was carefully calculated and designed to produce a rehearsed response from the audience'.[20] Gaskill said at the teach-in, 'Drama is the imitation of an action . . . there is no real baby . . . it's up to you to consider these actions, to look at them, think whether they are truthful . . . and for you to make your judgement on that . . .'.[21] The achievement of such a style is difficult to verbalise and runs the risk of sounding commonplace. Gaskill's views are shared by many directors. The problem is consistency:

> The text is always paramount. The style of the production and the style of the acting comes from the text. It seems very naive to say that, but it's not. So, quite simple things, like I'm a great believer in punctuation; how a writer punctuates his play is crucial. The fact that Edward never uses commas, or barely, and uses short sentences and never uses subordinate clauses, certainly didn't [in his early plays] absolutely dominates. If you play the sentence as written, it will produce a certain strictness of style which is personal to him, and has the same kind of separateness that his visual presentation has. It's not to make [actors] be more stylised or act unrealistically. You have to say it the way it is written. Once you accept that, you have already put a kind of limitation upon the wrong kind of emotional indulgence, or the kind of method tradition. As soon as you say 'that sentence matters', you have put a stylistic limitation on what you can do.

Equally, Bond's dialectical use of space in the play occupied Gaskill. He refers to its use, for example, in scene eleven, 'where the father is cutting the bread and butter, the mother is sitting on the side saying "My this, my that" and she has to cross the space. She moves the teapot; she goes back and sits down. That incredible, almost didactic demonstration of the separateness of two people, their fight over property'.

Bond asks of his actors an approach which is a source of frequent confusion and, sometimes, baffled annoyance. For character in a play such as *Saved* is not primarily seen as development and growth, except in the absolutely minimal case of Len. Character development only becomes possible in Bond's terms if and when the individual is able to use his resources to make sense of his world. In *Saved* (and subsequent works) the organised significance of the *play's* development is contained within the struggles of Len to free himself from his situation through a full apprehension of the nature of that situation. Len is surrounded by figures which merely exist, *are there* in the play. The fact that there is no development for these figures is a paradigm of their corruption. They are placed in a context which exerts pressure upon them and to which they contribute. It is the context which throws light upon aspects of these figures and not vice-versa. The thirteen scenes of the play are deliberately spread over about two years and their construction is such that they become episodes, extracts from the lives of the figures. What comes between the scenes is not presented, for it is both unnecessary and at the same time implies clearly by the method employed that the 'gaps' are taken up with the same motiveless and hopeless existence. The structure denies overall coherence of character in the traditional sense. Bond's ideas concerning acting proceed from a particular view of the world, a view of how people react to their circumstances:

> What is being done to the character and what does the character do? Very often it's a question of what is being done to the character. One is describing the processes of society. What one sees is not a character going from a to b to c, but a character whom we see from point a, then from point b. What you have to act is that situation. It's no use asking: 'How did *I* get here?'. You have to ask: 'How did *it* get here?'. What the actor has to define is 'What am I up against in this situation and what does that call out of me?'. The situations are designed not to show the development of his character but to show the crucial situations an individual has to cope with in order to produce what is of value to him.

It follows from this that acting Bond's plays requires a particular focus and discipline. Since each scene is a moment taken from the lives of the characters, it can only be played with reference to itself and to that specific situation. It is possible but misdirected to attempt to play a scene purely in terms of preceding scenes. To do so implies a steady growth of character and a situation designed to *demonstrate* growth of character. Jane Howell puts it well (and virtually paraphrases Brecht) in talking of her production at Coventry of *Narrow Road to the Deep North*. The actress playing Georgina (and her difficulties are typical) 'at times couldn't find the length *between the scenes* [*our italics*] and was looking . . . for a development. And it was only when we played each scene for what we thought it was intended, just played the actions of the scene, just concentrated on what was done, it seemed to solve all our problems'.[22] Elsewhere, Jane Howell talks of the need to 'play the moment' and to let the audience 'put the string through the beads'. David Carson suggests that 'the scene should finish, bang. You should have an entity which is a scene, and then the next one. But you had to have a division. You couldn't dissolve into them. They were written as divisions'. And Bond in commenting upon this issue distinguishes between Aristotelian models and his own work:

> What I don't do is say here are these characters, let us see what they will do. I say, given this character, what situations can I choose that will bring out what is significant and important about those characters? The idea that a character produces himself [is] the Shakespearian idea [and] I don't think [it's] true. You have to portray on the stage those situations in which they play various aspects of their part.

Thus it becomes vital that the acting of a part should not generalise. Figures in *Saved* do things as specific moments, but they do not connect up their lives as a continuous process and it clouds the truth if one detail is extrapolated to inform a subsequent detail. As an example, Fred moves, like the rest, from one moment, one situation, to the next. The quality of his life consists of moments – sleeping with Pam, fishing, killing, going to prison, beginning again and his desultory fragments are playable only as units, as Len points out: 'They ain' done 'im no good. 'Es gone back like a kid. Yer well out a it . . . 'E's like a kid. 'E'll finish up like some ol' lag, or an ol' soak' (scenes ten and twelve). Again, the text presents events which are not explicable in terms of acting by reference to what has gone before. An example is scene twelve, when Harry arrives in Len's bedroom. There is little to suggest prior to this that it will take place and only the barest of remarks to suggest Harry's feeling for Len. Harry's general inertia would lead one in conventional terms to deny the scene's credibility until it becomes clear that part of the point has to do with the optimism in the play, the fact that Harry, in spite of everything, 'Thought yer might like someone t'say good night'. For Gaskill, 'the psychology of the moment is always very important. Why people do things at specific moments I find more and more in plays now becomes crucial, which is not necessarily linked to the through-line of it'.

Presenting 'the psychology of the moment' is a means of persuading an audience to watch with a degree of detachment what is created on stage, to concentrate upon what is shown as another section of a series of enactments. Because *Saved* demonstrates effects rather than causes, it is important that the process is a dual one, the first part the responsibility of the production, the second (the questions as to causes) the responsibility of the audience. For the audience therefore to become over-involved in the presentation of effects runs the risk of disallowing the questions. Gaskill hoped that the audience 'will be able to watch it with great detachment. It's certainly the intention of the production, and I think to some extent the intention of the play; many of the scenes are very slow, in many of the scenes very little happens. This is just because we want to show you the whole of life, which includes the sudden accident in the street in which you see blood, but surrounding this the hours and hours in which nothing happens . . .'.[23] As Philip Prowse remarks: 'Emotive demands for sympathy from the stage can only muddle the issue. Once you sympathise with somebody, you make excuses for them. If you make excuses for that sort of behaviour, then you condone it and then you condone what creates the situation'. English-trained actors sometimes experience difficulty in working with Bond's text. Jane Howell: 'they think they've got to justify an author's text, but the text is its own justification. Sometimes they feel in a straitjacket. Actors have to do no more than the line and no *less* than the line'. Actors have to understand not only their part but also its contribution to the social situation depicted by the scene. The overall coherence of the scene is paramount. Since the stress is upon the scene's total effect, the presentation of an individual and emotional sub-text as performance is a distortion. This in turn imposes a particular discipline upon actors. Some of the actors playing Bond's *The Fool* at the Court in November 1975 illustrate the difficulties and the consequences of working in a particular way:

> . . . all you are is a contributor to a certain effect which Bond intends . . .
> I can't develop the character. All I can do is get better at what I am doing . . .

> . . . I have to work off every moment. That's the way the scenes are built up. It's a play of moments, instead of character . . .
> . . . It's just that if you just have one line you're just a part of the thing which is building up to the effect of the scene as a whole . . .
> . . . But I can't fill out the spaces. By its very nature the fact that my character fulfills a function limits the amount of new things I can try without detracting from the scene as a whole . . . But you know from watching the other scenes that no more is necessary.[24]

Such responses are both characteristic and honest. There is both an appreciation of the demands and a reluctance to be subordinated to, as they judge it, a function, so that the release of the actor's creative energy is directed not towards spotlighting the individual but towards illuminating the situation. Since Bond asserts, rightly, that what he puts on the stage are 'of course . . . understatements',[25] it becomes the actor's role to play those understatements. The audience's role is one of expansion. The situation and the lines have to be played exactly, and the text not used as a launching-pad.

Many of Bond's ideas on acting are similar to those of Brecht. Since their interpretations of society are similar in some respects, it is hardly surprising. Bond's views on the job of the actor at this stage are a consequence of his seeing the world in a way which Brecht would have agreed with. Thus: 'The problem is always to make actors interpret roles as social roles or social functions, to ask not "Who am I?" but "What am I?", not "Who does this action?" but "What is this action?", to define themselves in relation to other characters, to consider the nature of the action rather than the nature of the self. The actor must understand what goes on in the scene and the play, and not just what goes on in him'.[26] Brecht according to Bond is the great 'liberator'[27] but it does not follow, as he notes, that Brecht said all that was necessary on the subject. As Brecht often wrote, there is no such thing as an impregnable practice or theory. Would Brecht have disagreed with Bond's assertion that 'It's true that each scene must stand for itself as an aspect of the whole. But there must also be a cause and effect relationship between the scenes. This is necessary because life is ordered by cause and effect, incident and choice, problem and decision and this reality must be reflected in the structure of the play . . . Am I again biting the hand that feeds me if I say that there is a sense in which Azdak [in Brecht's *Caucasian Chalk Circle*] is used as a *deus ex machina*?'.[28] Bond readily accepts the influence of the visit of the Berliner Ensemble to London in 1956, and says that he 'came to Brecht before the theory – and perhaps I was, again, lucky'. He also stresses that the process was from there an evolving one: 'I have worked consciously – starting with Brecht but not ending there. Brecht's contribution to the creation of a marxist theatre is enormous and lasting, but the work is not yet finished'.[29] In some respects, Bond does begin where Brecht left off at his death. Brecht's later movement towards the allowing of empathy under careful control and the attraction of the collision of empathy and detachment, as expressed in the 'Conversation about being forced into Empathy' (1953)[30], may well have provided the starting point for Bond's work. It produced in Bond's plays moments which he later termed 'aggro-effects', as distinct from 'alienation effects' (see Chapter Eleven).

Talking of *Saved* nearly fifteen years after writing it, Bond offers important notions about the title and about the place of the play in his overall work. When asked, 'Why *Saved*?', he commented:

> I wanted a nice short title. There's an element of irony about it. I had a feeling that there is in the play an indication of moral attributes that are desirable, I think a certain consistency of behaviour and in that sense I think then one is not pessimistic because they are the foundations for creating a new society. The other reason is a very ironical one because the people in this play are the people who have much of the hardware of our technological, consumer society. They are not destitute.

Asked why solutions are not offered in the play, Bond replied:

> I know at that time I had no way of stating it clearly. My life was actually very like the one shown in this play. I was very surprised when people were upset about it. I say the play stands in its own right. It does. It doesn't do everything and obviously one has got to write other plays which do some of the other things. What it says I think is truthful. I show them [the characters] at their very worst but in doing that I also wanted to show beyond that the possibility of something better.

It is the 'possibility of something better' which the next play explores.

3

Early Morning

Early Morning would appear to be full of improbabilities. It describes a Victorian England ruled by a lesbian Queen Victoria whose two sons, George and Arthur, are Siamese twins; Gladstone as a trades union official and Disraeli as a conniving conspirator; Florence Nightingale as Victoria's lover and George's fiancée; Prince Albert as a plotter against his wife; a trial on a charge of cannibalism; decaying bodies and a ghost; the murder of all but one of the characters by Prince Arthur and their reappearance in a ghastly heaven where there is no pain and where people eat themselves and each other; and a resurrection scene to close the play. Though set in nineteenth-century England, the play reaches forward to include the technology of contemporary society by means of deliberately anachronistic references to radio broadcasts, walkie-talkie sets, cinema queues and airports. *Early Morning* is the first of Bond's performed plays which deploys such a technique and he explained this, in connection with *Lear*, in a letter to Gaskill of 18 May 1971 in which he stated that anachronisms are

> rather important and part of my style . . . The play isn't . . . a period piece. Any creation of any age on the stage is arbitrary . . . So I'm allowed to bend the arbitrariness in a direction I choose. The anachronisms are for the horrible moments in a dream when you know it's a dream but can't help being afraid. The anachronisms must increase and not lessen the seriousness. They are like a debt that has to be paid. Or as if a truth clutched at anything to save itself from drowning. So the anachronisms aren't careless or frivolous touches – they are like desperate facts. But 'mixed periods' is wrong. The anachronisms just occur.

The anachronisms prevent the play from being thought of as simple historical exegesis. They also are the means whereby Bond may show our society as burdened with and conditioned by the Victorian legacy. What is done in the modern world is a consequence of and imitates the priorities of the play's world. When Bond prefixes the play with the statement, 'The events of this play are true', he means that the events of the play present in surreal form the significance of the actions taken by Victorian and modern society. If people do not literally eat each other in reality, they effectively do so by destroying the humanity of themselves and each other. What might be termed the 'sub-text' in another work becomes here the main text.

Early Morning is written in the form of a dream sequence. Its development, organisation and structure is geared to and evolves with the progression in perception of its central protagonist, Prince Arthur. The audience witnesses the events of the play through Arthur's eyes. What is shown is not objective, but coloured by the responses of a figure who, throughout the play, attempts to come to terms with the nature of the world as he sees it. Arthur makes a number of decisions in the play, some of which are erroneous – he decides to join his father's rebellion against Queen Victoria; to annihilate the human race; to eat his father's flesh. All of these decisions move him a stage further towards a tentative understanding of his own situation, of the potential goodness of human beings, and the actual evil of political structures as shown in the play. The audience is invited to follow Arthur's evolution, and to understand how Arthur wins his freedom. The play is frequently treated as if it is not created as a dream. Consequently, to many critics it appears to be a mess of wildly-aimed, destructively unpleasant attacks upon historical figures, an emotional tirade upon the power of privilege and the evils of a corrupt society. The play, however, has a coherent logic, which cedes little to a casual observer. It is the most misunderstood of all of Bond's plays and it is central to his subsequent work. In order to test the thesis of the real possibility of individual freedom, Bond constructs a framework within which extreme representations of corruption are presented as a hideous nightmare. Arthur endures horrors, survives and escapes. What he escapes to is not shown.

What he will do with his freedom is left unsaid, for the play is a proving ground and not an analysis. The importance of *Early Morning* lies not only in what Bond experiments with, but also in what he subsequently discards. The play is therefore a summary of what Bond knew up to that time and it functions in one sense as a clearing house.

Bond began *Early Morning* in January 1965, a few months after the completion of *Saved*. It took over two years to write, during which time he revised *A Chaste Maid in Cheapside* (November 1965; produced at the Royal Court in January 1966), wrote the script for Antonioni's *Blow-Up* (1966) and translated *Three Sisters* (Autumn 1966; produced at the Royal Court in April 1967). *Early Morning*, after going through three extensive sets of notes and eight drafts, was delivered to the Royal Court early in 1967. Bond wrote to Geoffrey Strachan at Methuen on 15 August 1967 to say that the play would not be produced until January 1968 'because it needs long rehearsals and it can't be fitted in till then . . . Anyway, I want to work a bit longer on the last act'. The play was announced by the Court for production in January 1968, but on 8 November 1967 it was returned by the Lord Chamberlain's office, unmarked, and with the single comment that 'His Lordship would not allow it'. Quite apart from the use of historical figures in the play, the Chamberlain was presumably encouraged by the government's announcement in the Commons on 1 November that its bill to end theatre censorship would be dropped because of the pressure of other business. The Chamberlain was not to know that on 14 November, George Strauss (chairman of the Select Committee which in June 1967 had recommended an end to censorship) was to win a place in the Commons ballot for the right to sponsor a Private Member's Bill. Two days later, in consultation with the Home Secretary, he decided to introduce a Theatres Bill.

Nevertheless, the Royal Court was in real difficulties over *Early Morning*. The legal decision over *Saved* effectively meant that even a club performance was now liable to prosecution. Since *Saved*, the theatre was vulnerable, and the Chamberlain had informed William Gaskill that a club performance would result in papers being sent to the Director of Public Prosecutions. The Arts Council determined to withhold its grant from the theatre during the run of *Early Morning*, partly because of the legal difficulties and perhaps because the production might adversely affect the movement towards the abolition of censorship. During the later months of 1967 and the first part of 1968, the English Stage Company was faced with the greatest crisis of its short existence. It was compounded by the postponement of the proposed January production because Gaskill became ill with pneumonia. The dates were re-set for three Sunday night performances on 24 and 31 March and 7 April. Not even this schedule was to be fulfilled. *Early Morning* was finally given for the first time on 31 March 1968. The last play to be banned in its entirety by the Lord Chamberlain's office (Strauss's bill became law on 28 September) was performed, like *The Pope's Wedding* and like *Saved*, privately, and, unsurprisingly in view of the pressure exerted from outside the theatre, it did not work very well. Given the circumstances, it was a triumph that the play was done at all. Bond, returning from working on a film in Czechoslovakia (*Michael Kohlhaas*) gave an account of the production in a letter of 8 April 1968 to his American agent, Toby Cole:

> When I got back I got involved in the last stages of rehearsing *Early Morning*. Only three Sunday performances could be given – otherwise police prosecution was inevitable. Because of rehearsing difficulties (the actors were all earning their livings in other rehearsals!) this was cut down to two performances. One performance was given – but after that the police visited the theatre, and the licensee [Alfred Esdaile] banned the second performance. So a hurried performance was given for the critics in the afternoon [7 April] – and it was a disaster, badly under rehearsed and unconvincing. This isn't Bill Gaskill's fault – if he'd had time it would have been one of his best productions. Inevitably, after this, the notices have been terrible – but I don't care.

In place of the cancelled second performance, a teach-in on censorship was organised at the theatre. Esdaile offered his resignation as a consequence of the afternoon performance and demanded but did not get the suspension of Gaskill as Artistic Director. It is an extraordinary tribute to the integrity of the Royal Court and its Artistic Director that *Early Morning* was so fought for and that, once freed of the restraint of censorship (although not, however, from the threat of civil proceedings by a member of the public), it should affirm its commitment to Bond by presenting *Early Morning* and two of his other plays early in 1969. Defiantly, the production of *Early Morning* was accompanied by the statement that it 'celebrates the twelfth anniversary of the English Stage Company'. In May, Bond was given the George Devine Award for *Saved* and *Early Morning*.

As with producing the play, publishing it also became a difficult matter. Geoffrey Strachan of Methuen sent an internal memo to his general editor, John Cullen, on 10 April 1968 discussing whether to publish the play, after noting that by that time *Saved* was the best selling of the Playscript series with 2400 copies. He remarks of the play that 'Coming from a Dürrenmatt or an Arrabal one would find it less surprising. Coming from an English playwright it is rather remarkable'. A further memo of 11 April reports that Bond 'expects the Royal Court to be prosecuted and is anxious to see the play published quickly'. Methuen took legal advice as to the possibility of proceedings on grounds of either civil or criminal libel. Counsel's view (to John Cullen on 8 May) was that, with the exception of the name, Lady Flora Hastings, and the legend prefacing the play 'The events of this play are true', on balance, the likelihood of prosecution was remote. The fact that such opinion was felt necessary illustrates the sometimes precarious situation of publishers, as well as theatres. Methuen then offered at the end of May to publish *Early Morning* in the Playscript series, with the two modifications suggested by counsel. Bond, unhappy at the delay, had by then agreed to let John Calder publish the play, and Methuen generously, if reluctantly, waived their option on Bond's first play after *Saved*.

Early Morning begins with a series of plots against Queen Victoria. Prince Albert and Disraeli have been planning a coup for five years. Both of them want Prince Arthur to join their conspiracy. Victoria, sensing trouble, arranges a marriage between Prince George and Florence Nightingale, which would guarantee her popular support. The coup fails, Albert is killed, and Disraeli tries to persuade Arthur to sever himself from his brother and continue the rebellion. Arthur runs away, meets his father's ghost, who also urges the continuation of the fight against Victoria, and encounters Gladstone, who is busily organising his own rebellion. As all of the group meets, Disraeli is shot and Gladstone has a heart attack. Victoria, as always, survives with her lover, Florence. Arthur becomes insane and arranges by a series of tricks to kill everyone except Florence, who accidentally survives. The ghosts of Arthur's victims rise up, Arthur drops dead, and he is carried off to Heaven, where everyone reassembles. In Heaven, everyone is a cannibal, but whatever is eaten grows again. Gradually Arthur, by refusing to accept his fate, and by articulating his love for Florence, moves towards his escape. Victoria traps him into a coffin but while everyone else feasts, Arthur rises slowly from the coffin.

Prince Arthur is trapped in the world outlined in the first brief scene of the play, where Disraeli and Prince Albert meet secretly to discuss their impending coup against Queen Victoria. In an atmosphere of comic tension, Arthur is immediately talked of as a problem. His father wants him to join the revolution. Disraeli says Arthur's involvement would give the plot 'the appearance of legality'. The outlandish atmosphere of the play is created from the beginning but the first view of Arthur in the following scene shows a sullen, indifferent and self-pitying prince, who resists all attempts to drag him into the world of plot and counter-plot. As he chooses to remain an observer, he is able to see some things clearly but not, at this stage, how to act. He understands Disraeli's ambition and the threat he poses to the Royal family; he sees the consequences of the revolution more clearly than his father; he is capable of seeing behind Albert's rhetoric in scene two and he refuses Albert's persuasions easily. At this point, his conceit lies in his belief that he can somehow understand all this and yet keep clear of it.

Occasionally, Arthur emerges from his indifference into anger. If the world of revolution oppresses him, then he is more personally oppressed by one of the stratagems of that world, when Victoria, in scene three, proposes a marriage between George and Florence Nightingale. As a Siamese twin, he is to be subjected to the obscenity of a marriage by his other half, a humiliation blithely dismissed by Victoria's punning assertion that the marriage 'will call for some slight personal adjustment'. His anger at the fact that he was not informed of this is imperiously waved aside and finds its outlet in a sarcastic attack upon the besotted George and bewildered Florence. By the end of scene three, Arthur is hemmed in on all sides, a sacrifice on the one hand to the demands of the revolt and on the other a victim of Victoria's counter to the unrest in the country.

In the first three scenes Arthur is trapped between two forces. He can only talk of his own unhappiness and his resentment at his condition. Scene four brings him face to face with the notion that his condition is not unique. It is in this scene that Arthur begins to make connections between himself and others. It is in scene four that Bond establishes the normality of the nightmare which surrounds Arthur.

The 'story' of scene four of *Early Morning* is that of the trial of Len and Joyce on a charge of cannibalism. It, however, begins not with the trial, but with Albert's reporting to Disraeli the gist of the conversation with Prince Arthur which took place in scene two. Albert has the initial stages of the revolution clear in his head:

> . . . We close the ports and airfields, take over the power stations, broadcast light classics and declare martial law. The important thing is she mustn't recover: she must be shot dead.
> DISRAELI. Well, shoot her more than once.

The mood of grim levity is caught before the trial begins, as is the distrust between Albert and Disraeli. Albert lies to Disraeli about Arthur's talking of Len in the previous scene and, before Len is seen, his role in the revolution is determined by being chosen as Victoria's assassin. There is no sense in which Len is on trial for his life. The trial becomes a charade before it begins, conducted as high comic farce. The tone is created by Victoria's remarks as soon as she enters:

> Pass me that hat, dear. I'm sitting in a draught.
> (FLORENCE *hands her the black hanging cap. She puts it on.*) Black's my lucky colour. (*To* LORD CHAMBERLAIN.) Read the charge. Place?

No-one reacts to the charge of cannibalism, or expresses revulsion as the details of the killing and eating of Hobson unfold. Instead, the trial consists of parodies of formal procedure and of a protracted squabble between Len and Joyce. Len is henpecked by Joyce, silenced by Victoria, and finally manages to produce his rehearsed speech and prove himself guilty. Len is intent on proving his normality. He responds as anyone might in the circumstances: 'I got a right a be guilty same as you!'. He resents Arthur's 'fancy questions' when Arthur is summarily appointed his defence counsel by Victoria. Arthur attempts to follow normal court procedure by questioning a doctor as to the state of Len and Joyce. The court and the prisoners wave him aside. Arthur falls silent until, as the prisoners are about to be put down, he sees that they are handcuffed together and the parallel between Len and Joyce and his own situation as a Siamese twin attached to George strikes him with great force. For the first time in the scene, Arthur attempts the obvious question: 'Why did you kill him?'. The question is repeated by Arthur some four times. The answer might offer him help in his predicament, for Arthur can see that Len is as trapped as he is. The question remains unanswered, but the effect of the trial upon Arthur is to persuade him to acquiesce in Albert's coup, for there must be alternatives to a world organised in this way.

Scene four is characteristic of much of the procedure of the play. Its three sections, the coup, the trial, and the effect upon Arthur encapsulate the three central prongs of the play which are to do with plotting and counter plotting, the horrific basis on which the world is organised, and the transcription of these two into personal terms by Arthur. All three elements develop over the whole play and the first two elements are filtered by Arthur with the resources and experience he has acquired at any one point into the development of his own understanding and his own internal logic.

From the end of scene four, Arthur becomes involved in the plot to dethrone Victoria, and thus at the mercy of both sides. Arthur opts for Albert's route as a negative response to Victoria's way, even though he has acutely analysed the nature of Albert's proceedings in scene two. His first decision made in the play is as erroneous as a number of other decisions subsequently taken by him. He still acts in scene five as an angry victim. His antagonism to Florence is apparent and he watches helplessly. He observes the plot, makes an instinctive attempt to shield his mother, fails in an attempt to save his father and ends the scene covered in George's blood. The revolution he has endorsed is as farcical an event as the trial of Len and Joyce. As an alternative to his initial position it is a dead end, except that he is now, whether he likes it or not, part of that dead end.

Scenes six to ten tell the story of Arthur's flight from the chaos, his capture and his giving way to madness. It is during this sequence that the pressure becomes unbearable. Arthur is now a victim of the ambitions and exhortations of others. After the abortive coup, Disraeli urges him to cut himself free of his dying brother, so that the coup can retain its 'appearance of legality' (scene six). As he carries his dying brother away to seek refuge (scene seven), the parallel with Hamlet surfaces when his father's ghost rages at him to cut off George and carry on the revolution by killing Victoria. He continues his flight and encounters Len being attacked by Gladstone and some soldiers (scene eight). An obvious effect of the pressure upon him as he contemplates the nearly unconscious Len is that he expresses no surprise at the brutality of Gladstone and the soldiers, but reverts to his question at Len's trial: 'Why did you kill that man?'. The question shows that Arthur is no further on in understanding than he was in scene four. The world is run by the Queen whose instinct for survival amounts to genius, by the scheming Disraeli and by Gladstone, the union-organiser, with a copy of the regulations in his hand. They all pursue their own individual and sound logic, given the context of an insane world. Only Arthur is unable to chart a way through such normality. As Disraeli reorganises after the death of Albert, so Len, after his battering, goes to tell Victoria where her sons are (scene nine), after having first told Disraeli. Consequently, the entire group meets by the cave which shelters Arthur and George (scene ten). The farce of the first attempted rebellion of scene five is repeated, except that the total resignation of Arthur is established, apart from a brief flare of interest as his dead brother is reanimated. It vanishes as George refuses to answer Arthur's question about whether death is any better than life. The question is answered only at the end of the scene as George dies and Arthur is left alone on stage with a corpse.

It is in scene eleven that Arthur, for the first time, occupies the stage as a central figure. He is still a victim, but he comes now to act as interpreter of the logic of the world of the first ten scenes. He glosses the action taken by everyone else in the play so far. His summary of action and its consequences hinges in scene eleven upon his assertion that 'I'm a limited person. I can't face another hungry child, a man with one leg, a running woman, an empty house . . . I'm limited'. The scene moves from an elegy for his limitations through the great sadness of his dream about a mill which grinds people to dust, to a realisation of how, at last, he can act to overcome his limitations. From the dulled quasi-dialogue with his brother's skeleton and the joking remarks to the corpse of Len, Arthur moves from outlining his limitations to a vision of how he can be of service to the world. The world is right and normal. He is the eccentric, the limited one. The dialectics of this understanding lead him to assert the concept of 'the great traitor'. What is wrong with the world is not its morality but its lack of thoroughness. The light dawns on him. He joins the world of the play and becomes insane. If the whole activity of man is geared to destruction, then the only thing wrong with Hitler or Einstein were their limitations, for they protected their own people, when logically they should have destroyed their own side as well. It is a simple argument and a simple logic. Arthur's vision propels him into action and he plans to destroy as many people as possible, to become a benefactor. He outlines his plan to kill his own men to Victoria and Florence (scene twelve), Florence goes to the war front to give herself to the dying men (scene thirteen) and in the following scene, the two sides line up for a tug of war at Beachy Head. Arthur's real plan becomes clear as his side falls over the cliff, Victoria's side rush to the edge to cheer and the cliff gives way. They are all killed. Arthur brings the action, as he judges it, to an appropriate end. As everyone plunges over the cliff, Arthur thinks, in scene fifteen, that he has freed himself and everyone else. As the ghosts of the men he has killed rise up, he greets them: 'I'm proud. I've lived a good life. Arthur the Good. I set you free. You'll always be free'. But the consequences of his logic in scene eleven, the logic that precipitated action for the first time, carry also the consequence of entering the play's world which, ruled by Victoria and her gang, is not so easily defeated. The ghosts are joined together as surely as Arthur and George, as Len and Joyce, as, now, Arthur and this world he has joined. Arthur is still as trapped as he was when first seen. Instead of the play ending where Arthur wanted, it enters a new phase for now Arthur has earned the right to be part of that very society he formerly so resented.

In scene sixteen, Arthur, like Len in scene four, is pronounced guilty, and admitted to Heaven, where people eat each other. It is explained to him, as to a child, how this works. Victoria tells him that 'Nothing has any consequences here – so there's no pain.

Think of it – no pain . . .', but, as in the first scenes of the play, Arthur once again resists assimilation. He refuses to eat and, once again, he becomes the object of attention. The effect of his induction into Heaven is seen in scene seventeen as his brother suffers pain from Arthur's refusal to eat. Though separated in Heaven, the activity of one affects the other. Arthur's refusal is an attempt to negate his earlier logic which led to the attempted destruction of the species, but as then when his attempts to relieve the suffering of mankind failed so now he sees himself as the stumbling block to the happiness of others: 'Why can't I let them alone in peace!'. He forces himself to eat, so that everyone may exist peacefully in Heaven. He martyrs himself and eats part of his father. At the end of scene seventeen, Arthur prays to the God of this world: 'Eat and be good. Be good and die. Die and be happy . . . O God, let me die. Let me die – and everyone will be happy'. For the second time, Arthur acts in order to solve the dilemma; for the second time, the dilemma is unresolved, for the mob adopts him as its leader. The pattern of events in Heaven repeats the earlier pattern. There is a revolution impending, which Victoria sees and acts to prevent. However, this time, Arthur has begun the logic and accepted the conditions of existence which are to lead him, fumbling and unclear, out of the trap. In two scenes with Florence, he begins to articulate his awareness. He tells her in scene nineteen that he can never remain in this condition: 'There's something I *can't* kill – and they can't kill it for me. Pity – it must be nice to be dead. Still, if I can't die I must live. I'm resigned to my curse! I accept it. I'll probably even end up being happy'. What he resigns himself to is what earlier he termed his limitations. From that moment in scene nineteen, Arthur embarks on his way out of this context. Though he is tricked by Victoria into a coffin at the end of the play, his mistakes lead him to an apprehension of both himself and of his relationship with his surroundings. He frees himself and, though he cannot articulate the nature of his freedom, he is unable to be damaged by anything else done to him. He resurrects himself from the dead world and climbs out of a deadening historical and social legacy. Arthur, as he rises from the coffin, wears '*a long white smock or shawl*'. It is also shown that '*his hair and beard are still dirty and uncombed*' and that '*Parts of his old clothes are seen underneath*'. No miracle is shown, but a readiness to proceed differently. What changes is Arthur's premature mourning of scene eleven. It becomes, by scene twenty-one, as Arthur frees himself, a definition of his early morning.

For Bond, *Early Morning* both continues the process found in the two earlier plays and points the way towards the plays which follow. *Saved* and *The Pope's Wedding* are defined by their author as the equivalent of the early plays of Shakespeare and Ibsen who 'go through a series of history plays in which they create the conditions, describe the processes which bring them to their particular situation. I would regard my early plays as a sort of historical sequence [to do with] the development of what human beings are about and what their potential is'. What was clear was that he should not write *Saved* again: 'the obvious thing to have done would have been to write another play like that, instead of which I wrote something entirely different, on the surface, and that's not an arbitrary thing. It's just that I'm shooting from a different direction. That's why it might seem to be a different world but actually it's not'. Given the world described in the two earlier pieces, the problem then becomes one of investigating the possibilities of escape:

> What really happens in *Early Morning* is this. In *The Pope's Wedding* and *Saved* the problem is very concrete, very tight, it's a real problem for the individual. How does he find his freedom in that? In order to begin to establish freedom, you have to say how do I dissolve the problem, where can I see loopholes for the individual to grow? Then you have to say, well, what is the logical situation of this human being in relation to the social situation which is very negative? By the end of [*Early Morning*] I say that freedom is a possibility for human beings and that the negative social situation is not predicated by faults in the individual. So that it's a freedom play in that way, that having said in *The Pope's Wedding*, 'Look, that man is destroyed', in *Early Morning*, there's a totally opposite situation, in which whatever happens, whatever comes, it is possible for the individual to be free. That is really a sort of kicking-off point for the rest of the plays that follow. It makes the other plays possible. What I then have to do is reconcile the big distinction that I had to make between *Early Morning* and *Saved*, not merely in theatrical terms, but also in analytical terms. You have to say, there is the possibility of freedom, there is the cast-iron situation, how do you make the two come together, how do you make the freedom become a practical possibility in the present world and that's what the plays that follow have been about.

The form of *Early Morning* is one devised to demonstrate the slow emergence of the philosophical route to freedom as it is expressed in Arthur's living in the world, his movement from the condition of Len in *Saved* to the abstract and inevitably indeterminate awareness of an alternative.

Bond had approached the scale, style and themes of *Early Morning* in two plays written in the late fifties. These were *The Roller Coaster* and *Klaxon in Atreus' Place* (the latter was submitted to the Royal Court in 1958). *Klaxon* is set in a post-nuclear war setting, in which a series of groups are opposed to each other. There is a family group, headed by the Elder and his son, Unicon, which is pursued intermittently by a group of fascists. There is also a gang of Teddy-boys; the inmates of a mutant house; and a trio which speaks gibberish. The argument centres around the clash between the Elder and Unicon. Faced with a world full of hatred and oppression, the Elder evolves a defence which consists of rejecting it: 'I warned you to hate people – that's all you need to know if only you can get it into your head' (p. 23), to which Unicon replies: 'If you talk and don't act, in the end it doesn't matter what you say – it still turns you into an ogre'. Wherever Unicon looks, he sees acquiescence and consequential violence. The Teddy-boys are part of the system which oppresses them, the gibberers yield to fantasy, the fascists flourish and the Elder's is a philosophy of despair. Yet Unicon still manages to find some hope: 'Even if this world is like a drain you can still fight back. One day the grass will grow when we tell it to, there will be thunder when we shout for it, and the guilty men will creep away, the fish will leap in their nets when we tell them . . .' (p. 24). Balanced against this is the Elder's pessimism: 'We live in a madhouse where the sane attendants wear the straitjackets. We cannot act. They rob themselves in the name of trade, corrupt themselves in the name of entertainment, pervert themselves in the name of religion, stunt themselves in the name of education, deprive themselves in the name of opportunity and kill themselves in the name of the right to live' (p. 27). After a series of powerful scenes involving soldiers being scientifically taught to torture civilians, together with a farcical trial scene, the play ends with the Elder espousing his son's view that action is the only answer. As the Elder makes this resolution, the son observes, 'Well, it's good to start sometime'. *Klaxon in Atreus' Place* depicts a world where nightmare and cruelty are normal, where oppression and violence are everyday and where most of its inhabitants see no alternative but to take part and thereby perpetuate the structure. At the same time as the horror is depicted, the alternative is predicated. There is no romantic pretence, only a sense of possibilities. Unicon moves from fury to despair to controlled anger and a commitment to action in the face of overwhelming odds. The situation in the play is generalised and the investigation is of philosophical means of change. In *The Roller Coaster* the situation is made more specific. The play is set towards the end of the twentieth century with England ruled by a military governor, a puppet monarch, George VII, and a disaffected Crown Prince, Arthur. It concerns various attempts at revolution against the governor and is largely the story of Arthur's progress against the law and order practised by the head of state, who encourages crime waves, makes the law stricter and so controls the country by giving it its head. Arthur is initially neutered by the situation: 'Oedipus tore out his eyes after he looked at this' (p. 16). He opts in his despair for oblivion and attempts to abdicate from all responsibility. The governor's view appears to rule: 'Life wallows in anger, it thrives on a crisis, it gets a kick out of clinging to a ledge, it's happy in Belsen . . . The roller coaster is the big attraction at Vanity Fair' (p. 52). Eventually Arthur decides to act and joins the impending revolution because he wishes to exterminate the species: 'If they must have a war, they must. But let it be Armageddon' (p. 62). Finally Arthur is shot attempting to make everyone comprehend. He is destroyed as he begins to understand.

Both plays are preoccupied with the question of action. In a note-book of the same period, Bond remarks: 'Making moral judgements. The difficulty is to know *when* to ask if such and such an act is good. When are all its implications apparent? No-one is isolated'. Both of these plays, which Bond now describes as 'an anticipation of the possibility of freedom', trace the propulsion of the main character, Unicon in one, Arthur in the other, towards an understanding of the nature of moral judgements. They each move through a landscape which is both historical and contemporary. Both plays involve the deliberate juxtaposition of elements ancient and modern, so that Teddy-boys co-exist with Biblical groups (the Elder's family) and futuristic military regimes mix with Victorian royal legacies. It becomes a developing part of

Bond's style to indicate the continuousness of certain fundamental problems to set a play in one particular location and by the use of 'anachronisms' show the relevance of past events as contributory to the present situation. Where *Klaxon* ends with a determination to act, and *The Roller Coaster* ends with action leading to death, *Early Morning* analyses the careful progression of the movement towards action and freedom in a much more thoroughgoing manner than before.

By relating Arthur only obliquely to the centre of activity in the play's first ten scenes, Bond is challenging a theatrical convention. If 'the whole play is written from his point of view, from his experience ... the audience has to understand this ...'[1], then it follows that the audience must apprehend the crucial importance of Arthur as a figure precisely at the time when he is by his nature far removed from the main action of the play. Arthur, theatrically, exists on the edge of the play for the first ten scenes. We are being asked, deliberately, to 'place' Arthur in the middle of our sense of the play's development, when his attitude is one of resisting such evaluation as part of the world presented to the audience. The story of the first half of the play is how Arthur is dragged into the centre of the stage against his inclinations and in direct contradiction to the position he tries to maintain. It is like watching Hamlet's response to his world without the aid of the soliloquies. If Shakespeare's response to the problem of inactivity is to explore the mind inclined to stasis via the theatrical 'trick' of allowing that character some exclusive use of the stage, Bond's response is to eliminate the luxury of inside information, to demand of an audience that its dawning understanding of the world of the play should run exactly in parallel to and focus upon Arthur's understanding, so that his movement from inactivity to action exactly represents our developing responses. We see what Arthur sees. Instead of using direct explanation to inform the audience about Arthur, Bond chooses to present his evolving situation in visual terms. In a letter of 6 November 1969 Bond states that 'the argument in the play is dramatised by, for example, Arthur carrying someone on his back and slowly getting rid of him, and should be *felt*, as well as understood'. Arthur begins the play as two people, himself and George, 'and he's slowly whittled down to one'.[2] George, after a brief supremacy over Arthur at the prospect of marriage to Florence, declines in proportion to Arthur's struggles to extricate himself from the anarchy of civil war. He is apparently eliminated by scene fifteen. But because Arthur's solution is false (the ghosts are still joined together), he is attached to George again at the end of that scene. Ironically he is freed in scene sixteen only to find that he is to face an unchanged situation. As he moves towards his freedom, he is devoured by the inhabitants of heaven, reduced to a head and a laughing voice and, at the point of total disappearance, but with his intellect intact, he shows his dawning understanding and, when next seen, is restored to a complete body and escapes. The emotional and intellectual movement of the play is expressed visually as a series of simple physical images.

The drafts of the play show a marked change with regard to the character of Arthur. Beginning with the single image (a method entirely characteristic of Bond's writing process) of the Siamese twins (January to June 1965), Bond mapped out in the notes the general structure of the play. In three sections, headed respectively 'The Revolution, The Treason, The Trial', Bond debates the development of his main figure. Incited by Albert, Arthur revolts against the tyranny of Victoria and leads the rebellion. It is as a consequence of his leadership that he comes to despair: 'He acts from the best intentions – but he is appalled at the amount of misery & violence he releases – especially his own violence'. The degree of revulsion on Arthur's part proceeds here not from his oblique watching of events, but from his direct involvement in those events. What emerges finally as Arthur's philosophy of nihilism in the play (scene eleven) is here an attack upon his own activity. The focus is directly upon Arthur's conscience. As he sits eventually amongst the dead of the battle, 'Suddenly they stand – A. sees that they are all joined together – like Siamese twins. He is conscience-stricken, or frightened, & tries to bring them back to life'. Once in Heaven (or Hell), Arthur is indicted by the soldiers for being a bad ruler, for dishonouring himself and for betraying his accusers. At this point in the play's development, as Arthur faces consequences, he resembles Bond's Lear. There is no resurrection here. Arthur is tricked into climbing into his coffin, being nailed down and carted off stage. The ending is one without hope, for the logic of the notes leads inevitably to Arthur's destruction. This early logic gives way slowly to an account of Arthur initially as a victim who slowly begins to account for his situation. What modifies the despair of the ending in the early drafts is Arthur's later attempt to describe what he knows to Florence in the final scenes of the play. From the first notes in 1965, Bond was clear that the style and structure of his new play should mirror Arthur's development. He saw the movement of the play 'as short fragments, almost shaped like inductive mathematics. The search for an explanation, or some mental scheme of resolution, accompanies the drama – it is voiced in the dialogue, and is partly shaped by the action'.

It is therefore vital to grasp that Arthur is the protagonist of the play before the cumulative and multiple layers of meaning he carries begin to mount up. The first ten scenes reflect his impotence, so that he is seen as victim and comparatively silent observer. The drawing of the first ten scenes are a reflection of a note of February 1965, where Bond distinguishes between *Saved* and his new play:

> I have usually allowed my characters to indulge in a little self analysis at the end of a play. Len does this in *Saved*, at the beginning of the scene with the old man. This ought to be replaced with an intimating incident... In the new play, explanations should be given – but by incidents, and verbal tendencies or emphasis – not by verbal ideas.

Thus the decision to avoid direct, glossing statements leads to the attempt to work in a more oblique fashion. The play is not to include its own commentary but to use a method which characterises the nature of Arthur's evolving comprehension. It almost goes without saying that such a means demands considerable concentration on the part of the audience.

Gaskill finds Arthur 'a deeply unsatisfactory character [because] Arthur doesn't appear when you read it like the leading part until about halfway through. You don't get that sense of the play's going to be about him, so by the time you've cottoned on to that, something has gone wrong, and I don't think any actor can quite put that right'. However, Bond argues that 'Arthur intervenes in the scenes at vital turning points and so people become aware of him as they would a ticking time-bomb in a large ballroom. The director should be able to accomplish this – and much of the acting has to be played off the positions found for Arthur – I think I'm just getting away from some of the clichés about what is necessary in theatre, trying to use actors and stage in a new way'.

Gaskill's worry about the position of Arthur in the first half of the play led him to try to reshape and trim the play (see below) and it argues an insistence upon the through line of the story. Bond on the other hand plots the interventions of Arthur in a strategic manner, so as to pull the focus of the scene directly towards Arthur and away from the ostensible centre of a particular scene. Thus in scene three, he is bound to be one centre of the stage action because it is the first time that the audience sees the Siamese twins. This is followed by his angry interruption of formal court procedure as Victoria announces the engagement of George to Florence Nightingale. In the middle of the parodied ceremonial, he interrupts with 'Why wasn't I warned?' and Victoria drags attention away from him by dismissing her court. Only then does she rebuke him for public bickering. Equally in scene four, the comic parody of Len's trial is abruptly diverted by Arthur's interruption and his insistent questioning of Len, together with his realisation that Len is handcuffed to Joyce. In scene five as the Court settles down to its picnic, there is a brief stage direction: 'LEN *passes. He whistles "Lloyd George."* ARTHUR *notices this*'. No-one else does. There are other examples of such moments in the first part of the play and the problem, given Bond's definition of Arthur as 'a ticking time-bomb', becomes one of how to play these moments, how to ensure that the audience perceives their importance. For example, at the end of scene four, Len kicks Hobson's clothes at Arthur. The stage direction reads: '*Some of the exhibits fall on* ARTHUR. *He's draped in them*'. Bond says that in scene four there

> is an interlude in which *Saved* appears in the play. The character Len is brought in from the earlier play, and there is a trial of *Saved* in the first act of *Early Morning* and in this Arthur has made a great advance on the world of *Saved*, because he is able to see much more clearly the nature of Len's activity than Len could when he was himself in that play, but he is still very much tied up in that sort of character himself, and that's why Len kicks the clothes over him.[3]

The draping of Arthur in Hobson's clothes is bound up as a moment with that section of scene four where Arthur comes into the scene. He becomes part of it as Len and Joyce scuffle with the guards. The stage direction reads: 'LEN *and* JOYCE *are forced apart. It is seen that they are handcuffed together*'. This is a vital moment in Arthur's perceptions, for here he recognises that they are in a state comparable to his own. The playing of that moment has to show the moment's importance. If it is merely shown rather than stressed, then the pattern of images having to do with people yoked together, which began in scene three with the first real sight of the Siamese twins, which emerges again in scenes fifteen and sixteen, will not be grasped as a means of dramatising the coherence of the argument. The metaphor, which is basic to the play's development, will never be realised. Consequently, the sight of the ghosts of those whom Arthur has murdered will exist only as a moment and not as the great linking theatrical revelation it is. As Arthur celebrates his success, '*The ghosts move apart. They are joined together like a row of paper cut-out men*', and Arthur realises his mistake. He has achieved nothing. The next view of Arthur in the play, as he falls to the floor at the end of scene fifteen, is of his being joined once more to George and the third act begins with Arthur and George joined '*as before*'. An audience's understanding of this development hinges upon the playing of the end of scene four. Bond, writing to his former American agent, Toby Cole, on 6 April 1970, regarding an American production of *Early Morning*, refers to the importance of such moments as part of the underlying pattern of the play: 'It's shown in the movement and shape of the play – the silences and the mounting towards climaxes, what can be thrown away and what must be hammered at like a crucifixion'. Though this comment is true of all of Bond's work, it is vitally true of *Early Morning*:

> if I were directing that moment now, then you've got to get the clothes on him in some way but when they were on, then I would make a much bigger thing of it. He would look at them, and go into himself and touch them, and examine the clothes on himself. You have to analyse the scenes and say analytically what is the main feature of this scene. The passing around of the shoe for instance [scene five] is just a bit of theatrical fun and wit, but the clothes in the trial scene are of fundamental importance. That is an image which needs understanding, interpreting and demonstrating to an audience.

Elsewhere, Bond tries to spell out the process. Explanations of the play

> come later, and are helpful. But they don't substitute for the *theatrical*

learning (and I don't just say theatrical *experience*) . . . when I told the directors they had to tell the story I meant in terms of theatre. They had to look at the photograph (the audience had to) not keep turning the photograph over to see what was written on the back. The tendency was always to ask: what does that mean? and then: what does it mean exactly? – and so the play falls apart. You have to get on with the play and make the incidents clear so that the audience can then provide the meaning. And the audience can do this because we share common experiences and understand common images . . . the play works not by falling under a weight of symbolism and psychology, but by telling the *theatrical* story of the play in terms of *theatre* – and then the audience will learn from it, and even tell you what the symbols are.[4]

Telling the theatrical story of *Early Morning* is a matter of the appropriate style being apparent to the audience from the beginning. The play's first director, William Gaskill, saw the play's style as surrealist:

I never thought it made directorial problems in the way of how to work with the actors, or for that matter how to design it. I never thought that was difficult because I think you could say that the style was surrealist and one of the essences of surrealism is that you use realism quite consciously. It's the juxtaposition of elements in it which is startling. I don't think the play calls for any sort of stylization in the playing or really in the staging. If you do it realistically, then it has the quality of a dream, because things happen in a rather matter of fact way, but the things that happen that are written down, the events which happen, the dialogue people say, are not realistic, but if you don't *treat* it realistically you don't create the dream quality.

The design solutions for both Court productions aimed at simplicity. Deirdre Clancy produced for the 1968 version 'the absolute minimum, literally the things that Bill wanted to have on the stage. They were mostly props, furniture'. Even so, the production cost the unheard-of sum (for a Sunday night) of £500. The design remained substantially the same for 1969 but there was added a skycloth and a pair of green drapes for the interior scenes. The nature of the design reflects Bond's wish that 'Very little scenery should be used, and in the last six scenes probably none at all. Whenever possible the place should be suggested by clothes and actions'. It also proved necessary because of the expense of a large costume plot. Deirdre Clancy, provided in 1969 with 'the luxury of a cyclorama', felt the play should be done in a 'clean, surgical manner, because I thought that overlaying the mental horrors with a whole load of Hammer film gore wasn't right. I wanted people to look and say, how pretty, that's nice, and then there would be a sort of double-take. I think that's what happened because when the curtain went up on act three, it looked like a tennis party. The impact was that it was white and then when you looked again, the white was all rotting. It looked as if the cloth itself was bleeding'. In act three, Deirdre Clancy put everyone in the negative version of their earlier costumes. They were bled of their colours to produce whites and greys. And in what for the Court amounted almost to a fit of decadence, the lighting by Andy Phillips included colours and strobe-lights (for scene fourteen). Bond recalls that, having made the decision 'we spent the rest of the day in a state of deep shock and people were in the pub next door, saying "They're using coloured lights"'.

Gaskill however had doubts about the clarity of the story: 'I think the play does become mystifying and I was worried that the audience wouldn't follow it any more than I was sure I followed it myself'. In both the 1968 and 1969 productions, cuts were made. Scenes seven and eight were reversed, with Bond's reluctant agreement, because Gaskill felt the audience needed a clearer line to follow. This means that Arthur/George escape at the end of scene six and on their journey (scene seven) meet Gladstone, the soldiers and Joyce attacking Len before they rest at the site of Albert's grave. At the end of the grave-scene (eight), Gladstone, Joyce and the soldiers kick Len on to the stage. The scene ends with a new speech in which Len explains to the audience that he is now going to tell both Gladstone and the Queen where Arthur/George is. Scene nine, in which Florence first appears as John Brown, was then cut, and references to Florence in drag in scenes ten and twelve disappear. At one stage in rehearsal, Gaskill cut scene ten (the Bagshot scene): 'I couldn't analyse what is happening there, what symbolically is being presented'. At other stages, Arthur's 'mill-speech' of scene eleven was cut, as was scene thirteen. Finally, as Bond explained, Florence's opening speech of scene seventeen was replaced with the line 'An accident with a tin-opener': 'The speeches she had before were too grotesque for that stage of the play. Everything in the last act had to be very simple and direct – because in this act Arthur recovers his sanity; so the grotesque speeches belong to the middle act . . .'.[5] Thus the cuts made were basically of three kinds. One kind was to do with the through-line of the story, and the exclusion of what seemed irrelevant (scenes seven and eight reversed; scenes nine and thirteen excised and parts of scene eleven reduced). Another was a matter of unintelligibility (scene ten, which then proved essential). A third was a matter of the author's sense of what was appropriate (scene seventeen). Given Gaskill's respect for any text he directs, it follows that these decisions were not lightly made, but it is the case that there are aspects of the play which he found difficult to make clear to an audience. Perhaps, given the extraordinary circumstances of the premiere of the play, Jane Howell's view is a fair one. She played Joyce in 1968 and felt:

> we never cracked *Early Morning*. I did see two rehearsals when it was nearly cracked, and then it all went back to the beginning again and in those two rehearsals the actors were very tired and there was a lot of pressure. They started playing it rather fast and nervously, and it started to become farcical, and it was very funny and very fast, and you didn't have time to think because you were laughing too much. The third part seemed as if you'd done four days' work down the mines. A wonderful play but it has to be done like high-class Whitehall farce.

Gaskill's views were partly shared by Peter James who directed the play for the Everyman, Liverpool, in May 1970:

> One of the difficulties as well as one of its great interests is the problem of style. Scenes like the attempted execution of Victoria [scene ten] are burlesque (incidentally I think that the best written scene). So too is the picnic [scene five], but made very difficult by the fact that several things happen on the stage at once – according to Bond by design. But it makes the focus difficult to arrange since the audience is expected to glean almost everything from each incident. If they do not the plot becomes exceedingly difficult to follow. In a letter which Bond wrote to me after the Royal Court production he emphasised that I should get the *story* of the play clear above all things. This proved extremely difficult.[6]

James's sense of the setting of the play is that 'you need a very simple space so that the audience has nothing to distract it from the information that it must glean from the acting which I suppose is to some extent cartoon-like'. For James, as for Gaskill, 'Clarity is its great problem' and he underlines a recurring complaint as regards the acting of Bond. The style 'is so tight that the narrative becomes obscure. "There is no room to move in it" (an actor). One important sentence follows hard upon another too quickly. Somehow the style lacks the ability to emphasise and throw away, to build to crux etc.'. Peter James's worry about scenes of simultaneous activity in the play was countered by Bond elsewhere: 'When Peter James says the picnic scene is difficult because several things happen at once, I say you are missing one of the most important things you can do in a theatre, this multiplicity of action, which the audience can understand as long as the actors are technically efficient and don't look as if they are in a mess'.[7] Of the actor's reaction, Bond says, 'when the actor said, "There is no room to move in it", he really meant, "There's no room to do nothing in it. The text constantly makes demands on me as an actor"'. In the same letter, Bond's general comment both insists upon the play's coherence and also admits its difficulties:

> There are the quiet parts and the hectic parts . . . and I shaped the structure just as I do that of my other plays. The difficulty is that the play makes more demands – on technique, ensemble playing and so on – than most plays. Most plays benefit from these things, but without these things *Early Morning* doesn't even exist. But if they're there then *Early Morning* becomes exciting theatre. It becomes dynamic, releases its energy. *That* I do claim as a theatrical technician . . . If the play does anything else, or is worth anything, that's another question.

One of the problems in trying to assess *Early Morning* theatrically is that it has received so few productions. Apart from Gaskill and James, the only other British directors to mount it are Giles Havergal (Citizens' Theatre, Glasgow, February 1971), Howard Davies (Bristol Old Vic, May 1973) and Philip Prowse (Citizens', May 1974). Havergal, whose production went on in the tiny club theatre, the Close, says the play was too large for the Close, 'like Verdi in a chamber concert', and argues that it works only if 'you find a way in which there isn't a gap, [so that] the ball doesn't touch the ground'. Davies played *Early Morning* in the small Old Vic Studio, and used projections on the back wall in a deliberately expressionistic version of the play. Prowse adopted the device of a 'wipe' to clear away one scene and bring in another, so as to maintain a fluid, fast development. He noted that the style of playing demanded clarity above all. If the actress playing Florence, for example, played scene twenty (where Arthur's head is in her lap) emotionally, 'it made no sense at all. If she did it on very clear cut line readings, it then became a scene of considerable tension, of her absolute incomprehension, and what was left of him trying desperately to explain something which to him was perfectly clear and which she couldn't grasp because of her condition, the fact that she was really quite happy to be where she was'. The play has not been seen in the United Kingdom since Prowse's production.

There are difficulties about the play. It is occasionally too crowded with people and incidents. The movement of the play by means of the 'intimating incident' or by 'verbal tendencies or emphasis' can become obscure. Yet these are part of an attempt by Bond to shift his work in a different direction, not to write *Saved* again but to experiment with different forms. When he termed *Early Morning* 'my freedom play'[8], the comment is to be understood as applying both to a theatrical and a philosophical liberation. After the 1969 production, Bond conceded some understanding of those who could not see exactly what was happening all the time: 'I can sympathise with that, though it wasn't true of everybody. It goes through all I know about life and it was very difficult to get all that in one play'.[9] He subsequently remarked, perhaps ironically, that 'A more relaxed writer might have got three plays out of *Early Morning*, whereas I put all I had to say in one'.[10] Whatever else, *Early Morning* pointed the way forward in Bond's work. As Arthur rises above the world of Victoria, he is the embodiment of Bond's conviction that 'we are a society not in the process of decay, but in the process of birth'. The analysis of what that involves and the practical means of achieving it occupies the plays which follow.

4

Narrow Road to the Deep North

Bond began to make notes for his new play on 14 February 1968, at a time when rehearsals of *Early Morning* were under way at the Royal Court, and when the pressure on that theatre was at its most intense. The notes are headed: 'Play for Coventry Cathedral. The commissioned subject is People in cities. My subject is freedom'. The last sentence ironically reflects the turmoil over *Early Morning*, as does the next: 'You get nowhere if you stop to finish off an old battle before you start a new one'. However, the first draft of the play was not begun until 28 April. Between the two dates, Bond, as has been seen (see page 68), was engaged on a film and then in the final rehearsals of *Early Morning*. By the time he came to write the first version, *Early Morning* had been given two hurried performances and the notices it had received were generally very poor. His anger over the play's reception was still apparent a year later and led him then to be dismissive about *Narrow Road to the Deep North*: 'I regard the play as critic fodder really . . . it's a very easy, light little play. In a sense I wrote it so quickly just to prove that I could do it . . . because [the critics] . . . just hadn't understood a word of the first performance of *Early Morning*'.[1]

The play was commissioned by Canon Stephen Verney, chairman of the executive of the International 'Peoples and Cities' conference, held from 25 June to 2 July 1968, to celebrate the fiftieth anniversary of the restoration of the Coventry diocese after the first world war. Canon Verney approached Bond after three or four other writers had turned down the commission. Having accepted the commission and made his first notes, the pressure of other events was such that the deadline for the play was very close when Bond finally was able to find time to write it. What then emerged was something which bore very little resemblance to the original jottings. They are nevertheless instructive since in part they reflect upon the previous play and demonstrate a developing sense of the stylistic direction of the plays which follow. Thus on 14 February, before the production of *Early Morning*, Bond is noting: 'I want the form and the technique to be "modern" – which the comedy wasn't'. Because the new play is about 'cities, groups and organisations, the temptation is to use 1920s expressionism – putting a machine on stage. This mustn't be done. Need a simple, expressive, perhaps not elegant, but certainly cogent story – which contains all its drama *in itself*, and doesn't use expressionism to refer outwards. The story presents a simple, burning truth that could stand on the head of a pin'. The notes suggest that there are two routes which could be followed: 'I can take a specific People in Cities problem and try to solve it . . . or I can do something more general: ask why there are cities, ask what the consequences of cities will be'. In these notes, Bond, after toying with a number of possible stories, decides 'I must write the more general play. The relation of cities to men'. The play was then put to one side. The single, dominating image with which every Bond play begins its life was not found until the end of April. When it did, the February notes were left far behind.

A year or so before the play, Bond had begun to read an account of the travels of the Japanese poet, Bashō.[2] He began with the first piece in the book, 'The Records of a Weather-Exposed Skeleton' and:

> I don't think I'd ever done it before, I just shut the book and I couldn't read it anymore . . . I more or less forgot about it but from time to time it came up in my mind and when I had this play to produce I just went back to the book and I read it, and wrote a play.[3]

The section of the piece which affected Bond so profoundly, the 'simple, burning truth that could stand on the head of a pin', occurs as Bashō's account begins, where he encounters an abandoned baby by the side of the river Fuji. Bashō's response is 'that this child's undeserved suffering has been caused by something far greater and more massive – by what one might call the irresistible will of heaven. If it is so, child, you must raise your voice to heaven, and I must pass on, leaving you behind' (p. 52). Apart from the opening incident in Bashō's account, which became the play's introductory scene, Bond used very little of the rest of the book. The reference in scene one to 'a paper raincoat' is from 'The Records of a Travel-worn Satchel' (p. 73), and the *haiku* spoken by Bashō in the 'Introduction' is Bond's version of one of Bashō's most celebrated poems (p. 9). The title of the play is that of the fifth piece of Bashō's book and his translator notes that 'In the imagination of the people, at least, the North was largely an unexplored territory, and it represented for Bashō all the mystery there was in the universe' (p. 37). The play 'poured out of my indignation at this man . . . I turned Bashō into a sort of monster, a hollow zombie. One of those people who appear immensely cultured, with all the filigree of culture, all the outward show, but as hollow as can be . . .'.[4] It is perhaps not stretching judgement too far to see in the figure of Bashō and the action which so provoked Bond's anger, a synthesis both of Bond's constant preoccupations and of the resentment to do with the treatment of *Early Morning*.

Bond began the play on 28 April 1968 and wrote three versions of it quickly in two and a half days, which he drily noted was 'Not enough'.[5] He 'hardly rewrote at all . . . when I'd written it I just went through and changed odd words and so on . . .'.[6] Bond had reserved the right to choose the play's director, and it went to William Gaskill who, as he said himself, 'had very little response to it and suggested that Jane Howell, who was my Associate Director, should direct it herself'.[7] Before granting a licence, the nearly moribund office of the Lord Chamberlain required a number of cuts. The two the director recalls were the line, 'How many testicles has god?' (Part one, scene six), and an insistence that Shogo's mutilated body should not show his testicles (the stage direction reads: '*The genitals are intact*'. Part two, scene four). The Chamberlain wished to revise the first to 'How many testicles has a god?' and demanded the deletion of the second. After Bond initially refused to cut the play, Canon Verney and Jane Howell went to London and reached a compromise with the Chamberlain's office. Rehearsals began a day late and the cuts were ignored in the production which opened at the Belgrade theatre on 24 June 1968.

The central antithesis of the play's Introduction is that of

Bashō's quest for enlightenment set against his leaving a child abandoned by its starving parents to die. There is no means whereby the audience may avoid the fact that the peasants and their child represent reality as it is, and Bashō's poetic vocation consists of ignoring that reality, thereby relegating his 'art' to the false and immoral. Bashō does make charitable gestures. He gives the child what food he has. He tidies the baby's clothes. And he leaves it to die. At the same time, he appeals directly to the audience to acquiesce in his description of himself as a 'great' poet, quotes his best poem at them as proof and evades any responsibility for what he sees. Bashō's criminal action in the opening section of the play provides the basis on which he is to be judged throughout. Nothing he subsequently does should surprise. The peasants abandon their child and have no choice. The wife wanders between hysteria and rationalisations. She on the one hand laments the situation and on the other takes inevitable action. It is a scene she is used to, after all, as she is used to the casual beating from her husband. In a scene of a few minutes, Bond outlines the world of the play so graphically that what follows seems inevitable. Yet Bond's estimate of critical responses must have been confirmed by some of the reactions to the Introduction. The review in *Punch* worried that the audience laughed at Bashō's *haiku*. *Time* magazine saw Bashō on a quest for enlightenment, 'a radiant shaft of wisdom that will have the direct luminous perception of one of his poems'. *Record American* saw him as 'an old priest who also searches for enlightenment, but is trapped in ugly politics'. The apotheosis of such misreading describes Bashō as 'a kind, gentle, compassionate little man, full of charming self-effacement but very much aware of his own dignity . . .'.[8]

Ironically, these views are those of Kiro in scene one of the play. Kiro, who is the same age as Arthur in *Early Morning*, was rescued by a priest after his parents died of starvation. Since Kiro is ignorant of Bashō's leaving a child to die, he assumes Bashō to be enlightened and begs to be his disciple. If Bashō has not changed on his return, the place has, for now (thirty years later) there is 'a great city'. The basis of its development is shown by the soldiers leading prisoners to their death at the order of Shogo, an outlaw who killed the old emperor and built the city. What is apparent throughout the scene is Bashō's arrogance and his self-centredness, for amidst the killings, he wonders if his house and orchard are still where he left them. The condemnation of Bashō continues in scene one as he remarks that the northern tribes fed him when he was in need and that the net result of his journey is to realise that 'You get enlightenment where you are'. There are three separate strands here: Kiro's search, Bashō's self concern and the world continuing around them. The next scene takes place two years later with Bashō dictating his thoughts to an amanuensis. The killing of citizens continues unabated. So do Bashō's poems. Kiro has joined the seminary and, as he says in scene three, learnt nothing. As his companion priests get drunk and play hopscotch, Kiro initially sits apart from them, until he is pulled by the rest of the group into joining them. The joking horseplay as they get drunk is comparable to the boys throwing Pat's bag about in the first scene of *The Pope's Wedding* and the gang's pushing the pram about in the early stages of scene six of *Saved*. As the horseplay centres around the sacred pot, the sudden silence as the priests realise what is happening is again analogous to comparable moments in the two scenes from the earlier plays. As Bashō looks at Kiro, imprisoned within a thousand year old religious relic, he sees only the rightness of his decision not to take Kiro as a disciple two years before. It is a cleverly understated moment, with Kiro who has not learnt anything from the seminary standing centre stage with the pot hiding his head. It is also the means of arranging that Kiro and the tyrant Shogo will meet in the following scene, for Bashō determines that Shogo should solve this particular problem.

Scene four is set in Shogo's court and it opens comically with the death of the Chief Police Inspector from a spear intended for Shogo himself. Underneath the casual dismissal by Shogo of the Inspector's death, there is created the sense of Shogo's life being under constant threat, but he is never able to catch the assassins. The people in the city are forbidden to look at him when he goes out but one always does: 'It's always a different face, but the eyes are the same'. What Shogo says echoes Bashō's response to the abandoned baby in the Introduction. There the baby lying in his rags stares at Bashō 'as if I was a toy. What funny little eyes!'. As Shogo dwells on this, the words peter out briefly; some ideas surface, 'but it's gone out of my head . . .'. The links between Shogo and Bashō are developed in this scene without either of them realising it. At the same time, Bond is intent on suggesting that Shogo is both a caricatured tyrant and a victim of his situation. He is rarely two-dimensional and his puzzlement here, later in the same scene when talking to Kiro, and subsequently in the play, reflects a mind attempting to call up details of his earlier life which will make his present circumstances coherent. In his speech at the beginning of the scene, the stage direction makes Shogo walk behind the body of the Police Inspector and stand '*with his back to the audience*'. He muses about a 'circle that never stops getting smaller' and we are presented with an image of his ignoring the corpse (and everyone else), just as Bashō ignored the child earlier and as the unnamed survivor who closes the play will do, as Kiro lies dying. Shogo does not understand certain things and resorts to cryptic sayings as an alternative: 'I can't be on both sides of a door at once . . .'. As he speaks, Bashō is brought in and Shogo is faced with the man, who, thirty years before, left him to die. Neither of them realises it. And the audience will not realise it until Kiro does at the end of the play.

Shogo and Bashō are partially linked when Shogo's remark about being unable to be on both sides of a door at once is unknowingly repeated by Bashō when he enteres the scene. Shogo is startled by Bashō's remark. He and Bashō are closer than they suppose. Bashō challenges Shogo to remove the pot from Kiro's head. Bashō cannot because of his assumptions about the pot's sacredness. It is not a problem for Shogo and he has other matters to attend to. It is in this scene that the conflicting impulses in Shogo are obviously apparent. He will not kill the legitimate heir to the city whom he has kept in the palace and ironically gives him over to the care of Bashō's enlightenment. At the same time, he ruthlessly destroys a peasant, said to be a witness to the assassination attempt. The scene develops its twin centres. Kiro stands with the pot on his head. The peasant stands with a sack slowly enveloping him. Shogo solves both problems by smashing the pot and closing the sack. Kiro comes face to face with the tyrant. He virtually imprints himself upon his rescuer, as he puts his arms around Shogo's legs. The bond between them is carefully built up in their conversation upstage. As they talk, Bashō's outrage at Shogo turns into a plan with the Prime Minister to defeat the man who destroys religion and hope.

Kiro learnt nothing in the seminary, but his curiosity is undiminished. He is immediately attracted to the person who appears to have solutions. The section which concludes the fourth scene shows Kiro mainly listening to Shogo's logic. It is based upon the central notion that Shogo is the city 'but I made it in the image of other men'. Shogo's view of the world is comparable to the views later expressed by Georgina and similar to the views of Albert in *Early Morning* and Lear at the beginning of his journey. The reading of the nature of man leads Shogo to his practical conclusions as to the need for control, for 'law and order'. Kiro dissents from the view, but cannot argue it at this stage. At the same time, Shogo is conscious of his passive as well as active status. He is a prisoner of his gifts, as he says in the scene, and his sense of the truth of this is an echo of Scopey's situation and anticipates Bodice's feeling trapped (*Lear*, Act two, scene four). The expression of this is important for creating a sense of humanity and sensitivity in Shogo. He and Kiro represent the same impulses which have taken different routes towards their respective outlets. Because of what has happened to Shogo, he is in one sense helpless:

> what can he do in those particular circumstances? He obviously says and thinks that there are certain forms of social behaviour which will solve social problems adequately and basically they are – if it moves in the wrong direction, hit it.[9]

Shogo has found answers. Kiro has not, but he does not see practical alternatives at any stage of the play. Kiro's tragedy is neatly predicated by the end of the scene, as Shogo remarks about the welt left on Kiro's neck by the pot: 'I suppose that'll stay'. The investing of the line with more than its overt significance suggests briefly that Kiro will be unable to break out of his final despair.

Bashō and the Prime Minister travel to the deep north with the Emperor's son and encounter the West in scene five. Bond enjoys reversing the traditional Western view of the Orient via the two Japanese figures. The West is represented by the Commodore and Georgina. They are figures which could enter the world of *Early Morning* and feel at home. The Commodore throughout the play remains the same, Lord Mennings with more speeches. Georgina is seen later to be a more complex character, but her views resemble those with which Victoria agrees when they are listed by Arthur in scene twelve of *Early Morning*: 'I had no political experience. Now I've learned that justice depends on law and order, unfortunately. The mob's sadistic, violent, vicious, cruel, anarchic, dangerous, murderous . . .'. Both characters are parodied archetypes, as fixed in their conditioned reflex as Bashō in his. Bashō's enlightenment has led him straight to those who have more potential power than Shogo. His judgement is shown as faulty, since he thinks he's dealing with the Commodore: 'He's so stupid I *think* I can control him'. Both Bashō and the Prime Minister dismiss Georgina in advance, only to find that she is the real force, as the British Empire takes over Shogo's city and promptly acts in the same way as Shogo to control it (scene six). In the middle of the fighting in scene six, Kiro's ambivalence towards Shogo is apparent in his opening speech. Shogo deserves death. Nevertheless, Kiro wants to save him from death. His responses are not concrete, but an indication of his own turmoil and of his feeling for a part of himself. The scene builds to its climax comically as the British destroy the palace to the strains of 'Abide with Me'. Kiro and Shogo escape after persuading the Prime Minister that they are really priests; on the other hand, a refugee peasant and his wife, as always, become victims of the conquerors. The 'priests' are allowed to go; the peasants are proclaimed traitors and left on the floor '*with their hands on their heads*', an image of the dispossessed political prisoner.

A week later, Georgina has changed the city with the willing aid of Kiro's former priestly companions. It is in this first scene of Part two that Georgina reveals herself as a political animal, differing from Shogo in terms of the ploys used, but aiming at the same end as the other tyrant. She surprises Bashō and makes him revise his opinion of her. She rationalises her views at least as logically as Shogo, and, though it is comically given, it is clear that, like Shogo, she has arrived at this view out of her circumstances. Shogo views the world as a place where his vulnerability was exposed; Georgina had the same view beaten into her, as, she says, did all of the ruling *élite* of England. She employs 'morality' and holds similar contempt for most of those around her. It is entirely characteristic of Bond to invite an audience to form a particular view and, by reversing the portrait, force the audience to change its mind. Bashō, perhaps unwittingly, offers Georgina her own epitaph: 'people who raise ghosts become haunted'. He is not to know that it also applies to him.

The second scene, set in the deep north, shows the growth of Shogo's counter-coup against the British. It is also in this scene that there occurs the most intimate sequence in the play, as Shogo and Kiro talk to each other. Shogo's forced inactivity makes him restless as they wait for the tribesmen to arrive. As the scene opens, he stands ready to fight, wanting some sort of physical action, but Kiro largely wants to think, like Len, to puzzle out what has happened. Shogo eventually joins him and as they stare into the river, they both review their lives. It is a moment of calm and reflection (which Bond underwrites in the revised text for *Plays: Two* by the new stage direction: '*Their voices when they talk as they look in the water are calm and rapt. Individual words are not emphasized*'). Shogo's life 'goes on and on like a finger reaching out to point . . .', but Shogo cannot see at what. He feels guilty of 'the worst crime that's ever been done', but cannot define it. Nothing demonstrates Shogo's tragedy as clearly as this moment and nothing so effectively relates the causes of it. That he can impatiently dismiss Kiro's accusation about killing people as irrelevant reveals shockingly the degree of violence done to him as a child. Finally Kiro cannot help and the mood changes abruptly. The last event of the scene demonstrates Shogo's tragedy. As the gun fires and kills a tribesman, Shogo's only response is 'There! See how it works! We'll take the city in a day!'.

The city is taken and Shogo briefly reassumes power in scene three. He is then faced with the irresistible extension of his own logic, as he looks at the five children abandoned by Bashō. Without Basho to identify the Emperor's son, Shogo can act only in one way, since the child must not again be used as a political weapon against him. Bashō impinges on Shogo's life throughout the play and it reaches its terrible crisis in this scene. Shogo kills the children and pushes Georgina into insanity. After the near hysteria of the decision, Shogo reverts to peremptory instructions to his soldier about what is to be done. The picture of Georgina singing snatches of a hymn to herself and the heap of children's bodies provides a powerful account of the victims of the play. As Kiro returns from the north in response to Shogo's message (scene four), he is met with the reverse of his expectations, as the British once again and finally retake the city. The jolt provided by the fact that everything has again changed around is quite deliberate: 'The essential thing for me, for instance, to explain that structure in *Narrow Road* . . . is . . . Shogo in complete control . . . and then the next minute someone says that was last [month] and it's all over, it's changed . . .'.[10] What Kiro sees is the opposite of what he expected to see and it leads him to despair. The Commodore begins to take control because of Georgina's madness. He is aided by Bashō, who becomes Prime Minister. Shogo is put on trial. As parts of it come over a tannoy, Kiro, onstage, reads some of Bashō's poems as a kind of counterpoint to Bashō's account of Shogo's birth. The quality of the poems is made clear by Bashō's lies about Shogo. Bashō and the Commodore whip up the mob to butcher Shogo and speak of it as an exorcism. Shogo's hideously mutilated body is revealed behind a sheet. Its revelation is deliberately delayed and is therefore more shocking, a moment of violent effect. Kiro now understands at last the puzzle he and Shogo struggled with in the scene by the river. He lapses into silence. After the mob has moved on, the crazed Georgina watches his preparations and her sexual hysteria is daringly expressed as comedy: 'Murdered before I'm raped! I shan't know what it's like!'. The laughter stops as Kiro kills himself carefully and methodically. For the play's first director, the suicide is inevitable: 'I came to see those two as representing halves of the same person . . . So when one of the characters died, it seemed to me that the suicide of the other was inevitable'.[11]

> Kiro's suicide is not offered as a solution to anything: what is important for me is that I use Kiro to demonstrate the futility of his despair . . . at the end of the play, Kiro, with all his introspective enlightenment . . . and understanding, nevertheless puts himself in that same position [as Bashō], because he doesn't understand, or cannot accept, the necessity for social action . . .[12]

Elsewhere, Bond argues the irrationality of the act: 'There is never a reason for suicide. There's a lack of reason for living . . .'.[13] Kiro can see no reason for living, but the reason shouts at him at the end of the play. As he sits, dying, he, like Bashō, does not answer a call for help. Nevertheless, the near-naked man does climb out of the river and accuses Kiro, as the child's eyes had accused Bashō in the Introduction: 'He stares at me as if I was a toy'. The man survives, as did Shogo, and the man may well become Shogo. His will to live is unkillable. What he does with his life is not stated. What, however, is stated is that on one side of the stage, there is a near-corpse; on the other, a naked man drying himself and ignoring Kiro's fate.[14] Kiro opts out not, as Shakespeare later does in *Bingo*, as an indictment of his own activity, but as a futile gesture about the impossibility of living in the world.

The play's first director, Jane Howell, describes *Narrow Road* as virtually a primer for Bond's plays. Its setting, apparent simplicity of statement, its effect of spare, detached analysis of a context of violence, have all combined to earn it the label of 'Brechtian'. It is clear that in some senses this is true. Bond exploits 'Brechtian' moments (see below) and allows the 'shape' to be 'somewhat Brechtian'.[15] At the same time, given Bond's acknowledgement of Brecht's work (see pp. 63–4), it is also true that his source book is Japanese. More importantly, Bond asserts that the techniques of *Narrow Road* are the same as those in *Saved*, and that the only difference is that *Narrow Road* deliberately takes place in a context of three centuries, where *Saved* has a more specifically modern setting. Bond, in replying to a critic identifying his work closely with Brecht's, argues

> I build a lot of my alienation into the play's structure. Two or more points of focus on the stage, manipulation of time to serve the argument and not the story, showing characters in their various social roles and in various social situations (and so achieving 'wholeness') rather than developing a character from its *geist*...[16]

The processes and techniques Bond lists are as applicable to *Saved* as they are to *Narrow Road*.

Jane Howell directed *Narrow Road* three times in three years (see note seven). Two productions were in theatres with a large stage area, particularly as regards width; the third was in the more confined setting of the Royal Court. On a wide stage, she found that 'We could set part of the action on one side and part on the other. The picture-book element in the play was thus brought out in the right way – the actors were able to work in *demonstrated* relationships'.[17] The action in all three productions was set on a long platform (the 'narrow road') with the surrounding areas on stage painted black. At the back of the stage, the designer, Hayden

Griffin, constructed screens which, at the moment of the revelation of Shogo's mutilated body, were smashed down and the black spaces invaded. The importance of greater width for Jane Howell was to enable her to show the 'cross-cut action' both within scenes and from scene to scene. She aimed for an effect of 'presented' theatre, like a child's pop-up book. The effects common to all Bond's work became more apparent perhaps than before because of a wide stage.

Early Morning had investigated the route to freedom and had shown that it is possible. *Narrow Road to the Deep North* continues the process by asking what that freedom is for. How is it to be used? Kiro's reaction to his situation is a negative one. Such a reaction as Kiro produces is blocked off by Bond in the play's ending. At the same time, the ending stresses the difficulty of judging events and coming to terms with them. This to some extent comes about because in the plays up to and including *Narrow Road*, the central figure is tied in some way to another figure who is both the protagonist's opposite and also part of the main figure's own makeup. The development of each of these early plays is shown in terms of one figure freeing itself of those features which hold it down and prevent a rational view of the world. Without a view, the figure cannot free itself. The conflicting elements within any one figure are dramatised in the early plays by the creation of related opposites: 'Scopey/Alen, Len/Fred, the Twins, Kiro/Shogo – and a lot of the drama comes out of the conflict between these pairs of characters. They are all attracted and repelled by one another – and they all involve the other in death. The development of the plays can be seen most clearly in the developing situation between these pairs. Who is bait and who is victim?'.[18] This theatrical schizophrenia is employed to dramatise the struggle of warring elements within one figure. That figure advances each time a little more towards understanding. As the progression develops, the image moves from the simple extension of Scopey into Len, becomes literal in the creation of the Siamese twins, and develops into two separate but related figures with Kiro and Shogo. The fascination and repulsion felt by these figures remains a constant see-saw. The theatrical means used to show the process varies from Scopey's inarticulate attempts to discover Alen's secret, to Len's preoccupation with Fred, whom he is able eventually to judge, to the metaphorical and literal decay of George to a few bones on Arthur's shoulder. In *Narrow Road to the Deep North* the two figures of Kiro and Shogo demonstrate two conditioned routes. One baby was rescued from death, the other abandoned but survived in a crippled state. We are shown how what initially happened to them makes them what they are. It is vital to accept that, *pace* some critics, Bond does not deny causality. When it is asserted that, for example, Bond denies 'any simple causality based upon psychological trauma as the reason for Shogo's tyranny. He is emphatically not the way he is *because* he was abandoned'[19], there is a confusion between the acceptance of causality and the fact that stylistically it is not played in an obvious manner. When Bond says that 'this is a play about a non-existent child',[20] he means that in reality what is likely to have happened historically is that the child died. But further, he is referring to the destruction of the normality of the child, the complete perverting of its natural assumptions and expectations, and the consequences. Thus 'Shogo, who was killed (emotionally – it comes to the same thing) as a child, later kills five or ten or whatever number it is'.[21] The result of the deprivation is the clear relationship between victim and aggressor, expressed in terms of cause and effect. All of Bond's aggressors are victims of their situation. The difference between these figures is marked by their ability to make a coherent analysis of their situation. Scopey cannot. Len, a little further on, judges Fred but goes no further. Arthur begins to feel alive when in scene nineteen of *Early Morning*, he articulates the condition which is to afflict Shogo: 'Bodies are supposed to die and souls go on living. That's not true. Souls die first and bodies live. They wander round like ghosts, they bump into each other, tread on each other, haunt each other . . .'. And Kiro, seeing what Arthur saw, cannot face the truth. Or, as Bond puts it, in a letter of 14 April 1972: 'Shogo and Kiro are really one person. The tragedy is that they couldn't use each other's powers. Our society makes it difficult for us to do so – that is our tragedy . . . They are not incompatible, though most christians and most communists act on the premise that they are'.

What Bond writes is a series of scenes which both assert the links between the scenes and at the same time the self-contained nature of each individual moment. Both elements must be shown 'because life is ordered by cause and effect, incident and choice, problem and decision and this reality must be reflected in the structure of the play'.[22] Thus Shogo can only make decisions as a result of the damage done to him, but he also struggles at times against such inevitability. In Part two, scene three, he is confronted with the five children, and begs their help:

> SHOGO. . . . Which one of you's the Emperor's son? Please! D'you want to make me do something terrible? (*Shouts.*) Bashō! Bashō! Help me! Help me! Help me!
>
> *A long complete silence.*
>
> SHOGO. All right. Let's go on. I don't know who's the Emperor's son so I kill them all.
>
> GEORGINA. Monster!

The 'monster' Shogo, faced with something he does not want to do, begs to be released from his status as aggressor, is seen as a victim, and when no help is forthcoming, relapses helplessly. During the long, 'complete' silence, we are presented with a moment reminiscent of scene eleven of *Mother Courage*, where Kattrin beats the drum, of which Brecht said:

> the epic theatre is in a position to portray other occurrences besides excitements, collisions, conspiracies, spiritual torments, etc., but it is at the same time also in a position to portray these.[23]

It is used here to create a proper empathy with Shogo's situation and to provoke, as the moment ends, a certain detachment, a context for analysis by the audience. Shogo's struggle is also Kiro's. Like their predecessors, they involve each other in death. When Bond next dwelt on the idea of conflicting elements, he shows Lear ridding himself of such an element by rejecting the temptations of the Gravedigger's Boy's Ghost and, finally, Willy freeing himself of the idealised drowned Colin in *The Sea*.

5

Lear

In July 1968, a month after the production of *Narrow Road to the Deep North*, the Royal Court announced a season of three of Bond's plays for the spring of 1969. It was to be made up of the first public performances of *Saved* and *Early Morning* and Jane Howell's Coventry production of *Narrow Road*. Subsequently, the English Stage Company toured *Saved* and *Narrow Road* in September and October to Belgrade (where *Saved* was awarded joint first prize in the Belgrade Festival), Venice, Prague, Lublin and Warsaw. For the second year running, the English Stage Company consolidated its international reputation by following the success at Belgrade of Peter Gill's production of *The Daughter-in-Law* in 1968. When Bond returned from the European tour, he began his notes for *Lear* but he had been thinking about the play shortly after *Narrow Road*, and had spoken of it at the end of 1968 (see below).

Lear is a play about a society in the process of birth. It is concerned with the problem of how freedom becomes a 'practical possibility in the present world' and its conclusions present a figure who accepts moral responsibility for his life and who acts to show this acceptance. The ending of *Lear* reconciles the worlds of *Saved* and *Early Morning* by demonstrating moral actions within a concrete social setting. In the last scene of the play, the audience sees the wall for the first time. The wall is the pervasive symbol of the play and, as soon as the audience sees the wall on stage, Lear tries to tear it down. The gesture he makes is neither final nor futile. It is the demonstration of Lear's integrity to those he leaves behind that action is both necessary and possible. It also con-

play which rejects pastoral alternatives, golden age tions and mere theorising. *Lear* is the first play in which d argues that direct action is imperative, but revolution in *ear* is not a theory channelled into practice. It is not an ideology nade operational and it does not accept the idea of ends justifying means. The play continually demonstrates the nature and interaction of social and personal circumstances as the guiding determinant of subsequent action. In *Lear*, Bond relates effects to causes as he had done in earlier plays but he also shows the growth of organised and developing resistance to a repressive government in the last scenes. The play's conclusion is a measured account of the difficulty of action in an unjust society but it also demonstrates that action is the only moral response in such a situation. It would be facile to suppose that any greater optimism than this could reasonably be shown at the end of such a sombre and realistic work.

Because of the critical hostility which greeted the earlier plays, particularly *Early Morning* in 1968 and again in 1969, and because of the general incomprehension and political objections symbolized by the Lord Chamberlain's office when faced with *Saved*, *Early Morning* and *Narrow Road to the Deep North*, Bond's preparation for *Lear* was more extensive than for the plays before it. *Narrow Road* was partly the gesture of a serious writer whose work was not being treated seriously and *Lear* became for Bond the play in which the basis of his position would be made clear and unequivocal. His irritation is still apparent two months after the play was performed for the first time, when he wrote to his publisher about the 'Author's Preface' to the printed version: 'I've written an introduction . . . I'm tired of being told my philosophy is naive by people who don't understand it and really know nothing of the evidence on which it is based. So I've tried to say something solid that will give some background to my plays. I think this is the right time to do it'.[1] The 'Author's Preface' to *Lear* is a compressed version of a long series of essays and notes, written between 22 October 1969 and 4 June 1970. Twelve days after concluding these notes, Bond wrote the first draft of *Lear*.

The notes for *Lear* show that those eight months or so of 1969 and 1970 were one of the most intensive work periods of Bond's writing career. As he began the work on *Lear*, he also started a translation with Keith Hack, a Cambridge undergraduate, and subsequently a professional director, of Brecht's *Round Heads and Pointed Heads*, which itself is based on Shakespeare's *Measure for Measure*. For Bond, the process was partly that of a lesson in German and also a relief from *Lear*. He wrote to Geoffrey Strachan on 20 October 1969 that 'when I start writing a new play I find it really painful if I concentrate full time on it for the first few weeks – so the translation will help'. He also wryly observes, with a nod in the direction of the various film scripts which financial necessity more than anything else had occasioned, 'It's a good feeling to be writing something for myself again'. Hack's account shows that Bond worked on *Lear* during the mornings, and on the translation in the afternoons, that the translation continued 'for five to six months on and off', and that Bond was 'particularly interested in what Brecht made of a Shakespeare play'.[2] One consequence of the Brecht work was Bond's essay, 'The Duke in *Measure for Measure*', which forms part of the early notes for *Lear*. In it, Bond argues that Shakespeare, in spite of his original design, produced 'a total arraignment of conventional authority and the morality used to explain and excuse it'.[3] Also as part of the notes from December 1969 to May 1970 and therefore part of the process are a story, *The King with Golden Eyes*, a 'Play for Sharpeville 70', a short story called *The Kite*, a draft speech for a Cambridge Union debate, and notes for a story entitled *Buddha Dog*, as well as a long series of poems which run from 27 October 1969 to 1 June 1970.[4]

Bond's first public thoughts about his new play did not include the figure of Lear himself: 'It's a new version of the three sisters . . . Not Chekhov's . . . but a modern play about King Lear's three daughters . . . If you get rid of the King, the play becomes much more interesting. He is a renaissance preacher addressing himself to the Gods. He tells all the lies. He belongs to the seventeenth century, but he is irrelevant nowadays'. By September 1969, he is still on the same tack.[5] Three months after the *Lear* notes begin, in October 1969, Bond has brought Lear himself back into his play, and articulates his responses to Shakespeare's play:

> I'm not criticising *King Lear* in any way. It's a play for which (it's a stupid thing to say) . . . I have enormous admiration, and I've learnt more from it than from any other play. But . . . as a society we use the play in a wrong way. And it's for that reason I would like to rewrite it

> so that we now have to use the play for ourselves, for our society, for our time, for our problems . . .[6]

The *Lear* notes begin with a series of essays on general issues. A piece on aggression written on 22 October 1969 distinguishes between the lion hunting for food out of necessity but without anger and the situations in which it is proper to talk of aggression in animals.[7] It is followed by a note on 'Heliocentric Politics' (23 October) which argues the problems of living in a political and moral flat-earth society: 'If we remove force and authority people won't revert immediately to their basic nature (assuming that's gentle and tolerant and unselfish). On the contrary, they'll behave in this socially conditioned way – that is greedily, violently and selfishly . . .'. The consequence of this idea produces, in an essay entitled 'Revolution' (27 October), the prerequisite for successful change: 'To make a revolution now, you first *have* to make propaganda. It is necessary to show people the faults and the dangers of the present set-up . . . Unless a correct analysis is made, and is then widely understood, there won't be any change . . .'. It is a sentence which describes the impulse behind all of Bond's work, and it is allied in the same essay to the ever-present danger of violence engendering more violence. Following this is a group of notes to do with 'emotionalism' (28 October) which separates out instructive and protective ways of feeling from the emotionalism used as a substitute when a rational argument dictates the contrary. From this point, Bond ranges over a series of subjects – aggression again (31 October); survival (3 November) which '*doesn't mean* the survival through fighting of the fittest. We tend to think of evolution as an arms race . . .'; 'Man as a hunter' (4 November) – 'If he was set as a hunter, why would he develop into a farmer, since that would be against his skills and putative impulse?'; innate emotional structures and economic systems (9 and 17 November) and, finally in this section, 'Emotion compared to Economic/Rationalism in Politics' (27 November). It is only after these pages of analysis, speculation, questions and notes over a month that, on 1 December, there occur the first jottings on 'Queen Lear': 'This title is the working title *only* of my new play. It isn't meant to convey the contents'. At once, one of the central strands of *Lear*, the antithesis of justice against law and order, is apparent: 'The play

demonstrates one's rights, which can only be obtained in a soc
of justice and not one of law and order . . . justice is the experien
of liberation'. This antithesis is central to Bond's beliefs, so that justice is 'a human expression of evolution' against which is posited the institutionalised expression of authority, law and order, which is 'anti-life'. At this stage, the play's conclusions are not apparent: 'Is it therefore going to be a revolutionary tract, ending optimistically? Or will it show how law and order destroys justice?'.

The play's beginnings stress the links with earlier plays and suggest the next stage of the process. On the one hand 'The play is a continuation of *Early Morning*. Forgetting the Lear pattern for the moment, it is the individual's search for freedom' (1 December); on the other, the play 'ought to get away for a while from the Scopey-Len-Arthur Odyssey. This suggests the myth of the innocent destroyed by the guilty, the wicked – but this isn't good enough!' (3 December). Added to ideas from previous plays are the themes introduced by Shakespeare's and Chekhov's work:

> Why *Lear* and *Three Sisters*? *Three Sisters* partly because they've stayed in my mind since I translated them. Why *Lear*? Partly because of the moral imbalance . . . if you look at these three girls, you'll find they all suffer as much and die like Lear, and are no more guilty than him – that in fact, they are like the three sisters . . . Anyway, unlike *Early Morning* it isn't basically a comedy. The intention is more serious. *Early Morning* was like someone escaping from a prison. Tunnelling their way out. In the new play, they are outside and take a look around . . . (1 December).

Initially, Bond wonders about beginning at Lear's death and concentrating on the life which the sisters evolve. Or that Lear is alive and insane and the sisters have to cope with the insanity. What does occupy him is the image: 'I don't yet have the starting image. *Early Morning* was the twins, *Narrow Road* was the Basho-baby scene . . . My own version of *Lear* and the *Three Sisters* isn't enough. I must start from my own image, and not merely my own ideas'. What is vital at this stage is how the focus of the play will distinguish it from the two models in Bond's mind:

> The reversal of the academic moral/artistic/theatrical myth isn't enough, the making *reality* of Lear mythology isn't enough, because the play isn't to get its life merely from being a commentary on [*King*]

ttack on it or correction of it. The play must have a struc-
i itself, which then throws light across onto [*King*] *Lear*,
sters. The play must be its own dynamo and experi-
play interests me because it's about a family . . . (2

Early on it is clear that the play 'isn't set in the garden and the drawing room . . . but . . . in the execution yard, the street, on top of the roof, the police conference room, the school, the spinster's bedsitter'. Yet if the starting image is not yet apparent, neither is the movement of the play. What is seen so far is 'just those great big chunks of three sisters'. On 3 December, the analysis roots itself in King Lear's context – how he has been protected all his life, how he abandons his security: 'the unnerving thing . . . is that we see an old man going through the stages of infancy. And at the end he dies as a child – but we aren't shown him living as a man. The living child has to enter the dead world'. In this comment resides the eventual ending of Bond's play with a figure dying in action, and the distinction between this and the ending of *Early Morning*, for though it is true that 'Arthur has escaped. He's arrived at a just assessment of himself and his rights . . . he [nevertheless] hasn't reawakened Florence. He has to resurrect her'. In defining Arthur's limitations, he also defines how Shakespeare's play is used by certain audiences: 'Nothing sacred about him if you see him as a politician or churchman. There is a lot sacred about him if you see him as a child being led into the land of death. *They* see him as a hero of the land of the dead . . . Because there he's shown as the victim of fatality'. *They* 'read' *Lear* so as to gloss the play in the following way: 'The human spirit struggles but it's beaten down: that's how it must be. That's truth. The disaster is mitigated for them because they can still point to the persistence of the human spirit. That man's desires rise above his possibilities. But how gratifying the desires are, how they raise us above the brutes, how they ennoble us . . .'. It is noticeable in this that the objection is to the *use* made of the play, rather than to the play itself, and that what fascinates Bond is how King Lear as a figure contains elements both worthy of reverence (sacred), and worthy of condemnation (unsacred). His Lear is eventually cast as a figure within which the definition of justice and law and order co-exists, and his Lear's progress is a struggle for supremacy of those two mutually exclusive tendencies. On 4 December, Bond is back to the image hunting of the previous days: 'I must get my image from the world that isn't on the stage. The park and the siamese twins are real images, not theatrical ones'. At the same time, he is engaged in a critical appraisal of the way he has worked before. Thus 'the trouble with *Early Morning* is that it isn't real, and I had to make up for this by making it politically/royally offensive'. What exists for the moment in the notes are sketches for possible plots and a general analysis of the two models: 'This stage is like sitting by a mouse hole waiting for the mouse to come out, but with the expectation that when it does it will turn into a lion'.

From 3–15 December, the notes are occupied with an extensive group of images, without which the play's process cannot begin. The images centre upon blindness and perception, seeing and understanding, which is central to the play. Out of two or three line stories of, for example, a man with glass eyes, a car driver with glass eyes, a blind man looking after a child and gold teeth being removed at an autopsy emerges the story of *The King with Golden Eyes*, which not only opposes the conjunction of authority and blindness with perception and justice, but which also begins the linking of the old man and the child as an expression of Lear's beginning again as both child and man. The story leads to the picture of Lear as 'a man who has been in prison for a long time. He is released and goes through the tragedy of freedom' (9 December).[8] As he does, he is 'a child exposed to the phenomena of his environment, to the experience of kindness and unkindness by his associates . . . he impinges on society and the biological facts of growing, birth, sex and death'. The image which will provoke the play is not yet apparent. As Bond waits for the mouse to become a lion, one thing is resolved: 'There must be a crying scene in the new play' (15 December). On 16 December, there is a summary of how far the play has developed: 'The play is to do with a political revolution in a background of biological danger to the species. The disaster must be connected to the revolution. At the end perhaps the girls end up in the same prison – good and bad'. It will not be about 'kings, nobles, and their bastards and heirs . . . It's not a question of inheritance, who gets to the top: it's to do with the total structure, the complete dance, the force that holds it together. In my play there can be no Albany waiting in the wings'.

As 1970 began, the character of Lear becomes the dominant area of discussion. He is returned to the play by Bond but cautiously: 'It shouldn't be a series of scenes dominated by Lear's speeches and tantrums' (5 January) but nevertheless 'What is it that Lear realises or becomes – in the way that Arthur realises and becomes free?'. Lear then becomes a figure living in the conventional world. As a result of some sort of disaster, he enters the world of 'the living-dead' where he is surrounded by ghosts. He is 'a live man haunting the dead. His haunted daughters must therefore lay the ghost . . . So Lear's madness (In fact sanity – he sees clearly) is like an amalgamation of Acts 2 and 3 of *Early Morning* . . .'. At the end of this sequence of notes, there is another summary: 'I want a story . . . I have the core – the inner experience of the mad scenes. I need an ending, which can wait. But how do I start?'. It has taken from October to January to arrive at the elimination of attractive possibilities: 'Now I have nothing to write, so I can begin. I can begin at the simplicity of it, and clarify it from there . . . Don't observe the ripples in the pool, but the pattern they leave on the surface' (13 January).

After this conclusion, the notes begin to home in on the story which contains the simplicities. Where Shakespeare's Lear abdicates, 'In my play I think power should be taken from him. He has become arbitrary and dangerous, and his daughters depose him' (19 January). The daughters are divided between two who depose him and one who helps him. The play becomes one of revolutions, war and alliances between the three sisters, a foreign king and Lear. Throughout this upheaval, whoever is in power rules as badly as Lear had done. Nothing changes. Each repeats the pattern of the predecessor. At the end of this story, Lear and his family are dead, and the foreign king rules like Lear. As Bond observes to conclude the note: 'They change the left boot for the right boot and call it revolution' (19 January). Certain images recur. The autopsy has already been toyed with. Now, there is produced the possibility of Lear's 'fool' being a guerrilla leader. At the same time, the story so far involves constant betrayals and counter-betrayals, which eventually surface in the scheming of Lear's daughters. Cordelia begins to attract more attention at this point. She's described as 'a sort of unsuccessful Robespierre' (21 January), and seen as the great force that destroys Lear. When she dies, there is suspicion about the manner of her death and Lear orders a post-mortem: 'What do they discover? What indeed! A field-day!'. On 28 January the death of Cordelia sparks off an important thread: 'The image dominant in my mind during the last few days has been the post-mortem. Secondly, the use of ghosts . . .'. On 4 February, the discussion is about the play's ending and the suggestion that Lear leads some deserters against the government: 'This would entail . . . that he ends with some degree of political success, or at least ends in sight of it. Otherwise this isn't part of the series of freedom plays I've written. But, it isn't necessary to have a freedom ending. One can end a play pessimistically in order to provoke (or suggest) optimistic activities and views to an audience'. Though the play's frame is by now one of continual war, Lear's enemy is not an external one. He is a prisoner of his own convictions and activities, a moralist and therefore corrupt (9 February). He is the upholder of law and order which 'functions like a cage' (10 February). The cage image is passed over after this reference and there is one further sheet of notes for 11 February after which the specific play notes are not resumed until 1 April. As the play is left on 11 February, it begins with an arbitrary figure who tries and condemns a soldier. His daughters plot to depose him and he is given over to the care of Cordelia. The daughters in turn are deposed by a group of guerrillas who may put Lear on trial and side with Cordelia.

On 17 February, Bond began a 'Play for Sharpeville 70', which was produced at the Lyceum on 22 March. In one sense, *Black Mass* performed a function similar to that of translating Brecht, a relief from the complexity of a large-scale work, 'something short which I felt strongly, and about which it was possible to make a very direct statement and an unqualified statement that it was wrong and it was very important to try and remind people of that so the event wasn't forgotten'. *Black Mass* enabled Bond to clarify some of the issues to do with *Lear*: 'in a sense, writing shorter plays is like sharpening your pencil, putting a finer point on it again . . . it's very useful to take things down on to a smaller scale, structurally a smaller scale, so that one can experience almost within the grasp of one's hand the texture of a structure . . .'.[9] *Black Mass*, a twelve-minute sketch, is set out very quickly in the notes and is a distillation of the discussions to do with *Lear* from the previous October onwards. Its first director, David Jones, writing to Tony Coult, 16 September 1971, accurately gauges its intention and effect:

> The play itself works very well with a partisan audience, such as we had, and the final moments with the Police Inspector's cross mounting drill turned out to be a very effective piece of black humour indeed. Some of the earlier writing was not quite as sharp and funny as it might be . . . I think the play is very much an extended review sketch, written under speed for a special occasion; and I doubt whether Bond would consider it as an absolutely major piece of work, though it did its job very well indeed on this occasion . . .

The savagely comic attack in the piece as a style was to surface again a year later in *Passion*, another occasional piece for the Campaign for Nuclear Disarmament's Festival of Life on Easter Sunday, 11 April. Before resuming *Lear*, Bond also wrote a short story on 29 March, entitled *The Kite*. It is a children's story about a boy who becomes part of the kite he is given as a present. He eventually becomes a ghost living within the kite. After many years, the ghost dies.

On 1 April, Bond returned to *Lear*, and more of the eventual shape of the play becomes apparent. It opens with a soldier awaiting execution and Lear shooting him, sets up a later trial, where Lear calls a ghost to the stand, considers Lear blinding himself, and uses two locations, the court and a cottage with a family, to which Lear retreats. Equally, the notes begin to insist on Lear's motives: 'He wants to run his kingdom well, orderly, preserve his privileges, serve the people and be respected as God's anointed. The war (just or unjust?) interferes with this. He wages war "for the sake of the people", but it forces him to be arbitrary and despotic . . . His daughters side with (marry) the conquerors'. Lear is then put into a scene with his dead daughters and sees what he has made. Thus 'the play is a search for self-value – and the moment/moments/hours/days/years of experiencing self-value, validating one's self'. This decision is important, for it stresses the fact of Lear's misdirected but real integrity: 'He tries to do something as a king and fails. He goes on trying to correct his failure – and it's through this attempt . . . that he's "educated" – but along with this "education" . . . I have to show the political consequences . . . It's the relationship between Lear and his political activity that's interesting' (7 April). Hence, Lear looks for a key to understanding his own activity, a touchstone to guide him. The development of Lear for Bond is seen as that of a ghost who learns how to live again. For Bond defines ghosts as the living figures who are emotionally dead, 'in whom emotion becomes angry aggression, destruction, anti-life . . . Lear himself starts off by being dead. He's no better and no worse than the others . . . ghosts are the incarnation of law and order. The dead army' (8 April). As before, some of Bond's thoughts emerge through a consideration of what happens in *Early Morning*. Lear begins the play as a ghost 'or has his ghost – just as Arthur has George . . . So what happens to Lear? He lays the ghost in himself, and is he then destroyed by the other ghosts – daughters and allies – or does he free them? If the journey to freedom is fully worked out in *Early Morning*, perhaps in this play the liberation from politics ought to be played. But perhaps this liberation isn't possible, and there's no future for us, we drop out of evolution'. On 12 April, Lear is pictured 'sitting by a still pond. A visionary structure . . . Lear like an old Narcissus . . . not actual, but buried/submerged in the scene . . . looking at his dead self in the perfect circle of the pond'. A day later, the idea of the pond becomes that of a fountain. As Lear's 'living activity falls apart', his actions become 'a rhythmless dance – that is, before the . . . fountain' (23 April). By 23 April, the image of the fountain closes the play. Only in June is the story of the fountain of blood removed to Act One, and the image of Lear and the pool condensed into Lear's epitaph for himself in Act Three.[10]

By 13 April, there are signs of the movement of the play under six headings: 'Lear tyrant; defeated, outlawed, pursued; mad; rescued and sheltered; sane; destroyed (perhaps)'. The play is

> in a few, perhaps even only one, scene, continually unfolding in units, so that time passes with the progress of the units, and also place – because in some units the actors travel from a to b. The whole thing could be cut up into 2 (perhaps 3) parts. This cuts out blackouts and changes of that sort. I don't know yet about the style: whether Lear talks out his ideas, explains, criticises the anti-Lears, or whether it's all submerged, as in *Saved*. Mixture, perhaps.

As the movement is discussed, so are the beginnings of how Lear's developing understanding might be shown: 'he suddenly introduces a subject, not obviously related to what is being said or thought about, and with great vehemence, complication, circumstantiality – as though defending himself against a charge he has suddenly and secretly heard. Like Arthur and George's foot – only better' (14 April). This note on Lear's character becomes the basis of the struggle in Lear's mind, for his sanity. Lear is now seen as an aggressor, but his role as victim is more problematic. It is not sufficient, the notes remark, to see him go meekly to the slaughter: 'I want to see how it's possible for a free man to live, how he ensures his security'. Bond can now 'see' Lear:

> A quite tall man, with solid compact bones, a longish head, the cylindrical bone shape clear, quite a wide, full mouth, almost negroid but flat. Big hands, with long, almost square fingers. Square fingernails. His toes run almost in a straight line. Square, not barrel, chest. Treads with a spring, but contacts the ground firmly. Gestures with hands rather than points with fingers. Blue eyes. Of course, when the square frame collapses, some of the body surfaces seem to cave in, the lines of tension poke into one another, and broken diagonals appear.

As Bond constructs the physical Lear, he also decides that Lear should start in control. He does not begin alienated, as had Arthur. Here there occur three brief anecdotes about a gravedigger and his son, and one of the main structural segments falls into place: 'Perhaps Lear could go and live with the Gravedigger's boy and his wife. His wife objects to this. She says her husband lives in a dream – he's not a realist. She is a realist and understands the political trap that will shut on them. Lear is found, they shoot the Gravedigger's boy out of hand, but Lear is kept for a trial'.[11] From this, it is a short step towards floating the idea that 'Perhaps the wife then leads the guerrillas . . .' (27 April). This brings Bond once more to the discussion of violence, which had partly been explored in the notes for 27 October. The problem is once more set out, as if to remind himself that 'you can't employ violence for a limited objective and then leave off being violent when you've achieved that objective – because violence has its own logistics – and terror and fear will follow from its use. If the use is large (as in Stalin's regime) the terror and fear will be large – and this will enforce the use of more violence' (26 April).

The evolving discussion of violence and its relationship to the figure of Cordelia marks an important step towards the play. Throughout Bond's plays there is an analysis, sometimes implicit, of the nature of violence, its causes and its consequences. Each of the plays takes the analysis further on. Each play is part of a process rather than a conclusion. *Lear* is a conscious preparation for later statements about violence. Between *Lear* and the most recent plays there is no abrupt change in Bond's attitudes. Rather, the analysis of the biology and sociology of violence in a play such as *Lear* leads to discussion about the acceptance of the necessary danger of violence in revolutionary politics within a play such as *The Bundle*. The conviction apparent in *The Bundle* is a direct consequence of the probing in *Lear*. Cordelia's is a revolution which demonstrates how violence may be used to reinforce the very things it initially revolts against. She therefore for Bond becomes a Stalin-figure as the play proceeds (see p. 129).

By 27 April, the concern is with why Lear's daughters turn against him. They react against his arbitrariness and he makes enemies of them: 'But they must have – or give – an immediate reason: something is or goes wrong . . . Lear [is] building a grandiose wall to protect himself against his enemies, or actually engaged in a war'.[12] As the main symbol of the play is noted, the rationale of the opening becomes clearer, and the notes for *Lear* cease until 1 June. In the meantime, Bond drafts his speech for a Cambridge Union debate and makes notes for a short story called *Buddha Dog*. From 1–4 June, the notes discuss the wall image, the poem, 'Lear's Song' is written[13], and the relationship between myth and reality is set out:

> I think that Lear should 'stand for' something poetic and instructive and creative. The daughters and sons-in-law 'stand for' some sort of realpolitik, some industrial 'necessity' . . .

Virtually the last image of the notes is: 'Cordelia: pregnant woman with a gun'. Twelve days later, the first of six drafts was written.

Bond wrote to Gaskill on 21 July that 'Lear is now in a completed draft – *this is very good because I now have a play.* I'm not at the stage where I might have to give it up because I couldn't find a play in it. And now I want to work all my time on it for a while'.

He did for a year and then wrote to his publisher on 5 April 1971 to say that *Lear* was finished and to voice a worry which was to become a problem in subsequent casting: 'The difficulty will be to get a Lear. It's a role of classic length, but I don't like the idea of a classic actor doing it. He might make it too mannered and so on . . . this one has to be middle-aged'. Again, to Gaskill, Bond dwelt upon Lear's age: 'Certainly Lear has to be old – but not doddery. The advantage of a younger actor is just that he'd have more stamina. But I agree, a younger actor would have to be told to act the *development* and not impersonate old age . . . (There has to be lots of old men on the stage and all the young ones running amok)' (8 May). Bond's concern over the choice of a Lear recurred during discussions subsequently over the *Lear* shown at Yale. He wrote to Robert Brustein of Yale Drama School on 9 August 1972 that for most actors 'a combination of intellect and passion is beyond them. So they have to fall back on rhetoric – and there is *none* in this play. A scream from a wounded man is not rhetorical or hysterical – it is a precise description of a situation, and is reduced to essentials. So you also have to have an honest actor – I mean aesthetically honest . . .'. The problems of casting Lear are described elsewhere, as is the general evolution of the production which opened at the Royal Court on 29 September 1971, directed by Bill Gaskill.[14]

Bond's notes for *Lear* reflect both a profound admiration for *King Lear* and an insistence upon the use of the Lear story in terms which make it intelligible to and a parable for our own times. There are obvious features of Shakespeare's play which are used in Bond's play. Both, for example, show a king and father acting arbitrarily and being opposed by two daughters whose sole concern is to acquire power. Both Lears move from autocratic behaviour into a kind of insanity and come towards some understanding and pity. Incidents to do with the partition of the kingdom, blinding, the imprisonment of father and daughter and the general deployment of animal imagery are common to each of the versions. Bond differs in certain important respects. There is no loving daughter (for that matter there are no conventionally 'good' characters such as Kent, Edgar and Albany). Taking the Shakespearian cue of Cordelia's returning to England at the head of France's army to rescue her father, Bond turns the third daughter into his guerrilla leader. It is not only deliberately done, but the withholding of Cordelia's name until near the end of Act O at the very moment when the Gravedigger's Boy is about to be shot and his wife raped, is specifically aimed to destroy any lingering notions on the part of the audience that someone in the play will represent conventional goodness. The moment is not only inherently shocking but perhaps the point at which Bond emphatically thrusts Shakespeare's play well into the background of his own play. Another important change is how the function of Shakespeare's unnamed Fool is replaced by the Ghost of the Gravedigger's Boy, a figure which persistently offers illusory refuges for Lear and which he must finally part with in order to go on. The Shakespearian sub-plot disappears and the blinding of Gloucester transferred, albeit with the same metaphorical effect, to Lear himself. Where King Lear wishes to abdicate, Bond's Lear is intent on building his wall to keep his kingdom together. Most important of all, King Lear dies helplessly, unable to change the situation at the end of the play; Lear dies attempting to undo some of what he has made during his life. There are obviously other parallels and differences and it is clear that *Lear* shows a modern writer utterly absorbed in the tiniest details of Shakespeare's play but equally clear that the story is one which is capable of refashioning for the second half of the twentieth century.

The nature and purpose of the refashioning can be seen expressed theoretically both in the 'Author's Preface' to *Lear* and in some remarks by Brecht in *The Messingkauf Dialogues*. Bond's insistence upon the misapplication of technological progress, its exploitation by a small group within society and the need to understand this clearly echoes Brecht's worry that

> The more we can squeeze out of nature by inventions and discoveries and improved organization of labour, the more uncertain our existence seems to be. It's not we who lord it over things, it seems, but things which lord it over us. But that's only because some people make use of things in order to lord it over others. We shall only be freed from the forces of nature when we are free of human force. Our knowledge of nature must be supplemented with a knowledge of human society if we are to use our knowledge of nature in a human way.[15]

At the same time, Bond emphatically opens his 'Preface' with the overriding importance of addressing himself to the problems of

to demonstrating the causes to his audience, just as unces that what he terms the 'persecutors' may only 'once enough people understand the causes of their miseries, and the way things really happen . . . it's a question of communicating this understanding to as large a number as possible'.[16] Where Shakespearian man 'is helplessly handed over to his fate, i.e. to his passions'[17], both Brecht and Bond argue the modern equivalent to be 'social man'. The modern theatre for both writers 'exposes any given type together with his way of behaving, so as to throw light on his social motivations; he can only be grasped if they are mastered. Individuals remain individual, but become a social phenomenon; their passions and also their fates become a social concern'.[18] It is for this reason that Bond remarks in his 'Preface' that apart from the main characters of his play, the other parts are 'In a sense . . . one role showing the character of a society'. The society represented in this way indicates the influence exerted by the dominant figures of the play. To put it crudely, Bond's Lear progresses from a Shakespearian to a modern archetype.

Lear's progression is shown in three movements. These are described by Bond in his 'Preface':

> Act One shows a world dominated by myth. Act Two shows the clash between myth and reality, between superstitious men and the autonomous world. Act Three shows a resolution of this, in the world we prove real by dying in it.

The myths of Act one are all to do with the figure of Lear himself, his assumptions and his blinkered refusal to see and understand what is going on around him. Lear's chief characteristic is, despite the events of the first act, either to relate them to the evil represented by his daughters in rebelling against him or to retreat into a private world which cannot, he supposes, be touched by external happenings. For the first four scenes of the play, the consequences of his actions are played out in the revolt of Bodice and Fontanelle, the archaic and easily-guessed military strategy he employs against his enemies and his baffled incomprehension of the completeness of his overthrow. In the last three scenes of the act, Lear is equally a prisoner of his assumptions as he enters the pastoral world of the Gravedigger's Boy. Only intermittently does he wonder about where the responsibility lies for what has happened, but always to direct such blame away from himself. The myth of his rightness holds him a prisoner of his own wilfulness and in this he is remarkably similar to his Shakespearian antecedent. As King Lear, after his abdication and subsequent rejection by two of his daughters, is forced out onto the heath, so Lear is summarily expelled from his autocratic position into the countryside. Both figures, however, still act as if nothing had happened to modify their beliefs. Both have a great distance to travel before they are prepared to relate causes to effects.

The play begins with the imminent arrival of Lear to inspect the work in progress on a wall being built by forced labour to protect his kingdom. The people in the scene live in fear of the King. The workers and soldiers know that he is coming 'and that he always comes looking for trouble'.* What then happens grows directly out of the events of the scene. Lear does not come intending to murder a man. His two daughters, Bodice and Fontanelle, do not come proposing to tell their father of their impending marriages to the Dukes of North and Cornwall. These things are precipitated by Lear himself. He creates the conditions of his own overthrow by deliberately using the accidental death of a worker to force the pace of work on the wall, because 'otherwise my visit's wasted'. He acts with autocratic authority. Consequently, he is outraged when, for the first time, he is publicly contradicted, and by his own daughters. Until the crisis of the proposed court martial of a worker for sabotage, Lear and his party should be seen, as Gaskill suggests, 'like the Royal Family today visiting a shipyard, carrying umbrellas' (p. 23). Lear is accompanied, along with his daughters, by politicians rather than aristocrats. Bond describes Warrington as having 'a politician's manner. But he's quite empty – apart from probably rather liking military routines and being quite a decent fellow. He's not vicious, just wants everything to work well. With Lear, he observes the humane decencies but in the end tells Lear what he wants to hear' (p. 22). And Gaskill defines him as 'a Civil Servant . . . authoritative, and capable of running the country himself' (p. 26). The Old Councillor is 'a pink-faced, lovely white-haired, angry baby. He always makes Lear feel (and act) older. Because Lear sees him as a parody of

* *See note 14 which locates the quotations used here and subsequently in the chapter.*

himself' (p. 22). Lear is encircled on the one hand by those who tell him what he wishes to hear and on the other, although he does not initially realise it, by two princesses who will betray him.

From the beginning, Lear is faced with rebellion and his violent actions and outbursts betray his sense of events slipping from him. He is a King exercising absolute authority at the very moment of his own displacement. The rebellion is already in progress. The wall is being dug up by the local farmers. Lear's actions are those of a man utterly convinced of his own rightness. To protect his people, to put into operation what he has learnt from history and his life, makes the shooting of one worker a minor irritation. People are to be used to further the goal of security, just as Albert in *Early Morning* argues that 'The people are strong. They want to be *used* – to build empires and railways and factories . . .' (scene two). Lear acts from the best motives. His account of man argues the necessity of the wall. Lear has seen 'armies on their hands and knees in blood, insane women feeding dead children at their empty breasts, dying men spitting blood at me with their last breath, our brave young men in tears . . .'. Such an account of the realities of existence parallels Arthur's logic in the first part of *Early Morning*. Given man's nature to be thus, the consequence is Arthur's attempt to destroy the species or Lear's attempt to stave off his enemies. What Lear provokes, which he first treats as innocent kindness, is the moment of disassociation by his daughters. He cannot understand it and resorts to childish tears in his rage against them, as the workers and soldiers stand mute with the body of their fellow worker, executed by Lear himself, slumped forward on the post. His indictment of Bodice and Fontanelle is a self-indictment. What he will not own, and subsequently has to, is his responsibility for what they are. The stage is left to the daughters at the end of the scene. Lear is already defeated before he goes into battle.

As scene two begins, Bond presents the balance of private and public lives. Lear stands, a figurehead, saluting his soldiers, relying on the strategy which defeated the fathers of North and Cornwall and at the same time wondering aloud about his daughters: 'Where does their vileness come from?'. He is buttressed by the sycophantic Warrington and the inevitable churchman, as he announces the methods by which he is to lose. The scene shows Lear as he has always been and, at the same time, contains the essence of the change in circumstances which are to depose him. In some ways, Lear seems archaic in his suppositions and he is presented comically as a means of showing this. As in the first scene where he had to be moved out of the firing-squad's way, so in the second, the prolonged saluting of the march past is accompanied by his muttered conversation with Warrington. As Bond remarked, 'the secret of the scene is playing two things – being on parade and being secret'. The brief scene is followed by another of the same length, which significantly is described as the '*Daughters*' War Council'. North and Cornwall from first to last are treated as peripheral. The grim comic flippancy of Bodice and Fontanelle, which comes to be an index to their natures and to Lear's treatment of them, surfaces in their asides and is to continue into scene four. The Dukes are both 'clueless about war' and 'frightened of each other' according to Bond, and Gaskill felt they should be played with 'a movie-star virility' (p. 27). Fontanelle is disappointed with her husband, but pleased with her plan to acquire the whole kingdom. Bodice, in spite of what she says, is also disappointed with her husband and when she says 'So I shall have three countries', 'it should be like a greedy child. She never gets what she wants' (p. 29). The scene is deliberately written in a slightly farcical way, particularly as regards the sisters' asides, as a comic style is set against its content of sexual inadequacy, murder plots and territorial ambition. The scene has to establish the essential features of Bodice and Fontanelle, if the torture of Warrington in the scene following is not to be felt to be gratuitous. The audience's understanding of the early moral destruction of the two women will enable the torture to be seen as inevitable. So, Bond underlined the fact that the references to Warrington being invited by the women to betray Lear in scene three should be 'marked', so that the audience understands more clearly their punishment of him'.

Scene four begins with soldiers impatiently waiting to be sent home, now that the battle is won. Bodice and Fontanelle, who have planned the deaths of their husbands, are frightened to see them still alive. Warrington is caged in like an animal and, so that he cannot inform, has already had his tongue cut out. As North and Cornwall go, Warrington is left at the mercy of the two women: 'it is a sudden thought that prompts Soldier A to say, "Yer wan' 'im done in a fancy way?" and . . . this thought occurs to him because Warrington's entry as a prisoner is greeted with solemn looks and total silence on the part of the women'.[19] The status of Soldier A is cleverly suggested by Fontanelle's appraisal of him ('Good teeth, too') and his acquiescence in the violence is created by his suggestion of the manner of torture. Cornwall and North are not sent off so that the two women can torture Warrington in the way it subsequently develops onstage. Just as the killing of the child in *Saved* does not emerge full blown from the beginning, but escalates in intensity, so the mutilation of Warrington is a consequence of the developing situation. It is the situation which creates the events. As the torture begins, Fontanelle particularly is swept along by what happens and acts like a little girl in her excitement. The element of farce apparent in scene three is repeated in the torture of Warrington, particularly when the Soldier indignantly asks of Fontanelle, ''Oo's killin' 'im, me or you?' and, more chillingly, as Bodice sits aside from the action, knitting and commenting on Fontanelle's frenzy. Bond maintains, rightly, that 'there is no extraneous violence – it is all somehow justified' (p. 24). It is so because of the Soldier's professionalism, the daughters' anger at Warrington's refusal to aid them, and Fontanelle's direct attribution of what she is to her father. It is horrible because there are clear causes. For Fontanelle, satisfaction can only be achieved by the destruction of the thing she hates and her language collapses into that of a child with an opportunity for revenge on a parent: 'Kill his hands! Kill his feet! Jump on it – all of it! He can't hit us now. Look at his hands like boiling crabs! Kill it! Kill all of it! Kill him inside! Make him dead! Father! Father! . . .'. What has happened to Bodice, on the other hand, has given her a frightening control of herself. Apart from her knitting, she performs only one other action: poking her knitting needles into Warrington's ears and then stepping back to admire her handiwork: 'Like staring into a silent storm'. The scene ends as it began with a soldier reducing the events to the normal requirements of his job and matter of factly asserting 'Yer'll live if yer want to'.

Lear goes into a new world in the fifth scene, a pastoral context, and the staging becomes very simple. As John Gunter remarked, Bond 'minimises what he needs. The classic is the scene in *Lear* where he just asks for a bowl and a jug of water, and, of course, when it's there it's simply staggering'. The simplicity does two things. It emphasises the distance Lear has travelled from his court and it shows the kind of ordinary life he will find in the house of the Gravedigger's Boy. The war is still close, however, as Lear and the Old Councillor enter, and Gaskill felt that the entrance should present an image of 'two dogs panting. The Old Councillor is a hunted animal stuck with the wrong mate' (p. 28). Lear's self-concern is still uppermost in the scene, 'like someone with shell shock – he opens his mouth and out come the words . . .' (p. 29). In Lear's speech which begins 'My daughters have taken the bread from my stomach . . .', there is combined self-pity and posing, but also the beginning of a genuine re-seeing of the world, if only at a comparatively superficial level. As Bond put it, 'I think that in his first madness, there is an element almost of pretence . . . he is saying I have been a great king, now I'm going to be a great madman . . . so that in a way he acts his madness, but because I believe he is a person of real integrity . . . he can't make do with a pseudo-madness. He has to go on to a real madness'.[20] What he retreats from will not release him so easily, and, as the Old Councillor deserts him, the silent and mutilated figure of Warrington enters to hover briefly with a knife and then vanish as the Gravedigger's Boy enters. The Boy comes charitably to leave bread and water for Warrington, and finds Lear. Gaskill stressed to his Lear (Harry Andrews) that 'Even in the earlier scenes the Boy isn't important to you. You've been the King and have fallen on hard times and are, to an extent, dependent on him, but you have no real feelings towards him . . .' (p. 27). Even so, 'Lear is sane enough to know that if he stays he is endangering the Boy and the girl'. Lear nevertheless brings the war into the Boy's world.

As Lear enters the Boy's house (scene six), he takes with him his madness and the threat of destruction to the way of life evolved by the Boy. The Boy has moved from digging graves (and the metaphoric implication is thrust at Lear) to building a well for the spring water he found while constructing his father's grave. His account is one of economic simplicity, yet it carries its problems because of the wife he has taken. Cordelia in this scene and the following one presents a picture of unhappiness which is accentuated by the Boy's decision to let Lear stay: 'What Cordelia really wants is to learn how to live like the Boy, but it's impossible'. Like Bodice and Fontanelle, Cordelia is conditioned by her social circumstances. Bond had noted as early as the second draft of the play the need to establish her different background, 'something to demonstrate potential'. What is shown in scene six is her misery, her fear of outsiders, her sense that she cannot make the Boy happy. It is related ostensibly to her being pregnant, but the reference to her father's opinion that she would be unhappy in her marriage locates briefly her general state in something outside the immediate context. The audience has to wait until scene seven before the Boy spells out the difference in social status between himself and his wife and, further, to identify the similarities between herself and Lear: 'she'd like to put a fence round us and shut everyone else out'. Given her education and given what she sees, she, like Lear, eventually applies her logic to the circumstances. She should attract a certain amount of sympathy. Of her Bond says in a letter of 16 June 1978 that 'Her arguments are not without a just basis. She is defending herself against the intolerable'. Her defences, which later become systematized, are presented here simply as fear.

Lear's defences in scene six consist of a further retreat into madness. He trusts no-one in the scene: 'the mad speeches are not difficult for Lear. After the anger in the first scene, Lear shuts something off and refuses to allow himself to be hurt'. Lear is exhausted, living off what little reserves he has, but dwelling upon his defeat in gnomic phrases. The image as he lies down '*in an awkward pose and sleeps*' is of someone pursued by the recent events, unable to come to rest. At that moment, the confusion and threat in his mind is presented externally as Warrington makes another attempt on Lear's life. Lear sees the first of the play's ghosts and assumes his death is imminent.

Between scenes six and seven, Lear sleeps. As Gaskill noted, 'he has a long therapeutic sleep and suddenly he's back in the world. There should be a very clear difference between 1.6 and 1.7' (p. 29). A consequence of Lear's recovery is that the former arrogance asserts itself. The madness has passed for the moment and Lear muses about the possibilities of a new life. He supposes briefly, even though he knows it might damage the Boy and Cordelia, that he can forget what has passed and arbitrarily makes an attempt to expel Cordelia. The movement of Lear towards understanding halts for a while in this scene, seduced as he is by the idea of a pastoral alternative, not so completely however as to avoid sounding defensive about the Boy's offhand references to the mad king and the wall. In a scene which begins in a simple domestic way, Lear remembers parts of his dream which he tells as an allegory (a verbal disguise he adopts later in the play). The dream is about a king who discovers a fountain which has turned red. The Boy's wife pegs out white sheets to dry and as the Boy descends into the well to clear a blockage, Lear matches his strange dream to a more frightening reality. He realises that it is Warrington who has hidden down the well and that there is blood in the water. Lear knows it is blood and is frightened that his dream and the reality exactly match. As he understands that, the soldiers arrive at the house. It is almost as if Lear cues them on. Gaskill's note to his cast on the soldiers' entrance emphasises the ordinariness of what they do: 'The war is over, the soldiers have only two jobs – to find Lear and mop up generally. We must have the feeling that the soldiers desecrate Cordelia's place just by their presence' (p. 28). Just as Soldier A in scene four observes: 'Don't blame me, I've got a job t'do', so Soldiers D, E and F here systematically carry out their function. As Lear rightly says, 'You're soldiers – you must do your duty!'. He aids them by betraying the Gravedigger's Boy in the well. He goes and sits upstage to watch what he knows is going to happen, so that what confronts the Boy as he emerges from the well is Lear, who represents the destruction about to happen, a line of white sheets, which hides the soldiers, and silence. It is here the audience realises that the wife's name is Cordelia for the first time in the play; the pastoral alternative is shattered as the Boy is shot and a huge red blood-stain spreads over the white sheet he is clasping round him. As Lear relapses helplessly, the village Carpenter re-enters. His appearance earlier in the scene had been related specifically to his love for Cordelia; his second entry sees the beginning of Cordelia's rebellion, as he efficiently destroys the soldiers, some of whom are raping Cordelia. Lear is returned to the world which he thought he had escaped. The dramatic movement is ironically circular.

If Act one is, as Bond says, 'dominated by myth', the middle act proceeds to set that myth against reality. The movement of Act two develops by means of surrounding Lear with a series of obvious consequences of what was set in motion in Act one. There are three strands to the Act. The first deals with Lear's evolving ability to understand, if not to deal with, what is happening. The second shows the effect of the war upon Lear's daughters. The third traces the rise to power of Cordelia and the Carpenter. All of these have their origins in the first act of the play and they all are logical developments. What changes is Lear's response. Where five of the scenes of Act one had been exterior scenes, and had been designed to mirror Lear's self-absorption and his reluctance to 'place' the events in an order which would lead to a self-indictment, in Act two, the majority of the scenes are interior, as what happens surrounds Lear in a relentless fashion. He responds in two ways. At times, he retires into a private world and, as in Act one, tries to ignore what happens (in this he is aided by the Ghost of the Gravedigger's Boy). At other times, and more importantly, he begins to see in a novel way either, simply, the beauty of natural phenomena, or, more shockingly, that most of the criteria on which he has built his life are wrong. After his traumatic realisations of what he takes to be man's natural inhumanity in his trial (scene one), he attempts to find a kind of peace with the spirits of his daughters as small children in the scene following. Cordelia's revolution gathers pace outside the prison (scene three) and Bodice's war loses its momentum in scene four. The growth of the guerrilla movement affects the Act most obviously in the fifth and sixth scenes. It is in the latter of these two that Lear for the first time places myth against reality as an autopsy is performed on Fontanelle and he is forced to see that his image of her is utterly wrong. He moves from realisation and his blinding to the climactic moment of the act where, in the last scene, he kneels by his wall and begs the farmer and his family to go away from the wall. As in Act one, Lear is returned to the point at which he began. Lear, like King Lear, cries out against tyranny and injustice but cannot see a clear way. As the act concludes, Lear resolves to write to Cordelia in an effort to persuade her to stop work on the wall. It is obvious to the audience that the gesture is inadequate.

Lear's trial as Act Two begins is stage managed by Bodice. Lear has, says Bond, been in prison three or four months, and is much weaker as a consequence: 'Bodice . . . thinks she's broken him and that she's given everyone instructions to cover any emergency. The one emergency she didn't cover was that she had failed to break him'. The trial is organised publicly: 'The feeling should be that, because he is the King, they have to go through a formality, they can't simply shoot him in his cell'. As the trial gets under way, Lear finds from somewhere the strength to challenge all the participants. The Judge, acting under instructions, is immediately thrown by Lear's refusal to acknowledge his daughters. The mockery of a trial is in turn mocked by Lear's strength, and Bodice pushes Fontanelle to the witness stand to cover the confusion. Because she is a princess, she attempts to be formal but, comically, cannot help breaking into her usual girlish language. Lear's fatigue is demonstrated but also his refusal to be cowed: 'this is a scene of pain. It won't work if we feel that he can put two sentences together coherently'. In turn, the Old Sailor as a witness fails to affect Lear, and the Old Councillor loses his temper at Lear's insults. The Judge must be supposed to be looking continually at Bodice for instructions, and she sees her arrangements crumbling before her. The crisis of the trial is resolved by Bodice's sudden inspiration. She takes over from the Usher in her impatience. She gives Lear her mirror. Lear sees in the mirror a bruised and bleeding animal. As Bond explains:

> Lear, who has seen himself on postage stamps, . . . on monuments as a hero and father, sees himself for the first time as he really is – as a bad father and a bad king. If you see two cars crash and look through the window, you will see a man who is cut and shocked, trapped in the cage of the wreckage, squirming around inside. This Lear sees. The others can't, as they would be unable to do their jobs if they did. They couldn't be officials or dukes.

Lear becomes lost in his terrible realisations and his daughters goad him on; Fontanelle, seeing Lear's tears, relives her enjoyment of Warrington's torture. Lear's vision of injustice broadens so that his last two lines before he is taken away mean that Lear 'hears *all* the victims cry, all the people who have ever passed through the courtroom . . . Lear can "see" the blood of the victims of the daughters' injustices' (p. 29). He is, however, not yet ready to acknowledge his responsibilities. The cruelty is attributed to his daughters or, as he puts it, the monsters who have replaced them.

Lear comes into his cell in scene two still agitated about the trial and says 'I must forget' because he knows that he will go mad if he cannot forget. For Bond, 'the secret of playing the scene is to consider 2.1 and 2.2 as one scene for Lear', as Lear takes various ways to distance himself from the animal he has seen in the mirror.

Consequently he takes very little notice of the Ghost of the Gravedigger's Boy, who enters the cell, preoccupied as he is with the imminent destruction of the world. When the Ghost reveals that the banging on the wall, which Lear thinks is the caged animal, is only the noise of other prisoners, Lear is dismissive to the Boy and accusingly demands the help of his daughters. The Ghost has no access to the animal. It is exclusive to Lear and marks the degree of separateness existing between the two. Gaskill notes that in Act Two, 'the Ghost is always there when Lear wants to escape from reality and responsibility' (p. 25). It is the Ghost which calls up the ghosts of Lear's children, who then pathetically demonstrate why they are as they are. In calling them to relieve the pressure, Lear shows the audience how far his mistakes reach back. For a moment, the animal is at peace, but at a price. Lear disregards what he hears Bodice say of coffins and death. As Fontanelle sits on his knee, Bodice jealously puts on her dress and comes to him for attention. But it is her mother's dress and the gesture 'backfires' (p. 28). The scene develops visual complexity with Lear and his daughters, the Ghost watching, and then Ben, a young orderly, cheerfully entering with Lear's food. At this point, Lear sees an end to the pain in a vision of the future. Perhaps Lear has not yet earned the right to prophesy, any more than the right to peace, for the vision slips as soon as it is established. But some things are clearer: 'we have to see that Lear has learnt something, learnt he has to hear crying, because it's human . . .'. He still acts with selfish desperation to retain his daughters and his peace. As they leave, Lear's mind begins to give way and he cries that the animal has found someone. Bond explains that the 'someone' who is found 'is Lear. The animal is digging to find Lear and it's the horror of this image which causes Lear to faint. Lear talks himself into the relationship with the Ghost – it takes his mind off himself and his troubles' (p. 28). Before Lear joins with what the Ghost offers, he is presented with the picture of the Old Orderly, 'a survivor, because he finds everything that's left – cigarettes, a scarf – and because he never challenges anyone directly'. He has been imprisoned for years and for him Lear is just another victim. He stands, however, as Lear's victim, as one of the people Lear saw being dragged through the courtroom while on trial. Lear does not make the connection. He instead retreats to the Ghost, who takes his chance and begs to be allowed to stay with Lear. It's here

Left and top left:
Edward Bond (*photos: Bond*)
Top right: Edward Bond as Christ in *Black Mass* (London, 1970) *photo: Gascoigne*

The English Stage Company at the Royal Court, London: opening of the 1965–1966 season (*photo: Bond*)

The Pope's Wedding: Knut Hinz (*Scopey*), (Hamburg, 1971) *photo: Clausen*

The Pope's Wedding: Bob Peck (*Alen*), (Exeter, 1973) *photo: Toyne*

Saved: Elizabeth Bennett (*Pam*), Jack Carr (*Len*), (Leeds, 1973)
photo: Leeds Playhouse

Saved: John Castle (*Len*), Richard Butler (*Harry*), (London, 1965)
photo: Dominic

Early Morning: David Hayman (*Arthur*), (Glasgow, 1974) *photo: Henderson*

Early Morning: Shirley Anne Field (*Florence Nightingale*), Moira Redmond (*Queen Victoria*), Jack Shepherd (*Prince Arthur*), (London, 1969) *photo: Jeffery*

that the identification of the Ghost with that part of Lear which refuses reality is made clear, as Lear tentatively feels how thin the Ghost is. For the first time in the scene, Lear really 'sees' the Ghost, sees what he has destroyed, sees in fact what will offer him a false refuge until near the end of the play. Lear begins to feel compassion for others in his last speech of the scene. He responds to the pathos of the Ghost and the scene ends with a tableau of the two holding each other. It is the beginnings of compassion.

The Act leaves Lear and the Ghost in scenes three and four to show the effects of the civil war on Cordelia and her guerrilla army and on the forces of Bodice and Fontanelle. At once, the situation shows where Cordelia's circumstances have brought her. She is, as Bond outlines, 'a woman who takes everything in, that she knows she has to remember everything, that she will remember the Wounded Soldier when she talks later to Lear'. Her conviction and determination are absolute and Bond balances an account of why with a demonstration of what follows. Soldier 1, who has defected to try to join Cordelia, is shot because he is no use to the guerrillas and she calmly asserts the necessity for it in order to achieve power. Bond tersely states in a latter of 18 March 1977 that 'Cordelia represents Stalin, it is as simple as that' and elsewhere sets the remark in context:

> The simple fact is that if you behave violently, you create an atmosphere of violence, which generates more violence. If you create a violent revolution, you always create a reaction . . . Lenin thinks for example that he can use violence for specific ends. He does not understand that he will produce Stalin, and indeed must produce a Stalin . . .[21]

The scene moves quietly and tensely, guerrillas fighting professional soldiers and the 'situation of the Wounded Soldier is regrettable but inevitable' (p. 26). Yet the final image is of the dying guerrilla fighter, alone, counting stars. If Cordelia is inevitable in the context, so is the soldier's death.

From one army command to the other, equally dominated by one woman. There are two functions of scene five. One demonstrates Bodice's apparent control of affairs and the other demonstrates that affairs in fact control Bodice. More versions of this scene were drafted than any other. It is in this scene that Bodice and Fontanelle quarrel openly for the first time, and Bond asked his German cast to 'Remember how much [Bodice] has had to learn after taking power; she is angry that Fontanelle hasn't learnt'. Fontanelle is consistently a child, and her frivolity increases proportionately to the seriousness of the matter. The conduct of the war is taken on by Bodice alone. The dukes, terrified as ever, remain puppets, but Bodice then demonstrates that she is as much a puppet as the two men. She is a prisoner of the map in front of her and of circumstances. She produces a factual analysis of her situation. It contains no self-pity and no regret, and she is seen '*trying to understand what has happened to her*'. Faced with her position, she resolves to work even harder to prosecute the war. In this scene she is the embodiment, shown in all Bond's early work, of the victim and aggressor figure. After the second scene of the act, where Bodice was shown as a little girl, the audience is better able to understand Bodice and to see how her real abilities have been forcibly driven in a particular direction.

Scene five shows Lear in full retreat from the animal in the mirror. As before in the latter stages of the first act, he has closed his mind to the situation and allied himself with the Ghost's alternative. He is no further along in recognition. He has simply refused to think further. The group of soldiers and prisoners attempt to reach the security of Bodice's headquarters and the atmosphere of quiet tension parallels that of the scene which showed Cordelia's guerrillas. The effect of the war is one of massive dislocation for all. Bond insisted that Lear should be 'far removed from the fear of the scene . . . he is the only one not afraid . . . all the prisoners should feel that they are acting in a play within a play'. The chains and blindfolds the prisoners wear are a simple visual statement about them and the soldiers being lost. Lear is lost in a different way for his serenity is heavily ironic. His concern is for the Boy and here for the first time he acknowledges his betrayal of the Boy in Act one. The massive self-absorption involves his not recognizing Fontanelle who is captured and attached to the chained prisoners as Cordelia's forces take control. Just as the first two scenes of the act are to be played as one, so Lear's state in scene five extends into part of scene six. Within his serenity, Lear notices things he has not seen before. Throughout the early sections of the scene, there is a sense of Lear's wonder at recognising ordinary natural phenomena. Lear sits and thinks and ignores everyone except the Ghost. Outside his self-centred thoughts, the grimmer reality of political executions is forming. The Second Prisoner is taken out of the cell. Bond is at pains to explain that the Prisoner is 'not frightened; he is morally outraged by the fact that he is being shot by the very people he's risked his life for many times'. The ever present risk of violence leading to more violence is created by the increased stature of the Carpenter in the scene. His status has changed: 'up till now we've only seen him as a soldier or a carpenter. Now he's an important member of the Cabinet, sent to witness the execution of the Royal Family'. The Carpenter sees himself as morally correct: 'he thinks he's doing the right thing, so he's very puritanical' (p. 29). The Carpenter orders the death of Fontanelle, who is immediately shot. Only the fact that Cordelia does not wish Lear's death saves him. It does not save him, however, from damage.

Just as the Carpenter is concerned with efficient action, so the Fourth Prisoner, a doctor, is concerned to demonstrate his usefulness to the regime. As the Prisoner prepares for the autopsy on Fontanelle's body, Lear slowly re-enters the scene, and the Ghost cries out in terror. What is different is Lear's refusal to go away with the Ghost. He stays, childlike in his curiosity at the doctor's work, noting disinterestedly that the corpse on the table is that of his daughter. He is curious because

> he expects to find something hideous but can't. Just as for the first time he had seen the sky, now he sees a human being for the first time. It's important to Lear that he finds something hideous. He's killed thousands of people fighting her because she was wicked. But he can't find anything hideous. He should be insistent that she was cruel and angry and hard... When he says, "If I had known she was so beautiful...", it is a rejection of everything he's ever said or ever done – he wouldn't have built the wall ... etc. Be aware of the size of the moment. *Lear has wasted his life*... The autopsy speeches should be gentle and the pace should vary – some thoughts should be more difficult than others.

Lear's shock is balanced against the calm professionalism of the doctor, whose character 'especially with regard to the delivery of his lines, should be that of a University professor' (p. 29). Lear's wonder grows as he takes his full place in the scene, and truths are pushed further home to him when Bodice is brought into the cell. As Lear emerges, the Ghost has to retreat and the gap between the two is beginning to widen.

As Bodice enters, she attempts to act as if everything is under control. She asks 'In here?', as Gaskill points out, not meaning 'Is this the right cell?'; 'It is keeping up the pretence that she is being shown into a drawing room. It is this attempt to maintain the image of herself that is so pathetic' (p. 28). What she encounters is a different father, whose statements to her 'are an act of public confession'. In a gesture both shocking and pathetic, Lear shows to his remaining daughter the organs and viscera of her dead sister. He now, as at the beginning of the scene, withdraws into himself, but not in the same way, for now he thinks of how he is to open his eyes and see. Just as Lear wrecked his trial in the first scene of Act two, now here his massive intrusion into the autopsy similarly disrupts the orderliness of the proceedings. Things revert to normal with the prolonged and messy death of Bodice, who again, on the entry of the Carpenter, tries pathetically to act as if she will be able to avoid her sister's fate. Ironically, she demands 'justice in court', presumably not of the kind she offered her father. As Bodice dies, the Fourth Prisoner tries to regain ground with his scientific device for extracting eyes which he demonstrates as if he were a schoolboy inventor. The Commandant and the Carpenter do not ask what will be done and they leave before the careful blinding of Lear takes place. Here, as throughout the scene, the dramatic brilliance derives from the fact that no-one relates to anyone else in terms of the playing. They all, from Lear's withdrawal to the Carpenter's role as witness, to the doctor's scientific demonstration, to the soldiers' comic remarks about snake bite and rabies, pursue independent tracks of thought and activity. The expression of self-preoccupation is a large metaphor for the cruelty and indifference of all of the characters at some time in the play. Perhaps the only revulsion in the scene is expressed by the soldiers, who leave hurriedly, for, compared to the clinical blinding of Lear, their killing of Bodice seems at least compatible with their function as soldiers. The cruelty to Lear, quite apart from the blinding, is to affect his capacities radically: 'as he begins to understand he has to learn again how to act as a man and a politician' (p. 28). Only at this last stage of the scene does the Ghost 'enter' the scene again to lead Lear away: 'I can stay with you now that you need me'. But the Ghost's time is limited, as he helps Lear out of the cell, for the greatness of Lear asserts itself in the short climax to the Act of the scene which follows. Lear finds himself in the situation of the play's opening scene, near his wall. He encounters his victims in the farmer and his family who are refugees from Lear's land clearances. The process continues, as Lear learns that building has begun again and, as Gaskill says, 'We have to assume ... that Lear knows Cordelia is the head of the new government' (p. 26). The farmer testifies to the stubborn and natural instinct to build homes rather than walls, but he is a helpless political victim, who has no choice but to accept the situation. Their boy is forced into becoming a soldier, just as the farmer and his wife must work on the wall in order to live and eat. In a simple scene, Lear's understanding, as he stood with his hands in Fontanelle's body, is now further extended, as he tries to save the farmer and his family from death. It is a scene of crucial importance for Lear. Outraged by what he hears, Lear kneels by his wall and admits the sum of his mistakes. It occurs to him in his anger that he can convince Cordelia of the mistake she is making and his intention to write to her forms the basis of the developments of the third act, where he adopts a posture of non-violence, only to find that it is ineffective. A further consequence of Lear's resolving to do something rather than retreat is the beginning of the final phase as regards the Ghost. As Lear decides to write to Cordelia, the Ghost realises that his role as part of Lear's range of options is coming to an end. The Ghost

> becomes a destructive thing in the play. He starts off as a very innocent person, but what he wants to do is to live in a small community, in his own little private world, in which he ignores certain problems, and you can't ignore those problems. If you try to ignore those problems – they are problems of Lear himself, the questions he keeps asking – then I think you start inventing a myth about the age of the golden past. And if you try and live in the past, then that becomes a very destructive thing. And the ghost does live in the past, and he does belong to a stage of society that I think one can't go back to ...[22]

The rebuttal of the Ghost at the conclusion of the second act is a means of demonstrating the distance Lear has already travelled. His rejection propels Lear into the real world. The third act of the play is concerned with how Lear is to respond to what for him is a new situation. It is the third act which breaks most radically away from *King Lear*. Gaskill points out that the last act of *Early Morning* is 'a play in itself. There's a real sense of the play starting all over again. You get it in the third act of *Lear* and I think you get it in the second act of [*The Woman*]'. Lear himself had remarked towards the end of Act two: 'And now I must begin again' and essentially Lear's movement in Act three is from uncertainty in the opening scene to total certainty at the end of his interview with Cordelia in scene three. He begins Act three as a political dissident, once more located in the pastoral context of the last scenes of Act one, but now there is less of an attempt to see the context as a refuge. Others do, however, and Lear becomes increasingly a magnet for other disaffected people. The process for Lear is not simple. He believes that the regime may be countered by verbal means to begin with and his progression in the final act, particularly with his encounter with Cordelia, is from a passive to an active opposition. The tormented image of *King Lear* dying with his murdered daughter in his arms gives way to a figure resolved to demonstrate how he is able to live justly by refusing to accept what appears to be inevitable.

The scene which opens the final act takes place six or seven months after the encounter with the farmer. Lear has 'got used to being blind and ... his movement ... should be smoother. He asks daily whether there's any news from the village ...'. The atmosphere of the scene to begin with is one of pastoral calm, as Lear shares the Boy's house with Thomas and Susan, the successors to the Boy and Cordelia. Lear's image of himself, which still carries a kind of arrogance, is accentuated by what the Small Man, a refugee from the wall, tells him by way of flattery, and so he is allowed to stay. The Small Man is the first to tell Lear that he is talked about in the labour camps, 'that he's become an important symbol, and he decides to act out that role'. Lear in other words falsely supposes that, as he felt in the Boy's house in Act one, he 'could have a new life here' and Bond points out that the only reason Lear says he is not a king at the end of the scene 'is because he thinks he's God Almighty' (p. 26). Lear still lives an illusion, as he has done for a lot of the play. Lear is trying to re-enact the goodness of the Gravedigger's Boy in the latter scenes of Act one and he realises the parallel. Since he was not turned away as a refugee, he in turn will accept whoever comes, to the increasing despair of Thomas and Susan. The emaciated Ghost, Thomas, Susan and the Small Man all pressurize Lear to be more careful. Lear, blandly, with good intentions, resists. Gaskill suggests that 'The relationship of Susan and Thomas to Lear is like that of having an impossible, but kindly uncle to stay' (p. 26), but since Lear acts spontaneously as the scene develops, he is not easily controlled. On the one hand, Lear enjoys his status as *guru*; on the other, he is still feeling his way in his new role. The soldiers arrive, looking for the Small Man but are deflected from their purpose, and the scene ends with an uneasy calm, for everyone except Lear.

The technique of showing Lear's state of mind overlapping scenes which is intermittently apparent in the play is a means of demonstrating that Lear's understanding is regularly slightly behind the events. As he reaches a particular stasis, events then move on again. As scene two begins, Lear acts out his role as a living symbol. He tells stories to the group who have come to hear him speak. The story he tells 'is Lear's prepared story of the day . . . Lear is the bird who speaks the truth, because birds speak the truth, but they can only speak truthfully when they are free, not in a cage. And if they are free, there is a danger because the soldiers (King) will then come and punish them. But if you don't tell the truth, your life becomes mad . . . Strangers have to understand that if Lear spoke openly, he'd be arrested tomorrow, so he's developed this clever way of talking to them about their lives without being openly antagonistic'. Lear feels he has found his role, how to act truthfully under a repressive regime. Yet his action consists of words, and his role is shattered as the Soldiers return and take the Small Man and Ben away: 'The reality of the world cannot allow escape into a passive, contemplative life. If you are surrounded by violence you can't escape from it . . .' (p. 26). Gaskill's point is made forcibly by the return to the play of the Old Councillor, a natural survivor, who has not been seen since Lear's trial. Now as then, Lear insults the Councillor's time-serving acquiescence but feels helpless to go further. He lapses into despair. Bond asked in his Vienna production for, on Lear's part, 'the feeling of searching. Lear keeps opening doors and they keep shutting in his face. Now he thinks there is no way out . . . This is not a scene of a man in his study contemplating life, it is a scene of action, the moment of a big decision. It is a measure of

Lear's greatness that, at the moment of personal despair, he can embrace the sufferings of the world'. As Lear articulates his truth, 'I can do nothing, I am nothing', the words cue the Ghost's appearance, who, at his most unpleasant, offers Lear a last refuge in fantasy by destroying the people who surround Lear, just as the Gravedigger's Boy's well was polluted by the blood of Lear's victims. Lear is being offered the opportunity to regress and his lying down to sleep without answering leads the Ghost to feel that at the last, Lear is imprisoned again, this time by the Ghost's alternative. But Lear has not listened to the Ghost for some while. As the Ghost is rejected (and described in the stage-directions as 'It' for the first time), so John, whose love for Susan parallels that of the Carpenter for Cordelia, leaves the house to marry the girl in the village. He leaves a crying Susan who is calmed by a Thomas with new authority. The Royal Court cast noted the changed attitude of Thomas: 'in the previous scene there hadn't been enough people – he was too isolated, too vulnerable. Now he is thrown into a situation where he must act, he has no choice, he considers himself to be less vulnerable and has, in fact, to adopt this role'.[23] The emergence of Thomas, forced or not, is to a position where he becomes the legitimate heir of Lear's understanding. He and Susan benefit from what Lear is to do.

Lear and Cordelia finally meet in scene three, and Cordelia is outmatched, but resolute. Lear's calmness is a consequence of the previous scene and it is demonstrated in the brief sequence with the Ghost before Cordelia arrives, about the owl and the fox. The owl 'is a symbol of wisdom, which because [Lear] has seen the sky, heard voices etc. he can hear; he cannot hear the fox, as the Boy can, because that is a primitive, intuitive way of life, the life the Boy led before his death. He has been destroyed by Lear and now even the pigs scream at him'. The Ghost understands that the very ordinariness of tone, the conversational manner of Lear at this point, signifies that Lear will never again listen to him. Lear, for Bond, 'is now another figure in the play. He is the only character left from the beginning of the play that has kept his sanity and perspective'. He has earned the right to speak the truth. As earlier in the play, Cordelia's situation in the scene is not presented unsympathetically. She would not have Lear killed earlier and she comes now as a ruler but not a vindictive figure. As she releases Lear's hand, she calls into the scene her indelible memory of the soldiers killing her husband and raping her. Bond establishes her reasons, and allows her her conscience. As she concedes that she cannot prevent people listening to Lear, she admits her failure and Lear recognizes his strength. The Ghost's pathetic interjections are ignored and the cue for Lear's last great speech is provided by the Carpenter's trying to silence him. Lear articulates his compassion and achieves a legitimate mythical status as he finds himself to be part of the minds of the people: 'Finally, you cannot make people inhuman. People like Lear or Tolstoy become symbols. The rest of the speech explains what it is to be human. Lear has compassion – if you lose that compassion, you become mad' (p. 27). Lear understands as he says the words, and Cordelia sees that there is nothing she can do to destroy the truth of what Lear says. She can only continue irrevocably along her chosen route and it is one which necessitates Lear's death. The effect of Lear's speech is to make the matter very simple for him. The Ghost exits to watch his wife go away and Lear explains part of his intention to Thomas and Susan. As he resolves to commit himself to action, however insignificant, the death of the Ghost closes the scene and that lingering temptation to avoid reality, which has persisted intermittently with Lear, vanishes completely. Lear feels pain for the last time as the Ghost is savaged by pigs and dies. One of the final images of the scene is that of the Boy's body dropping from Lear's arms to the ground, as Lear summarises his own life and offers his epitaph.

Lear goes to his death calmly in the play's last scene. It is the first time in the play that the wall is on the stage. He tells Susan that Thomas will understand what it means and he is shot as he digs at his wall, like the worker in scene one of the play is shot, deliberately and efficiently, by the farmer's son of Act two, who has become an officer. He is disposed of as a minor interruption in the work of rebuilding the wall. Yet in acting, Lear 'sets an example . . . to the young people who are left . . . at the end of the play. They are the really important people in the play – they represent for me a new possibility for change in society. They are my equivalent of Fortinbras . . .'.[24] What Lear presents to Thomas and Susan is 'the clarified problem' which is in turn 'the basis of optimism'.[25] The phrase is precisely chosen:

Lear was, in many ways, a very grim play and I think it's right that it

> should have been. I didn't want to create any false optimism, any easy optimism at the end of the play because . . . my portion of the twentieth century has been pretty stunning . . . and I felt that . . . one had to write the truth . . . in all its horror. But I wanted very much to maintain the feeling of strength and moral resolution, purpose, in the play . . .[26]

Lear is a play which for Bond is concerned with the necessity to identify the nature of contemporary problems as a fundamental antecedent to solving them:

> Our problem isn't a wall that we can dig up like Lear does. His action simply means that he understands the things he's done wrong in his life, and that he has to go back and undo them. If we can identify what our real dangers are, this is the only way I can see towards making genuinely revolutionary activity.[27]

One of the facts which makes *Lear* a compelling play is its refusal to endorse easy alternatives.

6

The Sea

Bond's next play is subtitled 'A Comedy'. It was written, straight after *Lear*, as an antidote to the remorseless theatrical experience of the earlier play. In *The Sea*, Bond shows the ability of human beings to survive the worst, to retain their optimism, and not to be brought down by the lunacy and injustice of the world they live in:

'I wanted very much in *The Sea* to look at the same sorts of problems but this time to put the emphasis on the strength of people, on their ability to change their society . . . So I wanted to make people laugh and experience human strength.'[1]

This is not to say that *The Sea* in any way encourages complacency. The tightly knit society of a small town on the East Coast of England is a battleground over which the victims of an oppressive and morally impoverished culture wander in mad distraction. Alternatively, they hide away in disgust at what they have seen. The town is isolated on the edge of the sea; the effect is of a society sealed off from the outside world and from any potential for change. Bond sets the play at a precise moment in time – it is 1907, and the iron-clad values of Edwardian England are leading inexorably to the disasters of the early twentieth century.

It is a world ludicrously bent on self-destruction – just like that of *Early Morning*. The central character is another Bondian innocent. Willy Carson, like Arthur, is a young man who slowly awakens to the horrors around him. He is not a heroic figure, but a very ordinary man who is forced by circumstance into trying to understand his world: 'He isn't consciously searching for anything. What happens intrudes into his day to day compromise with living.'[2]

Willy and Arthur both come close to being overwhelmed by cynicism and despair, but they survive, and Bond expresses through them his conviction that society *can* be changed, while people like them continue to question its values. Their reactions inevitably involve a rejection of the world as they know it: at the end of both plays, they are seen moving out of the irrational world the other characters inhabit as though abandoning it as lost. Their action is a rejection of their present (and *our* present), but it also signifies the chance for a better future.

In *Lear*, Bond is concerned with different kinds of political oppression and the violence he shows is exclusively political in nature. In *The Sea*, Bond shifts the focus and shows a more characteristically English form of repression – the operations and influence of a rigid class structure, which is carefully worked into the whole fabric of the play. It is the source of the strong thread of social satire that runs through it. Mrs. Rafi, the village dictator by virtue of her supreme upper middle-class self-assurance, is the Edwardian equivalent of the lady of the manor; she and her entourage of genteel middle-class ladies are characterised as figures of fun, unaware of the emptiness of their posturings and the hollowness of their values. To mock their pretensions, Bond uses a more conventional comic approach than in any of the earlier plays – although there is a marked family resemblance between Mrs. Rafi and Victoria in *Early Morning* or Georgina in *Narrow Road to the Deep North*, Mrs. Rafi is essentially a *grande dame* in the tradition of English high comedy. In the same way, the farcical events that disrupt the funeral service on the cliff-top have earlier forerunners in scenes like the one with the young priests and the holy pot in *Narrow Road to the Deep North*, but without the sustained pitch of comic anarchy and the sheer ingenuity in the handling of the farcical mechanics that Bond attains in *The Sea*.

The satirical comedy is, however, only one element in the play. Bond is concerned to show the effects of a rigidly sectionalised society on its victims. Mrs. Rafi practises a form of mental and emotional violence on all those beneath her – as Rose says late in the play: 'The town's full of her cripples.' Her main victim is the draper, Hatch, a tradesman who uneasily straddles the two worlds – that of the working class (Hollarcut, Thompson and Carter, the village men whom he influences with his ideas) and that of his genteel middle-class customers, to whom he is obliged to display an attentive servility. Unable to give direct expression to the antagonism he feels, he redirects his hostility. His fears of an alien invasion of England from outer space may be lunatic and unreal, but they find very real expression in his attitude towards Willy and Evens.

Willy is an object of suspicion because he arrives, in strange circumstances, from outside the village; Evens is equally suspect because, in removing himself from society to his hut on the beach, he has rejected the same social pressures that constrict Hatch – he has found a solution which Hatch, still grappling with them in his own way, is unable to accept. Evens and Hatch represent two extreme poles of social response, as Bond explained: 'My play is pointedly about sanity and insanity, and the town represents the dilemma of entrapment. The 80-year old man, Evens, is the sane one. The rest are manic about their entrapment.'[3]

What finally drives Hatch mad is not so much his sense of the unjust way that his society is organised, as the fact that he is forced to suppress his feelings about the real causes of these injustices – his aggression is directed not at Mrs. Rafi but at alternative scapegoats. As a result his views border on the fascist; although this is not made explicit in the play, in interview Bond has made the point very directly: 'There is no doubt but that Hatch is a Hitleresque concept on my part.'[4] While Willy works steadily towards a view of his world that allows grounds for hope and optimism, Hatch's inability to reach an intellectual understanding of his situation culminates in the futile intensity of his knifing of the corpse washed up on the beach.

The progress in Willy is from the shell-shocked state he falls into after the drowning of his friend, Colin, in scene one to a fuller understanding of the problems of his life and his society. Above all, he 'has to learn to face and accept Hatch's fury, but not be seduced, corrupted or intimidated by it. He must avoid it and its deeds. But he mustn't pretend it isn't there.'[5] Hatch, however, has an increasingly insecure hold on reality – he invents fantasies to explain the tensions in the real world: 'he lives in a world as illusory as that of the play which is rehearsed in Mrs. Rafi's drawing-room.'[6] His false diagnosis of the reasons for his own unhappiness and discontent is a form of irrationality which, Bond suggests, in the end wreaks its own revenge.

Three main elements, then, are interwoven in *The Sea*: the

world of Mrs. Rafi, expressed mainly through high comedy; the barely controlled paranoia of Hatch; and Willy's growing maturity and understanding, partly under the tutelage of Evens, together with his dawning relationship with Rose, Mrs. Rafi's niece and the fiancée of Willy's drowned friend.

The dramatic pattern that Bond forges from these three elements is very carefully shaped, as an examination of the distribution of main characters through the play's eight scenes shows. Willy is there almost throughout. The only scene in which he does not appear is scene five (the confrontation between Hatch and Mrs. Rafi which precipitates Hatch's madness); he witnesses only the *effect* that Mrs. Rafi has on Hatch. In scene two, he comes into the shop *after* Hatch's fawning attempt to sell the curtain material and gloves to her, and Willy's other meetings with Hatch consist entirely of the series of bizarre encounters on the beach (scenes one and six) and on the cliff-top (scene seven).

Hatch appears in six of the eight scenes; the prominence Bond gives to this character underlines the importance he attaches to keeping Hatch's failure to cope with the social pressures exerted on him constantly in the audience's mind. There is no call for him to be involved in scene five (the rehearsal of the play Mrs. Rafi and her ladies are putting on), but far more telling is his exclusion from the last scene; clearly, he can have no part in the rational deliberations between Willy and Evens about the state of the world and Willy's best course of action.

More interesting still is a breakdown of the respective appearances of Mrs. Rafi and Evens. They appear together in the same scene just once – at the cliff-top funeral service, theatrically the climax of the play. The remainder of the scenes contain either the one character or the other, a structural pattern which emphasizes how Willy is shuttled backwards and forwards between the kind of society to which, by birth and social station, he belongs and the influence of Evens, the old recluse, whose support Willy needs if he is to face and to comprehend the lunacy around him.

Given that the three elements in the play involve considerable variations in mood and tone, where does a director or actor place the main emphasis? What is the balance between the fun and the intensity? Bond would want to stress that any production should reflect the comic nature of the play *as a whole*, and not just go for the humour in the scenes which are obviously comic – otherwise the intended effect of the play will be lost: 'I simply cannot reconcile myself to a life that will ultimately end in violence and chaos. I do believe in the triumph of the human spirit. If *The Sea* starts violently and noisily, it should end with the profoundest sense of tranquillity. I gather from the reviews that the German productions treat the play as something very grim and serious. PLEASE remember it is labelled A COMEDY and for a reason! It should be played lightly and with as much fun as possible.'[7]

Bond's instruction is clearcut and straightforward. It precisely matches his intention 'deliberately to say to the audience "You mustn't despair. You mustn't be afraid. You must be conscious of the dangers but nevertheless be conscious of your strengths."'[8] How useful, though, is this general observation to an actor playing, say, Hatch or Willy? Each of these actors is presented with a number of situations of a seriousness and intensity that must be reflected in their performances: Hatch's stabbing of the body, for example, can't be played 'lightly'. The task for an actor in *The Sea*, or in any play by Bond, is to avoid letting moments such as these colour the rest of his performance or form the basis for an overall characterisation of the part. To do so is to misunderstand the way Bond constructs the characters and the function he gives them – as he has explained: 'We see the character from different facets, we see the character acting in different situations, and what the actor therefore has to act is *simply that one situation*.' In other words, the situation is never to be used by the actor as a basis for *generalising* about his character elsewhere in the play. As Bond describes it: 'The situations are designed not to show the development of his character but to show the crucial situations that an individual has to cope with in order to produce what is of value in him. . . .'

Scene one of *The Sea* is the most directly theatrical of all the openings to Bond's plays. Although the first lines of *The Woman* also plunge the spectator right into the thick of the dramatic action, the opening scene rapidly demands an attentive *intellectual* response to the excitement and tension displayed on the stage. In *The Sea*, Bond aims at a very different effect. At the start, there is only the darkened empty stage, and a wall of sound that stuns the senses:

Beach.
Empty stage. Darkness and thunder. Wind roars, whines, crashes and screams over the water. Masses of water swell up, rattle and churn, and crash back into the sea. Gravel and sand grind slowly. The earth trembles.

Two subsequent stage directions indicate that this is only the beginning – the assault intensifies in the course of the scene, as '*The tempest grows louder*'. The sounds, the empty stage, Willy's offstage cries for help, twice eclipsed by the noise of the water, combine to disorientate the spectator. To begin with, there is no fixed point of focus for the audience to look at; when one arrives, in the shape of Evens ('*A drunken man comes on singing*'), the result is to add a layer of strangeness to the general pattern of chaos, disorder and despair. It is not only what Evens *says* that seems so strange, but even more his behaviour. Two young men are struggling for their lives in the sea, yet he makes no effort to help them. His one gesture is to offer Willy a drink from his bottle – and even this minimal gesture has a chillingly surreal quality about it, since Willy is *still in the sea*. What one sees is a drunken old man proffering his bottle to the raging waters offstage.

An audience's first response might be to view the situation as a combination of accidental and tragic circumstances: Willy is unable to save his friend from drowning because, through an unfortunate freak of fate, the only person on the beach is an old drunk. Such a view at once appears too easy and reassuring with the entrance of a second, even stranger figure. In the published script, Bond's only direction is '*Hatch, a middle-aged man, comes on with a torch*.' This is expanded in his script for the B.B.C. Television production to include a brief description of Hatch's movements: '*Hatch, a middle-aged man, is marching stiffly towards the camera with a torch. He looks like an automaton*.' In this case, it is not only the character's attitude – nakedly hostile to the young man in distress – which strikes a chill: his lines ring with the sound of a harsh, crazed morality: 'Filthy beast . . . I know who you are. You thought you wouldn't be seen out here.' The failure of the drunk to offer help was one thing: suddenly, it seems the whole world is crazy, incapable of one single natural response.

The whole scene lasts two to three minutes: the audience does not have time for a considered, rational response. The function is to shock and disturb – and incidentally to make Willy's traumatic state throughout most of Act one seem convincing and understandable as a reaction not only to Colin's death but equally to the callousness and inhumanity he has encountered. Yet one inescapable question stares out at us from what we see: what kind of world is this, where basic human impulses are so blunted and attitudes so deranged?

The thought might also cross our minds that another play has started in a very similar fashion – even without the help of Bond's tongue-in-cheek stage direction: '*The tempest grows louder.*' Bond has openly confessed his indebtedness: 'Yes, the play is strongly influenced structurally by Shakespeare's *Tempest*. I even have it start with a storm too.'[9] But he has also explained how what matters in the end is the essential difference between the two plays rather than the similarities: 'The basic idea behind *The Tempest*, I think, is the idea of conflict and resolution. The image of the sea conveys this very well – the storm is a destructive image, it reflects social and personal conflicts; the sea is finally able to resolve these images into a powerful continuity. That's what Shakespeare, I think, had in mind. That's not finally a satisfactory image for our own age.'

For Bond, conflict is rooted not in basic human nature but in the constrictions forced upon it by society, and conflict can only be resolved by human action to change society.

In an early note on the play, Bond wrote: 'The storm at sea is to image the storm in the draper's shop'[10] – a reference to Hatch's onslaught on the curtain material, and on Mrs. Rafi. (One of Bond's two early titles for the play was 'Two Storms'.) Scene two, although set in Hatch's shop, offers no hint of the man-made storm to come.

The tone is very quiet. Hatch's opening lines are full of the ingratiating servility of the tradesman: 'Art serge is coming in now, Mrs. Rafi. Very fashionable for winter curtains.' Dropped softly into the sudden stillness and silence after the end of the storm, their effect is to bring one back with a jolt to what seems a reassuringly familiar world.

Evidently the sound-effects of the storm need to continue beyond the end of scene one and through the scene-change for the sharpness of the contrast to be fully registered. The effect Bond is after is more easily achieved in film or television than on the stage, as Jane Howell, who directed the play for television, explains:

> The marvellous thing that you could do in the television production was make changes in a flash, so you could get the counterpoint of the relationship between the scenes, the rhythm of the scenes against each other – something you can never truly do in the theatre . . . Bond does hand one scene into the next and you can never quite get that in the theatre, where something has to be taken off the stage, or characters have to go off . . .

Hatch's hushed tones are also in violent contrast with his last lines in scene one, railing demoniacally at Willy above the booming of the guns from the shore battery. Within the space of a minute we have seen a Jekyll and Hyde character, the two facets of his personality clinically juxtaposed. When the audience recognises him as the madman they saw on the beach, the inevitable question which arises is: can this be the same man? There is no apparent link between the two extremes of behaviour we have witnessed.

The first clues are laid as we watch Mrs Rafi systematically humiliate Hatch. She grudgingly selects her curtain material, then rejects the gloves he has on offer; the tension caused by his subservient social position and by the precariousness of his livelihood, at the mercy of Mrs. Rafi's whims, are clear to see. In the television script, when Willy enters the shop, Hatch reacts by '*watching nervously as he pretends not to notice and tidy the gloves away instead*'. Is this an expression of guilt? Or is it out of fear that Willy might publicly condemn his behaviour on the beach? The former seems unlikely since, when Willy and the two ladies have gone, Hatch persuades the other coastguards that Willy is the advance guard of an invasion force from another planet.

As he talks to the three men about his beliefs, Hatch's manner changes. His words have a directness and confidence about them: 'They come from space. Beyond our world. Their world's threatened by disaster. If they think we're a crowd of weak fools they'll all come here. By the million. They'll take our jobs and our homes. Everything.' But this is different again from his expression of these selfsame fears when he confronted Willy during the storm.

In a way, the changes we see in Hatch – the different 'versions' of his character presented over the short space of two scenes – make perfect sense: it's a truism that human beings behave differently in different situations. What is distinctive here is the compactness and terseness of Bond's dramatic technique. The changes in Hatch are shown not as subtle gradations from a secure and established reference-point, but as a series of apparently contrasting statements. The audience's perception of the character is formed out of this dialectic and, what is more important, can only be formed from an understanding of the *situations* in which we see him. The key to the first part of scene two, for example, is the difference in class and social standing between Hatch and Mrs. Rafi.

Several implications for the actor spring from this. He must play the character in each situation *and that situation only*; he will not get very far by inventing an overall psychological base for the character as a launching pad for the performance of individual scenes. As Bond explains: 'There *is* a continuity within the character . . . because although things are done to them, they do still react with a certain consistency. The actor has to ask what type of person am I – and then define this in terms of a situation . . . It's no use asking: "How did *I* get here?": You have to ask: "How did *it* [the situation] get here?"'.

So far, the play hardly sounds much like a comedy. There *is* comedy, even in the first scene, as Jane Howell points out: 'It comes from Evens during the storm. But it seems so improbable. I don't think an audience can *laugh* at it. It's so difficult for them to know what is going on. So much so that I love it when Hatch comes on and says "I know what's going on here"'. But until scene four the comedy is mostly on a slow fuse; it is used to point the strangeness of the situation and to set up questions in the audience's minds. The exception is Mrs. Rafi. Bond gives to this character lines which in their polished wit trigger memories of Oscar Wilde, particularly when she gives vent to her feelings by way of epigrams: 'Leave her. Never show any interest in the passions of the young, it makes them grow up selfish.' The language reflects her continual disdain for everyone she comes into contact with. What is missing from her words is any sense of human feeling. With the blithe, unquestioning self-assurance that derives from her social position, she queens it over the other characters, sweeping all before her on an imperious torrent of words; the casual viciousness with which she treats her social inferiors goes hand in hand with her haughty, *grande-dame* manner. It is this one facet of her character that Bond holds steadily before us until her last four speeches in the play.

Willy's appearance in scene two is limited to the one brief conversation with Mrs. Rafi and Mrs. Tilehouse. He is cautious and withdrawn. There is no evidence of how the events of the first scene have affected him. There is more than a suspicion of the stiff upper-lip in his bearing – Mrs. Rafi's world is not conducive to the open expression of personal grief. It is only when he visits Evens at his hut on the beach, prompted by Mrs. Rafi's suggestion that the old man will know where Colin's body might be washed ashore, that he gives vent to his feelings:

> WILLY *sits down on a box and starts to cry into his hands.* EVENS *looks at him for a moment and then goes slowly into the hut.* WILLY *cries a bit longer before he speaks.*
>
> WILLY (*trying to stop*). So stupid – doing this – coming here and . . .
>
> EVENS (*inside the hut*). Is there a proper place?

This small incident lays the ground for the vital conversation between them in the last scene; as scene three develops, there is the sense that we are in a different world from the one over which Mrs. Rafi presides, a world with at least the potential for an open exchange of thoughts and feelings. At this stage Bond allows no more than a hint of this potential, while Hatch and Hollarcut watch suspiciously from not far off, forcibly reminding us of the warped aggressiveness that Mrs. Rafi's values can provoke. (Hatch's interpretation of Willy's tears as a signal to his fellow space-creatures is itself a sign of his reluctance to tolerate any display of natural human feelings.)

Evens tells Willy what he wants to know about the tides. But his long speech giving this information contains a lot more than is needed to answer Willy's questions:

> Perhaps not. We're into the spring tides now. He'll be washed up where the coast turns in. (*Points.*) You see? People are cruel and boring and obsessed. If he goes past that point you've lost him. He should come in. He's hanging round out there now. He could see us if he wasn't dead. My wife died in hospital. She had something quite minor.

I sold up. They hate each other. Force. Make. Use. Push. Burn. Sell. For what? A heap of rubbish.

This extract, and the remainder of the speech, is a characteristic Bond 'soliloquy'. Evens's lines switch continually from one train of thought to another; the subject is changing all the time, from his description of the movement of the body in the sea to his account of his view of the world. At first sight, it might seem that these abrupt changes in subject also represent a movement from the external to the internal. On closer examination, this is clearly not the case – it is hard to imagine how an actor could pitch half of the lines on an emotive, interior register and then switch back to an impassive description of the tides without making the whole speech topple over into melodrama. The variations in the speech demand only the very slightest changes in the vocal and emotional register; its distinct sections need to be played as simply a succession of individual statements. The method is analogous to the way in which Bond constructs a character, showing the character from a number of fixed points and asking the audience to draw the necessary conclusions. In the same way, the actor here needs to deliver the lines trusting in the information they convey about Evens, not complicating them by trying to construct a hidden network of emotional linkages.

Played this way, there is no danger of Evens becoming a sentimentalised figure, a wise old man of the sea. Even at this early stage the character needs to be kept in perspective: 'The old man on the beach has weaknesses – and he indulges in the luxury of admitting this without doing anything about it. Perhaps he can be excused more easily than other people in the play – but perhaps he should be condemned more than any of the others.'[11] Evens's comments on human beings in scene three are entirely negative; he has withdrawn from society and sits outside it, staring balefully in. Bond does not want us to be too easy on him: 'He is a man of enormous potential and intellect, and also a man of personal taste and conviction . . . and he has done nothing with his talents – or only enough to show what he could have done. Was anything done again?'[12]

The reverberations from this early note on the character carry through to the next play, *Bingo*, where Shakespeare, like Evens, sits watching with disgust the way men behave towards each other, yet does nothing to interfere with the injustice he sees. The question Bond has him frequently ask of himself is phrased in the same words: 'Was anything done?'. It is echoed, in a significantly modified form, in Mrs. Rafi's burst of self-analysis – and self-pity – in scene seven: 'Has anything been worthwhile?'. Bond's earliest projected title for *The Sea*, before 'Two Storms', had been 'Was Anything Done?'.

By the end of the scene, it must seem possible that Evens's negativism will carry the day. There is no question that he is a more powerful figure than Willy and the fierce irony of his reply when Willy asks him why he was drunk during the storm has a convincing ring to it: 'I drink to keep sane. There's no harm in the little I drink. Li Po: you who are sated with life, now drink the dregs.' His explanation prompts further questions in our minds. Can he honestly claim there is no harm in his drinking? What if he had not been drunk? Might Colin have been saved? Later, Willy voices this thought for us: 'If you hadn't been drunk.' Evens disposes of it with a reply which implies far more than it says: 'I answered that question long ago: *if* he hadn't gone to sea.' Nothing can be gained by wishing things different. Colin is dead, Willy is alive, and he must face the world as it is.

To begin with, Willy shows no inclination to question his condition; his mind is still locked on thoughts of Colin and his death. It has been argued that the character on stage presents much the same problems as Arthur in *Early Morning*, because Willy too seems to hover on the edge of the main action rather than being directly involved at the centre of it. It is easy to see how Willy's role could be overshadowed by the more virtuoso parts of Mrs. Rafi and Hatch. 'These are the "vital" characters,' wrote one critic, 'the ones to whom you respond, for whom you care . . . If the death matters . . . then it matters to the stony-faced, the silent, the young automatons Willy and Rose – as "dead" as the dead man, but representing the hope of the future.'[13]

But Willy, as we shall see, is very far from being dead by the end of the play. What truth there is in this stricture might fairly be applied only to Willy's characterisation in the early scenes. His appearance in scene two amounts to only a very brief conversation with Mrs. Rafi and Mrs. Tilehouse. Scenes three and four present more difficulty, because he plays a large part in both yet his state of mind remains something of an enigma. How, then, does an actor playing Willy negotiate these two scenes without creating the kind of totally negative reaction stated above?

To a large extent, it comes back to the point made earlier about the character of Hatch. Bond's method is to show different facets of a character, either from scene to scene or within a scene. There will always be the danger of an actor or an audience unconsciously combating this by striving, too hard and too soon, for a generalised, composite view of the character which glosses over Bond's emphasis on the primacy of the situation in favour of a more conventional consistency of character. Jane Howell points to the distortions that can result:

> Willy could be played as the perfect hero – a generalised performance of Willy would make him always quietly spoken, never raising his voice, very intelligent – which he undoubtedly is – calm, all-seeing, wise – totally wonderful! . . . If you let the actor generalise from scene to scene, the logic will go something like this: he has lost his best friend in the storm, the rest of the time he is shell-shocked, he is in mourning for his life, he is in mourning for everything else. And the actor won't actually look for the changes in the scene.

In scene three, Willy *is* self-absorbed and relatively withdrawn. The 'changes' in the scene, as far as Willy is concerned, are minor variations on that one note. What must not happen is that the Willy of this scene should come to characterise and colour the part as a whole. It is clearly significant that Willy is young – twenty-one years old – and that in the course of the play he starts to come of age. The intelligence and maturity he shows later should not strike the audience as extraordinary or come as a surprise.

In scene four Bond switches back from the beach to the unnatural climate of the town. With imperious authority, Mrs. Rafi presides over an event which – characteristically – represents a triumph of art over life – the rehearsal of a play on the subject of Orpheus and Eurydice, to be given by her group of local ladies in aid of the Coastguard Fund. The irony that this play within a play is on a theme which, according to one critic, contains strong correspondences with the remainder of the play (one only needs to substitute Colin, Rose, and Willy for Orpheus, Eurydice and

Pluto)[14] cannot be completely ignored. But thematic ironies of this kind are infinitely less important than what Bond shows in direct stage terms – the juxtaposition of Willy and Rose (the dead man's fiancée) with the arid inanities of the rehearsal.

The rehearsal scene is one of two comic highlights in *The Sea*. It is a wicked parody of the worst kind of village hall amateur theatricals. By the standards of, say, *Early Morning*, the comic effects are quite conventional – the scene is structured on one basic comic principle: the idea of constant interruption. As Mrs. Rafi struggles to inspire her cast, she is frustrated by a combination of external circumstance and individual recalcitrance. Mrs. Tilehouse questions the appropriateness of Mrs. Rafi's star turn – a solo rendering of 'There's No Place Like Home'. Mafanwy objects to playing the dog. Jilly is so overcome with emotion that she breaks down and cries. The Vicar is incapable of delivering his lines without indulging in constant digressions about the life of the parish. On top of all this come two major dislocations of Mrs. Rafi's insubstantial pageant: Willy's arrival, and the sound of guns, which finally and conclusively shatters the elaborate cocoon Mrs. Rafi has carefully spun ('one can't play lutes to the sound of gunfire').

Mrs. Rafi's first action in the scene is to send her ladies scurrying to close the curtains on the windows overlooking the sea – nominally to prevent Rose from tormenting herself with thoughts of Colin. However, as John Dillon remarked, describing his production at the Asolo Theatre, Florida: 'The closing off of that light is an important moment. The women scurried over to the curtains – and the three curtains fell as one. And you had that idea of artificial light, which is very much Mrs. Rafi's environment.' The alternation between indoor and outdoor scenes, between the town and the beach, between the tight enclosed environment of Hatch's shop or Park House and the natural world outside, is fundamental to the structure of *The Sea*; the contrast between the two worlds is built into the narrative rhythm. In the Royal Court production, the backcloth of sea blending into sky was always visible behind interior and exterior scenes alike; partly, as the designer Deirdre Clancy explains, 'for its symbolic effect, but also because it was practically impossible to get rid of it!' The impression of the wider natural world waiting outside heightens our sense of the cramped artificiality of Hatch's and Mrs. Rafi's behaviour. In

David Carson's production at the Marlowe Theatre, Canterbury, 'six or seven feet were left clear each side of the shop set; Hatch's shop seemed like a small island.' The effect of the world outside the windows should be one not of threat but hope: in the television production, Bond's suggestion for the lighting of the exteriors was: 'I think everything should be bathed in light, cocooned in white.'

The rehearsal is well under way and the comic momentum well established by the time Willy appears. For the remainder of the scene, until his conversation with Rose at the end, Willy is onstage but silent – after stuttering out a few words to Rose when they are introduced, he returns to the sidelines to watch the play. It is vital that the audience remains aware of him there during the rest of the rehearsal, but this presents the director with an immediate theatrical problem – in the words of William Gaskill, who directed *The Sea* at the Royal Court; 'How do you make it clear that the passive figure is also the central figure?'

Bond's only stage direction for Willy after his entrance is close to the end of the scene. The rehearsal has broken up. 'ROSE *crosses to* WILLY. *He sits alone on a chair. While they talk the others are admiring and giggling at the designs.*' But what of Willy earlier on? In the Royal Court production, Gaskill had Willy and Rose sitting on a sofa in the foreground, stage right, with the back of the sofa towards the audience. Thus, two characters who have little direct part in this scene, but who must remain in the forefront of the audience's mind, were placed in a strong position downstage. At the Asolo Theatre, the director found the same solution, placing them on a downstage sofa 'as if putting a frame around their meeting'.

From this vantage point, Willy – and Rose, until her turn comes to appear in Mrs. Rafi's play – watch the rehearsal. Rose's first lines in the character of Eurydice – 'I am queen of this dark place. My heart burns with a new cold fire.' – are an ironic comment on her own reaction to Colin's death. They introduce a moment of genuine feeling into the general posturing and histrionics around her, but they also mark Rose out as a potential victim – like Willy, she is in danger of letting her feelings close her off from life. Meanwhile, the actions and gestures of the other participants in the theatrical travesty point up the ludicrous hollowness of their lives. The grand declamatory style of the play they are rehearsing, the constant interruptions, Mrs. Rafi's attempts to keep things on an even keel, all cry out for a calculated comic exaggeration in the acting. The exaggerated comic style is important for another reason – Bond wants to show not only the ridiculousness of their values but the *unnaturalness* of their behaviour. The final effect of this play within the play, together with the alarums and excursions that surround it, is to project a bizarre vision of a dead world.

Willy's presence as an onlooker at these weird and artificial rites focusses our attention more keenly on the chasm that separates Mrs. Rafi from the real world outside, but it is easy to overlook the fact that this is also a vital scene in terms of the development of Willy's character. Jane Howell explains: 'In the play scene he goes into hell, if you like, and sees these strange fantasy figures, and then suddenly the curtains are drawn and there is light on his face, and it's like recreating the whole experience of the storm for him in a different form – something like the torch Hatch shone on his face; suddenly there's light on his face.'

The opening of the curtains, following on from the sound of the guns, firing as they did during the storm, jolts Willy out of his trance-like state. (The script for the television adaptation contains a direction that perfectly describes the image of Willy sitting gazing at the rehearsal – 'WILLY *appears as a pale, ghostly, unmoving shape in the background*.') On television Jane Howell had sought to underline the metaphysical connection between the play scene and the storm scene by adopting a suggestion made by Bond. When Willy first enters, the curtains have been drawn and '*He looks round at the darkness*'. Bond's suggestion was that, as Willy makes for a seat, he has to clamber past the chairs and other furniture, pushed to one side to make space for the rehearsal; his movements through the darkened room should suggest his struggling movements through the waves in scene one. This is a difficult effect to bring off – it is more likely that Willy will simply look awkward – although this kind of visual simile, like the 'pale, ghostly' image of Willy, is probably easier to realise on television than on the stage.

What must be registered is the change in the scene – and in Willy's state of mind – after the curtains have been opened again. The change of attitude comes at a precise moment in his conversation with Rose:

ROSE. Mr. Carson, you must go home.

WILLY. No. I sat in that hotel all yesterday. No. And what has been happening here this afternoon, I noticed nothing till the guns . . . ? There were people on the beach when the boat turned over.

The last sentence signals a complete change of tone. For the first time he talks to Rose directly about Colin's drowning. The platitudes he'd spoken a few lines earlier ('I can't say how sorry I am. There's nothing I can do.') are replaced by an urgent need to describe the experience to her. On the evidence of the character we have seen so far, this has to be regarded as a positive step. But two cautionary notes are struck. Willy is still obsessed, just as he was when talking to Evens, about what might have been: 'We were so near the shore. If only I'd been able to get to him.' And Rose closes her ears to his account, preferring her role as tragic heroine to the disturbance Willy's new tone would cause her.

Willy's 'reliving' of the storm is a prelude to the storm that erupts in Hatch's shop. Unlike the natural storm at sea of the first scene, this one is unnatural, man-made, the consequence of intolerable social pressures. In scene five, Bond shows a man driven into madness; but the tone of the scene is by no means unrelievedly serious. As in the play scene, comedy is used to satirise and to deflate. It acts as a frame within which Hatch's outbreak of emotion stands out that much more starkly.

The mood of the scene switches from comedy to near melodrama to periods of calm – the audience is never allowed to relax into a settled response. Ironically, we see two sides of Hatch with which we are already familiar – they are different sides of the same coin, in that both are ways of coping with his role in society, but whereas his ingratiating manner towards Mrs. Rafi is consciously adopted, his vision of alien invasions, although rationally and coherently expressed, is not a *conscious* mechanism for survival: it is a form of displacement activity, a transference of aggression from its natural target in the real world (Mrs. Rafi and those who hold sway over him) to a fantasy substitute. The connection between Hatch's paranoid interpretation of other people's behaviour and his own struggle to survive is made in his conversation with Hollarcut and the others – his instinct is to see anyone who poses a threat to him as in league with the creatures who are out to subvert his world: 'You soon spot them behind this counter. You get a fair indication from the way they pay their bill. That shows if they respect our way of life, or if they're just out to make trouble by running people into debt.'

Hatch still has the cool logic of the self-assumed prophet. But his mask of rationality, or reasonableness, crumbles in the face of Mrs. Rafi's ultimate blow to his livelihood: because of his dereliction of duty in failing to help Willy in the storm, she refuses to accept the 162 yards of blue velvet curtain material he has ordered for her. Her action triggers off the comic frenzy that typifies the rest of the scene. Hatch's first reaction is to make excuses for his behaviour, but there is more than a trace of exasperation in his voice: 'Did you see the storm? What could I do – Christian or not! – calm the waters, Mrs. Rafi?'. Mrs. Rafi's immovability rapidly pushes him into further excesses – he hints darkly that she is in league with Willy – but he is still torn between a compulsion to retrieve the situation and the need to speak his mind. Bond's way of representing this in the dialogue is succinct and graphic: 'Feel the stuff, ma'am. Really, an educated person of your taste can't resist a product as beautiful as – (*Crying.*) but oh the pity of it is you don't see the whole community's threatened by that swine, yes swine, bastard, the welfare and livelihood of this whole town!'. The shift in the tone and rhythm of the speech is another instance of Bond's characteristic method of juxtaposing contrasted statements. There is no sense of a slowly mounting hysteria in Hatch's remarks; it is the suddenness of his display of open emotion that shocks and works on the mind.

In a conversation with William Woodman, who was about to direct *The Sea* at the Goodman Theatre, Chicago, Bond stressed how important it was for the actor not to anticipate Hatch's breakdown – and acknowledged the technical difficulty of the sequence when he cuts, tears, rips and slashes at the material, all the time commenting on his life in the trade: 'The cutting scene is the most difficult to stage. Ian Holm wanted a glove, it was such arduous work. The actor playing Hatch mustn't be obvious at all in this scene that he's cracking. It's a temptation to be avoided . . .'.[15]

The attack on the material is yet another displacement activity: shortly afterwards Hatch actually strikes out with the shears at the real object of his aggression – Mrs. Rafi. But the seriousness of Hatch's predicament, and the sense of the agony of long years of oppression bursting to the surface, is counterbalanced by sharply comic sequences: Hatch's hacking of the material is prefaced by Mrs. Rafi sternly leading Thompson, her gardener, out of the shop by his ear; Hollarcut watches the height of the drama from a safe position behind the counter, ducking his head down beneath it when things get too hot; Mrs. Tilehouse swoons; and there is a continual, increasingly frantic coming and going, marked by the clanging sounds of the doorbell which Bond scrupulously indicates in the stage directions on each occasion. One consequence of the way he has written the scene is that, although we are made still more aware of Hatch as a victim, we are not encouraged to feel empathy with the character. The overriding principle is one of demonstration.

Hatch's breakdown and the preceding scene of the rehearsal expose the hollowness and frailty of the protective shells which individuals like Hatch and Mrs. Rafi grow to avoid any real contact with other people. In the remaining three scenes, Bond shows through the characters of Willy and Rose that there are alternatives to the irrationality we have seen.

Reviewers and critics have tended to sentimentalise Willy and Rose by referring to them in a lazy shorthand as 'the young lovers' – the vision conjured up is of them walking hand in hand down the beach and into the sunset as they leave for a new life together. But what Bond shows is Willy and Rose learning to live in the real world, learning to face the worst and not to grow protective armour but to plunge back into life: 'Like the young couple in *The Tempest*, Willy and Rose have to create their own personal maturity. The ideal figure is drowned and lost – he would have been impossible either to live with or live up to – and the couple have to find their own strength by learning to solve the problems of their own lives and their society. They find that strength in the process of learning, they don't bring that strength to the process.'[16]

Our last sight of Willy was of him trying to convey to an unwilling Rose what he remembered of Colin's drowning. After only a few lines of scene six, talking to her on the beach, he again confronts her with his thoughts about Colin. It is like a continuation of his earlier, fruitless conversation with her – except Willy has changed. The calmness and directness of his words is one aspect of this change – although he had shown evidence of this capacity in his talk with Evens in scene three. More striking is what he actually tells her.

Rose's attitude is remote: as Jane Howell puts it: 'She still has an image of herself sitting in black on the beach.' Their early exchanges consist of separate trains of thought which overlap, rather than an actual dialogue. Willy is now capable of being objective about Colin; Rose continues to romanticise both Colin and her own position, and her stance is entirely negative: 'I can't bear to lose him. I don't think I can live without him.' This self-regarding quality in Rose goes hand in hand with a passive despair: 'How can you escape from yourself, or what's happened to you, or the future?'

Willy offers no easy comfort:

> If you look at life closely it is unbearable. What people suffer, what they do to each other, how they hate themselves . . . you should never turn away. If you do you lose everything. Turn back and look into the fire. Listen to the howl of the flames. The rest is lies.

This is Willy's strongest speech in the play, echoing Evens's long speech to him in scene three but with a maturity and power which alert us to how changed he is from the ghostly figure of the play scene. Deliberately, Bond shows the *change* not the *development*; this scene could be happening two days, three days, a week after his visit to Park House, and we are neither shown nor told anything of his thoughts in the interim. All that matters is that he is now capable of confronting reality, however grim, with the voice of reason.

The whole sequence between Willy and Rose is played out in front of Colin's dead body, washed up on the shore and lying upstage, at first unnoticed by them. The drowned man's appearance, down to the last detail, had been one of the formative images in Bond's mind when he started to think about the play: '. . . I heard about somebody who had been drowned after a ship had sunk, and he was found washed up, dead, lying on the beach. And he'd been trying to get his jumper off over his head so that he could swim better – his head was covered by this jumper, and his hands were stretched upwards, still caught in the thing, and he'd drowned like that . . . it seemed to me so extraordinary, that he'd pulled this hood thing over his head trying to escape.'[17]

The body clearly has a metaphorical significance: the action of 'trying to escape' is analagous to the situation of Willy and Rose, who have both come close to being swamped by their own despair. But any metaphorical connotations give way to a more immediate theatrical reality: Willy has come to terms with the death and has achieved a sane perspective on life and so reacts undramatically to the body, but the same is not true of Hatch, who arrives on the beach and, thinking himself to be alone, stabs and hacks at the corpse in the delusion that it's Willy he is killing. The parallel with his earlier slashing of the curtain material is obvious, but by now Hatch has lost all hold on reality and his alienation is expressed through a vicious and calculated act of violence. Our immediate reaction might be horror and repulsion, but the parallel with his attack on the material reminds us of the pressures that forced this action by driving Hatch into madness. Willy's comment to himself as he watches – 'Hit it. That's an innocent murder' – is true not only because Colin is already dead but because Hatch, in the fullest sense, is not responsible for his actions.

The body is used as a focus for the contrasting states of mind – and views of the world – that Willy and Hatch have arrived at. Willy's newly-born determination to 'look into the fire' is put to an acid test. He is not horrified by what he sees. He does not react with conventional moralising. His observations on the innocence of Hatch's fury is not a ham-fisted attempt by Bond to ram home a message, it is evidence of the clarity and maturity of Willy's perception.

As if to test our readiness to confirm Willy's judgement, Bond makes the desecration of Colin's ashes the centrepiece of the comic action in scene seven – the scene where he gathers together all his characters for the play's dramatic climax. The funeral service on the cliff-top disintegrates into chaos when Hatch bursts in upon it; Colin's ashes, already dropped, scattered, and carefully swept up by Mrs. Tilehouse with her handkerchief, become a weapon in Mrs. Rafi's self-righteous hands – she throws handfuls of them in Hatch's face (in the Royal Court production she also hit him with the urn!). The effect is overwhelmingly funny; it also emphasizes the desperation of Mrs. Rafi's efforts to keep control of the empty ritual which she has so carefully stage-managed. The similarities with the play scene are inescapable: the merciless parody of the Church of England funeral service (with the accompaniment of a piano whose sound is '*hollow and spread*') takes the place of the bloodless Orpheus play, and the false piety Mrs. Rafi imposes on the proceedings is again undermined by interruptions. She is confronted, as before, with niggling challenges to her authority: the rivalry for the most elaborate descant between Mrs. Rafi and Mrs. Tilehouse is a comic *tour de force*. The sound of the guns again shatters the spurious solemnity of the occasion.

It is another broadly comic scene, but the comedy is played off against a number of very sobering moments. Hatch enters in a frenzy of messianic zeal, believing he has saved the town (the world, perhaps) by killing Willy; he comes face to face with his supposed victim, very much alive. His bafflement and despair intrude on the mood of farce, just as his last speech in the play intrudes on the mind. It starts with Hatch afraid: 'I don't know if you're all ghosts or if you still have time to save yourselves', and ends with the warning: '. . . no one can help you now.'

In his delirium, Hatch offers a piercing observation on the town's inhabitants: they *are* all ghosts, as Mrs. Rafi admits to Willy later in the scene, living a dead culture, exercising a morality which consists of stock responses and pious faces. Although the shakiness of their morality has been exposed, it reasserts itself as Hatch is dragged away 'to the town lock up'. Mrs. Rafi regains control of the situation, bossing a surly Hollarcut into promising to atone for his part in the anarchy by digging her garden.

Then Bond gives Mrs. Rafi a speech which, for the first time in the play, shows her as a vulnerable, frightened human being 'afraid of getting old'. The placing of the speech is deliberate – any earlier in the play, and the critical amusement with which we have viewed her might have been clouded by sympathy. Like Hatch as he hacked at the curtain material, she talks of her life having been wasted. Like Hatch in that scene, her mask drops and we see the tense and twisted face behind it. But even now we are not asked to waste too much pity on her – what she does is to find excuses for the harsh way she has treated people, and Bond's attitude towards that is unequivocal: 'I think what she says about herself is ultimately unacceptable. I don't think you can push people around in the way she does and then find a legitimate excuse for it. That's wrong. That's the excuse of a lot of leadership – and it's absolute nonsense . . .'.[18] We should be wary of misinterpreting Mrs. Rafi's plea for sympathy as an occasion for extending it to her: 'She looks into her soul when she is alone with Willy on the beach – but even as she does so she admires her courage for doing so, and this is also an illusion, as Rose points out a few moments later with her cutting remark about cripples.'[19]

Rose's remark not only undercuts Mrs. Rafi's speech, it also tells us a lot more about Rose's strength of character. The change in her from the previous scene is as pronounced as the changes in Willy from scene five to scene six, although her acceptance of what Willy told her is still tentative and hesitant:

WILLY. The dead don't matter.
ROSE. I'm not sure.
WILLY. Then you're like your aunt. You talk and have no courage.

It is inevitable that Willy will leave the town: Rose might stay and turn into a version of Mrs. Rafi. Bond never has her actually state her decision to leave with him. He indicates it through two simple actions. First, 'ROSE *covers the piano with a green or faded dirty white sheet*' – exactly the same colours Bond specifies for the blanket used to cover Colin's corpse on the beach. And when Willy announces his intention to go for a swim in the sea – it is as if by swimming in the same sea in which Colin drowned he is asserting that he has exorcised his former self and *can* look life in the face – Bond shows Rose coming to her own decision. It takes no more than a dozen words:

ROSE. Will you?
WILLY. Oh yes.
He looks at her for a moment and then turns to go.
ROSE. Wait. (*He stops.*) I'll come down and hold your clothes . . .

She follows him off, leaving behind the dead past – the covered piano and, by association, Colin's drowning.

Bond might have ended the play here, if he had merely been aiming for a satisfying theatrical resolution. Instead, he wrote a last scene which most critics have seen as a postscript, an addendum in which 'enactment gives way to philosophising'.[20] At a cursory glance, Evens's speeches in this scene – in particular the fable of the rat and the ratcatcher – might seem to bear all the marks of an epilogue, with Evens as the author's spokesman, but this view ignores the context in which Bond has set them and the interaction between Willy and Evens, of which the speeches are only one part.

In the two preceding scenes we have witnessed Willy's new strength and resolve. In this last scene we see that he is still a prey to doubts. The old man confirms what Willy knows – the world *is* full of savagery and aggression – and Willy openly expresses the weakness he feels: 'How can you bear to live?/I'm not sure if I can bear it.' In the following speeches Evens offers Willy a positive vision; he still emphasises the difficulties, but he counsels hope: 'What the old man says is that there is certainly a lot of violence in life. And that life kills other forms of life in order to exist. And that on this planet, most life has been lived this way – that's why life has survived. But what he really says is that this is unacceptable to human beings. It's not the sum total of all life. Human beings have other possibilities open to them.'[21]

It is important to note that Evens shows considerable hesitation before telling Willy all this:

EVENS. . . . Have faith.
WILLY. In what?
EVENS (*shrugs*). Well. (*Looks round.*) Would you like some tea?

He pours himself a mixture of tea and whisky. Even then, in a stage direction Bond added for the collected edition of his plays: '*The silence lasts a moment longer.*' There is a strong sense of deliberation, as if Evens had often *thought* about what he says to Willy, but has never before *said* it to anyone. The distinction is vital. It is not only what Evens says that is important, but the fact that he is saying it: 'The old man doesn't say anything that Willy hasn't already told Rose, in essence, when they talked on the beach just before they found the body – but the act of saying it and listening to it *demonstrates* their belief in the possibility of a rational, sane society.'[22]

The scene is convincing *because of what is being enacted*. Not that the intellectual content of the speeches is unimportant, but the interplay between the characters, as Jane Howell emphasises, is vital to its meaning: 'It's like two people testing each other. They've both been through an incredible experience, they both respect each other, and they discuss the root causes of what's been going on. And they test each other out as they do so.' In a way, Willy and Evens serve as a model of the rational, sane society in which Bond wants the audience to place their trust. We should take hope, as much from the relationship we have seen them work their way towards as from Evens's parting words of advice: 'Go away. You won't find any more answers here . . . Remember, I've told you these things so that you won't despair. But you must still change the world.'

There is no guarantee of success. That much is implied by the unfinished sentence that ends the play – Willy's reply when Rose asks what he has been discussing with Evens: 'I came to say goodbye, and I'm glad you –'. Bond leaves room for a literal-minded interpretation, something like 'I'm glad you are coming with me', but the effect is to leave us in a state of suspension: 'I left the last sentence of the play unfinished because the play can have no satisfactory solution at that stage. Rose and Willy have to go away and help to create a sane society – and it is for the audience to go away and complete the sentence in their own lives.'[23]

The Sea stands at the end of Bond's first cycle of plays. In an interview in 1975, Bond explained how he had conceived of the relationship between *The Sea* and *The Pope's Wedding* before he wrote any of the plays. An image for the beginning and the end of the series, which he then thought would take him his entire working life, was in his mind from the start: 'I would begin with a tragedy in which the old man would not talk . . . Scopey never gets an answer from him. I wanted to end the series of plays with two people sitting on a beach after the storm has died down, talking to an old man. They try to come to terms with the problems that they have to face.'[24]

The connection between the two plays becomes even clearer when we realise that Scopey is there in *The Sea*, in the figure of Hollarcut, a character whom Bond treats with great sympathy – he alone of Hatch's three disciples remains loyal; he has a mind of his own, and there are a number of indications that he doesn't really swallow all of Hatch's strange beliefs; and he speaks out forcefully against Mrs. Rafi after the *mêlée* at the funeral. There is a strength and dignity about Hollarcut which is impressive. Like Hatch, he feels frustrated and alienated by the way he is made to live, but because he never clearly understands the nature of his problem he is reduced to expressing his feelings by way of a cheerful aggression. At the beginning of scene eight, he stands outside Evens's hut, holding a big stick. He could be Scopey, about to murder Alen, since in his muddled anger he still fixes on Evens as a scapegoat; 'Who drove him wrong in the hid? Why'd he take up all they daft notions? I don't know no one doo that if that weren't yoo.' As his parting shot, he indicates that he also intends to ensure that nothing will grow in Mrs. Rafi's garden. It's an appropriate gesture of defiance, but it will do nothing to change his life.

Hollarcut is a character who will appear again in Bond's later plays. He is the working man, conscious of the injustices to which he is subjected, but with a blurred vision, without the same degree of rational consciousness that Bond gives to his central characters. He reappears, with a more substantial role, in the second cycle of plays – in the shape of Darkie in *The Fool* and the Dark Man in *The Woman*.

7
We Come to the River

Before starting *Bingo*, the first in his new series of 'history' plays, Bond turned aside to work on a very different kind of project – a libretto for an opera by one of the leading contemporary European composers, Hans Werner Henze. The suggestion had come from Henze, who had seen the Théâtre National Populaire production of *Early Morning* at the Avignon Festival in 1970 and had subsequently read, and been impressed by, a number of Bond's other plays. In the summer of 1972 a meeting between them was arranged by a mutual friend – director Volker Schlöndorff – to whom Bond had once expressed his admiration for Henze's music.

Henze's idea was that Bond should write for him a version of Marlowe's *Edward II*. In October 1972, Bond sent him a finished libretto – not based on the Marlowe play, but on an original subject. There was a further meeting between the two of them in Vienna the following January, when Bond was directing *Lear* at the Burgtheater. In the light of their discussions, Bond made some revisions to the script, and then again in January 1974, after a year's gap while Henze was working on other projects. During this hiatus, Bond wrote *Bingo* (Henze, in fact, saw the production at the Royal Court on a visit to London in September 1974, and was enthusiastic about the possibilities of basing a chamber opera on it). Bond continued to provide Henze with minor revisions to *We Come to the River* up to October 1974, so technically the libretto was only finally completed at the same time that he finished writing his *next* play, *The Fool*. Henze started to compose the music early in 1974, and the opera opened at the Royal Opera

House, Covent Garden, in July 1976.

Because of the long gap between the first drafts of the libretto and the first production of the opera, the relationship of *We Come to the River* to the plays Bond wrote from 1973 to 1976 can easily get confused. The period of roughly a year (from early 1973 to early 1974) which spans the writing of *Bingo* and the major revisions Bond made to the opera libretto is an important time, because in these two works Bond pushes his analysis of individual responsibility in a capitalist society one stage further. In the plays up to *The Sea*, he had shown individuals struggling to achieve a full consciousness and understanding of the need for change; in *We Come to the River* and *Bingo*, as in *Lear*, he explores the difficulty of translating consciousness into action. In both these works the central character is a man who is responsible for causing suffering to others, who is tormented by his vision of the suffering around him, and who dies having made only the faintest of gestures to change the society he helped to create.

To interpret either work, we need to confront a simple question: how sympathetic do we feel towards the central character? How do we view the agonised conscience of a man who is aware of his complicity in causing suffering and injustice and who ignores the one opportunity given to him to make a stand against it?

Bond's own priority would be for the audience to understand the situation he presents: how they react and what they do with their reactions is their responsibility. But his treatment of the General in Act Two of *We Come to the River* is detectably harsher than his treatment of Shakespeare in *Bingo*. This may be due to the fact that the opera is more overtly political than the play; in the final version of the libretto Bond makes a strong and unequivocal statement about the overthrow of capitalism and the use of political violence. In doing so, he anticipates the end of *Stone*, which opened in London shortly before the opera but was written two years after it.

For Henze, the importance of Bond's 'actions for music' was that they freed him from an *impasse* he had encountered as a result of his earlier ventures into music theatre: 'From the moment that Henze embraced Communism, he began to look for new dramatic material and for new means of projecting it without invoking the apparatus and rhetoric of conventional opera . . . Yet he has confessed he remained thwarted. He felt that music was condemned to play a passive role in the face of what he describes as "contemporary reality" . . . he could not see how it could be used to present "real social conditions". It was Edward Bond, Henze claims, who showed him the way out of this predicament.'[1]

Bond sets the action in 'Europe: nineteenth century and later'. In Henze's production of the opera at Covent Garden, the costume-design conveyed a general impression of early Edwardian England, while the soldiers' uniforms suggested a slightly later period: any more precise a sense of time or national identity is deliberately blurred – the opera is a parable about any modern European militarist society. It shows the crisis of conscience of a General, recently victorious, after a bitter campaign against a rebel province. He is characterised as an ice-cold, efficient professional soldier, but when his doctor tells him that he is going blind, his awareness of his own vulnerability brings home to him the suffering he has brought in others. He speaks out against the violence that his society sanctions and condones, and is locked away in a madhouse. The Emperor asks him to make a public statement of support for his regime. The General refuses, but he also ignores an appeal from the rebels to join them and lead a revolt of the oppressed. The Governor of the province is assassinated and the Emperor, fearing the General's influence, has him blinded – 'Even my enemies wouldn't follow a blind leader.' Still haunted by visions of his victims, the General is killed by his fellow inmates in the madhouse.

The libretto calls for over 120 other characters in addition to the General. As with the seventy-odd minor characters in *Lear*, in effect they are 'one role showing the character of a society'.[2] Scenes showing the progress and downfall of the General are set in counterpoint to scenes showing the society of which he is a part – the shooting of a deserter, the assassination of the Governor and the government's reaction, the General's soldiers celebrating after the victory, the reception in the General's honour at the local Assembly Rooms. Often these scenes are *presented* contrapuntally – on several occasions in the opera, two or three scenes are played concurrently on different stages.

The idea of staging a number of scenes simultaneously had originally come from Henze: 'I wanted simultaneous action for dialectical reasons, but also for formal reasons – writing simultaneous music means writing polyphony.' The drafts of the libretto which Bond sent to Henze were carefully tailored to meet the composer's requirements: 'the whole libretto has been written with an understanding of music such as I have never had before. Bond designed the whole work for the music, more than perhaps he even realised'.[3] Henze has also remarked how Bond 'must have been thinking as contrapuntally as I was able to think in my music, to prepare all those possibilities for me.'

It needs stressing that Bond's 'actions for music' cannot be assessed independently of Henze's music – far more than the plays, *We Come to the River* must be seen and heard in performance. There is a strong temptation to treat it as another play, albeit in a slightly different form, particularly on the strength of the text published by Eyre Methuen, which reads very much like a condensed and compressed Bond play. The impression one gains from reading this text is bound to be vague and misleading, since individual *sections* (which might be either complete scenes or those parts of a scene that are played on just one of the stages) are printed separately, with only a general note as to which sections are played wholly or partly together. To gain an accurate impression of the interrelation between sections when the opera is performed, one has to turn to the version published by Schott, where the words and actions are printed under the stages on which they occur and the points of overlap, when there is action simultaneously on more than one stage, are very clear to see.* Even then, there is a vital element missing: the effect of the music in reinforcing the dramatic contrasts inherent in the libretto. It has been suggested that Bond's script could be staged as a play, dispensing with Henze's music and with actors treating the choruses and songs as they would ballads, but it is difficult to imagine what scenes with simultaneous action *and simultaneous dialogue* would sound like without the unifying effect of the music.

Henze's remarkable talent as a composer for music theatre is immediately apparent in brash set-pieces such as the military

**References hereafter will be to the numbers of the scenes, as they are performed in the theatre, not to the sections as printed in the Eyre Methuen edition. The Schott edition is published by B. Schott's Söhne, Mainz, 1976.*

parade or in sequences of great lyrical beauty like the sequel to the death of the Old Woman and Child in the river, or the Song of the Victims. Henze, however, like Bond, is intent on making a rational appeal to the audience's intelligence and understanding. The score is full of musical references, both internal (to indicate connections between separate parts of the action) and external (that is, references to other composers and to musical conventions). In itself, this is unremarkable – merely part of the stock-in-trade of any composer. What is distinctive about Henze's intricate system of musical allusions is not only the sheer theatricality of many of the examples, but also the way he uses them to make pointed, often ironic, comments on the action.

A minor, but very effective, example comes in the scene when the Assassins sent by the Emperor arrive to blind the General. They enter immediately after a desperate monologue by the General: 'When will I go mad or die? You promised me long ago I would go blind. How much more must I see? . . . Is it so difficult to vanish off the face of the earth? I am like an evil ghost that upsets the hands of the clocks other men live by.' For the end of this monologue, Henze writes a striking musical climax, a massive classical sound in which the music that has been used to characterise the General goes into multi-layered counterpoint, and then fragments and virtually eliminates itself. This is at once followed by the sound of a harmonica playing, in a style that is irresistibly reminiscent of the background music in Hollywood westerns: it conjures up celluloid memories of the two hired guns stalking into town.

This piece of musical irony matches and reinforces Bond's characterisation of the two Assassins: they are dispassionate professionals, but with more than a touch of caricature about them – and with a good line in black humour, as they stand over the General, who is strapped in a straitjacket:

FIRST ASSASSIN (*admiringly*). Like his suit.
SECOND ASSASSIN. Natty.
FIRST ASSASSIN. Convenient.
SECOND ASSASSIN. A joke really.
FIRST ASSASSIN. Can't shake his hand before he goes.

Henze writes music for these two parts which has them singing as if they were characters in an *opera buffa*.

As the First Assassin takes out a knife, an organist plays a variation on a very distinctive tune heard earlier, also on the organ, when the General condemned a deserter to be shot. The effect is not just to sound out a similar note of foreboding in two very similar situations. The repetition also forces a connection between the events; according to Henze, it is 'like saying that the General condemned himself when he condemned the deserter'. Henze is continually looking for ways of using the music analytically.

A similar analysis could be made of any other scene in the opera. It is more appropriate, however, in the context of an overall study of Bond's plays, to examine two other features of *We Come to the River* – Bond's treatment of the main character of the General, and the problems associated with presenting scenes with simultaneous action.

We Come to the River is played on three separate stages. Stage one is in the foreground: it 'should extend as deeply as possible into the auditorium. The orchestra pit is to be covered.'[4] Although it would be misleading to make a generalisation about the use of any of the three stages, it is fair to say that stage one is mainly used for monologues and to show the world of the oppressed. Stage two, 'which could perhaps be elevated or sloping, is on the first part of the main stage';[5] it is the area where most of the central events occur. Stage three, 'which is higher than Stage 2, is to be constructed at the back of the main stage';[6] there, in the background, scenes of violence and suffering are placed.

Each stage has its own orchestra, situated alongside it, and the music is designed to run through the three stages; if a character or a sequence of action moves from one stage to another, the music too is transferred from one orchestra to another: 'the idea is that an orchestra plays only when there's an action – somebody rushes from stage one to stage two, and this orchestra will stop and that one start.'[7]

The problems for the audience begin when characters and events move from one stage to another in this way, while at the same time another action is taking place elsewhere. It is a problem of focus, not so much visually (one can quickly scan the whole scene and then focus on particular aspects of it), but aurally.

Although there are many occasions in *We Come to the River* when separate strands of the music and the vocal line are interwoven in a relatively traditional manner, allowing one element in the total sound pattern to gain prominence at any given moment, very often simultaneity of action also means simultaneity in the music, with blocks of sound overlaid one on top of the other. What is more, there are *six* potential sources of sound – the singers on each of the three stages and the three separate orchestras. The result can be a mass of sound which blankets the ears and prevents any more than a very generalised response to the events on any one of the three stages. All this was further complicated at Covent Garden by the problem of the acoustics; Henze found it very difficult to get the balance he intended between an orchestra positioned in front of the proscenium arch and another situated behind it.

Simultaneous action on all three stages occurs in five of the eleven scenes (in two of these – scene seven, where the Old Woman is crossing the river and is surrounded on both sides by soldiers, and scene eleven, when the mad people scatter over all three stages – the simultaneity is not in fact very complex). In the other six scenes, although all three stages are in use most of the time, the action on any one of them is faded or frozen as the action starts up on another stage; at most, two actions might very briefly overlap, or be staggered so that they do not conflict and compete for the audience's attention.

The opera opens with two separate activities in direct counterpoint. On stage two, we see the General in his tent, dictating a dispatch to the Emperor: the enemy is routed, the General has lost 22,000 killed or wounded. The stage is dimly lit: '*Dark, quiet. Candles.*' Further back, on stage three, his soldiers are celebrating in the canteen – '*Drink, smoke, movement.*' The contrast in tone and rhythm between the two stages leaves a prevailing impression of the General's coldness; he seems untroubled by human feelings – there is a terrible gap between the picture of carnage conveyed by his report and the dispassionate way he dictates it, the sentences chopped into terse business-like words and phrases; 'The – enemy are routed, all – survivors pursued and taken. The rebel army no longer exists. I – am sending the leaders to the capital –'. The character is established within seconds and the contrast between the General's music on stage two and the orchestral description of the men noisily carousing strengthens our impression of him.

What is easily lost, though, in the thick of these combined sounds, is Bond's introduction of another important character, among the soldiers on stage three. While his companions discuss the battle and argue over military tactics, the Second Soldier sings of peace: 'Get out of the army. Marry and have children. I'll get up in the morning and there'll be no killing that day. I'll work hard. It'll be cold, it'll rain – but there'll be no killing.' In the Covent Garden production, as in the B.B.C. Radio broadcast, most of these words were inaudible, since they are sung at the same time as the final sentences of the General's dispatch on stage two. Although Soldier Two can be given a certain prominence through his position on stage and his music has a noticeably different timbre from that of the others, the audience has no chance of hearing and understanding the precise nature of his views.

Scene two consists of an independent action, performed in the foreground on stage one. At the court-martial of a soldier who had wandered away from the battle in a state of shock, the General passes the death sentence. His reasoning has an impeccable logic: the victory has only bought time to prepare for the next war, which will inevitably come; soldiers will always want to run away; the deserter must be shot as a warning to the rest.

Scene three interweaves three separate sequences of action: in the Guard Room (stage one), the deserter sits and talks of his childhood in an orphanage, while his guards play cards or try to sleep; in the Assembly Rooms (stage three) in the neighbouring town, the local bourgeoisie give a formal reception in the General's honour; after receiving their plaudits, the General leaves and walks across to stage two; there, in the tent, his doctor is waiting; he tells the General that an old wound is beginning to affect his eyesight – he is going blind.

This is a crucial moment in the scene, and it is managed with great skill and dramatic power. As the doctor breaks his news to the General, in the Guard Room the Deserter asks Soldier Two if he is a good shot: '(*touches his forehead*). Shoot here.'; at the same moment, at the reception the civilians have all left and the formal festivities are about to turn into a stag party. The relevant lines are sung not simultaneously but in sequence, from one stage then the next: 'Shoot here./You are going blind./I've ordered your whores, gentlemen.' The strongly contrasting tone of the last statement adds to the intensity of the events on the other two stages. At the same time, a connection is implied, rather than stated, between the General's blindness and the shooting of the deserter.

This scene demonstrates more successfully than any other part of the opera the uses to which triple staging can be put, but the success of the scene has a lot to do with the fact that true simultaneity (on all three stages) is kept to a minimum – it occurs only once, briefly and insignificantly, at the point when the Ladies leave the reception. The most striking effects in the scene are created not by the simultaneity but in a more traditional, linear manner – by focusing attention on one stage at a time and allowing the shift in focus from one stage to another to set up the contrapuntal effects. What is more, this method at least ensures that no key element is lost, as happens with Soldier Two in the opening scene. We are constantly aware of the Deserter, awaiting his execution, on stage one; his lines come over without competition from voices on the other stages – although phrases of the dance music played by the stage three orchestra come through, the vocal lines never overlap.

The entrance of the Doctor provides Henze with the opportunity for a straightforward theatrical coup. He comes on not from the wings but through the audience; the music associated with the character begins to play before he appears, as if in anticipation, and then bursts forth very loudly as he enters. Henze's intention was 'to underline that, almost like in ancient theatre, he is a messenger of change'; the dark note he introduces into the scene stands out all the more starkly against the highflown – and very comic – coloratura aria (a close relation to Mrs. Tilehouse's quavering descant on the clifftop in *The Sea*) with which one of the young ladies on stage three is saluting the General's achievements. Only near the end of the scene does the clarity of focus wobble slightly – the coarse revelry as an officer attends to a whore obscures the last part of the exchange between the Doctor and the General after the Doctor has pronounced the sentence of blindness.

In a letter to Henze on this 'diagnosis scene', Bond stressed that it should be done coolly: 'The Doctor is like a judge. He gives the facts and says to the General "if you behave inhumanly, you will become unlike a human being.'"[8] Bond's comment is, an indication of the strength and precision of his theatrical imagination: what the Doctor tells the General is important, but so too is the connection between the Doctor's 'judgement' on the General's condition and the General passing the death sentence on the Deserter in scene two. It is a connection which can only be made in performance, and only by playing the scene in the way that Bond intends. The Doctor's manner here should stir a memory of the General's manner during the court-martial if the harsh irony in the parallel between the two scenes is to be felt.

Shocked by what he has been told, the General characteristically keeps a grip on his emotions; at the end of the scene he calls in an officer and makes ready to resume dictating the dispatch to the Emperor. The stage direction in the Schott edition of the libretto carefully notes that '*they sit as in scene one*'. Only 21 minutes separate these two images in performance (evidence of the economy of Bond's words and of Henze's music – and of the effects of simultaneity in telescoping the action); the correlation between them is inescapable and it marks a turning-point in the characterisation of the General.

Scene four, in which the General wanders about the battlefield, where wounded men are still lying, sees the beginning of the General's awakening to the suffering he has inflicted on others. He encounters a Young Woman and her mother, searching for the body of the Young Woman's husband; she scratches at one of the corpses, insisting it is him, and the General pulls her away. His feelings remain blunted: he urges her to be logical – it can't be her husband. Then, for the first time, we hear one of his victims speak out directly against him: 'Have you killed so many men, seen so many bodies! You don't know what you look at anymore!' The Young Woman's situation demonstrates not just the sufferings caused by war but the impossibility of ignoring and escaping the consequences of the kind of society one lives in.

The General falls back on anger and rationalisation in the face of the Young Woman's challenge: 'I killed no one. They are war dead. They gave their lives.' It is his last attempt to deflect his feelings of guilt. In scene five, the Governor arrives to take the salute at a victory parade; the General is abstracted, preoccupied by what he has seen, and he causes consternation by voicing his concern for the wounded and the victims of the war. He returns to the battlefield in the following scene and again encounters the two women. His experiences have now led him to the point of reassessing his own part in it all – when the Governor and soldiers follow him there, he makes his stand: 'Go away. I'm not a soldier now. I've left the emperor's service.'

All that follows in the scene makes it clear that a mere change of heart or change of mind is not enough. The Governor has the two women shot because they witnessed the 'sordid affair' of the General's breakdown: what is more, he has them shot under an order issued earlier by the General himself that all looters of corpses should be executed. The General protests, but he is now powerless, having renounced his former authority. His actions to assuage his guilt are no more than desperate, ineffectual gestures.

While the broad effect of this is likely to be apparent from any performance of the opera, there remains the problem that many of the finer details in the libretto will inevitably get lost when simultaneity of action and music is employed to any great extent. The main casualty will always be the words, unless the librettist is willing only to provide so much verbal padding. It remains an open question whether it is possible to achieve the particular kind of dramatic counterpoint Bond and Henze aimed at – the use of contrasting actions for an *analytical* purpose – through simultaneity. Bond also uses the device in *Bingo* and *The Fool*, the two plays he wrote in the course of his work on *We Come to the River*, but only in a very limited and restricted form.

Part Two opens in the garden of the madhouse to which the General has been committed. '*The* MAD PEOPLE *are quiet, slow and withdrawn. They move like clouds on the tops of mountains. Many of them sit in isolation and sing monologues . . . During this other* MAD PEOPLE *start to build an invisible boat.*' Bond's evocative stage direction describing their drifting movements captures perfectly the sense of a strange and remote world, very different from the urgency and intensity of Part One.

The overriding concern of the Mad People is the building of their make-believe boat, which they imagine themselves sailing down a river to an island where they can escape from the world they know: 'We are happy there. Peaceful and free.' They play out their fantasy, raising invisible sails and moving off down the imaginary river. The General stands in isolation among them. He rejects their fantasy – 'Tell them there is no river! No island! The river is dead!' – but we see that he too has turned his face away from reality. He is visited by the Second Soldier, who describes what is happening outside the Madhouse garden: arrests, torture, a state of emergency, people disappearing without trace. On behalf of the people, he appeals to the General to give help and advice: 'The people write your name on the walls. You are their hero: you attacked the emperor. None of the leaders had spoken against him before! Help us now. Tell us what we shall do.' The General is given his one chance to use what power he has to influence events. Wrapped in his own thoughts, he seems not to hear the appeal. Like Shakespeare in *Bingo*, he sits on in the garden, preoccupied and troubled.

The view that the audience takes of the General both at this point and in the last scene could too readily be one of undue sympathy. It is an easy emotional response to make towards a character who is locked away and apparently going mad. It might even be ventured in his defence that, although he turns a deaf ear to the Second Soldier's plea, he then scornfully turns down the Emperor's request for him to lend his moral support to the Government, now faced with civil war. This is not what Bond and Henze would have us feel. The sequence with the Second Soldier brings home to us the consequences of his refusal to help the oppressed. The Government is showing signs of cracking. Its reaction is to increase the terror and repression, but the clear message of the scene is that with the General's support the revolutionaries could have seized power. As it is, Soldier Two takes his own desperate form of political action and assassinates the Governor. Ironically, the General is implicated when it becomes known that the Second Soldier visited him in the madhouse. The Emperor orders that the General be blinded.

All of this gives a context to the General's blinding and death which makes it plain that we should not waste too much sympathy on him. His blinding (after many years living with the threat of going blind) is ironic, not tragic. He is guilty not of the crime for which he is punished but the exact opposite – having done nothing! When he learns that the Second Soldier has killed his wife and children and then committed suicide, he feels, rightly, that he is to blame. Instead of learning a lesson about his earlier inaction, he plunges into hysterical despair: 'I was promised blindness and madness and death! Let me put out my eyes!' It is the reaction of an old-style tragic hero; there is a massive self-indulgence in the way that he persists in the contemplation of his own misery and guilt. He becomes the archetype of the ineffectual liberal – racked by his insights but incapable of action, holding back while others fight the battles for him. We are bound to feel outrage at the cruelty that the two Assassins inflict on him, but we are not asked to *sympathise* with the character.

When the Assassins' knife has been drawn across the General's eyes, he is blindfolded. As the blindfold goes on, the characters who were his victims in Part One appear. The remainder of the opera belongs to them. The General's death is no more than a confirmation of what we already know: he is redundant, because he cannot bring himself to join the struggle for a more rational world. Lear had at least made his gesture on the wall; the General makes none and he is swept under by the Mad People's imaginary waves. His death, like his blinding, is ironic. He is destroyed by the madness he helped to create. The Mad People kill him because they see him as a threat to their imaginary haven on their island; it is truer to say that he and his kind are a threat to the very real and tangible world that his Victims might achieve.

The death of the General must not be seen as the tragedy of one individual but as a political statement. We are encouraged to take a harsher view of the character in the final version of the libretto than in the earlier drafts. The first script that Bond sent to Henze in October 1972 put most of the emphasis in Part Two on the General's awareness of his responsibility and guilt coming up against the attitudes of the Government, seeking to suppress his influence. The opera ended with the Assassins shooting the General on the Emperor's orders; the last stage direction is. '*The ghosts go out. A few* MAD PEOPLE *are left drifting over the stage.*' The changes Bond made early the following year were aimed at redirecting attention from the General to the Victims. The Mad People were given more prominence, turning on the General's body after he is shot and dismembering it. A Madman slithers in the blood like a child sliding on ice, and a Madwoman dips her fingers in it, painting her face and admiring herself in an imaginary mirror.

By January 1974, Bond had decided that the Mad People should kill the General – he can no longer be seen as a victim of fascist repression: '*They push him over and smother him with the sheets and blankets. The GENERAL struggles as if he was fighting waves.*' It is as if he were struggling vainly against historical inevitability. It is another 'innocent' murder, like Hatch's assault on the corpse in *The Sea*, except that the moral here is more clear-cut and has more political force. Bond modifies the image he had previously envisaged: now, a Madman and Madwoman stay by the body and play with the sheets/water. The action denotes their innocence – but innocence is not enough. Alongside their actions, we hear the Victims singing to the child, offering their own commentary on the General's death:

> We stand by the river
> If there is a bridge we will walk over
> If there is no bridge we will wade
> If the water is deep we will swim
> If it is too fast we will build boats
> We will stand on the other side
> We have learned to march so well that we cannot drown.

Henze has described how 'we tried not to make a grand affirmative statement – not like *Fidelio*: like a flower in winter, like the child as a lone figure of hope; the music becomes very quiet and tender, almost like a folksong.' It remains Bond's strongest and most unambiguous political statement in his work up to then.

8

Bingo. Scenes of Money and Death; The Fool. Scenes of Bread and Love

> When I first started seriously to write plays I thought my life's work would be the span of plays that began with *The Pope's Wedding* and in fact ended with *The Sea*. But when I'd finished these plays I found, of course, that there were many other plays I wanted to write. I next wrote three plays (*Bingo*, *The Fool* and *The Woman*) in which I tried to deal with society at three important stages of cultural development. The past often works as a myth on the present. It is like a burden on our back and from time to time we have to rearrange it so that it becomes comfortable and we can go on with our journey . . .[1]

The Sea both concludes a group of plays, as suggested above, and implies the next cycle. Willy's last line in *The Sea* is not completed 'because the play can have no satisfactory solution at that stage. Rose and Willy have to go away and help to create a sane society – and it is for the audience to go away and complete the sentence in their own lives'.[2] Though Bond himself later characterized the final sentence of *The Sea* as being rather naive[3], the impulse which produced it had far reaching effects, both structurally and stylistically, on the plays which followed. *Lear* is about 'the difficulty of changing the world' and *The Sea* ends 'with people being as honest and open as they could'.[4] The next play examines the problem of how the first proposition cannot be resolved if the second proposition is absent. *Lear* had been concerned with the demystification of *King Lear*. It showed Lear himself understanding the necessity of rejecting his own private mythologies and it demonstrated the imperative need to avoid comfortable acquiescence in Shakespeare's conclusions. *The Sea* as a companion piece to *Lear* insists upon 'the strength of human beings and their ability to deal with the difficulties of changing the world'.[5] *Bingo* sets out the consequences of ignoring obvious implications in the pursuit of those things which assert a cynical and corrupt view of man and society. It shows a man ignoring his own truths, a writer denying his integrity, someone allowing a gulf to separate what he knows from what he does.

Set in and around Shakespeare's Stratford house during the last years of his life, the play is built upon Bond's interpretation of Shakespeare's involvement with a plan to enclose the common fields at Stratford from which Shakespeare derived his tithe income. The plan originated with Arthur Mainwaring in league with the prominent landowner, William Combe. The enclosed land would then be converted from arable to sheep pasture, which inevitably would lead to greater unemployment and higher prices. To protect his own interests, Shakespeare entered into an agreement guaranteeing him against any resulting loss. Combe ignored a plea from the corporation of Stratford that he should not enclose and began digging ditches around the fields. There were attempts by some to fill in the ditches. Combe's scheme was finally ruled against at the 1616 Lent Assizes. There is no evidence that Shakespeare actively resisted the enclosures, and as the author of a recent account of Shakespeare's life says, Shakespeare's 'apparent detachment renders provocatively apt the large questions Mr. Bond raises about the social responsibilities of the artist in an unjust society'.[6] Bond argues that 'that we don't know his attitude is an indictment of him. If you lived opposite Auschwitz and said nothing and did nothing, I don't necessarily know your attitude? But I do you know! His silence condemns him terribly, and that's why I haunt the earlier part of the play with William Shakespeare's silences' (letter to the authors, 22 April 1979). Bond's reaction to his reading about Shakespeare and the enclosures is one of the first things to surface in his notes for the play and details from historical accounts of the period are strikingly juxtaposed with the writing out of Timon of Athens' diatribe against gold (Act 4, scene 3; the same reference was, six years later, to appear on the title-page of the rehearsal script of Bond's play, *The Worlds*). Certain decisions were taken at an early stage and affected the evolution of the play. These were that the history of the enclosures would not be followed through: 'It is how it makes WS. act that concerns the play'. There would be no attempt 'to show WS. at work . . . or how the great man eats an egg'. Thirdly, Bond noted to himself: 'Be careful *not* to criticize WS. Even the poor don't. Just state the facts'.

The choice of Shakespeare is deliberate because of the synthesis afforded thereby of Bond's preoccupations:

> art to me is one of the things that creates human nature and it is a necessary element in that it is a necessary part of a culture. It is the self-critical, the self-reflective, the self-examining part – and that's one of the reasons why two of my plays have dealt with writers as major figures simply because they can be clearly seen to be caught up in this process. What I have done is try to find representative figures from the past in Shakespeare and Clare [in *The Fool*] to see how they were functioning as writers . . . I don't think that there is a special problem for the writer any more than for a dentist or a bricklayer. What those two plays with authors deal with is the problem of what is a culture. You see, what I want to say in those plays is unless you have something called a culture as opposed to a simple organization then the issue is not that a writer commits suicide, or a writer will be locked up, but that you will have H-bombs like those ten miles up the road from here . . .[7]

Bond maintains the primary function of the artist is one of helping people to understand their society: 'A lot of people assume this role. There is always some embarrassment when an artist uses it, but it is inescapable'.[8] The life of a great writer is used in order to talk of the life of anyone. *Bingo* says 'that Shakespeare may be the greatest dramatist of all times, but he is subject to the same laws as you or I or the man who drives your bus'.[9] But because a writer is a writer, it is also true that his public responsibility is greater, since his work may influence other than those within his immediate context. To object that this stance is elitist seems to deny writers any particular function.[10]

Because *Bingo* on one level concerns a writer and his function and the relationship of a writer to his society, there is inevitably a degree of autobiographical preoccupation consequent upon the conclusion of one series of plays and the beginning of another. *The Sea* had been started very soon after *Lear* (the earliest notes are dated 17 April 1971 and it was completed by August 1972). There is then a gap before the initial notes for *Bingo*, which begin 2

April 1973. During this time, Bond was in Vienna rehearsing his own production of *Lear* for the Burgtheater (January 1973). The rehearsals began in November. On his return from Vienna, Bond attended rehearsals at the Royal Court of *The Sea*, the first performance of which was in May. Yet already in the earliest notes for *The Sea* there appears what later is to become Shakespeare's grimly repeated question in the later scenes of the play, 'Was anything done?'.[11] On 30 April 1971, Bond cites a quotation from Leonardo Da Vinci's *Notebooks* and glosses it himself:

> Leonardo: Tell me if ever anything was done?
> [Bond]: Tell me if anything has ever been done. Or have all things only happened and have all our efforts been wasted? When I look at the wreckage of other people's lives, which are part of my own . . . Tell me why it's not possible to do the things we see so clearly have to be done . . .
> Possible title: Was Anything Done?

While the play was being written, Bond was contacted by Hayden Griffin, the resident designer at the Northcott theatre, Exeter, on behalf of himself and the theatre's artistic director, Jane Howell. Under Jane Howell, the Northcott had courageously opened with *Narrow Road to the Deep North* (April 1971), staged Bond's *Three Sisters* (September 1971) and *The Pope's Wedding* (June 1973). Griffin recalls that:

> We were really stuck in the last year. We got through the first year quite well. We nailed our colours to the mast with *Narrow Road*, and then we did a Brecht and we were on 60% houses of young people. The second year was more difficult, but we struggled through it and then in the third year, the first half was easy [but] then I said we must get a new play from Edward. So I 'phoned him, and he said he'd think about it and about two weeks later he said he was halfway through a draft.

The play opened on 14 November 1973 at the Northcott, directed by Jane Howell and John Dove. Bond had been to see *The Pope's Wedding* at Exeter in June and Howard Brenton's *Measure for Measure* the previous September. *Bingo* was not written for the Northcott, but Bond did know the theatre reasonably well. He was also clearly impressed with the quality of work being done at the Northcott by Griffin and Howell, as his agent, Margaret

Ramsay, said in a letter to the Northcott 15 October 1973: 'It is Edward's gesture to Jane to ask her if she wished to do the first production at her theatre . . .'. By the time rehearsals began in Exeter, theatres in London were vying with each other for the play and Bond wryly observed that 'The RSC, the National, and the Court all want to do it, which makes me think of the time when no-one wanted to do anything I wrote, and how happier I was then . . .'.[12]

Structurally the play divides into two movements, each of three scenes. The first half of the play sees Shakespeare in his garden, using it as a kind of sanctuary which is then intruded upon by figures which represent the reality outside the confines of the would-be voluntary exile. He is in a sense trapped between what is represented by his own house – his abandoned and sick wife and an embittered daughter – and what is happening in the world beyond the garden gate – the schemes of Combe and the oppression of the poor. These matters allow him no rest and he is forced to leave his sanctuary and, in the third scene, to wander the heath-like area of the land beyond Stratford. The climax to the first part of the play is his outburst downstage from the hanged Young Woman, in which, like one of his own play characters, he is made to force conclusions home to himself. The vision of the baited bear is terrible in its insistence upon the cruelty of the world and, like King Lear, he indicts the social structure of which he is a part. In the second section of the play he drinks with Ben Jonson and this scene (four) in the pub again suggests a kind of refuge. It is, however, as intrusive upon his longing for quiet as the earlier scenes in the garden. Again, as in the first half, Shakespeare is driven out on to the heath, and again he is faced with the realities he has consistently attempted to avoid as his gardener is accidentally shot and the work of fighting the enclosures goes on around his totally self absorbed figure. Where however at the end of part one, Shakespeare produced an outburst on the evils in the world, now in scene five, he begins to accept his part in the perpetuation of those evils. He returns to his house to die and even here the figures who, because they exist, pose questions he cannot answer, intrude into his bedroom. For the only time in the play and as a gesture of acceptance, Shakespeare acts to demonstrate his understanding of his own betrayal. He kills himself.

In an early note, Bond begins with the proposition that Shakespeare as a writer 'has been to Golgotha and the clay will always cling to his boots. So he has come back to be W S dying, and not a local gentleman making money' (10 April). The first scene counters Shakespeare's attempted withdrawal into his garden on a day in late autumn with a rapid series of figures and incidents which will not allow him to rest. As he attempts to abdicate from any concerns, his emptiness and silence is disturbed by the Old Man clipping the hedge and then by the Young Woman, a beggar, whom Shakespeare attempts to dismiss with the glib gesture of charity. Shakespeare holds a piece of paper which turns out to be the basis of an agreement with William Combe about the enclosures. Those who will suffer from any agreement are represented by the Young Woman and the deranged Old Man. The two of them form a natural alliance. The Young Woman's attempts to speak more formally to Shakespeare as opposed to the Old Man not only emphasise social distinctions but also become an ironic expression of what Shakespeare's pact with Combe will do to people like them.

Before Combe, who is in the house, comes on, two others, in addition to the gardener and beggar, have been in the garden briefly. Judith, Shakespeare's daughter, has appeared to announce Combe's arrival, and the Old Woman, the gardener's wife, has tried to sound Shakespeare out about the rumoured enclosures. Shakespeare hardly reacts to any of these four people. Yet they are all victims in some way. The Young Woman is obviously so; Judith is eventually seen to have been corrupted by her father; the Old Man is a victim of a press-gang; and the Old Woman's life is dominated by the needs of her damaged husband. They are all depicted unsentimentally as victims of the system which Shakespeare is about to endorse. The consequences of that system are then made clear as Combe enters the garden and explains the proposal. Shakespeare is shown to understand the effect on the people of the enclosures but his need for security is stronger.

As Combe nears the goal he has set out to achieve, Shakespeare shows his comprehension of the critical moment: 'We've come to the river' and Combe who, by now, knows he will be successful, can produce his pragmatic and cynical response very quickly: 'We needn't build a bridge if there's a ford downstream. Will you reach an agreement with me?'. Shakespeare weakly avoids saying yes, but speaks Combe's language by the end of the sequence. The sheet of paper turns out to be, not a sequel to *The Tempest*, but his calculations: 'I want security'.

> . . . by making these arrangements with Combe, he has to accept the enforcement of those relationships. And that means accepting a certain series of laws, and a certain series of punishments to enforce those laws, and a certain mythology to explain those laws. And when those things are involved, he can't say 'I will sign this piece of paper and stand back'.[13]

In the notes before Bond began the first of six drafts of the play (April–August), Shakespeare in the first scene is shown as more actively preoccupied with his business concerns and the encounter with Combe is in fact dominated by Shakespeare. It is Shakespeare, for example, who cynically finds the way around any difficulties arising from the agreement. The line 'We needn't build a bridge if there's a ford downstream' is Shakespeare's to begin with. Subsequently, the line was transferred to Combe and Shakespeare then begins to be more withdrawn. What this section aimed at from the beginning is caught in a note of April: 'The hard, factual world of commerce; the logical contriving and arranging; constructing, and detailed defining of consequences'.

As the episode ends, Shakespeare is immediately faced with the consequences of what he has just agreed to, for the Old Man's son discovers his father making love to the Young Woman in the orchard. He locks the gate on the girl and she is forced to enter the garden to face Combe in his capacity as a magistrate. The Son, who stands later on as the representative of those who opposed the enclosures, exhibits a prurient disgust at what his father does and takes a self-righteous satisfaction in what the law will now do to the Young Woman. She is caught between Combe's perfunctory dismissal of her and the Son's vehement gloating. They are aided by Judith's callous question regarding the girl's parents' graves and, unwittingly, by the Old Man's delight in so thoroughly upsetting his son. Through all this, Shakespeare watches, breaking his silence only to disconcert the Son, for whom his dislike is at least as strong as that for Combe himself. As the Young Woman had lied desperately about her Bristol aunt out of her fright, so the end of the scene sees Shakespeare lying to the Old Woman that

'Nothing's decided'.

Scene two shows to Shakespeare, already established as an alien in his own house, the lives of the victims of Combe's world and now his, as well as Shakespeare completing the land deal by signing Combe's paper. Here the antics of the Old Man in the first scene are explained in a matter of fact manner by the Old Woman, which serves to make the explanation both horrible and comic: 'Some man were killin' a man lay on the ground front on him an' when he swung his axe back he hit father top the yead. Not the sharp end, though. That'd a kill 'un'. The serious care the Old Woman takes in describing the accident so carefully both accentuates the random cruelty of the world outside Shakespeare's garden and establishes the Old Woman's dignified pragmatism. It is a feature of her life and response which is to be used later in the play. Here it is employed as a gentle rebuke to Judith's self-pitying remark that the Old Man 'should be happy. No responsibilities. No duties'. However, Judith's situation is shown at the same time by her asking about the Old Woman's marriage and the effect on her of hearing that the marriage was happy for seven years. Hard upon this is the first reference to Shakespeare's wife which establishes both Judith's forced responsibilities and Shakespeare's neglect. Judith does not appear in the play until the second draft, when she replaces Shakespeare's other daughter, Susanna. Bond, as he notes in the 'Introduction', decided to give to the Old Woman 'the more comforting and strengthening role that I think Susanna played in his life'. Initially, Mrs Shakespeare was to make a brief appearance, but only at the end of the play: 'Then she must appear shocking, old and ill and weak-palsied. But she'd have to have been mentioned quite a bit often before' (Mrs. Shakespeare in fact does appear in the second draft but nowhere else).

Shakespeare is sufficiently alive to the impending contract with Combe to be irritated when the Old Woman, as she does throughout, tries to mother him in the same way as she does her husband. Shakespeare and Judith now meet only on the neutral ground of discussing the outbreak of arson in Stratford. There is perhaps the briefest of contacts between father and daughter, but it is not what Judith wants. In the Exeter production, Shakespeare never looked at Judith during the exchange and clearly wanted her off the bench; Ron Daniels of his Yale production (January 1976) remarks on the irony of apparent closeness while discussing an objective topic. Patrick Stewart, who played Shakespeare in the Stratford and London revival (1976–7), noticed that because of the change in playing Shakespeare at the Warehouse, London (see below), the character became less sympathetic to the audience. Consequently, the exchanges with Judith in the first two scenes became 'harsher, crueller, uglier' (Stewart). However, it is important to establish Judith's situation and Bond told Meg Davies (Judith in the Stratford production) that Judith should not feel like Regan or Goneril. Rather one should always look at what her life is like.

Judith, frustrated, leaves, and Shakespeare is left briefly alone. As he begins to rest, he is startled very quickly by the Old Man who constantly in his childlike manner asserts his naturalness against Shakespeare's confinement. Shakespeare is presented graphically with two figures, the Old Man and the Young Woman, the one imbecilic, the other constantly shaking from the effects of a whipping, who then proceed to laugh at the strangeness of the world. The Old Man is cutting back the new spring growth in the hedge and the Young Woman earnestly vindicating her judgement about her beating: 'I warned 'em straight'. She treats it as unremarkable, clucks over their refusing to listen to her prediction. Together, the two present a remarkable and poignant account of what has been done to them, and their sanity, as they giggle at the peculiarities of other people, is one of the most moving things in the play. Shakespeare reacts by trying to feed and clothe the Young Woman. His concern for her reacts upon Judith, who wavers between pity and resentment and the lines are designed to elicit, not contempt for her, but to measure her complex and angry responses. She moves from calling the Young Woman a 'poor thing' to a brutal cross-examination of the Old Man, to taking the girl's shivering to be a result of fear. Out of these moments early in the scene, the Old Man provides the link between personal concerns and public policy by saying that his son rages against Shakespeare for siding with Combe and that Combe is trying to enclose the best land. His speech anticipates Combe's entry, and the threads of the scene come together as Judith, rejected by Shakespeare, enters to assume that the Old Man is again in the orchard with the Young Woman. She contributes to the girl's death by her mistake and regrets it, but the

Young Woman is doomed anyway by the structure Combe embodies, of which Shakespeare is now a part. Judith launches her attack upon her father, to be met by the flat dismissal of her banality. The Young Woman's imminent hanging is cleverly prefigured by the Old Man's tearful account of what hangings are like and his compassion contrasts strongly with the helpless frustration of Judith. As the scene closes, Shakespeare leaves his house. He returns only to kill himself.

What must animate the first two scenes is not only the figures around Shakespeare, but Shakespeare himself. Patrick Stewart and Bob Peck (Shakespeare at Exeter) insist upon the importance of a figure who is not passive:

> I had been [in Stratford] concerned with a man in isolation. The man I played here [the Warehouse] was a man who was firmly in the world, alive and aware and perceptive of everything and reacting to it. Before, it put him too much in isolation intellectually and emotionally and as soon as I brought myself into that world, it changed everything. He became always inquisitive, right to the very last moment of the play. (Patrick Stewart)

> ... every sense is out and it's listening a lot and also, particularly in the two early scenes, anticipating what was coming. He knew how people were going to react. He was aware, critically aware of what was being said. His awareness should be the focal point of the audience's attention. It's how what happens around him affects that central character that matters. (Bob Peck)

The awareness and anticipation referred to here is shown in the carefully-punctuated lines given to Shakespeare. Frequently, his lines act as a summary, a 'reading' of the situation and the intention behind the lines of others. Thus in the dialogue with the Old Woman in scene one, he responds to her talk of the enclosures by divining that she is concerned about her son. As she says 'Yo'll be brought in – you stand t'lose', Shakespeare remarks flatly 'And your son.' and as the woman asks what Shakespeare will say to Combe, he 'reads' behind her line again with 'Your son told you to question me.'. This dramatic method serves to set Shakespeare at a distance from the other characters during the play. He 'reads' accurately in this instance as the Old Woman eventually says she told her son to call on Shakespeare, who replies unemphatically and dryly, 'Did you.'. The absence of the question mark is important. Shakespeare is confirming what he already knows, not asking for confirmation. Consequently, Shakespeare's lines often possess a summarising quality. As he looks at the Old Man and the Young Woman in scene two, he interprets the dialogue: 'You give her bread and lie with her.', and at other times, his monosyllables indicate his sense of what is going to happen. As Judith enters and thinks that the Old Man and Young Woman are down in the orchard (scene two), he produces 'No', which both denies Judith's conclusion and objects to what is going now to happen with Combe present. Bond has remarked more generally elsewhere upon his sense of public and private language:

> My public language, as it lies shrouded by the page, may seem to some people to be flat. But it is designed to provoke that richer language, in performance, that I think is the red-blood of any true culture. Don't think that I am content with this almost hidden language. It is totally necessary to capture the public language and to learn how to use it with subtlety and distinctness, but if it replaces that other language then I think we would impoverish our species as much as if we'd taken the gloss off a starling or the plumage off a parrot.[14]

The task of any director therefore is 'to create *from the language*. The language interprets the play to the actor and he has to interpret the language to the audience: that's where his creativity comes in'.[15] It is a statement relevant to all of Bond's plays and particularly true with regard to the apparent sparseness of the 'public language' of *Bingo*.

The comments of Peck and Stewart cannot be stressed too much as a guide to the playing of Shakespeare, for it is the difference between reading the play as a cry of despair and appreciating the play Bond wrote. Shakespeare when played as a passive spectator makes his action criminal in an irrelevant sense. Such a pose also turns the play into an epilogue. The dramatic force of Shakespeare's being seen to accept his conclusions and act upon them is the point of the play's processes. Each scene adds another strand to the development of Shakespeare's understanding, actively, what is happening and what he has done. Shakespeare signs the piece of paper for Combe not by a process of rationalising the ways of the world, which is what Combe's speciality is, but in full knowledge of what he is doing. What is made clear, however, is that his action is also brought about by his circumstances, by the desperate search for security, to which he refers both in scene one and again in later scenes. Because of his need, he compromises. As Bond says, 'there is no rational argument that's going to stop Combe . . . And so that means that he [Shakespeare] has to be forced into a different strategy, and it's that situation which he withdraws from'.[16]

Scene three is the first of three consecutive scenes which move from daytime to night in the inn (four), to Shakespeare wandering around in the snow after leaving the inn (five). Where the initial scene is described as a 'pleasant warm day', the last scene of the three is set in the aftermath of a snowstorm early in the year. The three scenes are very carefully linked in terms of causation, for Shakespeare's mood in the pub scene (four) is related clearly to the gibbetting of the Young Woman in the previous scene, and scene five is equally specifically triggered by the dialogue with Ben Jonson. As scene three opens, Bond shocks his audience with the sight of the gibbetted Young Woman, with the effects of Combe's and Shakespeare's world. It is tranquil spring weather and she has been hanging for a day. Bond debates the means of presenting the fate of the Young Woman in the April notes. The problem 'is the difficulty of staging the hanging or whipping, that both of these things are melodramatic on the stage, but that it would be dishonest to avoid them if they're really relevant. Later (W S) goes to see her hanged. Or, *much better*, she has been hanged and is in a sort of gibbet (Ref. Rembrandt's drawing of the woman on a gallows). I think this is the solution!'. The audience is shown a scene with two centres, the girl, and Shakespeare sitting downstage, staring away into the auditorium. The two centres are visually set apart, but the link between them is unavoidable. Shakespeare sits with what he has done shown behind him. Carefully, Bond leaves Shakespeare to sit and concentrates instead upon other victims, as Joan and Jerome rest from digging stones out of their strip of land. They are middle-aged and have spent their lives scratching a living. What is noticeable is their vitality, resilience, and readiness here to endorse the execution of the Young Woman. They are initially shown to be an unresisting part of the structure which condemns them to the life they lead. At this point, Jerome maintains a level of quiet defiance, which is not to become active until later. He has no time for the Son who, with his disciple, Wally, arrives to justify his beliefs. Joan casually describes the girl's death, but her sympathy is mixed with a belief that the hanging was right.

The Son's speeches are all directed at Shakespeare, attacking him for his part in the enclosures, and his comments drive Shakespeare out. As Shakespeare goes, and Judith enters, she becomes the object of the Son's attention and is frightened, both by the Son and by the gibbet. Bond had noted in the third draft of this scene: 'Judith to call father during this', and what emerges is that the image of the dead girl changes its function according to who is speaking or looking. As Bond suggests, 'it's not a static thing. It's also a fluid, artistic, creative device which you use in different ways'. For Shakespeare, 'the storm breaks outside'. As he returns to the hill, he calls into the play a memory of a bear-baiting in London. If he had managed to calm 'the storms inside me', that is to say, rationalise what London offered by confining it to London, and leaving for Stratford, he now cannot prevent the realisation that the baited bear and the gibbetted Young Woman are precisely co-related. It is one of the few times in the play where one sees Shakespeare the artist for, as Howard Davies, who directed the Stratford and Warehouse productions, points out, he has been communing with the dead girl and in the first half of the baited bear speech, he constructs pieces of a jigsaw, notes to use to make an artistic whole, which then become the second half of the speech, provoked into coherence by Judith's unthinking line: 'You don't like sport. Some bears dance'. Shakespeare, out on the heath, virtually re-enacts one of his own characters. He rages like King Lear at the injustice and cruelty of the world, but as he does so, reaches new conclusions, which carry him beyond despair, for he realises that 'There's no higher wisdom of silence', which in the first draft Bond glossed as 'No wisdom beyond your own responsibility'. What the line does is to root the terrible things he describes firmly in the sphere of individual responsibility. Out of the self-accusations of the middle speeches comes the precise analysis by Shakespeare of the gulf between what he has said and what he has done: 'To have usurped the place of god, and lied . . .'. The rest of the scene shows Shakespeare hammering home to himself the evidence of his culpability. He confirms his realisations, and is confronted by the realism of the Old Woman who, lovingly, tries to persuade him to live in the real world, but who in fact stands as a moral condemnation of Shakespeare's activity. If Shakespeare laments that he cannot formulate the correct question, she plainly says her life does not afford the luxury: 'I yont afford arkst questions I yont know y'answers to . . .'. The gap between the artist and man is set out by Shakespeare's contrasting the beautiful vision of the swan flying up river with what surrounds him on the heath. It is crystallized by his knowing that the corpse of the Young Woman is 'Still perfect. Still beautiful', and that he has killed her.

In scene four, Shakespeare faces another despairing writer, sent by the theatre to ask for a new play. The early notes include the figure of Drayton who, however, is omitted from the first draft. Ben Jonson's animosity is apparent from the beginning of the scene: 'the pub scene is a dialogue, although one character does most of the talking and Jonson does feed off every single little thing that comes back to him' (Patrick Stewart); 'Jonson is goading him all the time, to make a response and he hardly responds at all' (Bob Peck). What Shakespeare brings to the scene is not simply that he is not writing, but that as a consequence of seeing the dead girl hanging, it is vital that he writes no more. Shakespeare has to be seen to react to Jonson, be, as Bob Peck puts it, 'absolutely tormented by everything that Jonson is saying'. If there is no reaction, then the audience cannot be taken into the fifth scene 'because they haven't been through the process which triggers the snow scene'. If Shakespeare had gone to the pub in an effort to avoid the realisations of scene three, what he encounters instead is confirmation. Jane Howell argues that there is needed the 'same violence from Jonson as you have from Combe and the Son over the other side of the stage – they both claw and tear, so that Shakespeare is torn from both sides like the bear, he's ripped from both sides. Then it will work and be funny. But that balance is very, very difficult'. What Jonson cannot forgive is the Shakespeare who appears 'to make no effort, just does it' and is serene. Everything that Jonson produces in his desperate flippancy must be seen to damage Shakespeare further, as a result of scene three: 'What's your life been like? Any real blood. . . ?'. As Jonson continues his self-laceration, and unwittingly attacks Shakespeare more than he knows, he evokes the London of which Shakespeare talked in scene three, and the two writers sit in one corner of an inn, while over the other side of the stage, another aspect of the world is being shown, that of individuals taking action, as opposed to two old men talking about it. Everything after the end of scene three is added proof to Shakespeare, for the labourers, united by the Son, and radically affected by the enclosures, fight a system endorsed by Shakespeare's piece of paper. He understands it very well: 'Lie to me. Lie. You have to lie to me now'. The two centres of the scene come together with the simultaneous speeches of Jonson, Combe and the Son, the lyrical pastoral alternative from the writer and the hard faced threats of Combe. Combe delivers his pragmatic rationale to the labourers and his truths are forceful and logical. He allies himself with a long line of figures in Bond's plays from Albert to Shogo to Lear who, given a certain view of the species, evolve a hard logic to demonstrate its undeniable truth and the consequences: 'there can only be one master'. The scene is cleverly constructed, but unless Shakespeare is shown to be the focus and the scene effectively about his realisations, then the danger is one of its declining into a literary interlude, to be prized only for remarks about *The Winter's Tale* and the Gunpowder Plot.

Initially, the effect of Jonson's bitterness and hatred in the closed context of the pub produces a drunken despair in the frozen landscape of the fields above Shakespeare's house (scene five). The conditions are extraordinary, for the snowstorm is late on in the spring. Shakespeare takes it as confirming his view of his world as sterile. As he wanders around, musing, the life of the scene is generated by the Old Man, for whom the snow is magical and exciting. He has been for the last time to the hill where the gibbet stands, to pay his respects to the Young Woman, and now he carries on with his life. His energy contrasts vividly with Shakespeare's inactivity, and it is directed not only at playing in the snow, but also at providing food for himself and his wife. Shakespeare is so immersed in analysing his thoughts that he does not notice the four or five dark figures, who are filling in the enclosure ditches, running across at the back of the stage. They exist on the fringe of the central activity and it is deliberately unclear who they are, here, and subsequently in the scene. They are vague figures because the point is to do with the focus on a self-concerned drunken central figure. Some directors found this moment problematic. Jane Howell, even given the considerable depth of the Northcott stage, spent three days rehearsing the running figures, and still found it technically difficult. When the production transferred to the Royal Court's stage (August 1974), the problem was, she felt, virtually insurmountable. Ron Daniels at Yale had a depth of only about eighteen feet, so that the dark figures were very close to Shakespeare. The same difficulties were apparent in the production at Stratford's The Other Place.

Bond's comment (to the authors, 22 April 1979) on the running figures is that 'it worked perfectly once at the Royal Court in rehearsal – the figures ran on and passed straight by Shakespeare, two upstage and one downstage of him. He was kneeling, and as they swept by he looked up – and it was just like a drunk who knew something had happened but didn't know what . . . The *problem* is something else: it's the actual running, not the runners' relationship to the main figure. Now if the actors stand in the wings and then say "Right, lads" and dash clumsily across – then you have a problem. You have to work at the movement, at their panic, and the snow slowing them down . . . Then they become men running for their lives – think of them running along an empty street, behind them in the square, policemen with guns, and they pass a drunk with a bottle . . .'.

Shakespeare recognizes his similarity now to Jonson and when Judith enters he uses Jonson's definition of hatred in an attempt to explain what he has done to his daughter. What is carefully shown is Shakespeare's objectivity in his speeches to Judith and his realisation that it is too late to change. As Shakespeare enters upon his soliloquy, the figures return over the stage and a gun fires. This is the moment designed to pull together the two activities in the scene:

> take a simple effect like the pistol-shot. There, the effect is a shot, followed by the man appearing with blood and moaning, it's not just a pistol-shot. It's followed immediately by a visual complement. The effect there – the whole scene is a sort of wandering scene – is to bring the whole scene into focus, it's not just a man talking. Here's an old man wandering in the snow. How do you make them aware he is discussing matters of life and death, culture and non-culture? Well you do that by putting in the pistol shot, followed immediately by this image of the wounded man.

The visual complement was made more explicit in the Yale production by Bond's asking Ron Daniels for some blood to be left on the snow as the wounded figure goes off. Shakespeare's ignoring of the wounded figure is designed to affect the audience's response to his vision of harmony which follows, as he for a moment lives in an ideal fantasy. As Bond noted in the third draft, 'Snow = perfect ideal. When it doesn't melt, WS lives in the perfect ideal. The perfect ideal is false because it is unreal. An ideal is always a lie'. It leads here to the deliberate echo of *The Tempest*: 'A dream that leads to sleep'. Bond describes the soliloquy in this way:

> the snow is a sheet of white paper and Shakespeare is so consumed with his crisis that he becomes an embodied pen writing out his history on it: what could be more natural for a writer? . . . it is, actually, very simple – but the actor must know absolutely what he's doing and what each paragraph in his testament means. Then he can move easily from statement to statement. It makes for difficulties sometimes in rehearsals because the director hasn't interpreted the speech as a consecutive argument and so allows the actor to wander into panic or make him act drunk or some nonsense . . . the problem is the through-argument: and that means the director interpreting the whole of the play because here Shakespeare sums it up and himself in it. Shakespeare ignores the wounded figure: this is the essence of his situation (he ignores other things throughout the play). Here he is so drawn into the discovery of self-knowledge, so concentrated in his self-judgement, that you could probably set fire to his coat and he wouldn't notice it (to the authors, 22 April 1979).

Yet Shakespeare then abandons the ideal and returns to his despair, as he reaches his lowest point with 'Was anything done?'. The scene ends with the Old Woman again helping him down to the house which at the beginning of the scene he refused to enter. He goes as the Old Woman makes the connexion between the gunshot and her husband. It is here that the full force of her statement about the Old Man is recalled when she said in scene three: 'His 'ole loife's a risk'.

As Shakespeare in the final scene waits to die, he is presented again with the issues he has tried to avoid throughout the play. One of the most moving moments comes with the Old Woman's commonsensical account of her husband's life at the beginning of the scene. Her gentle analysis is set against Shakespeare's absolute withdrawal to begin with, and the quiet dignity is shockingly broken with the assault by Judith and Shakespeare's wife upon the bedroom door. Jane Howell points out that the idea of intermittent and violent noise offstage is comparable to the baby's sobs in scene four of *Saved*. Shakespeare is unaffected by it, for he now cannot and will not do anything about it. He is now beyond accountability except to himself, so that his writing comes towards Jonson's definition of 'White worms excreting black ink'. What has to be grasped at this point is not that Jonson is correct but that Shakespeare has by his actions made himself into a Jonsonian figure.

The Son arrives to escort his mother to the Old Man's burial. He then stays behind to find out if Shakespeare saw him shoot his father. He has lied to his mother. Shakespeare has passed from his mood of despair to the extent that he will not lie any longer to himself or to anyone else. It is the first time in the play that Shakespeare has talked to the Son and in his last speech of any length, he judges himself fairly, clearly and coldly. He summarises a wasted life and what his freedom has cost others. The effect of the speech is vital to any reading of the play which finds its processes other than pessimistic. The final version of Shakespeare's death is radically different from the early drafts. In the first two versions of scene six, the Son helps Shakespeare over to the window to watch the burial of the Old Man, after which he drops dead and Susanna (subsequently Judith) enters to search for the will. By the third version, Shakespeare does not watch the burial. He dies and Judith enters alone (in the second version, she had brought her mother on). Thus up to the fourth version, Shakespeare dies in humanist despair. Scene six was then rewritten in the fourth draft and then Shakespeare swallows some tablets. It is also at that point that the line 'Was anything done?' is carried over into scene six. However Combe does not unwittingly give Shakespeare the poison until the same revised Northcott copy which also shows Shakespeare entering scene five with Jonson's poison bottle. The revisions are important and hinge upon the decision that Shakespeare commits suicide. The link is established thereby between Jonson and Shakespeare and, in Combe's giving the bottle to Shakespeare, there is the suggestion that the appearance of Combe precipitates the final action. These changes shift the ending of the play from despair to one which shows Shakespeare clearly taking responsibility for what he has done. Those who find the play pessimistic would have more justification if the play had been concluded with the third draft. Shakespeare in the final version sees causes and consequences. He sees also the real nature of justice and he says it to a man who is making the same mistakes. The Son responds to Shakespeare's clarity by admitting he shot his own father. Yet the Son supposes he can avoid this by taking action against the enclosers or, alternatively, going away and beginning again. He 'deceives himself. Shakespeare acts fraudulently but he doesn't deceive himself mentally, he judges himself. The Son does not. He, I think, accepts a series of false values, false beliefs . . . I think he lies . . .'.[17] The Son has enmeshed himself in political violence, but his response is to emigrate. It is no more a solution than Kiro's suicide. Even Combe when he enters is prepared to allow that one of his men may have carried a gun. The Son and Combe briefly represent the coming struggle, but the Son's corruption is established. Combe stands briefly as the formidable enemy he is, and neither Shakespeare nor the Son can oppose him. Shakespeare kills himself because of his recognition of his culpability and because he is old and tired. The important thing about the play's ending is his understanding. His death is not an evasion. It is a self-critical comment.

Bingo was only so titled in the sixth version of the play, in the copy Bond sent to his agent, Margaret Ramsay. The running title up to that point was 'New Place'. There was always, however, a sub-title which was 'Scenes of death and money'. The reversal of the sub-title came in the sixth draft. Early in April, the play was being described as 'Death and Money or Money and Death. Notes for a Chamber Drama'. The title of the play was explained by Bond as a comment upon the aridity of certain definitions of culture: 'it's a sort of attack on that kind of culture which is seen as something outside life, a sort of gilding on life, or something removed from life . . . It should be *about* our lives and it should help us to be able to solve our problems'.[18] Equally, the title opposes 'cultural appreciation': 'Art has very practical consequences. Most "cultural appreciation" ignores this and is no more relevant than a game of "Bingo" and less honest'.[19] The sub-title of the play marks a new and important development both structurally and thematically in Bond's work. The relationship between death and money is established as a title as early as 2 April, and the first draft is headed by the phrase 'scenes of . . .'. Bond points to the plays with similar sub-titles (from *Bingo* onwards) as ones where 'there's a more obvious dialectical contrast between money (which ought to be a good thing and a source of power and prosperity to the society) and death. In what sense is money associated with death? What is the relationship between bread, or if you like, money, and love. Unless you feed, you cannot love. In *Bingo* money always leads to death'. Plays since *Bingo* revolve around the connexions and antitheses between bread/love, money/death. The analysis of this central problem dictates the subject and form of the plays after *The Sea*. For Bond, the analysis is 'totally to do with the overall structure. The stories are chosen in order to illustrate that particular antithesis, because I think they are basic social problems inherent in historical processes'. The form described here leaves the play's structure open-ended: 'I want to get away from the well-made play, and to do that I called *Bingo* "scenes of something". These scenes of something don't just tell a story, they also, I hope, make a statement to those watching, a statement the audience is invited to finish'.[20]

What Bond means by the idea of a 'Chamber Drama' is the presentation in as precise a manner as possible of story and statement, the latter to be offered for completion by the audience. Bond noted to himself before beginning the writing of the play that the scenes should be 'short, dry and factual, especially at the beginning'. The writing is to be 'pithy; not flashy, though. No long set pieces of reflection. All words to be involved in the progression. Even W S's speech in the snow can be quite short. Interrupt with [Judith]. Send her away. She returns with others etc.'. This intention to a large extent stems from a refusal to make the focus of the play a comfortable arraignment of its central figure, to make a romantic attack. From the outset, the intention is to show how easily and understandably Shakespeare becomes enmeshed in a world which destroys him:

> The play isn't telling any secrets. It tells what everyone knows about the way our wishes and intentions and consciences and ideas are turned awry – by money. W S's 'crime' isn't a very bad crime – he doesn't wilfully exploit anyone, or steal wilfully from them, or punish them for criticising him, or claiming back their own things. It is all only part of his security and prosperity . . . The play is about the compromises W S makes. But what right has he to call on the poor to make

> these compromises . . . Even if he shows commercial restraint he still has to make compromises with his own humanity, his compassion . . . The crime relates to W S. It is brought out by his life. By his pact with society. Not a criticism of W S, because there is no alternative for him; other than hanging or beheading . . .

If Shakespeare, as Bond puts it, 'acted within the restraints of his world view, which is imposed on him by his time and place', he can then serve as a model for Bond's argument that 'it would be wrong to say that our problem is such and such now because of something that happened in the past. Our problem is created all the time, constantly re-created. And it's because we don't interfere with the re-creations of our problems, that we can't solve our problems . . .'.[21] *Bingo* shows 'the working of a coherent pattern of justice: behave in this way and you will have to bear the consequences'.[22] The audience is left to determine the relevance of the statement to their own lives.

In *The Fool*, Bond takes as his main character the early nineteenth-century poet John Clare. Unlike Shakespeare, Clare is more a victim of society than a transgressor: he suffers at the hands of a culture with no interest in his kind of art, which offers a critical comment on its values; he is taken up by polite society as a passing fancy and then casually dropped; he is unable to earn a living or to support his wife and family, and when the strain of his position begins to affect his physical and mental health, he is committed to an asylum. In one respect, then, the play is about the destruction of a writer by a society which automatically quashes and punishes any attempt to challenge or question it – and yet *The Fool* is only incidentally a play about the role and position of the artist. Clare is seen as only one member of a whole section of society – the agricultural labourers whose culture and livelihood is threatened by the beginnings of the Industrial Revolution; in Bond's description: 'The play shows destruction. The social and economic system then existing was destroyed . . . life is turned into a wound as the old culture is destroyed.'[23] Although the theme of destruction runs as heavily through the play as it does through this early note on it, the ending is positive: there is a flickering resistance in Clare even in the madhouse, and we are shown the strength of ordinary people, their ability to survive and to endure. Clare's imagination and articulacy are only one element in a play which puts a whole society on the stage.

Clare may have the first line in *The Fool*, but the opening sequence, in which the labourers perform a mummers' play for Lord Milton and the local gentry, is there to establish the social world of the play, not the main character. The immediate and obvious division between the classes hardly needs comment: it is built into the language the different characters use, which in turn underlines their views of the world and their habitual responses to it. The flexibility and directness of the dialogue spoken by the working-class characters, including Clare (an East Anglian dialect, though Clare was a Northamptonshire poet), is in stark contrast with the polished phrases Lord Milton and the Parson use as a mask for their real intentions and as a rationalisation of their actions: 'The East Anglian accent I do claim to know. I use it because of its curious concrete feel, its repetitiveness, it's like a sort of hammer knocking, knocking, knocking. But at the same time it can be very agile and witty. It's language which imitates experience. Because language shouldn't be just words, it should be something that moves in the mouth and forces gestures and forces action.'[24] The Parson uses conventional rhetoric to describe the momentous changes – and economic deprivation – which are about to overtake the labourers: '. . . we are entering a new age. An iron age. New engines, new factories, cities, ways, laws. The old ways must go.' He does not try to explain and discuss what this entails: the labourers are patronised and humoured in the knowledge that they have no part in such discussions, nor any say about what Lord Milton has in store for them.

The atmosphere of scene one is of an age in transition. The mummers' play is an indication of what will be lost. Clare, Darkie and the others are participating in the last rites of a folk tradition which is about to disappear; the vitality of the mummers' play washes against the rock-like solidity of Milton and his house-guests, ranged in a line, glasses in hands, watching the performance with benign amusement. Bond's description of this part of the scene to an American director of *The Fool* emphasises the strength and conviction which the mummers' play should convey: 'The Mummers' play shouldn't be gauche – like the rustics' play in *Midsummer Night's Dream*. We should feel they have their own expertise, that their clothes have a real eye for colour and design – they aren't at all Walt Disneyish. They should be very competent dancers and singers: it is their culture, and they can still express themselves in it. They can, of course, poke fun at Milton and the Parson, but they still have to show their respect: it has to be suggested, not stated aggressively.'[25]

Clare's part in all this is not very significant. At the start of the scene, he is simply one of the lads and, when the mummers' play is over, it is Darkie who speaks out rebelliously against the hardness of their existence. All we see of Clare in scene one is his sexuality – 'It's a passion that can rise up at any time and completely overwhelm everything else about him.'[26] What is more, there is no direct reference to his writing until the fourth scene. Clues are laid, but that is all – at the beginning of scene two, set in a wood at night, the stage direction reads: 'CLARE *alone. He sits. His lips move and his fingers tap a rhythm. He is saying something noiselessly to himself. He has a piece of paper in his hand but he doesn't read it.*' It is small actions such as this, as much as what is stated in the dialogue, that forms the basis for our view of Clare in the early scenes – like the sequence later in scene two between Clare and Mary, the servant girl from Lord Milton's house. On the face of it, it may seem that Bond is merely enlarging here on the portrayal of Clare's sexuality but what is interesting is that the stage directions make it clear that for some time they do not touch – in fact, not until Mary offers Clare the bread:

CLARE. . . . On't bin out my head. That night. Never forget you.
MARY. Hungry?
CLARE. Allus hungry.
MARY *takes out bread and gives him some. They eat.*
MARY. Stole it.
CLARE (*touches her breast while he eats*). Well built gall. Never seen a gall like you. Like t'live in this forest. The two on us. Tread the reeds an' creep in.

It is an important moment, and it demonstrates how vital it is that the stage directions are played exactly as Bond wrote them. This conjunction of 'bread and love' gives us a new perspective on Clare: it suggests that his joyful vision is idealised and romantic, since it takes no account of the economic necessities of life – he finds it hard enough to feed himself; it is a healthy, but partial, view of life. Clare increasingly links this vision with Mary; by scene three, he is totally obsessed with her. But he is in love with an abstract person of his own imagining, not the character that we see on stage: 'Clare wants to romanticise her – to see her as a body without a critical mind, merely an assenting mind. But she judges, makes decisions: she's too strong to fit into her situation, but not strong, perceptive, or organised enough (how could she be?) to change it . . . Clare thinks she knows about freedom and happiness in a way he doesn't – in a way outside reality, above the constraints of living in or off society, but she doesn't really know either.'[27]

The image of the eating/lovemaking gives a momentary glimpse of a unity which Clare is unable to achieve at any point thereafter. At the beginning of the scene, and then again at the end, he briefly holds the centre of the stage, but in the next two scenes he is brought up against the reality of the world he lives in and his character is defined strictly through his relation to two central incidents – the night of rioting when the villagers protest against the enclosures, and the events in the condemned cell at Ely prison.

The central image in scene three is the stripping of the Parson by the rioters. The salient fact as far as the character of Clare is concerned is that he is conspicuous by his absence. He comes on very briefly early in the scene, but he is not involved in any of what happens. While Darkie and the others are facing the reality of their lives, Clare is in a dream, chasing over the fields in search of Mary; it is like an inversion of the snow scene in *Bingo* – there, the protest against the enclosures is represented by four or five figures passing quickly over the top of the stage, while Shakespeare is the focal point of the scene; here, the protesters are at the centre of the action and Clare makes only one very fleeting appearance. His absence from the scene is even more pointed in that Mary, the object of his search, is onstage, seizing the opportunity to capitalise on the temporary overthrow of order by robbing the homes of the wealthy; her shrewdness and eye for the main chance is highlighted by her actions while the Parson is being stripped – while the others are comparing the softness of his skin with the hardness of their lives, Mary is busy hunting for the pearl buttons that have fallen on the ground. For a second time, her astuteness and aptitude for surviving is contrasted with Clare's romantic vision of her – he is offstage chasing an illusion.

Darkie, the instigator of the protests, acts, like Mary, as a complement to Clare. He is the man of action: while Clare mourns the loss of the fields and the wood, Darkie actively opposes Lord Milton's plans. He has no chance of success – Bond wants it to be shown that the action of the villagers 'isn't very well organised, it's not an example of sound political organisation, it's a spontaneous resistance to legalised robbery'.[28] Like all of Darkie's actions, it is emotional and hasty, dictated in this case by blind rage. By the end of scene three, the relation between Clare, Mary and Darkie has been clearly delineated: each has a very distinct standpoint for dealing with the world, but each standpoint has its limitations, and the impression is given that, if only their distinctive strengths could be united, they would amount to a force which might resist even Lord Milton.

The analysis so far has emphasised Clare's limitations. We should also see that he presents as much of a threat to his society as Darkie – as Bond has observed about the historical Clare: 'when everything is being regulated, organised, and told its exact place in society, he was saying "No, I want to sing now" or "I want to dance now"'.[29] Unless the fragmentary glimpses that we get of Clare in the early scenes suggest this aspect of him, we can too easily develop an over-critical attitude towards the character, as in this comment by Martin Esslin: 'The passive central character is designed to draw the spectator into the position of such a person, who sees the world revolve around him without fully understanding what is happening. It is this lack of understanding which makes Bond's Clare a *fool*.'[30]

Clare is not, in fact, a *passive* character, as the critical orthodoxy about the play would have us believe; it is just that for much of the time he is not given the centrality we would expect of a main character. Nor is it Bond's intention to draw us into the play in such a way that we view the action through Clare's eyes: the scenes are designed to show contrasting elements in the social world of the play (Clare, Mary, Darkie, Lord Milton, the Parson) and we are asked to assess the significance of each action without the benefit of a 'central' character through whom we can route our perceptions and feelings. Finally, what Bond had in mind with the title of the play was not Clare's 'lack of understanding' but a kinship with characters like the Fool in *King Lear* or Ariel in *The Tempest* – 'the idea of some knowing resilience'.[31] Although both

Clare and Darkie are disposed of by society – and Mary, too, ends up raddled and destroyed – the final impression we should have of them, and of Clare in particular, should be a positive one; for Bond, '"The Fool" connotes not mystical insight but strength . . . the world of the play is that of strength'.[32] He is careful to show that, although Clare and Darkie do not fully understand one another, there is a mutual sympathy and a bond between them. This is established in scenes one and two, and then restated in scene four, where Clare visits Darkie and the other men who have been condemned to death for their part in the riots.

Bond's method of presenting the relationship between Clare and Darkie in scene four can be better understood if we first examine two other aspects of the scene – the lighting and the set-design. While the lighting is obviously governed by the specific nature of the setting ('*Quiet. Dark. Pale light from two small high grated windows.*'), it is important to grasp the relation between the lighting for the prison scene and that for the other scenes before the interval. All four scenes take place in a very subdued light. There are naturalistic reasons for this – two of the scenes are set in the evening, two at night: but this only begs the question why Bond should have chosen to set them in this way. The clue is to be found in the contrast in the lighting for the scenes after the interval; as Bond explains: 'The first half should be played in darkness, and the second half should be played in bright light, except for one scene.' In the first half, the main focus of attention is not Clare, but Darkie; Clare becomes prominent after the interval. The movement from darkness to light is connected with the relative weight Bond gives to these two characters in the two halves of the play and the lighting is used to comment on the values that we are shown through the two characters. This is not to say that Darkie represents some force of darkness, but by the last scene in the play, when Clare is no longer romanticising or evading reality, Bond wants to emphasise his importance as a symbol of the spirit of resistance which Darkie had shown earlier, but with the addition of the creative and imaginative capacity which Darkie lacked and which, Bond implies, is essential for the creation of a healthy culture.

The lighting, then, becomes as much an object on the stage in its own right as it is a means of showing the other objects; in *The Fool*, as in *The Pope's Wedding*, it is used to comment on the action in a far more systematic way than elsewhere. There is one other function of the lighting on which Bond lays great emphasis and which applies to all of the plays: 'You have to light a scene in a way which helps to tell the story and puts the situation clearly, but the other thing is that, if you are going to put as much weight as possible on the acting – which is my ambition – then you have to find a way of lighting the play which enables the audience to read the faces and hands with great clarity.' The need to do so becomes absolute as Bond more and more consciously uses physical expression and gesture as a vital element in a scene, to the point where in *The Woman* an entire scene is characterised by the different gestures which the characters in it make with their arms and hands.

Scene four is distinct from the other dimly-lit scenes in *The Fool* in that the actors are literally confined within the tight space of the set for the prison cell. In the first production, at the Royal Court theatre, Bond has described how William Dudley's design for this scene consisted of 'a rectangular formation of six benches which gave a tight inner space. A door slung inside a metal frame was let into the upstage corner. That was it. No window. There was a downward light to help shape it.'

Bond would have preferred, in addition to the real door, a real wall and a window. In scenes like this, set in a small room or a cell, he is usually concerned to convey the sense of a world outside the space which the audience sees. In this case, a key part of the scene is the noise coming from elsewhere in the prison. As Bond explains: 'One big advantage, if you have the walls, is that the effect of the sounds from the other prisoners is much more intense – the sounds clearly come from beyond the cell. I also wanted the prisoners inside the cell to bang on the walls, so that you had the feeling of them trying to get out of their box.'

The sounds he refers to are the cries of laughter and relief from the prisoners offstage who have just been told that their sentences have been commuted. At this point neither the characters onstage nor the audience know the reason for these sounds: they at once create a feeling of expectancy and tension. Bond has first one, then several of the onstage characters beat on the cell door. It is easy to see why he would have wanted to reinforce this action by having them bang against the wall as well – the effect he is after is of the whole cell becoming a drum with the prisoners hammering on it, beating against the wall like butterflies against a window. It is an extreme, unnatural moment:

BOB (*banging on the door*). Here! Here! Here! Here!
DARKIE (*to* BOB). Shut up, boy!
HAMO, BOB *and* PATTY *beat on the door and shout.*
HAMO. / BOB. } Here! Here! Here! Here!
PATTY. Let's out! Let's out! On't a prisoner!
Outside the laughter goes on and on. Screams, shouts, peals, groans – of laughter. No one laughs in the room. Their hysteria is dry.

Peter Gill, who directed the play at the Royal Court, described the effect of this moment within the context of the scene as a whole in this way: '. . . the prison scene in many ways can be seen in kind of conventional John Ford western terms – the boys caught, a kind of hero figure going to be hanged, the good friend, and the sister who is the girlfriend. You can play that scene in a kind of realistic, poetic, romantic way, which is very much in the scene and underscores the scene. But on top there is this element introduced of the people outside the scene, laughing at their release, in a way that becomes unrealistic.'[33] Gill accurately describes how Bond can make a scene turn on moments like these, which illuminate a character or a situation, but to suggest that they are 'unrealistic' is misleading, particularly because this would seem to suggest that they are invariably signalled by a marked change in style. This is not the case, as another example from the prison scene shows.

Patty, Darkie's sister and (by scene six) Clare's wife, has come with Clare to visit her brother. Darkie and the other prisoners, who are given bread and soup by the Warder at the beginning of the scene, continue to eat while they talk to their two visitors. As they discuss whether or not the authorities will go through with the sentence and hang them all, Patty becomes increasingly tense and uncomfortable: her composure finally breaks when one of them asks her what people are saying in the street:

PATTY (*irritated*). How'd I know *what* they say? (*Silence. She collects the bowls and stacks them neatly by the door before she speaks.*) O boy *I* don't know what t'say. Thass a fact. (*Trying not to cry.*) Allus a good boy Darkie. Stand up for the right. On't hurt a fly out askin' pardon. All a you. They on't know.

Unless this sequence is played for its social reality, it will come over as a routine dramatic moment. In fact, it tells us a lot about Patty's character. She has walked miles to visit Darkie and, within minutes of getting there, she loses her temper. After an embarrassed silence, she collects the plates. In Gill's production, the prisoners collected up the plates themselves and gave them to her – it was made into a smooth and tidy piece of action, marking a dramatic pause until Patty continued with the second part of her speech. Instead, the audience needs to be shown the reality of the situation – Patty, because of her temperament and social conditioning, finds it impossible to repair the damage her outburst has caused by openly apologising or showing any obvious affection for her brother, sc she makes up for it by adopting the role of a housewife and clearing up – that is to say, tending – for the men. Her action is an indirect expression of the character's feelings and it is an index of the way that the scene needs to be treated; as Bridget Turner, who played Patty in the Royal Court production, remarked: 'It's such a powerful play. But you've got to be careful not to act the impact you know it's going to have on the audience. Like the prison scene. It's a dreadful situation, but you can't act that. Even though you're personally moved by it, you can't act it. So you act different moments within the scene.'[34]

The actor playing Clare has of necessity to adopt this approach of acting 'different moments within the scene', since his part in this scene is virtually confined to two outbursts of laughter. They occur suddenly and without explanation. The first comes soon after Patty has told the others that some of Clare's writing might be published:

DARKIE. No thass good John. On't be ashamed a that.
MILES. What you write boy? Write 'bout this place. What goo on.
CLARE. Who'd read that?
PATTY (*pride*). Gen'man come though on't he boy? (*Silence*). Well thass a long way gettin' here but I'm glad I made the effort. Hev t'go soon Darkie. Git a start fore it's dark. Any errands? Miles?
MILES. No, gall.
Silence. CLARE *starts to laugh. He tries to stop*.

There is a ripple of embarrassment and puzzlement in the cell. Darkie interprets the laughter as an expression of Clare's conviction that the prisoners are bound to be reprieved: 'Thass right. On't goo through with it.' – but it is so transparent that he is trying to convince himself of this that we are made to doubt whether this can be the real reason for Clare's outburst. The second occurrence comes after the other prisoners, whose sentences have been commuted, have been taken to another cell: Clare and Patty are left alone with Darkie: '*The* WARDER *goes out and shuts the door.* CLARE *sits on the bench with his head in his hands.* DARKIE *and* PATTY *stand.* CLARE *begins to laugh. It is easy, not hysterical, but not calm. It wells up in him and overflows.*' This time, his laughter is more protracted: he falls on the floor and rolls about under a blanket, trying unsuccessfully to stifle it. This action has to be played with great clarity and precision. The longer the actor can sustain it, the more likelihood there is that the reason for Clare's laughter will fully register on the audience.

Clare is neither insensitive to Darkie's situation nor heedless of his attempts to hold down his feelings of despair. The first laugh is a reaction to the ludicrous injustice of the different positions the two men find themselves in: he himself has avoided capture and punishment because he was so preoccupied with Mary, and his luck seems all the greater in that his writing is beginning to gain some recognition. The second bout of laughter is more dramatic and it is designed to show the audience the most important facet of Clare's character. In his first notes, Bond described his intention as follows: 'Clare's vision *not* socially impossible/unworldly/ indifferent – laughing over death/joy.'[35] In the script, the specific nature of the laughter is brought out by setting it in counterpoint with laughter from outside the cell: '*Off, there is a short burst of laughter. It becomes hysterical – like sobbing. It lasts for a few seconds.* CLARE *laughs happily through it.*' Clare's behaviour may well strike us as inappropriate, given that he is sitting with a man who has been condemned to death, but the counterpoint of the two sounds underlines for us that it is not unnatural or hysterical, and certainly not a sign of the madness which is to come later. On the contrary, it is a wholly natural and spontaneous reaction to an absurd and unjust situation.

Bond might easily have hinged this last part of scene four on Darkie's courage in the face of death. Instead, he gives prominence to these two actions by Clare. There is no explicit statement or comment on their meaning. There is just one very short sequence of dialogue between Darkie and Clare at the end. It has a dual function: Clare's questions about Mary remind us of the obsessional element in his character, and their last exchange underlines that ultimately there is no conflict between them:

CLARE (*after a pause*). On't quarrel Darkie.
DARKIE. No.

Although their lives are different, they are united; although the routes are different, both characters will finally be destroyed by society.

In the second half of the play the character of Clare assumes a more traditional dramatic function – he becomes the focus of each of the four scenes. Even now, however, he is presented very much in juxtaposition with his society. In scene five, Clare is in Hyde Park, being courted by Mrs. Emmerson, a refined, middle-aged lady whose literary sensibilities are so far removed from life as to be ridiculous. Through her, and through Clare's meeting with Charles and Mary Lamb, we are shown the hollowness of the world which Clare hopes to break into. Lamb is a worn and ineffectual Romantic, making speeches on Truth but forced to work as a clerk and sustaining himself with drink. Mary Lamb obsessively buys up more food than they can possibly eat, until it is left rotting around the house; as Bond has explained: 'I wanted to show that in this society even the vegetables were rotten – they became obsessed with food but couldn't enjoy anything.' Finally, Admiral Lord Radstock, Clare's potential benefactor, insists that, if the poetry is ever to be published, the lines criticising the landowners and the poem on Mary must be cut.

The censoriousness and unhealthiness of their world is amply illustrated by these exchanges, but Bond goes one stage further in order to demonstrate the inhumanity on which it is based. While Mrs. Emmerson, Lamb and Radstock are engaged downstage in patronising Clare in their different ways, upstage a prize-fight is in progress. The fight lasts for the duration of the scene and it can only be staged in one way: for the viciousness of the fight and, by association, of the society itself to come over, the contest has to be made to seem as realistic as possible; it needs to be fast and furious. Although the two actions take place simultaneously, the dialogue never overlaps; the comments of the fighters and their backers are interspersed between sections of the literary conversation downstage. The danger in production is that the formal contrast between the two actions will become the main focus of attention; that is important, but more important still are the attitudes of the characters downstage towards the fight. In his notes for an American director, Bond pointed to the difference in their reactions: 'Clare gets drawn into the fight. Mrs. Emmerson would ignore it as crude, till Radstock connects the fight with the navy – so that she can then see the black man as a British Jack Tar and wave her handkerchief enthusiastically at him. At the end the two halves of the scene – the fight and the debate – should become one. Perhaps the boxer runs round on a victory run: till, right at the end, Clare is left with the boxer – the antithesis of the way he started, with Mrs. Emmerson.'[36] This antithesis is as ironic as the parallel between Clare and the defeated Irish fighter: the boxer has been knocked about without even being paid for his pains; meanwhile, Clare is still expecting to be paid for his verses.

Clare's identification with the defeated Irish boxer is an idea which is reinforced by having it carried through to the next two scenes. In scene six, Clare is already on the edge of defeat. His health is failing, and Bond works in a verbal reference to the sequence between Clare and the boxer, whose first line to him had been: 'Me gut. Jazuschriss he must chew granite for breakfast.' Clare describes to Patty, now his wife, the pains which prevent him from getting a normal job and also from writing: 'No grip left in me hand! Pain in me head! Gut burn! Thass terrible gall.' The connection is made more explicitly later in a remark by Mrs. Emmerson: 'He still thinks he's a boxer.' Both Mrs. Emmerson and Patty see this as another of Clare's fancies or delusions, but our sense of the truth in the parallel Clare has made between himself and the boxer should prevent our taking the same no-nonsense attitude towards him which is voiced by Patty, who rejects his complaints of ill-health as an excuse for not working to support her and the baby, and is hostile towards both his writing and his continuing obsession with Mary. The sequence between Clare and Patty works on one level as a piece of intimate domestic realism, but it can only be fully understood in the context of the play as a whole if the audience is capable of viewing the relation between Patty and Clare with the same objectivity that was needed for assessing the relation between Clare and Darkie. There are two easy options open to the audience: one is to side with Patty against Clare and to accept at face value everything she says about him; the other is to see her as a nagging shrew. The conflict of interests between Clare and Patty ought not to blind us to the fact that the contrast between them is as instructive as the contrast between Clare and Darkie, or Clare and Mary: in the words of Linda Atkinson, who played Patty in the American première of *The Fool* at the Folger Theatre, Washington; 'Patty is a survivor. Clare as the man doesn't survive; his spirit survives. Patty survives in the real world. It's the real world that she deals with. She has no visions or illusions. Her feet are on the ground.' In this respect, there is a strength in her which Clare lacks, but it is this same practical, hard-headed attitude which causes her to go along with Mrs. Emmerson's plan, in collusion with Lord Milton, to have Clare committed to the asylum. When Milton's Keeper leads Clare off, his arms tied with a rope, the image is immediately reminiscent of Hatch's last exit in *The Sea* – with the one difference that Clare, unlike Hatch, is not, in fact, insane.

We see and hear nothing of the process by which Clare is driven mad in the asylum. Scene seven confirms what we already know from the dramatic method Bond has employed in earlier plays – the narrative is important, but what Bond chooses to show in a scene is finally governed by dialectical considerations. In this scene, Bond has Clare confront the conflicts in his life and try to resolve them; in order to show this, Clare is seen once more in relation to Darkie and Mary. It is four years later. Clare, having escaped from the asylum, is on an open road at night. Like the snow scene in *Bingo*, the first part of the scene is a kind of hallucination; in effect it is set inside Clare's mind: 'It has a strange appearance: the blind boxer (Clare's fantasy), the sudden appearance of the destroyed Mary (totally unlike the free Angel Clare had imagined) . . . So it is mad and irrational – filling in the audience about some of Clare's lunatic experiences . . .'[37] Bond follows this description with an apparent paradox: 'Clare is a rational man, in this mad scene, even more than at other times.'[38] It is vital that Clare's rationality is what finally emerges for us from the scene, because otherwise his return to the asylum can only be read as a defeat.

Clare comes on '*exhausted and in rags*'. He encounters Darkie and Mary, the former as a blind boxer, the latter '*a tramp. Grotesque, filthy, ugly.*' At this stage Clare reaches his lowest point in the play. Not realising that the figure of the boxer is Darkie, Clare attempts to show his strength to Mary by picking a fight; he is knocked unconscious. Mary tries to feed Darkie with bread, which he is unable to swallow. The force of both these actions is to show us that, although all three characters have been destroyed in one way or another, Mary and Darkie still remain stronger and more capable than Clare. His inability to come to terms with the real world is further emphasised when Mary and Darkie leave, and the sequence inside Clare's mind is followed by an encounter with the outside world in the shape of three Irish labourers. Like Clare, they are itinerants, but they know how to take care of themselves.

Clare's realisation of the illusion he has been living comes in two stages. First, he is forced through starvation to agree that the Third Irishman can have Mary sexually in return for some bread and cheese; the Irishman goes in search of her, but without success. Then, more positively, he accepts the lesson of his meeting with Mary and Darkie – that is to say, he draws a rational conclusion about the way in which he should have lived:

> I wandered round an' round. Where to? Here. An' a blind man git here before me. The blind goo in a straight line. We should hev come t'gither. She git the bread. He crack the heads when they come after us. An' I – I'ld hev teach him how to eat.

Each of the metaphors Clare uses is simple and direct, grounded in what we have already seen in the previous action. Given that the contrast with his weakness and uncertainty earlier in the scene is made clear, there should be no difficulty for the audience in seeing this as the turning-point of the play. The responsibility at this point rests with the actor and the director. The change in Clare's perception of the world is contained solely within this one speech; if its effect is not crystal-clear, Bond's presentation of Clare in the last scene will be wide open to misinterpretation.

The last scene is set some twenty or thirty years later. Lord Milton and Patty are visiting Clare, who has returned to the asylum. Patty remains as tough and hard-headed as Bond's description of her in his poem 'Patty's Speech':

If asked she would say:
I make do with what I have and go without what I haven't
And no man can snap her[39]

Lord Milton, however, is a broken man; his way of life has been overtaken and he hates his son: 'A vicious bastard. I was cruel sometimes. Foolish. But did I hate? No. Never a hater. He hates. Flicks his wrist as if he's holding a whip. Don't see much of him – except his back. Busy. In love with his factories. It's changed.' Bond expects us to treat Milton's remarks with the same scepticism we needed for Mrs. Rafi's speech towards the end of *The Sea*; like her, Milton indulges less in self-analysis than in self-justification. The fact that Milton has lost his fields and the old life – he, too, is something of a derelict – is not intended by Bond as a cue for our sympathy.

The characterisation of Lord Milton raises again a problem we have met before. In allowing characters like Milton a measure of humanity or self-awareness – in making them rounded dramatic characters rather than caricatures – Bond also makes it possible for those members of the audience who automatically respond to drama exclusively on an emotional level to thoroughly misinterpret the play. The most flagrant example in connection with *The Fool* was the review by Harold Hobson, who maintained:

> Not only do the upper class in *The Fool* possess all the grace and intelligence; they have all the kindness too. In contrast to this adulation of the well-born Mr. Bond represents the common people as brutal, vindictive, sadistic, and perverted. They fall upon a gentle-spoken clergyman . . . and strip him of every shred of his clothing, and then try to tear his humiliated and trembling body to pieces. This is a contemptible scene, though I daresay that some amateurs of unavowed emotions will take pleasure in it.'[40]

It is as if Hobson had only seen one part of the scene – the central action of the stripping of the Parson – or had relegated everything else in the scene to the category of incidental dramatic trimmings. The dialectic of the scene is perfectly straightforward: the rioters, after great hesitation, move in on the Parson and tear off his clothes; they grab at his skin, but this is no casual violence – at the same time as they pinch his flesh, they describe how they are oppressed by him. The Parson weeps and mumbles prayers; they cry out loud at their condition. The Parson stands covered with a piece of blood-stained linen, but it comes from a wounded man who spends the whole scene crawling about in agony. The scene is constructed in such a way as to pose one simple question: whose suffering is the greater?

The same principle applies, just as plainly, in the last scene. Milton's self-justifying remarks are addressed to the aged figure of Clare: '*He's in a bathchair. A shrivelled puppet. His head nods like a doll's. His face is white.*' Clare is his victim – not his alone, but Milton's part in Clare's destruction, however well-meaning his intentions, should be in the front of our minds. And yet, despite Clare's state, Bond also wants us to see his resilience, and the imaginative energy still flickering inside him – the early notes contain this description: 'Image of Clare. He begins as a healthy, spunky young man and ends as a white-faced, red-cheeked, grey-haired clown with a nodding head. An image of decay and ruin, yet with some manic life in it . . .'[41]. It asks a lot of an actor to communicate to the audience this double-image of intellectual energy and physical decay; he will stand no chance at all of succeeding if the change in Clare's perception of the world in the previous scene has not yet been registered.

Only one effect, however, is likely to be too oblique for the audience to understand. It occurs when Lord Milton leaves to fetch Patty, who is waiting outside; he opens a glass door which leads out to the garden: '*The door swings slowly open. It catches the sun. It flashes once into the room. Brilliantly. Silence. An owl calls in the trees.*' The sound of the owl refers back to Lamb's speech on Truth in the Hyde Park scene: 'The goddess of wisdom is a bird of prey, the owl. But the fools have hunted *her* and put her in a cage . . .'. The connection with Clare is obvious enough when it is described in this way, but whether it would be made by the audience in a theatre is another matter. The brilliant flash of light is another reference to Clare: it represents the light still shining inside him. In this case the allusion seems more difficult still to communicate. Unless the flash of light is exaggerated, it will go unnoticed; if it is vivid enough to be noticed, but not fully understood, it will merely seem odd.

Bond uses these devices, just as he uses the image of the hectically nodding Clare, to avoid having characters make speeches which will spell out the meaning of the last scene. The governing principle in *The Fool* – in the characterisation, in the construction of a scene, in the structure of the play as a whole – is that the audience should be shown the evidence Bond chooses to present, but not *told* how they are to respond to it. His instructions on how this last scene should be played are precise about the implications of this for the actors: 'Don't play the scene in such a way that you try to make the audience realize the truth by making them cry at it: play it so that they cannot cry and are forced to realize the truth.'[42] Bond's own views are implicit in the way he shapes the dialectic, but he wants the audience to follow the logic and make the connections for itself: 'I don't believe in reducing characters to caricatures of their class role or function. That can only confirm audiences in what they already know, or surprise them. But learning is a more subtle experience – after all, you can always get over your surprise.'[43]

9

A-A-America!, Stone and Other Works, October 1974–February 1977

The period from October 1974, when Bond finished *The Fool*, to February 1977 was a time of experiment and investigation. *The Woman*, the third and last play in the series on history and culture, had been in Bond's mind since 1973; he continued to work on his ideas, but only began to draft it in December 1976. Most of his energies were given to a number of short plays and adaptations, together with a text for a ballet and a full-length farce, all written in response to specific requests. Three of these works have never been performed – his adaptation for television of Ibsen's *The Master Builder*, the ballet script, and the farce, which is called *The Palace of Varieties in the Sand*. Each of these unproduced works has distinct individuality and merit, but it is in the three short plays written for London fringe theatres – *Grandma Faust, The Swing* and *Stone* – that Bond consciously tries out and tests new techniques, in particular, ways of using, and subverting, an audience's expectations and assumptions about the nature of the characters and the action they are watching. This process of experimentation is allied to another notable feature of all three plays; in each case, Bond makes a clear statement about the overthrow of an oppressive capitalist ethic.

The Master Builder and *The White Devil* (adaptations)

Bond's version of *The Master Builder* was written soon after

The Fool, at the invitation of an American television company, KCETTV of Los Angeles. It goes much further than any of his other four translations or adaptations in making extensive alterations and additions to the original play. In his translation of Chekhov's *Three Sisters* for William Gaskill in 1966, and again with the translation of Wedekind's *Spring Awakening* for the National Theatre eight years later, he had concentrated on providing a good contemporary acting edition. In the same way, the language of Bond's adaptation of *The Master Builder*, reworked from the translation by Michael Meyer, is contemporary in idiom and eminently actable; but the play as a whole is a very free adaptation indeed, with large chunks cut out of the original text and a completely new ending grafted onto it.

The cuts do little to interfere with Ibsen's intentions. But Bond is far more radical in his treatment of the latter stages of Ibsen's play, where he draws his own conclusions about the characters and situations Ibsen has presented him with, and declares his findings by adding a number of short scenes of his own. Solness still climbs the tower, but in this version he does not fall to his death. Hilde (who in Ibsen glories over his heroism and death) rejects both Solness and her former romantic idealisation of him: 'What a pity you climbed the tower! It was so nice before. You see, it wasn't at all high. When I was a little girl your tower seemed enormous. Now it isn't. I realised that when you got to the top today. (*Laughs slightly*). You – well you looked so silly clambering down again.'[1]

In the original, Solness is convinced that he 'willed' the fire that burned down his wife's ancestral home; Bond gives the wife a speech explaining that she started the fire, so that Solness could build the new redevelopments he had set his heart on. She resolves to 'get him through' now that Hilde is leaving him. The scenes that Bond adds fillet the romantic symbolism out of the play and replace it with a more down-to-earth reading of the characters and their motivations. The effect and meaning of the play are altered. Ibsen's Solness is a powerful central hero who wills his fate, a heroic rebel; Bond is concerned to show he has feet of clay. This sacreligious treatment was probably the reason Bond's script was not put into production. It has yet to be performed.

The 'acting version' of *The White Devil* was made early in 1976 for a production of Webster's play by a new company which was to take over the Old Vic theatre, left vacant after the National theatre company moved in March to its new home on the South Bank. Bond arrived at his version by editing the text, cutting it heavily so as to give more weight to his interpretation of the play:– 'it's not about sexual violence and intense personal emotion, but power and money.' Again, the ending is pure Bond – but this time, instead of writing new scenes, he simply cuts the last two lines, subverting the token morality of Webster's ending:

> Let guilty men remember, their black deeds
> Do lean on crutches made of slender reeds.

In the original, these lines are delivered by the young prince whose arrival denotes the restoration of order. In the Old Vic production, the prince and his courtiers remained offstage, battering at the door, with the prince screaming his moralising comments through it – not only pure Bond, but pure *Bingo*.

The overall effect of Bond's cuts is to defuse the melodrama and to encourage a more dispassionate appraisal of Webster's action: it plays down the extravagances and invites one to draw the obvious parallels with the corrupting influence of money and power in contemporary society. At the Old Vic, director Michael Lindsay-Hogg sought to underline the connections with the present day by putting the play into modern dress (the set, with a large pair of revolving doors at either side of the stage, resembled the lobby of a Grand Hotel). Unfortunately, in an attempt to strip the actors' performances of any rhetoric, he also encouraged an excessively low-key delivery of the verse which too often degenerated into Method-like mumbling, accompanied by a plethora of finely detailed gestures and expressions which might well have underscored the realism of the action, had most of them not been lost somewhere in the vast reaches of the set. The result was a production which made it very difficult to assess the strengths and weaknesses of Bond's text.

The Palace of Varieties in the Sand

Bond had first been approached in 1975 to write a comedy for the same company, which was to be headed by Glenda Jackson. The play he provided, *The Palace of Varieties in the Sand*, was written in about three weeks, at the end of December and the beginning of January, 'to clear a block in a way. My sister had died earlier that year and I hadn't written anything for some time. It's the only time I've sat down without knowing in advance what it was I was going to write – except that it would be a farce.' When it was submitted, it did not meet the company's requirements.

It is a farce with a hard cutting edge to the humour, resembling *Passion*, the short play Bond wrote five years earlier for a C.N.D. Festival, in its mixture of anti-royalist satire and caustic social comment. For the first time in his plays, the main character is a woman – Winnie, a typist living in a small London flat. Through the services of a medium, she makes contact with her grandfather, who died in the First World War and turns out to be the Unknown Soldier buried in the tomb at Westminster Abbey. He persuades her to blow up the Cenotaph, and the Royal Family with it, at the next Commemoration Day Service.

With the help of Jim, an electrician who happened to serve in a bomb-disposal unit in the army, Winnie comes within a hair's breadth of accomplishing her task. In a scene of freewheeling farce set at the foot of the Cenotaph, the Queen, the Prince of Wales and the Queen Mother just escape coming to a sticky end (through sheer luck rather than good judgement, since their main characteristic is a slow-wittedness which makes even the simplest official duty a searching test of their intelligence). Winnie succeeds only in shaking the edifice. The Queen Mother collects the pieces that fall off it for her rockery.

Winnie is subjected to the same fate as Clare in *The Fool* and the General in *We Come to the River* – scene three is set in a Madhouse Garden. Jim follows her there and gets a job as a gardener. The forces of inhuman, petty officialdom are parodied in the figures of the Director of the Asylum and Mrs. Thompson – formerly the medium who put Winnie in touch with her dead grandfather, but now a Cadet Policewoman who is keeping a watchful eye on her. The inmates perform a play written by Winnie: St. Peter and God are at the gates of Heaven, refusing to let anyone in. God complains bitterly that so many are ready to give up their lives in his name: 'Couldn't someone live for me for once?'

Jim is killed one night climbing up to Winnie's window. For the last scene, the action switches to Westminster Abbey and to the Coronation of the Prince of Wales. (The Queen has decided to spend her declining years sorting her collection of Commonwealth stamps.) As the Prince and the Queen process up the aisle, the Unknown Soldier reaches out of his tomb and grabs the Prince's leg. He refuses to let go until the Prince promises to marry Winnie – to make the family respectable. Winnie is rushed from the Asylum by helicopter. It is nine years since Jim died and she has hardly spoken in that time. She turns down the proposal and marries instead a member of the working class – a corporal on guard outside the Abbey.

The Queen Mother wanders on, more senile than ever, searching vaguely for the Great West Door to put out the milk bottle she's clutching ('I was told that if you put out an empty milk bottle outside the door a milkman would come along and exchange it for a full one'). Mistaking the steps down into the tomb for the stairs to the servants' kitchen, she disappears down them, only to bob back again and stand, head and shoulders out of the grave (a parody of Winnie in Beckett's *Happy Days*?, unpacking kitchen utensils from her shopping bag and starting to make a cake.

It is easy enough to identify many elements from earlier plays that Bond mixes into *The Palace of Varieties*, but particularly intriguing are the parallels with the play which immediately preceded it. Winnie, like Clare in *The Fool*, is viciously punished for daring to step out of line. Like Clare, she is reduced to sitting in a wheelchair, barely speaking, clinging to her sanity – in the words of the Old Gardener at the Asylum: 'They're not all mad when they first come, not by a long chalk, but they are after the first year.' But the same spirit of resistance that Bond wanted to show in the last scene of *The Fool* characterises Winnie's attitudes here.

Grandma Faust

The next play continues in the same comic vein – and with similar serious intent. It is the shortest of the three plays written between January and May 1976 (running for about 45 minutes in performance) and together with *The Swing*, it forms a double-bill under the collective title *A-A-America!*, first seen at the Almost Free theatre in London as part of a season called 'The American Connection'. It comes at an important juncture for Bond as a writer – *The Woman* is yet to be written, but he now begins to test the ground in preparation for the significant new step he is to take, over a year later, with *The Bundle*. It seems very likely that Bond had this in mind when he stressed how *Grandma Faust*, *The Swing* and *Stone* should be regarded as part of the canon: 'I don't want the plays to be seen as minor or occasional pieces outside my main development. I'd like them to take their places along with the others.'[2]

Grandma Faust, which Bond describes as 'a burlesque', is a comic parable in which caricature and parody are used in an onslaught on slavery, racism and the capitalist ethic. The theme is serious enough, but for much of the play it is as if Bond has for once decided to let the audience off the hook – the action he shows is sharply satirical, but it is held at one remove by the parody of Deep South folksiness that runs through every line of the dialogue. It is only through one running gag, pushing at the limits of good taste, that Bond actually tightens the screw enough for the audience to feel uncomfortable and to examine their own reactions. His attack on rabid racism and the worst symptoms of America's devotion to the Consumer Society is made by showing it in such a violently exaggerated form that it becomes comic. Gran (who is in fact the Devil) is more bizarre than threatening; she '*brings herself in, in a wheelchair. She is a cross between Whistler's Mother and Grandma Moses*'. The keynote of her character is its grotesqueness; her actions may be sinister, but the actor isn't asked to *play* that – the Almost Free production hit just the right tone in having Gran played by a man in drag. As for Uncle Sam's appearance, the name says it all: top hat and tail coat, bedecked with stars and stripes.

The tone is set in Uncle Sam's opening speech: 'Those little silver fish are so purty if I ever catched them I could buy the whole world. Every river an mountain an the fields an seas. But not one of those little critters jumps on the end of my little tin hook. Hot diggety.' It's a good burlesque of the slow Southern drawl, and the final exclamation is carefully planted to trigger an explosion of laughter. Bond first eases the audience into the play with straightforward jokes and standard comic routines: for example, Gran needs to break the bad news to Uncle Sam, if he's to help her get what she's after – the soul of a simple Negro:

GRAN. . . . It's this son: your gran is the devil.
SAM. Shucks gran you ain that bad.

Then the screw is tightened. Bond has to ensure that we also remember the viciousness and cruelty they represent, so he invents a new American festival – 'Nigger Foot Pie Day'. Gran enlists Sam's help by tempting him with all the riches of the world, but also through his stomach: 'Now I can give you all the Nigger Foot Pies you ever could eat. An nigger roast and fricassee of nigger . . . Spare nigger fingers with coleslaw as side-dish. Nigger fat soup . . . And nigger elbows to take away from table afterwards an pick by the fire.' It's not so easy to relax into comfortable laughter at these disagreeable exaggerations. Like the images of cannibalism in *Early Morning*, they force on us the need to calculate for ourselves the gap between exaggeration and reality.

Bond immediately provides a focus for our ambivalent reactions in the figure of Paul, the simple Negro who comes on stage singing a spiritual. The same comic idiom is maintained – temptation for Paul is a loaf of bread with a silver hook inside to snare the unwary soul, and Sam makes a good job of 'selling' it: 'You hear me stroke my loaf boy? My my that crust make a purty sound. Hmm mmm. You like the sound boy? That sound's called succulence.' Even when Bond wants to show the naked hatred and prejudice beneath Sam's mask of reasonableness, he does it through the standard device of the comic aside:

SAM (*aside*). I'll lynch the bastard. (*To* PAUL.) Ain you never seen agony before? Knew all them moaning spirituals was a fake. (*Off,* GRAN *laughs.*)
PAUL (*tears a corner from his vest and offers it*). Here. You stop cryin now.
SAM. Can't stop cryin you stupid son of a bitch. (*Aside.*) I'll swear at him a little so's he don't git suspicious.

Despite the comedy, it is important that the seriousness and cruelty of what Sam is doing comes over – in his first page of notes on the play, Bond spelled out the charge against him: 'Faustus sold his soul to gain knowledge ... You sell other men's souls to protect your ignorance. The American needs the negro to be mentally and racially inferior so as to whitewash his own immorality.'[3] But the actor playing Sam can only show the caricature, since that is what he is given to work with. It is Paul who must confirm the reality of what we are seeing, and this makes different demands on the actor, as Bond explained during rehearsals at the Almost Free: 'He finds his reasons for living during the play. So we have to show him destitute at the beginning and then show him getting up off the floor. A real quality of starvation has to come through.'

The main weakness in the play is that the transition from Paul's 'destitute' state at the start to his triumph over Gran and Uncle Sam is so quickly managed. He is merely a passive (and silent) victim in the auction scene and during the squabble between the two all-American Ladies ('*Bermuda shorts, sun vest, big floppy sunhat and dark glasses with diamante frames*'), both itching to put Paul, body and soul, in their home-baked Nigger Foot Pies. This is followed immediately by the lead-in to the soul-fighting match in which Paul shows his underlying strength. Because Bond is writing a comic allegory, he satirises oppression and racial prejudice but shows little of the specific conditions which give birth to them – or how they might be countered. The final stages of the play simply offer a symbolic statement to the effect that they can successfully be overcome.

Although Sam fails to capture Paul's soul, it is frightened out of his body: 'PAUL *picks up his soul. It is a large black doll*'; when Sam approaches, it rises and hangs in the air; when Paul calls, it floats down to him. The soul-fighting match is set up like a cross between a world heavyweight championship fight and a fairground sideshow, with Gran as the M.C., the two Ladies as cheerleaders, and enough dirty tricks up Gran's sleeve (or skirts) to make Sam odds-on favourite. The 'ring' – a chicken-wire cage, unrolled by attendants – is exactly the right venue for a serio-comic struggle for a man's soul. But the representation of the fight and its eventual result are less convincing. The method of combat – 'It's a duel with this here soul as weaponry. Jist take turns t'crack each other cross the head – or elsewhere where it's injurfiable' – doesn't amount to a very consistent use of the soul imagery. Paul's combination of passive resistance and wily intelligence comes over strongly (he refuses to fight back and each time drops the doll a few feet in front of him, crawling along after it, until Sam courteously helps him out of the ring to retrieve it and Paul promptly refuses to get back in!). Sam is unable to follow him because 'I ain never been out the cage my whole life!' We are shown that a man will keep his spirit free if he has the will – and the wit – to resist. Paul ends the play a free soul.

Given the play's distinctive tone, what kind of balance between comic exaggeration and realism does a production of it need to strike? The clue, as always, is to be found in the language: 'The language interprets the play to the actor and he has to interpret the language to the audience . . .'[4] What, though, is an actor to make of *Grandma Faust*, in which the dialogue ranges in tone from the enormities of the catalogue of varied nigger dishes to similes like this one from Sam: 'Glory be my stomach's rumblin like the ghosts of them dead bisons runnin on the great plain.'? The temptation might be to send up the folksiness of the dialogue, but how then does one accommodate the seriousness of the theme as opposed to the comic treatment of it? What's important is that the actors use the language to satirise the characters' *attitudes* – it is a distancing device, as Bond hints in an early note: 'Language – a parody, to relate to actual American as Brecht's English relates to English.'[5] The performances need an ironic edge – if *Grandma Faust* is played aggressively, it will topple into ludicrous melodrama. Bond sums it up in another observation: 'I think that if it was spoken like a Restoration comedy it would be fine. Can you imagine trying to make Swift's 'Modest Proposal' sound angry? It has to be cool.'[6] Gran, Uncle Sam and the Ladies give evidence of the monstrous cruelty that a bad society can breed, but they cannot be played as if the characters knew they were cruel.

Stone

Only four days after finishing *Grandma Faust*, Bond started work on *Stone*. This time the request had come from Gay Sweat-

Narrow Road to the Deep North: Diana Raworth (*Georgina*), David Sterne (*Kiro*), (Exeter, 1971) *photo: Toyne*

Narrow Road to the Deep North: David Sterne (*Kiro*), (Exeter, 1971) *photo: Toyne*

Lear: Richard Münch (*Lear*), (Vienna, 1973) *photo: Pflaum*

The Sea: Costume sketch by Deirdre Clancy (London, 1973) *photo: Clancy*

The Sea: Marianne Hoppe (*Mrs Rafi*), Doris Schade (*Mrs Tilehouse*)
Herbert Mensching (*Hatch*), (Hamburg, 1973) *photo: Clausen*

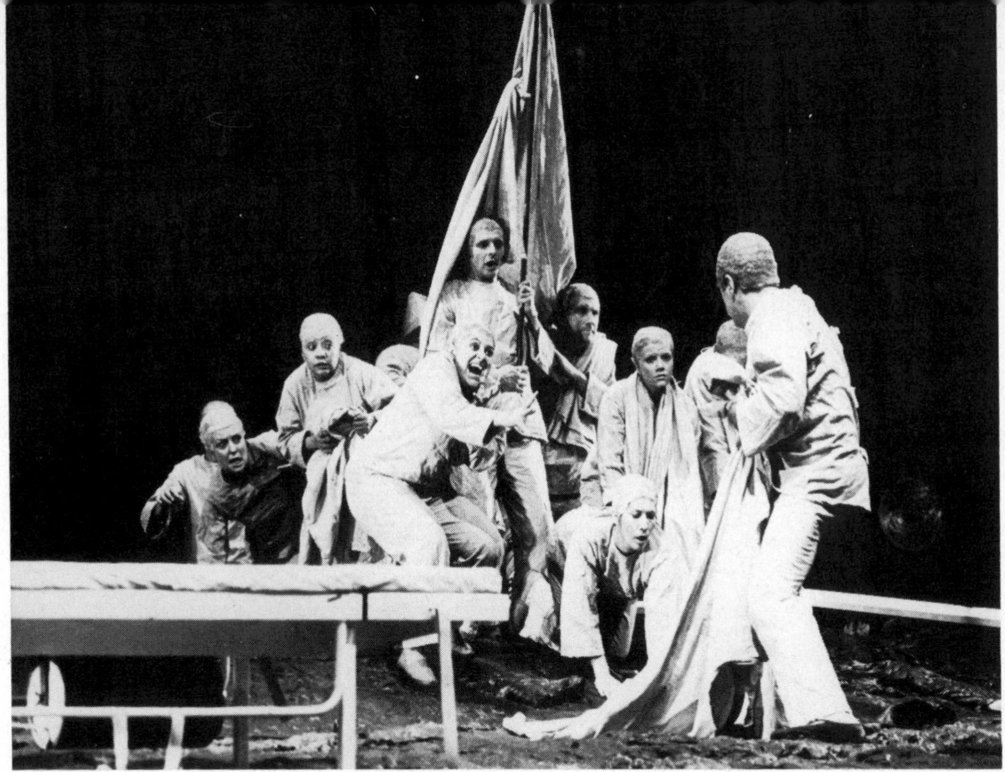

We Come to the River (Cologne, 1977) *photo: Odry*

Bingo: Bob Peck (*Shakespeare*), (Exeter, 1973) *photo: Toyne*

The Woman Part One (London, 1978) *photo: Davies*

The Woman Part Two: Yvonne Bryceland (*Hecuba*), Susan Fleetwood (*Ismene*), (London, 1978) *photo: Davies*

The Bundle: Mike Gwilym (*Wang*), Bob Peck (*Ferryman*), Margaret Ashcroft (*Ferryman's Wife*), (London, 1978) *photo: Davies*

shop, a theatre company based in London and committed to homosexual liberation. *Stone* does not deal specifically with homosexuality, indeed nowhere in the play is it mentioned (although Bond decided just before the play opened to insert eight lines on the subject before the first scene – 'a sort of chorus – a question and answer – a catechism' – to guard against any simple-minded interpretations which might see *Stone* as saying that homosexuality was a burden)[7]. Bond wrote instead a parable about oppression in general. The Man who sets out optimistically into the world in scene one is forced, just like Paul, to fight for his soul; he is again an innocent who finally shows his strength, but in *Stone* this is only after he has first knuckled under to the system and has come close to being totally corrupted by it. In *Stone*, far more than in *Grandma Faust*, the emphasis is upon the forms that oppression takes and the difficulty of resistance.

Since the play is in the form of a parable, it is vital that every element in a production, particularly the acting and the design, is used to support the meaning of a scene; there is no room for interesting but irrelevant detail. The idea of the journey, which provides the basic structure, was considerably strengthened in the first production, directed by Gerald Chapman at the Institute of Contemporary Arts (I.C.A.), by having the play performed on a platform stage, twenty-four feet long and eight feet wide, with the audience on three sides (the long central platform, although less than half the distance of the stage opening at the Northcott Theatre, Exeter, created a very similar visual impression to the one Jane Howell and Hayden Griffin achieved there in their production of *Narrow Road to the Deep North*).

Bond uses two main theatrical symbols to convey his parable about capitalist exploitation and the way in which an individual's talents and virtues can become corrupted by the kind of society in which only opportunists can survive. The symbolism of the coins, or 'talents' (each is given a name – Prudence, Soberness, Courage, Justice, Honesty, Love, Hope), which the Man carries with him and which turn from virtues in the course of his encounters and transactions, may well have been suggested by Brecht's *The Seven Deadly Sins*, where each of the 'sins' Brecht shows is in reality a virtue – except in a cut-throat society.

To this Bond adds the symbol of the stone – in the first scene it is no more than a large pebble which the business-suited Mason persuades the Man to deliver to his house, but before long it becomes an enormous rock which the Man carries chained to his back. Both these symbols serve their purpose well. The transformation of the stone to a rock on the Man's back is a forceful and clearcut theatrical image, while the shifting 'identity' of the coins is a device that Bond uses to subtle effect. In the second scene a Tramp tries to get the Man to part with his coins; with a feeling of self-satisfaction, he hands them over (after all, the Tramp's need for them is greater than his own), but he holds back one of them for himself – the coin that represents Hope.

By scene three the Man has already been corrupted. In order to ingratiate himself with the Girl who runs the inn, he makes a violent attack on the Tramp and throws him out; he also reclaims his coins from the Tramp's pockets. The fight is described – and must be staged – with a sharp realism, but the Man's relationship with the Girl is then expressed through a stage metaphor which, in the questions it asks of an audience, is as effective as anything Bond has written – the Girl's dance of the seven veils. We are encouraged to expect some kind of striptease. What we get is a striptease in reverse. She starts the dance naked. There is nothing sexual or lascivious about her performance; the effect, as Bond explained during rehearsals at the I.C.A., should be 'like a child running naked down a beach'. As the dance continues, '*Each time she asks the* MAN *for a coin, he gives it to her, and she covers herself with a white sheet*'. She dances more and more slowly and by the end she is '*shrouded from head to foot*'. It is one of those compelling stage metaphors that Bond so often uses not for a self-contained dramatic effect but to challenge the audience's moral preoccupations. Both characters were involved in the ruthless assault on the Tramp and the money the Girl collects from the Man now has the Tramp's blood on it; but the image of degradation and shame she presents at the end of her dance offers no scope for any moral censure. She too is a victim. The purpose of the dance is not to excite the emotions but to show the relationship between the Girl and the Man, a relationship which is conditioned by money; it amounts to a form of mutual exploitation. It is a process which is destructive of both their virtues – as the money changes hands: '*After each coin he eats and drinks a little more slowly. The dance ends with the* MAN *crawling back to his stone to sleep and the* GIRL *stumbling to a standstill. She is shrouded from head to foot and cries quietly under her shrouds.*' In the next scene, the Man discovers that the coins have changed from virtues to vices.

The metaphor of the dance offers the audience a key to the moral issues contained in the first three scenes; it is a forceful illustration of the observation Bond made in the 'Author's Preface' to *Lear* (on that occasion, about a man condemned to spend his working life in routine factory or office work): 'Because he is behaving in a way for which he is not designed, he is alienated from his natural self, and this will have physical and emotional consequences for him . . . he becomes a threat to other people, and so his situation rapidly deteriorates.' It illustrates the process not by a cool presentation of the issues, but by showing the audience an action which agitates the emotions – and by doing so forces us to reflect on our earlier preconceptions. Bond is developing and sharpening here a dramatic technique which is put to even more pointed use in *The Bundle*.

For the remainder of the play, Bond systematically blocks off any bolt-holes through which the audience could take refuge in easy, automatic responses. Consider the deliberate ambiguity with which he treats the death of the Tramp. The Man's attack on him in the inn is an outburst of suppressed rage which, since he is unable to direct it at the real cause for his sufferings and frustrations (his self-imposed burden), he turns against another victim like himself. Like Hatch's behaviour in *The Sea*, it is a displacement activity, and the analogy with Hatch is useful because it helps to explain Bond's treatment of the Tramp's death in the subsequent Trial scene. The question of who was in fact responsible for the killing is left open. The Policeman's speech in defence of his own actions might appear to be self-incriminating – 'I've been kicking people all my life . . . my kick is controlled. Now if the accused is suggesting that I kicked a man and accidentally killed him, that suggestion is palpably ludicrous' – but Bond was adamant during the first production of *Stone* that the staging should not identify who was guilty (it was suggested, for example, that the Policeman might carefully wipe blood off himself as he entered at the end of the Girl's Dance). The problem Bond sets is not to identify the murderer but to consider the reasons for the death. If the Man is guilty – which is still possible – it would, Bond suggests, be an 'innocent' murder.

In Bond's plays the aggressors are also victims – even the Policeman, the one and only clearly comic character in *Stone*, is shown wilting under the Judge's stern scrutiny. In the last scene the Mason, in marked contrast to his previous appearance, is now a pathetic creature, mumbling over his heap of stones. Bond invites us to see him as a frightened, fragile figure, neurotic because of the power he wields. Since he is not portrayed as a sub-human caricature, considerable weight is attached to the moment when the Man kills him. This is a real death, yet in the final line of the play we are asked to view the Man's action as an innocent one: 'MAN. I want to wash my hands.' To underline the point, Bond has subsequently decided that the Washerwoman offstage should reply: 'No. They are clean.' As the confrontation between Man and Mason mounts through the short last scene, the dominant note is of the Man's outrage at the desperately evasive answers he gets to his insistent questions – why has he wasted his life carrying the stone? why has he been corrupted? The force of this outrage and the weight of the whole play combine to persuade us that the killing is justifiable.

There can be little doubt that Bond endorses it. The ending of *Stone* is closely related to two general observations he made elsewhere in 1976. In an interview before *Stone* opened, he said: 'I do think you have to look for points of confrontation, but it's difficult because they get out of hand. But there must be those situations where oppression is made to identify itself. You must tread on its toes and make it declare itself.'[8] There could be no better description of the last scene of the play. Earlier, in the 'Author's Note – On Violence' in *Plays: One*, he wrote: 'I believe in solving political and social problems in rational ways whenever possible. The dangers of violence, even in a just cause, are too obvious for me to think otherwise . . . Right-wing political violence cannot be justified because it always serves irrationality; but left-wing political violence is justified when it helps to create a more rational society, and when that help cannot be given in a pacific form.'

Bond does not show in *Stone* what kind of rational society he is advocating nor how it may be brought about; he shows the pressures out of which it will be created. According to Gerald Chapman: 'For the actors, it's more complex than simply looking for the character motivation behind the words of the text. There is a continual sense of the pressure of the forces which make a character behave in a certain way.' At the same time, Bond stresses that 'if you're telling a parable story, you have to tell it with a *zest* for the telling of it'. There is a boldness and directness in the writing which is reflected in the use of six songs to comment on and clarify the process the Man goes through. Two of these songs – 'Stone' and 'Song of the Seven Deadly Veils' – have a marked Brechtian flavour, and the reader may also see several parallels between *Stone* and Brecht's short *Lehrstück, The Exception and the Rule*. Both plays are political parables which make use of the idea of a journey; the Judge in Brecht's play uses the same pseudo-logic in justifying his acquittal of the Merchant for shooting the Coolie that we hear from the Judge and the Mason in *Stone*; the characters of the two Policemen, the Innkeeper and the Widow jog memories of Bond's Policeman and Woman; and the message in Brecht's prologue could equally well be used to preface *Stone*:

> We ask you expressly to discover
> That what happens all the time is not natural.
> For to say that something is natural
> In such times of bloody confusion
> Of ordained disorder, of systematic arbitrariness
> Of inhuman humanity is to
> Regard it as unchangeable.[9]

As we shall see when we consider *The Bundle*, comparisons between Bond and Brecht, particularly with regard to dramatic technique, can only be taken so far before they become misleading. And, although a number of characters and situations from plays by Brecht may have entered into Bond's thinking about *Stone*, another major influence was in fact two of Bond's own early plays – *The Outing* and *The Golden Age*, both written in 1959–60 for the Royal Court theatre Writers' Group. *The Outing* contains a number of speeches and situations which are found again, only very slightly modified, in *Stone*; it also contains a story which reads like an early sketch for *Stone*: 'There was some bloke. 'E was goin up this road see. 'E clocks this stone. It's out in front a 'im on the road. It's a rock, see, know what I mean? – twice the size a your nut. There's a bit a new string tied round it. It's all done up like a parcel . . . 'E picks it up an takes it with 'im. The road goes phut, or 'e loses it, or somethin, y' know. So 'e puts this stone on the ground. 'E takes off the string. 'E undoes the parcel.' The details may be different, but the connection is unmistakable.

The Golden Age is closer still. It is a parable play with songs (similar in style to those in *Stone*), retelling the story of the Good Samaritan. It opens with a middle-aged man walking down a road; this 'Good Man' is a prototype of the Mason, a manipulator of every social situation to his own advantage – he persuades a Poor Man to work for him, against the Poor Man's better judgement. The whole play is aimed directly against the comfortable notion that Man is naturally aggressive and argues that it is the way society is organised that makes him so.

The fact that Bond should have quarried material for *Stone* from two plays written seventeen years earlier is interesting enough, but there is a further, more significant, dimension to the connection between them. *Stone*, by virtue of its uncompromising political statement and Bond's use of a form of controlled theatrical shock effect in sequences like the Girl's dance, is unmistakably a forerunner of *The Bundle*; and parallels with *The Golden Age* also feature in *The Bundle*.

The Swing

The last of the three short plays written at the beginning of 1976 was *The Swing*, which, with *Grandma Faust*, makes up a double-bill under the title *A-A-America!*. Bond subtitles it 'a documentary'; it is based on actual historical incidents, described in a prologue by Paul, a negro who is clearly meant to be seen as a descendant of Paul in *Grandma Faust* – he would most probably be played by the same actor:

> In the fall of nineteen eleven in Livermore Kentucky a blackman was charged with murder. He was taken to the local theatre and tied to a stake on stage. The box office sold tickets accordin to the usual custom: the more you paid the better you sat. The performance was this: people in the pricey seats got to empty their revolvers into the man. People in the gallery got one shot. An pro rata in between. Course he died very easy compared t'the style of some lynchins.

We are deliberately encouraged to expect the play to be about Paul's murder. In fact, it is hardly about Paul at all. There are only three occasions when he has any appreciable part to play in the action; for the rest of the time, he comes on and goes off, doing chores and running errands for the whites, a silent figure in the background. By conventional standards, he cannot in any way be regarded as the protagonist. He stands and waits, and watches while a community goes mad and starts to tear itself to pieces. In *The Swing*, as in *The Sea* or the 'history' plays, Bond looks at a society which is at a historical crossroad; the roughness and rawness of the American frontier is becoming 'civilised' and the result is a society which retains the irrational violence of the old frontier life, but with a new top-dressing of culture which proves to be as spurious as the middle-class culture of Mrs. Rafi in *The Sea*.

The first half of the play is deceptively calm and quiet. Bond introduces the five characters who represent different constituents in the make-up of the small town community. Mrs. Kroll, the owner of the run-down theatre in which three of the four scenes are set, is a mixture of the would-be genteel, the hard-headed and the ludicrous. All these facets are combined in Bond's characterisation of her as a faded vaudeville star; at the beginning of scene one, Bond originally gave the following description of her, sitting on a swing which has been decorated with bright paper flowers and bunting: '*She goes to the swing and sits on it but doesn't swing. This makes her look curiously lumpy, like a stranded bird.*' It is a deft summing-up of how out of place Mrs. Kroll seems in a society where the values of commerce and capitalism are taking a firm hold.

This new world is represented by Skinner, a shopkeeper who has bought a lease on the theatre and intends to turn it into a new store. Brash, insensitive, cunning rather than intelligent, he is a dominating force in the action and his influence scars and maims everyone who comes in contact with him, except for Paul. But the hollowness and hypocrisy of their culture is most strikingly seen in the character of Greta, Mrs. Kroll's daughter. Bond shows through her the way in which education and cultural pretension can be used to ward off contact with real life. Greta's character and the values she embodies are finally summed up in a single image.

This occurs in scene two, as she sits at a table in her room with Ralph, Skinner's son; she is tutoring him in literature – because Skinner believes it might make him a better salesman: 'I'd like him taught so's he can carry on like you did jist now – bout civilization and so on. If he came out with that he could sell a real classy line of goods.' The scene becomes an illustration of Greta's obsessive and guilt-ridden sexuality; she reads a translation of Virgil out loud to Ralph and '*As she reads she uncovers one of her breasts and takes it out*'. Compare this with an analogous image in scene two of *The Fool*: there, as Mary and Clare sit in the wood, Clare holds her breast while they eat bread; it is an image of natural sexuality. Here, Greta refuses to let Ralph touch her, but instead provides a commentary on her state of arousal: 'How firm the nipple is. It glows. It means I like you Ralph. When the lady's breasts are firm it means she likes the man.' Unable to give direct expression to her feelings, she hedges her remarks by hiding behind her role as teacher. The tension between Greta's natural feelings and her guilt at having them leads to what for Bond is an inevitable outcome – she goes mad. The ostensible reason for her madness is the assault she claims is made on her in the yard that night, but this may or may not be fictitious; what is more important is that her madness is inherent in the way she feels constrained to live – as she tells Ralph: 'We must understand our lives and then act as if we didn't.' The second part of her creed is a flat contradiction of Bond's own philosophy.

The calm of the first scene and a half is shot through with underlying tensions and frustrations. Paul remains outside all this. His one sequence of dialogue is with Fred, a young white man whom Paul has introduced to the wonders of the new science of electricity. Fred is eager to set up in business, with Paul as his right-hand man. When Paul objects that blacks are in no position to accept offers like that, Fred maintains that things change. For the first time, we hear Paul state his views: 'They don't change that easy. Not for anyone. You git fixed on the past like you pumped it into your arms. It's a terrible habit t'shake. One day your people are gonna lynch each other in the gutter over a drop dime.' Encapsuled in Paul's statement is the main theme of Bond's 'history' plays – change is far from easy, but a society which lacks moral understanding is always likely to tear itself apart. Paul's strength and certainty show through the lines, as does his contempt. We see the figure who has been standing on the sidelines in a new light – it is as if he is watching and waiting for the time to come when he can make his move. But he is still a potential victim. The vandalising of Skinner's store, the attack on Skinner himself, the assault on Greta (if it ever happened) – all committed by unknown assailants – bring out the self-righteous vigilante in Skinner. The attack on Greta, which remains unproven, is rapidly converted into a 'rape', and Paul is the natural target for suspicion.

Bond's handling of the remainder of the action shows a playwright in absolute control of the effects he wants to create. At this point, the audience is bound to remember Paul's prologue and to steel itself for a violent and bloody display of racialism. But the ground is cut from under our feet, first when Paul clears himself with a perfect alibi, then when the tone of the scene suddenly switches completely. Skinner has cast round and found another scapegoat – the 'nigger-lover' Fred. When Greta comes on, distracted and raving, events seem set on a highly dramatic course. Instead, Bond turns Greta's madness and the hysterical reactions of Skinner, Ralph and Mrs. Kroll into a source of amusement: '. . . the second scene ends with a farce. It should be directed as a farce, the actors moving in unison and with efficient (stylised?) theatrical gesture. It isn't an intellectual farce – it should be played like a vaudeville farce.'[10] The change in tone is not introduced in order to provide a momentary relaxation of tension. Bond plunges the play into farce so that the audience can view the events with the necessary scepticism and objectivity: 'I want the scene to start very earnestly . . . and end in pure farce because I want to say that these people aren't caught up in the unalterable course of a tragedy; it would be possible to change, it would be possible to change them: they are only figures in a historical farce. That makes the fact that the lynching goes ahead depend on the absence, at that moment, of human responsibility – not the unalterable hand of fate.'[11] Jack Emery, who directed *The Swing* at the Almost Free theatre, has stressed the demands that this makes on the technique and ability of the actors: 'It needs a company with copper-bottomed confidence to play a high tragedy scene, to get it to work, and then progressively to break it apart and say "laugh at us". For a performer to do that is to risk a great deal.'

The end of the scene is calculated to disorientate the spectator. The farce abruptly turns serious when Skinner hits Fred – and then, just as suddenly, we are into the beginning of the next scene, and watching Mrs. Kroll dispense a brand of tatty theatrical magic as she struts her way through the song 'I Wore a Little Grey Bonnet'. (At the Almost Free, the music was taped by a school band and the atmosphere it gave was exactly right, wrong notes and all.) We have to adjust not only to the change of mood but to the realisation that it might change again at any moment – since we are cast as members of the audience watching a show in the town's small theatre, the stage seems set for an enactment of the ghastly incident that Paul described in the prologue. At the end of the song, these suspicions are confirmed. Stagehands lay protective sheets over the stage and Skinner, adopting the role of M.C. just like Gran at the soul-fighting match in *Grandma Faust*, warms up the audience with rousing appeals to its sense of patriotism and justice. On tape, we hear sounds of the audience shouting and cheering its response.

At this point the members of the real audience might well feel inclined to reject the roles they have been given as accomplices in this black charade. Bond hits them with two hammer-blows which force them to consider their reactions to the events on stage. The first comes with the identity of the victim – Fred is led on and tied to the swing. The assumption that Paul is the one who will be murdered has been an inevitable part of the audience's response to the play ever since the prologue. Bond's second challenge is directly to the audience's perception of the scene. He juxtaposes Fred's fear with a sequence of grim farce: the Clown, having begged Skinner to allow him the first shot at Fred, makes great play of not being able to take proper aim at him.

The sequence devolves into a comic routine in which, every time Skinner asks the Clown to look down the sights on his revolver, 'he immediately develops this into his *own* interpretation of the only thing that's worth looking at: girls. So that the clown is made into an obsessive character – and at every mention of the word "sights" the clown goes into a comic hunting routine, as if he's running round the stage like one of the Marx Brothers looking for women . . . it makes the scene much more dangerous (and funny) for the audience: they realise they are watching a man, and a society, out of control. . . . Finally, the Clown's obsessive madness takes over in extreme sexual imagery (which connects him with Greta's obsessions) and the shooting of Fred comes out of the Clown's mounting hysteria.'[12]

It is with this frame of reference that we finally witness the shooting. Bond makes few concessions to the difficulty of staging the scene – the impact of the bullets is meticulously described, blood spurts and flows, and 'FRED *spins, twists, jerks, screams*'. It is the most harrowing sequence of violence Bond has ever set before an audience.

He follows it with a short scene on the same stage the following morning. The reality of what we have just seen is still in front of us – Fred's body is being taken down and photographed. At the same time, Bond brings back Paul to offer a parting comment which serves to explain the substitution of Fred for Paul on the swing. Paul announces that he is leaving Mrs. Kroll's employment; before he walks off, he drops a dime on the stage, which the stage-hands laughingly fight over. The connection is not hard to make. As you remember, three scenes earlier Paul had told Fred: 'One day your people are gonna lynch each other in the gutter over a drop dime'. It has not quite come to that point yet, but Fred's murder is evidence of an unhealthy and immoral society moving towards self-destruction, as it turns its violence in upon itself.

Text for a Ballet – for Dancers, Chorus and Orchestra

In September 1976, four months after completing *Stone* and *The Swing*, Bond turned again to his ideas for *The Woman*. He had written a first draft of the play by early January, and he then gave his attention to another project which, like *We Come to the River*, had been originated by Hans Werner Henze – this time a ballet, for the Stuttgart Ballet Company, for which Henze hoped to write the music. In the event, Henze found the script unsuitable and consequently it has remained unperformed. Its interest lies in the fact that Bond gives clear expression in it to political ideas which had already been indicated in earlier works such as *Stone*, but were not to surface prominently until after *The Woman*, when he set out on a new series of 'answer' plays with *The Bundle*.

The script is fourteen pages long. There is no dialogue, but it includes fourteen songs for a chorus,[13] generally to be found at the beginning of a new scene, which provide a commentary on the action; it also gives detailed descriptions of the characters' actions and movements. The story is in two parts and it is an explicit political parable. Part One is set in London in 1884, in a 'factory where artificial limbs and appliances for wounded soldiers are made'. The Factory Owner takes his family and a group of official visitors on a tour of inspection. They see the workers, many of them deformed by their labours, and limbless soldiers and sailors being fitted with new limbs; 'the medical care is elementary. They practise using their new limbs, they are awkward. No one helps them enough or shows them what to do.'

The factory thrives on war; when peace is declared, the workers' pay is cut and they riot, but the police are called in and the riot is put down. Other scenes show life in the slums – derelicts sleeping out under an arch, beggars in a town square. A girl from the limb factory helps a crippled soldier to learn how to use his new leg. She takes him back to her slum room, where he dies of malnutrition – 'the soldier rises from the bed. He is covered in feathers: a bird. The bird and the girl dance together . . . Their dance creates a world of peace, where the innocent are also the strong and the just are fed.' Another war breaks out, to the relief of both Owner and workers, since work at the factory returns to its previous hectic level.

Part Two is set in the present day. The factory is now a Medical and Training Centre for the rehabilitation of workers injured in industrial accidents, threatened with closure on account of the country's bad economic situation. Workers and other demonstrators mount a protest outside and there is a violent confrontation with the riot police and with a group of Young Fascists. Characters from Part One reappear as ghosts – the Owner, his clerk, some of the visiting party; they watch the battle with horror and show their contempt for the workers. The bird/dead soldier also returns: 'the bird's reactions are the opposite of those of the ghosts: rational and dignified. The bird is the figure of revolution. It dances its austere judgement over the police and managers. It greets the workers and demonstrators.'

The authorities capitulate and the Centre is spared. But the workers refuse to go back in and run it – in a chorus titled 'Song of Tactics' Bond draws the moral: isolated local victories are not the answer, society as a whole must be changed. In the final section, he shows a vision of the future. The workers and demonstrators are sitting by the side of a canal. With them are the staff of the Centre. 'Some of the factories . . . have been pulled down. Some of those that remain have been converted to recreational buildings. The factory windows have been painted in bright colours. Some of the walls have also been painted.' The ballet ends on this scene of communal relaxation.

There are a number of occasions when Bond makes use of stylisation and expressionistic elements (the bird, or the workers in the factory 'fitted into the machine . . . like a half-human frieze'), but in the main any production would need to work at conveying the social realism to a degree which is uncommon in most Western ballets. It was for this reason that Henze decided not to work on it: 'Ballet dancers can't make believable beggars or policemen – and dancers don't want to spend a year learning to use only one leg.' However, he subsequently made the interesting suggestion that it could well be performed as a mime piece, either by actors or by professional mimes.

The script remains of great interest as a sign of Bond's increasing readiness to call out for revolutionary action to change a society. His previous work for Henze had closed on the defiant 'Song of the Victims'. Now he shows the victims taking action. A clear line leads through from earlier plays: situations and issues recur, they are subjected to further analysis, and step by step the answer comes through more clearly. In the 'Text for a Ballet', Bond states it in the 'Song of Tactics'; the third verse runs as follows:

> Who can pass by the child left to drown at the river?
> But who feeds the tenth child? Will you shelter the hundredth?
> Who owns the river? Whose fields
> Does its water make fertile?
> Today the river runs calmly and smiling
> Why do the people who live on its banks
> Shiver as though they were trapped in a flood?
> While you are asking the landlord these questions
> For the sake of the child
> The child might drown
> But ask and be answered!

The issue he describes here, the answer he gives, even the metaphor he uses, all reappear later that year in *The Bundle*.

10

The Woman. Scenes of War and Freedom

Bond started to develop the idea of a play set during the Trojan War at the same time that he began work on *The Fool*. On 12 March, 1974 he sketched a one-page outline for a play called 'The Trojan Woman'; on the same day he also wrote a separate page of notes for a play about John Clare. At that time, his intention had been to write 'The Trojan Woman' first. As a result of his work that day, first on one play and then the other, he saw the Clare play so clearly that he decided to work on that play first. It was February 1975, nearly a year later, before he returned to 'The Trojan Woman'.

That initial page of notes on *The Woman* separates the action into three sections. The first is 'The war at Troy. Total chaos. Swarms, noise, patterns of events . . . the universal idea of the moment of war.' Then follows a section when Hecuba, the Queen of Troy, confronts the Greek heroes who have destroyed her city and murdered her grandchild; Hecuba blinds herself and 'smears them with her blood and tears'. The third section has Hecuba living in exile by a sea-shore, her presence tolerated by the local fishing community. She is joined there by one of the Greek heroes who was at Troy. He seeks reconciliation; she refuses. But he lives with her as her companion until one night she dies during a storm.

In the set of notes on the play dated from February to May 1975 Bond considerably expands on the structure he laid down in the earlier one-page outline. Even so, at this stage many features of the finished play are still missing: there is no Ismene, and consequently no alliance between Hecuba and Ismene to try to end the war. The scenes on the sea-shore now form Part Two; but Bond explores the possibility that Hecuba and the Greek hero *are* reconciled. There is no sign of the Dark Man, or the foot-race, or the assassination or death of the Greek hero, the character who in later drafts becomes Heros. All these missing elements are introduced in a final series of notes over a year later.

In the intervening period, Bond had been occupied mainly in writing the works discussed in the previous chapter. He had also spent two holidays on Malta: 'I wanted to soak myself in the Mediterranean background . . . just to face the sun on the rocks, as it were, as simple as that. I re-read all the extant Greek tragedies while I was there, and the comedies too.'[1] One result of this further reading and thinking was Bond's realisation that the action of the play needed a radically different resolution from the one he had sketched earlier: 'I wanted to go back and re-examine that world and how moral and rational it was, and whether or not it could be a valid example for a society like ours. I came to the conclusion that it wasn't. What I had to do was to reverse those values so that in the play there is a man, Heros, who stands for the classical values of beauty and order, and he is opposed by a miner who stands for a new order, for a new proletarian direction of history. There's a conflict between them and the miner wins.'[2]

All the subsequent drafts (from December 1976 to April 1977) progressively clarify the political allegory the play now contained. The new ending – the victory of the miner – is a very significant development. The series of three 'history' plays now ends on a statement of faith in man's ability to change the world. The last two scenes of *The Woman* deliver a far more positive statement than Bond allowed himself in *The Sea*, at the end of the first cycle of plays. And it is a political statement. Hecuba and the miner (Bond calls the character the Dark Man), both Heros's victims, combat his tyranny by killing him. Their motivation is not revenge; it is a revolutionary action: 'I show them acting out the logical development of history. And . . . I have represented history as a woman with a sword under her skirt.'[3]

Thematically, though not in style, the second part of *The Woman* anticipates *The Bundle*, the play which was to follow it. Both plays present unjust and irrational societies and explain the practical and moral paradoxes involved in confronting and changing them. At the same time there are a number of obvious points of comparison between *The Woman* and a much earlier play, *Lear*. Bond has said that he saw the character of Hecuba as 'a female Lear', and the pattern of the development each character undergoes is certainly broadly similar – an enforced education in the horrors man is capable of inflicting on his fellow man; an attempt to withdraw from the world, followed by a decision to take action. What is more, the description of *Lear* which Bond appended to the 'Author's Preface' can very easily be applied to *The Woman*: 'Act One shows a world dominated by myth. Act Two shows the clash between myth and reality, between superstitious men and the autonomous world. Act Three shows a resolution of this, in the world we prove real by dying in it.'

Part One of *The Woman* shows two societies, Athens and Troy, in the throes of an absurd struggle not for Helen but for the stone statue of the Goddess of Good Fortune, which Priam, King of Troy, had originally stolen from the Greeks (throughout the play Bond allows himself considerable licence in adapting the Greek myths for his own purposes). In the early notes for the play, Bond defines the social situation he wanted to present: 'The societies have gone mad through being based on injustice and the protection of injustice.'[4] Part Two presents a contrast between the irrationality and authoritarianism of Heros and the natural community of the island society, threatened with destruction by the Greeks. The shift from the chaos of Part One to the growing sense of an overall purpose and design in Part Two is reflected in the way Bond structures the scenes. The fourteen scenes of Part One cut swiftly from the Greek lines outside Troy to the city itself, from Heros's tent, the Greek headquarters or the battleground to the Palace, Prison and Temple Precinct inside Troy. In contrast, the events of Part Two unfold inexorably in one place, beside Hecuba and Ismene's hut on the island. Common to both Parts is a strong narrative drive which is closely related to Bond's view of the play's function: '. . . we have to do that highly subversive thing: tell a story with a beginning, a middle and an end . . . unless a story has a beginning, a middle and an end its events can't be fully understood and it can't lead to an action that results in change. Telling such a story, describing history, needs a new sort of acting.'[5]

The first production of *The Woman*, which opened at the

National theatre in August 1978, was directed by Bond himself. Working with him was the same design team, Hayden Griffin and Andy Phillips, that had collaborated with Bond on his production of *Lear* at the Vienna Burgtheater. Bond's decision to take complete responsibility for the first production of this play – and possibly of all the subsequent plays he wrote – came out of his clear sense of the need to confront the problems which his plays presented to actors in a more direct way than was possible simply by attending rehearsals and making suggestions to the director: 'It seems to me that I've reached a position where I'm making new demands on actors in my writing. I have to interpret the making of these demands.'[6] The production was important not only as an illustration of Bond's views on how a play of his should be acted, but also as an exercise in how to use the challenging space of the stage he had to work with. The Olivier theatre has a large open stage and a fan-shaped auditorium holding 1160 people, with three main banks of sharply raised seats sweeping down to the stage. Bond had not written *The Woman* directly for the Olivier: 'It wasn't commissioned by the National Theatre. I didn't say when I was writing it, "I will send this play to the National", although I think I had in the back of my mind a description of the Olivier theatre that I'd read in a newspaper. But I didn't go and see any play there until I'd finished *The Woman*.'[7] It is tempting to claim, in retrospect, that *The Woman* could only have been successfully played on an open stage the size of that at the Olivier, yet the play is no more sizeable nor more ambitious in its theatrical demands than *Lear*, which Gaskill succeeded in fitting onto the Royal Court stage. Although a number of the effects obtained by Bond in the Olivier would have been difficult to achieve on many other stages, it would be wrong to generalise in any way from this one production.

In the fifteen productions put on in the Olivier since it had opened in October 1976, little advantage had been taken of its potential for open staging. Only about two-thirds of its depth was normally utilised, and only about one-third in productions like *The Cherry Orchard* or *The Country Wife*, with a large set built well downstage and across its whole width. The first time Bond explored the stage, he found, across the rear and masked by black drapes, a tall metal fire wall painted black. Together with Hayden Griffin, he decided that for *The Woman* the stage should be opened right back to this steel wall. The black paint was stripped off and the huge, dully glittering wall served, not as a backdrop, but as a major element in the action and in the design, dominating the events of Part One as the wall of Troy and lit in Part Two to suggest the endless horizon of sea and sky surrounding the island.

For the large circular stage which had now been created, Griffin designed two floor coverings. In Part One the whole area was acid red in colour, with the stage raked down to the steel wall at the back. The effect was to suggest the blood and suffering caused by five years of war:

> H. covered the great stage
> With a red floor cloth
> That looked like the tongue
> In an open mouth.[8]

For Part Two the floor was grey, with a mosaic of cracks and fissures, like baked earth. The central disc was raised and tilted towards the auditorium, giving the impression of an island isolated in the middle of the sea. Stage right was the low hut for Hecuba and Ismene, with three large rocks stage left.

The design elements were deliberately kept simple so as to leave the stage uncluttered. In an article written after the production had opened, Bond emphasised that both the design and the use he made of the Olivier stage were a way of putting the main weight of analysis and interpretation squarely on the actors: 'Usually only part of the Olivier stage is used. A smaller stage is built onto it so that the rest of the stage is hidden and wasted. This symbolises the way we often largely waste our chances to create a new theatre. I used the whole stage not because I was sure how to use it, but because it was important that the company and I faced the challenge, and took the opportunity, of using it. It's a stage that can help us to create the new sort of acting we need to demonstrate our world to audiences.'[9]

In a poem written at the time of his work on the production and pinned on the notice-board of the rehearsal room, he described the basic acting-style that he was after:

> Each man on this stage is a crowd
> He gestures like bridges crossing great rivers

His head is raised like searchlights filling the sky
His face is a placard[10]

This is not intended as a recipe for an expressionistic or agit-prop acting style. Bond's point was that the Olivier stage was unsuited to any interiorisation in the playing; if the actors were to succeed in communicating the play to audiences, they would need to adopt a very different approach: 'It needs broad, unfidgety acting that moves from image to image, each image graphically analysing the story. When the audience's attention has been won in this way it's possible to do very small, subtle things. This combination of large and small, far and near, is a visual language of politics.'[11]

The first scene of *The Woman* establishes the absurd and malevolent political climate that runs throughout Part One, a mutual suspicion between Greeks and Trojans which stands in the way of any rational solution being found to the war. At the start of the play, the new situation caused by the death of Priam and the passing of power to Hecuba presents an opportunity for the deadlock of five years of war to be broken. Influenced by the arguments of Thersites, the Greeks show a superficial readiness to adapt and be flexible by agreeing to send a delegation to negotiate with Hecuba. Ismene, Heros's wife, is allowed to speak at the council. She is sent on the delegation with Thersites, in the belief that her presence might influence Hecuba to listen to reason, but the decision to send her is a cynical one – a reflection of a chauvinistic male world.

In counterpoint to this show of reasonableness by the Greeks runs the demonstration of their true attitudes. Heros's review of the events leading to the war, and the situation both sides are now trapped in, establishes the pattern for all the succeeding political arguments. The contorted chop-logic with which he describes the dispute over the ownership of the statue of the Goddess is calculated to raise a laugh, but a deadly intensity runs under the surface of Heros's lines. At any point in the play when the statue is discussed, the same tone is heard: 'What I wanted was a certain classical loquacity – they did write and think in a contrived, at times even tortuous, way. I wanted to get that feeling in intense situations of danger, always thinking and talking and commenting on them; it seems to me that's the strange thing about the classical world, it doesn't really shout, it thinks passionately. I tried to get that feeling into the language.'[12]

The Greeks' mistrust and hatred of the Trojans is shown more directly through the short scene-within-a-scene which gives the Greek view of events inside the walls of Troy. As it appears in the script, this short sequence could be taken as simply a device for introducing the main characters on the Trojan side. So it is, except that the audience sees them solely through the eyes of Heros – the exaggerated attitudes the Trojan characters strike are Heros's vision of them. In an early note on Hecuba's character, Bond had begun to develop this idea of showing her from the Greek viewpoint early in the play: 'a queenly, sophisticated, smart, dangerous, clever, sometimes cynical woman. She could also be shown through the eyes of the soldiers: then she would appear irrational, something out of a fairy story, glamorised – but stupid, because her actions would appear arbitrary . . .'[13] Soon after, this idea had developed to the point where the Trojans would be played by Greeks: 'Perhaps there could be a soldiers' entertainment in which soldiers dress up as the enemy and act scenes – caricatures. Heros to be excited by this.'[14] In the finished play, the naturalistic framework of the soldiers' entertainment is abandoned, and the scene inside Troy becomes Heros's vision. In Bond's production, the actors playing Nestor, Ajax and Thersites stood up and detached themselves from the council meeting, moving away downstage from Heros and Ismene, where they enacted the scene-within-the-scene. In the course of rehearsals Bond had encouraged the actors more and more to emphasise the element of caricature in Heros's view of them through a corresponding theatricality of expression and gesture. The scene was finally played as a straightforward parody: Thersites/Cassandra lay prostrate at Hecuba's feet, clasping her mother's legs as she pleaded with her; Ajax/the Son twitched uncontrollably when Hecuba placed Priam's ring on her finger, then prowled up and down like a petulant schoolboy; Nestor/Hecuba alternately preened herself at her newly-won power and hugged it jealously to her like a female Ivan the Terrible, a stereotype of the powerful, manipulative, scheming woman. Heros's view of her allows no possibility that the Trojans might relent in their attitudes: 'Trust the Greeks? No, I'll never do that.' The entrenched positions the

Greeks and – as Heros believes – the Trojans have taken up is firmly established;

After a long war
Minds go rancid
Even children talk
As politicians
And men play
As children
Hate settles everywhere
Like dust.[15]

And the audience is presented with a double-image of Hecuba/Nestor which can only be brought into focus when Hecuba herself first appears in scene four.

Scene one ends on a short, private sequence between Ismene and Thersites, only three speeches long. It acts as a brief introduction and transition into the following scene, by raising the question at the heart of scene two – how serious is Heros in sending Ismene on the peace delegation to Hecuba when, as Thersites claims, 'He must destroy Troy – his power in Athens depends upon it'?

One of the general notes Bond made before writing the play dealt with the idea of building an internal structure through the alternation of public speeches and private conversations and arguments. This switching from the public to the private appears not only in the broad movement from scene to scene but also within scenes. Scene two, between Heros and Ismene, is not, in fact, a private scene, except in the literal sense that no other characters are involved. The situation between them has to be very carefully defined and clearly demonstrated by the actors: Ismene is about to go as ambassadress to Troy, but she is doubtful whether Heros is sincere in his desire for peace – and the scene is defined by the question Ismene asks Heros halfway through it: 'Will you keep your word? No killing or looting?'. The way the scene is played must show the importance of the question. Unless the scene is anchored on Ismene's question – and the fact that it goes unanswered – her dilemma cannot be made real for the audience. She is concerned with her own conscience, as she prepares herself to meet Hecuba. Heros's reply is effectively a lie; instead of the direct answer she wants, she receives the equivalent of a guarded public statement issued by an astute, careful politician. Heros offers her no assurances about his future conduct. He is eager to use her on the delegation because he is so intent on regaining the statue, but his political position and the mood of his men militate against his being able to keep his side of the proposed bargain not to sack Troy. Ismene is left unsatisfied; what is more important, it means that she meets Hecuba in scene four without her conscience having been salved.

Scene two is set in a bedroom. It might be a love scene, or an intimate scene between husband and wife; but it works against expectations, since the characters' preoccupations are not private ones but arise directly from the political situation shown in scene one. What the audience sees is not a minor domestic drama, a tense situation between husband and wife, but two characters involved in issues over and beyond the subjective and the personal. Heros, misinterpreting Ismene's 'I wonder what she'll look like', launches into a brief diatribe against Hecuba; Ismene's response – 'I meant the statue' – is not calculated to draw from the actress playing Ismene a display of anguish and concern at the lack of contact between them. There need be no implied emotional comment in the way the line is delivered. Ismene is concerned – but at what Heros says, or leaves unsaid, about his intentions towards Troy. Throughout the scene Ismene's lines consist of short phrases or questions; she is not given a single speech of any appreciable length. Her silence is not because she is brooding over her relationship with Heros, or why he fails to react to her; her mind is fixed on her own role on the delegation and the honesty of her mission. Any tendency to load the part with irrelevant subjectivity will simply miss the point of the scene.

It is worth comparing the method by which Bond creates a character with the approach an actor needs to make towards playing the part. One of Bond's early notes on the play reads: 'Ask of all your characters what and when they last ate, and when they will next eat. Also ask with whom they have sex and when they last had sex? . . . Know the answers to these questions for each time the characters appear. Also know about their temper, when they last washed, had new clothes, saw an accident, overheard a conversation, saw something they couldn't understand. Know their opinions about things which aren't involved in the play.'[16]

This account of Bond's approach to writing a character, Stanislavskian in its detail, is probably no different from the process the majority of playwrights go through. In Bond's case, what it provides is only background knowledge about the character; it is a necessary process of preparation, but no more – few of the answers to these questions are incorporated directly into the play. The same method and the same discipline are required of the actor. The actors playing Ismene and Heros might find it useful in discussing scene two to explore the past relationship between the two characters, but it is irrelevant for them to show any of this to the audience. During a rehearsal of scene two, Bond explained: 'You should know everything about the characters. But we must avoid reducing the scene to that level.' This observation holds good not only for individual scenes but for the playing of a character over the whole length of the play. Bond's characters are far from being abstract ciphers or representative 'types', but their human qualities, their strengths and weaknesses, are presented through their reactions to different situations in the play. Characterisation is rooted in social rather than personal relationships.

Take the case of Ismene. In Part One, the steps by which she arrives at her decision to make a humanist appeal against the war are clearly marked. First, she decides to stay with Hecuba in Troy as a hostage to the Greeks' good faith; then she openly joins the Trojan side and informs Heros she intends to stay in Troy until the Greeks return to Athens; finally, she walks round the walls of Troy, openly accusing the Greek officers in front of their own men. At each stage she is forced into a more extreme statement against the war, and so also against the Athenians and her husband. Although in scene one her bright enthusiasm for peace gets her into a position where she is allowed to speak at the council meeting, her experience of political manoeuvering and in-fighting is limited. Her moves are not carefully considered or plotted; she thinks from moment to moment. As we have seen, after scene two she has effectively decided to compromise with her conscience and to suppress her doubts about Heros's intentions. In scene four, when Hecuba tries to break the deadlock in her negotiations with Thersites by asking to speak with Ismene alone, she finds Ismene as unwilling as any other Greek to admit to the truth – 'Your husband will burn Troy to the ground.' All the arguments and tactical manoeuvres between them centre on Hecuba's attempt to strip off the mask of self-deception that

Ismene is wearing. Hecuba herself is capable of dropping her role as politician and ruler of Troy – she talks freely and openly about the origins of the war: 'Troy is senile. Priam took me to bed . . . to make the city young again. It didn't work. So he stole the statue.'

Ismene's immediate response is on a personal level – she sees Hecuba in a new light; but it is immediately clouded by reverting to her lie: 'You've been misjudged. But what can I do? Return the statue – then we can leave you in peace.' When she is finally forced to admit the truth, her extraordinary decision to stay in Troy is the product of impulse, not a considered action – Hecuba asks her how it will help, and Ismene doesn't know: 'I can't go back now we've spoken. Send for Thersites.' Only afterwards does she come up with the pretence that she is being held as a hostage.

Her decision to stay in Troy is made under extreme emotional pressure – Hecuba clinches her arguments by displaying her grandson, one of Heros's potential victims. But the scene is not about Ismene's emotions; it is about the decision she makes and the thought processes which lead her to it. Similarly, in scene six, when she explains to Thersites that a rational solution to the war can be found, she is not angry with him for failing to support her, she is stating her belief in reason – an emotional delivery of the lines will only obscure this. It is vital that the audience understand Ismene's increasing decisiveness and sureness of mind, and also how much her actions cost her – she renounces husband, country and security of any kind. By the time she openly accuses the Greek officers, in the two short scenes under the wall of Troy (scenes nine and eleven), Ismene is fully conscious of the action she is taking. In these two scenes we see her tiredness, but also her strength; we must be shown through the performance why she takes this action – her love for truth, rather than a hatred of the Greeks.

In the trial scene (scene thirteen) Ismene is still intent on making the Greeks understand her case against them: 'In Troy I saw the people suffer. Young men crippled or killed, their parents in despair and dying of disease. I told them as they were dying – they couldn't hear but I told them because I'm Greek! – I shall do all I can to stop this.'

Although Ismene has a series of speeches in the scene, the effect is of one long speech, anchored on the one word 'tomorrow', a word to which she returns time and again. It is a speech continually interrupted by the officers who are her judges. The effect is to show the strength of her determination to do all she can to prevent the following day's massacre. As with other scenes, it would be possible to reduce the situation to a superficial theatrical conflict between Ismene and the officers, with Ismene reacting angrily to their charges. The effect then would be as if her arguments were drawn from her by the blindness and prejudice of their attitudes. In fact, her arguments are already in her mind well before the start of scene thirteen, and to base the scene on her reactions to the officers will only get in the way of a full understanding of the central development Ismene's character goes through. She persists with her arguments *despite* their reactions.

In the National theatre production, her inability to get through to them was marked by the Officers breaking in ones and twos from the long row of stools on which they sat and moving upstage to play a game of ball. Only Nestor, Thersites and Heros were left listening to Ismene's words. Her curse on the Greeks for what they are about to do is both her strongest speech in the play and the moment when she recognises defeat. Heros, the court now cleared, condemns her to death. Her previous strength temporarily deserts her; she is lost, bewildered – Ismene's lines become short questions, as she struggles to understand the implications of what has happened: 'Many people die saying what I've said. Who are they? Who killed them? How many more will die – and who'll know?'. The speech could be read as a personal attack on Heros; but the arguments are over, she can no longer hope to persuade him, and out of the death sentence she draws fresh resolve. She insists on still proclaiming the truth: 'I shall sit in the dark and listen till the last wail. Not to tell tales when I go to heaven, but so that the truth is recorded on earth.'

To play Ismene's relationships with Heros or Thersites or the other officers on a level of personal anguish and affront is to distort Bond's intentions:

> There is an appeal against the waging of the war, which is a humanist appeal; that is, Ismene takes the line – it's all she can do – that if she appeals to people's reason, that will have some effect. She also says more than this, because she says she believes that the world is fundamentally a rational place and therefore simply to record the truth is a valuable thing because it becomes part of the experience of other

people and changes them. What she does is more than just make an appeal; she does affirm a belief in the values of faith and understanding and reason.[17]

Hecuba, the 'Woman' of the play's title, appears in only five of the fourteen scenes in Part One. Her relationship with the Son and with Cassandra is cool and distant – Cassandra is completely ignored, the Son regarded as a tiresome and dangerous political opponent. Hecuba's key role in Part One is to make Ismene face the truth of her situation and then to support her in her stand against the war. The crucial scene for both Hecuba and Ismene is the prison scene (scene seven). Both characters have dropped out of the action of the play. Hecuba was given power, exercised it as well as she could, then had it snatched away from her by the Son and the Trojan Priests. Ismene has thrown in her lot with the enemy, but has achieved nothing. Both are imprisoned – Ismene literally, Hecuba under house arrest. Hecuba begins the scene by saying there is nothing to be done: the Son will insist on keeping the statue and Troy will be destroyed.

Although they are no longer involved in the political events, in prison they discover more about themselves. It is this knowledge that makes Ismene determine to take further action. The lines are full of intellectual energy and the excitement of knowledge. The scene is built on parallel statements: each character echoes the other, as if encouraging the other to reveal the truth. Ismene talks about her future and a city which will be rebuilt, Hecuba about the past and Troy being destroyed. Hecuba describes Priam's strength, and the metaphor she uses – of an old man whose life is like a raft on a great river – is a statement of support for Ismene: she too can develop that kind of strength, if she is on the right river. Ismene uses the metaphor of the child – one of the weapons in the armoury Hecuba had used against her in scene four. Before, Hecuba had insisted Ismene tell the truth. Now she does so. She admits to her lie – 'I knew when I came here my husband had lied, but I pretended I didn't' – and she decides on her new course of action.

Each character is first given a political speech, then talks about something very personal. Each understands political life in terms of her personal life; the gap between the two, which we have seen embodied in the character of Heros, is bridged. The process in the scene is very similar to that in the prison scene in *Lear*, where political discussion gives way to the sequence when Fontanelle's body is cut open. Lear's action as he puts his hand inside his daughter's body is allied to his accepting responsibility for her death and for the consequences of his earlier actions. In *The Woman*, Bond places all the moral responsibility and all the moral development in the characters of the two women: 'Instead of writing from the woman's "point of view", I tried to treat the women in the play as normal human beings. I showed them capable of facing and understanding and resolving the same moral and political problems as men.'[18]

At the opposite extreme from Hecuba and Ismene are the attitudes of Heros and the Son. Heros, 'the elitist and privileged general',[19] is motivated by vanity and an overriding ambition. He sees the destruction of Troy as necessary for the realisation of his great purpose – the creation of a new Athens. Despite Heros's republican and democratic claims, the city he means to build is to be laid on a foundation of slavery, violence and cruelty. He seems incapable of genuine personal emotions – when in scene five he is given the opportunity to leave Troy with the statue he wants so badly, he is concerned less for Ismene than his public reputation: 'What sort of welcome would I get in Athens? Come home with a stone and no wife?'. The most striking example of his denial of basic human feeling is when he condemns Ismene to death; he treats her not as his wife but as a public nuisance which has to be dealt with. And in scene fourteen his callousness goes even further: no longer hemmed in by the endless political debates and arguments, he gives full vent to his anger and cruelty, though with an icy control.

What Heros shares with the Son is a kind of fatalism. In the Son it takes the form of a lust for power which he recognises as useless – the city will be destroyed whoever rules it. His vision is despairing and nihilistic: 'I shall be the man who stands on the street corner of history with a rope round his neck and beckons the spectator to come and be hanged.' Heros sticks doggedly to a fatalistic belief that he must get the statue if he is to ensure the prosperity of his new city. While Hecuba is rational about the statue – it's just a stone – and the Son is cynical, in that possession of it seems to him to guarantee nothing, Heros interprets everything in terms of the Goddess and the Greeks' inevitable success, even the plague which threatens his men in scene three: 'Can't you see? – the goddess has taken us one more step closer to victory!'

Heros's character switches violently between two extremes – at one time cold and logical, while at others the intensity of his emotional rages comes as a shock. First one facet of his character is shown, then another. Bond searched in rehearsals for those moments which crystallised a situation or an individual character into a simple stage image, a moment of summing-up. One such image occurred at the beginning of scene five. Heros, who has just received Hecuba's ultimatum – take the statue and go, or lose your wife – stood, hunched, with his chin resting in the palm of one hand, physically and emotionally wrapped in himself, not knowing what to do; not a god, as he half suggested in scene two, but a little boy. As the short scene with Nestor began, Heros snapped out of this stance and his attitude became something very different – his expression now not glowering but neutral, as he asked Nestor business-like questions about the danger of Ismene's position.

An even more striking example was provided by the actor who played the Son. When offered power by the Trojan Priests in scene six, his reaction was a loud, orgasmic cry. The combined sound and image was expressionist in effect, revealing the Son's inner psychology – the actor offered a sharp, graphic image which presented an analysis of the character. There could be no clearer example of the essential first criterion in acting a Bond play: the play tells a story, and the actor's task is to speak the lines and make the meaning clear, while illustrating the story – not with decorative embellishments, but with carefully selected actions and images which crystallise a situation.

The acting method implied by this kind of example is the opposite of the one where an actor seeks to inhabit a character, digging down into his emotional core as though into a well. Instead the emotion is externalised and the energy is in the head, the fingertips, the feet. It is the athletic style of acting which Bond called for in an interview in 1975.[20] The same principle should apply to the way the narrative is put over. An important characteristic of Part One is its narrative drive and excitement, the clash and exchange of ideas. The rhythm and pace of the performance needs to reflect this: 'This means that as actors we should use each scene to prepare for the next. We must not become bogged down in each scene –

weighed down with emotion, trapped in too much detail – we must reach forward to the next scene.'[21] In Bond's production, changes of scene were effected by briefly overlapping one scene with another; there was no attempt to clear the stage and wipe clean the image at the end of one scene before the characters entered for the start of the next one. In part this was a practical decision – on a stage the width of the Olivier, the overall pace of Part One would otherwise have been damagingly slow. In conjunction with the lighting, this device also gave a sharpness to the narrative line. Part One was lit by shafts of light which cut from one area to another, just as successive scenes cut from the Trojans to the Greeks and back again: the feeling created was one of frenzy and chaos. Between scenes, the normal convention of scene-change lighting was reversed. Instead of the lights going down, they were brought up. The scenes were strung together visually as if on a connecting thread.

However much design and lighting may support the analysis of the situations in a play, stage imagery has finally to be realised through the acting. Take any of the large-scale scenes in Part One of *The Woman*, where several groups of characters are on stage – the scene where the Greek soldiers are attacked by plague-women (scene three), the scene in the Temple Precinct (scene twelve), the Trial scene (scene thirteen), or the last scene. Although they are big scenes, visually they are simple. They benefit from a stage the size of the Olivier in that their structure and the strong visual effects within them can come over clearly; they will not become compressed and cluttered, as they would in a smaller space. In the Trial scene, Ismene's curse is set against the action of the Officers' game upstage; as with the snow scene in *Bingo*, Bond's distinctive use of simultaneous images seems to imply a stage with enough depth adequately to contain them while retaining a clear focus on the relation between them. The same is true of scene three of *The Woman* – the entrance of the plague-women, coming over no-man's-land towards the three soldiers, also demands space. The mainspring of this scene, however, is the way the soldiers react. Scene one has already shown the quarrelling among the Officers; at the beginning of scene three there is a more natural feeling of community and cameraderie – the soldiers know and trust each other. Then, as the women appear, move slowly towards them and remove their veils to show their plague-ridden faces, the soldiers' reactions move from suspicion through sexual anticipation to fear, in the space of a few short lines. This progression is swift and clearcut and calls for a comparable clarity in the acting.

Two contrasting examples of the relation between stage imagery and acting style were provided by Bond's handling of the crowd sequences in scenes twelve and fourteen. In the Temple Precinct scene, the threat of violence from the Trojan *'poor, starved, wounded, sick, lame, crazed'* towards the respectable Bystanders, together with the assassination of the Son, was orchestrated so that individual members of the crowd had very little personal identity. Instead, Bond gave them a corporate identity, expressed through gesture:

> I tried to show their common purpose through their hands. First their hands are flat and extended, the hands of beggars; when they come closer to their enemies their hands become fists; when they carry out the statue their hands are weapons, claws and flails; and when they're united in one moment of choice (to give the statue to the Greeks) their hands swing in the direction of the harbour like the leaves of a tree turning in the wind.[22]

The sense of a common purpose is vital to the scene's meaning. Although violent, the crowd are behaving very rationally: they seek to end the war by seizing the statue and returning it to the Greeks. The motif of the hands, built into the structure of the scene in Bond's production, is not an aesthetic effect; as Bond underlines in his poem on the scene, 'Hands'[23], every gesture and every movement of the arm or hand by any character – the Trojan poor, the rich Bystanders, the Son, his assassin, the soldiers – was used to express the relation between the characters and to describe what was happening in the scene. It is a method akin to Brecht's concept of 'gestus', a term for which it is hard to find any precise English equivalent, but a method which involves expressing a character's relationship with others by means of a consistent system of concrete physical or verbal images.

In scene fourteen, the Greeks' destruction of Troy results in a series of individual sequences with an intense emotional effect – Ismene calling from the wall in which she is immured, the child being torn from Cassandra's arms, Hecuba's confrontation with Heros, Hecuba blinding herself in one eye. The scene as a whole is almost operatic in its scale and emotional range. The group of Trojan women (eight in number at the National theatre, although Bond's conception of the scene calls for rather more) are far more than passive onlookers sitting at the edge of great events. As with the Trojan poor in the previous scene, the Women's attempt to protect Cassandra and the child from the Greek soldiers needs precise choreography since the struggle between the women and the soldiers takes place at the same time as Hecuba is pleading desperately with Heros and is also punctuated by Ismene's cries from the wall. In contrast, the dialogue between the women which opens the scene calls for more particularised playing. Their exchanges express a numb horror and convey an underlying tension about their fate. It is a crucial sequence because it anchors the rest of the scene, with its outbursts of great emotion, in an immediate reality. The Women's situation provokes down-to-earth questions: how long have they sat in the sun with their bundles, who has been there the longest? The image should have a grainy reality. The moment when they are rounded up to be taken to the ships springs from Bond's memory of a documentary film he had seen: 'I have in mind an image from a documentary film of the last war. There was a line of women, about to be taken off somewhere by soldiers; they were so terrified that, when the soldiers moved behind them, they immediately started moving in the direction they had to go. It's that effect we want.' These Trojan Women are not a formal chorus, as in Euripides, but prisoners awaiting transportation.

This scene is a controlled and bitter demonstration of the savagery that man can inflict on his fellow men. It is the culmination of the relentless inhumanity shown by Heros throughout Part One. The most violent events – Hecuba's blinding and the killing of the child – happen offstage. At first, the destruction of Troy is stated simply in the First Women's: 'The city's quiet. They're killing the old people.' As the scene increases in intensity and Hecuba finally confronts Heros, the description is more terrible in its detail: 'Teach me. Not how to herd women through the streets and goad them with your swords so you can chase them, or how to jeer when the old run and fall down, or how to mock when you lean over them with your sword, or kill a woman and wipe the knife in her husband's grey beard, or throw a man's blood down on his own doorstep – not all these skills of violence . . .'.

Hecuba, unable to persuade Heros to spare her grandson, tries to blind herself in a 'nihilistic outburst of passion and despair. The self-mutilation of victims to terrorise the victors. It is uncontrolled. It is the summing-up of the lack of calculation in human affairs.'[24] It is a gesture of desperation, and a rejection of the world, 'so that she wouldn't ever have to look on human destructiveness again . . .';[25] it echoes Cassandra's earlier despair: 'This world is cruel. If the whole sky was a cloth and I wrapped it round my wound the blood would soak through in one moment. I cannot bear this. I don't know how.'

The short sequence at the end of the scene when Nestor and the two Soldiers return with loot from the burning city adds a final layer of irony. Nestor's moralising comments and pseudo-profundities on 'the solemnity of the world and the awfulness of the war' are morally bankrupt. His account of his actions during the massacre brings to mind Hecuba's comment about Priam in scene four: 'When the old play games they mistake that for youth – it's only senility.' His lines are juxtaposed with the actions of the soldiers; as he moralises, they sort drunkenly through their loot. Like the Trojan Women at the beginning, the actors playing the two soldiers must drive home to the audience the reality of the situation. In their production, Bond and designer Hayden Griffin raised the central steel wall some twelve feet for scene fourteen, to create the impression of a breach in the wall of Troy. Behind it the smoke and the flickering glare of the lighting suggested the fires in the city. It was an impressive scenic effect, but the reality of the scene had first to be established through the acting, and in particular the acting of the minor characters.

After the intensity of this scene, the opening of Part Two shows a calmer, less inhuman world. The village festival – the song, the dance and the start of the footrace – at once establishes a feeling of natural community life. But Bond does not intend that the image should be idyllic: 'I'm certainly not saying that the community is idyllic. I'm saying that it will have to face the problem of the Greeks. It will eventually be invaded and colonised.'[26] The dance is a simple folk dance, but Hans Werner Henze's music for the song that accompanies it is atonal in style. Although the transition from Part One to the calmer world of the festival is clearly marked, Bond does not want to allow the audience to relax completely: 'I don't want to record. I want to comment. So I only record as much as is necessary for people to recognise, then I start analysing in order for them not to recognise but to think, to resituate the situation that I show. I didn't want the audience to be able to say: "Oh yes, we know where we are." '[27]

Hecuba and Ismene have both escaped with their lives, but their situation is harsh – and so is their relationship. They are outcasts, tolerated by the villagers, but no more. Ismene, freed from the wall by soldiers who opened it up to rob her of her jewellery, has lost her memory: 'What I say is that the mind she has – the concepts and attitudes she has – are really inadequate; they haven't been successful – she didn't save Troy and she was bricked up . . . Therefore her mind is no use to her, because it couldn't allow her to fulfil the objectives that she wanted as a full character. I had to wash out the ideas and the intellectual concepts she had so that she could go back to square one. So that if she was the most intelligent woman in the world, she then becomes the stupidest, so that she can learn again.'[28]

Her only sense of identity comes from the stories she persuades Hecuba to tell her. She has lost the ability to act on a responsible level: her innocence and vulnerability are those of a child troubled by the ways of the adults around her. From the independent-minded character of Part One, she has become a slave and a drudge, her range of emotions limited to what is needed to survive. Her relationship with Hecuba is one of mutual dependence – each relies on the other, Ismene for Hecuba's protection and Hecuba for Ismene's eyes and physical strength.

Hecuba is now a female Lear; she has suffered everything and she is now dead to the world. She has withdrawn into a set, limited pattern of existence on the island and through it has developed a false sense of security, by blocking out her memory of the past; she is blind only in one eye, but she has covered her other eye with an eyeplug: 'I left the world when my children were killed.' Her withdrawal, however, is not into an easy form of escapism. Bond: 'I don't think it's a pleasant paradise – it's very hard and very cold, very withdrawn and repressed – she has her walks on the beach and that's all.'[29]

To mark the change in Hecuba from Part One, Bond asked the designer to add to her costume something that would suggest the image of a chrysalis; Griffin supplied a piece of material which

Yvonne Bryceland used as a shawl, wrapping it tightly around her and cocooning herself from the world outside. But escape and withdrawal prove impossible. Nestor's arrival, his absurd questions to her about the whereabouts of the statue, his projection to her of a picture-postcard view of the glory of the new Athens, all pave the way for the inevitable arrival of Heros at the beginning of scene four. Again, the stage imagery graphically encapsulated the situation and the characters of the two protagonists. In his stage directions Bond emphasises the self-concious pride of Heros's bearing – he '*looks like Michelangelo's Lorenzo de Medici at the Basilica of San Lorenzo*'; later, when he talks with Hecuba alone, he removes his helmet and studies his face in its highly-polished side. At the start of the scene Hecuba, in Bond's production, stood in the wall of villagers grouped on one side of the stage, her back turned to the Greeks and buried even deeper in her shawl.

By the end of scene four, Hecuba has been forced back into the world. The change in her occurs under the pressure of the new situation caused by Heros's arrival. The agent of change is Ismene. In the short sequence after Heros and the Greeks have left, Ismene and Hecuba break through to the unity they had managed in the Prison scene. Their respective roles in Part One are now reversed: it is Ismene who forces Hecuba to face the facts. Hecuba takes off the band and eye-plug with a determination to face the problems of the world again: 'If I were a priestess a god would come down now and tell me what to do. Instead, my enemies come – and I must be ready again. Yes, ready for all my old anger to sweep through me, like the fire in Troy. Help me to take it off.' When they discover she is totally blind, it's as though the horror of Troy has come back again – 'that day has come back!' But this time Hecuba doesn't cry out or mutilate herself. Instead, she reaches out to Ismene: 'I wounded myself too deeply. I jabbed round with the knife. I had no chance. But you – perhaps you'll start to remember.'

The way is now open for Hecuba to take action against Heros. Her ally in this is not Ismene but the Dark Man, Heros's natural enemy, who has escaped from the silver mines of the new Athens. He is closely related to the minor characters in the crowd scenes in Part One: like the Trojan Women and the others, he is a victim; like the crowd in the Temple Precinct scene, he is physically twisted and deformed. From the end of scene four he assumes a major role in the action, and Ismene's role decreases in importance. Hecuba can only get rid of Heros by using the new source of strength the Dark Man provides and by linking it with her own intelligence, insight and political skill, but Bond is careful to ensure that the Dark Man is in no way a romanticized figure – his initial treatment of Ismene is opportunist and, like Ismene, he survives in the world without fully understanding it.

The key point in his relationship with Hecuba comes towards the end of scene three, and Bond's direction of the sequence afforded a very interesting and significant example of how little importance he attaches to a naturalistic consistency in the playing of his characters. Hecuba has offered to ask Heros to spare the man's life; the Dark Man's reaction is at first sceptical and suspicious: '(*craftily*). And what d'you want out of me?'. Hecuba succeeds in making him realise that it is *natural* for her to want to save his life – and it is a turning-point in the play. The questions Bond had the actor who played the Dark Man ask himself are instructive: 'if the Man has escaped from the mines, why did he escape? Why did he not just kill himself, if life was so unbearable? What did he see on his journey to the island – more suffering and cruelty?' Bond suggested that his escape was not a negative reaction, a blind escape from intolerable conditions – it contained the seeds of positive resistance. Then, from the example of Hecuba, he sees that positive human values do exist – they are real and tangible.

The problem for the actor is to show this, without moving through a gamut of longwinded, interior emotions. Bond suggested that at this point in the scene the Dark Man should stop limping, or at least walk more freely, though with the rhythm of a man with a limp; as the character's understanding of his position and of the world changes, so does the physical representation of his disability. The Man's limp 'disappeared' for the remainder of the scene, but then in scene five he is confronted with Heros; when the scene begins, he is sitting watching Heros down on the beach, and then scuttles off to the hut when he sees Heros coming. Bond felt that now the Man should be limping badly again. The principle is a simple one: the playing of the scene must reflect the character's *situation*, and this particular application of the principle amounted to the clearest possible rejection of naturalism as a basis for constructing a character in performance.

At the moment in scene five when Heros agrees to spare the Dark Man's life, Hecuba has not yet developed a plan of action. In the course of the scene, she becomes convinced that there is only one way of dealing with Heros – as she tells the Dark Man: 'He must be killed! I've walked on the beach and daydreamed of killing him myself. Sheer fantasy! I'm blind and I haven't enough strength to scratch him with a pin. He'd chop *you* down like a stick.' By the following scene, she has decided on the stratagem of the footrace. Bond staged the early part of scene six with Yvonne Bryceland sitting unseen in the hut. The conversation with Nestor became like an old man consulting an ancient Sibyl. Her physical entrance into the scene was delayed until her lines anouncing the 'dream' in which the goddess gave her instructions for the race; having listened from the hut to Heros refusing to go back with Nestor to Athens and having heard evidence of his still mounting obsession with finding the statue, Hecuba knows the time is ripe. When at last she appears, the audience sees a new, controlled, decisive Hecuba. From this point on she is in control of the situation: 'She takes the initiative and once she does so she has a chance of controlling her situation. She becomes an image of human thought and human purpose acting within the developments which are created historically.'[30]

Although Bond wants the main characters in Part Two – Hecuba, the Dark Man, Heros – to be clearly identified with larger political and social forces, their roles are obviously still rooted in the individual characteristics established in Part One and the early scenes of Part Two. Heros, for example, shows the same deadly, calculating side of his character; his attitude to Hecuba is one of continual suspicion: 'I look at the face that Priam kissed – and it's a mask. If I could see your eye I'd know if you lied.' When he questions Ismene about the statue, he approaches her with the cool calculation of a general planning a military manoeuvre. The arguments he uses are similar to those he used at the end of the Trial scene: 'Ismene, in war the good hides behind the bad. You're the only one I've seen stay innocent through a war: I had to stop that – the bad was hiding behind the good.'

The language is tight and epigrammatic and Heros's argument is clear: Ismene does not understand how hard it is to do good. His philosophy is unchanged, but it has been sharpened and honed by twelve years of ruling his new city. The sudden switch to violent emotion, when he loses control and threatens Ismene, is already familiar from Part One, but his behaviour becomes progressively more irrational; as he continues the search for the statue, he 'deteriorates, gets nervous, supports his hopes and beliefs with patently false reasons.'[31] His inability to give up the statue puts him in Hecuba's power. In effect, Hecuba simply pushes Heros further along the path towards self-destruction.

It must be made to seem inevitable that Heros will rise to the bait of the footrace. In Bond's production, Heros's gesture as he issued a challenge to anyone willing to run against him – legs spread, arms flung wide, head thrown back – condensed his obsessional drive to have the statue into a single intense image. It was followed immediately by another: the Dark Man shuffled across the stage to Hecuba, his limp more pronounced than ever – and she revealed that he was the other runner.

For the first time, the Dark Man discovers his own strength. Heros asks him who he is and – after an uncertain and tentative start – the Man's description of his life in the mines turns into an open accusation of all that Heros stands for. It is a powerful speech because it is so strongly rooted in character. We recognize that he is saying these things for the first time in his life. It is also a dramatic situation: he is indicting the man who is ruler of the world, and considerable tension is generated by our uncertainty about how Heros will react. When he makes a conciliatory gesture (after all, he needs the Man to run the race if he is to win the statue), the Man's rejection of it reinforces the message underlying his earlier speech – Heros and the Man cannot be reconciled because they are class enemies.

The correlation between the characterisation of the protagonists in Part Two and the political ideas Bond wants to convey is all important. It is vital to Bond's intention that Heros's irrationality should appear to lead inevitably to his death, because through this Bond seeks to illustrate the idea that an irrational society carries within it the seeds of its own destruction. The Dark Man is identified as the representative of a new working-class consciousness. It is he who kills Heros, because the death must seem the result of historical, rather than tragic, inevitability – like the killing of the General in *We Come to the River*.

Hecuba's role is to engineer and control the situation by which

Heros is finally trapped. She uses her intelligence to lure him into running the footrace. Maintaining the pretence that she can still see through one eye, she judges the race – and tells Heros that he fell asleep. The audience is aware that she cannot see – and knows that she intends to kill him. On one level, the action leading up to the killing is a demonstration of the power of human intelligence to shape and change events.

At the same time, the weakness and untenability of Heros's position is continually emphasised. When Hecuba gives her judgement on the race, she also tells Heros the truth about his life – he is spending his life like a sleepwalker, and his irrationality has deprived him of any understanding of his society or of himself. The footrace and its aftermath serves as a metaphor, a series of images, which illustrate and sum up Heros's political biography.

Bond is careful to show that Heros's death will have no dramatic effect on the course of events, apart from removing the immediate threat to the island community: 'It is part of a long process by which freedom is won.'[32] The play does not propose solutions: 'In a way the community at the end is like the young people at the end of *Lear*. The problem of their future has to be faced.'[33] It is a characteristically muted ending, with emotion held in check by the last scene, where no hint of sentimentality or rhetoric is allowed to intrude. The Dark Man and Ismene, like the community, are poised on the edge of new possibilities. The situation is open – they have been granted a measure of choice about their future. Hecuba has set a pattern of rationality after the irrationality Heros had created.

The central verbal images in Part Two are those of the storm and the water spout. In scene one, Hecuba's great speech describing the storm is also a metaphor for her belief in an overall purpose and design in history – inside the heart of the storm is a still, calm centre: 'Then the wall of water hit us. It seized the ship and jerked us inside and half way round the circle and suddenly dropped us out inside, yes, inside the waterspout. It was calm there. The white wall was spinning round us. I looked up and through the top far above I saw the stars.' Within the apparent chaos of events is Hecuba's strong, secure vision of a better future. Similar imagery is used to express Hecuba's fears at Nestor's arrival: 'Now there's a storm blowing up. Millions of drops of rain, each one with a human face.' This time the imagery is linked more explicitly with the idea of the force of history – not as an abstraction, but in tangible human form ('each one with a human face').

On the night before the race, the storm becomes 'real'; through sound and lighting the audience is placed in the centre of the storm, while Hecuba shouts above it, asking the Man to describe it to her. She is identified with the elemental forces which for her represent the possibility of change. Her death, when the storm hits the island again on the night after the race, reminds us of the cost of bringing about change. It also brings to mind the image Hecuba had used in the storm speech in scene one, a metaphor for her own role in the play: a tree grows, flourishes, gives help and protection to men until eventually 'it's knotted and rimed and the tree stops bearing fruit. Then it's cut down and burned.'

It is doubtful whether the full meaning of the play's verbal imagery could be apparent to even the most alert and attentive audience at just one sitting. As with some passages in *Lear*, the difficulty lies in the particular meaning which Bond intends the audience to attach to the imagery – it is likely that the connection Bond wants to make between the storm imagery and the process of history will simply not come over. This problem can arise even with a concrete stage image; the spiral of light which Bond asked for in scene six, flickering briefly on the steel wall at the back as Hecuba walked down towards the beach and into the storm on the night before the race, was not intended to be seen as a self-contained lighting effect, merely part of the effects which combined to create the storm. Its shape was meant to suggest the water-spout and to refer back to the earlier verbal imagery of the water-spout and the storm. As with the flash of light in the last scene of *The Fool*, the reference may prove too indirect and oblique for the audience even to be aware of it.

More direct in their effect are the crowd scenes in Part Two. The importance of the minor characters of the islanders cannot be overstressed. Although the Dark Man becomes their representative in the final scenes of the play, the role of the crowd is vital if the audience is to appreciate the full significance of the Dark Man's killing of Heros. In Bond's production, at the moment when Heros is killed, chaos and pandemonium are let loose for a few seconds (recalling the man-made chaos at the end of Part One); the stage is full of people running in all directions. Then Hecuba calls out and takes charge, and in one co-ordinated movement all the characters look out to sea, then back again at Hecuba. From this point on Hecuba controls the scene, persuading Nestor to leave for Athens and prompting the islanders to resume their normal lives.

This one co-ordinated movement was an exception to the way the crowd scenes were handled in general in Part Two. Unlike the crowd in the Temple Precinct scene, Bond worked at encouraging an individuality of response from the islanders towards the Greeks:

> In the second half of the play the group is used for a different purpose. An island is occupied by foreign troops. In rehearsals the actors discussed the ways in which they could react. Some wanted to resist, others to quietly comply because they saw their situation as hopeless . . . All these reactions are recorded in performance. As the pressure mounts the reactions change and develop until at the end – at the moment they are freed from their enemy – they move in one united movement to face the sea – and then back to face the audience.[34]

The Woman contains a number of major characters who are as fully drawn as any in Bond's previous plays, but it is important that the audience doesn't interpret the play as a conventional tragedy played out between the characters of Hecuba, Ismene and Heros. One guarantee against this is the weight which any production gives to the minor roles, particularly the Trojan poor and the Islanders – the term minor roles is in itself a misnomer, when the significance and the authenticity of what Bond shows is so strongly dependent on the conviction that the actors bring to these parts. In any of Bond's plays, the minor characters have an important function in that they represent contrasting elements in the society Bond shows us. In *The Fool* and *The Woman* Bond tries to reconcile his primary intention – which is to examine a diseased culture and to suggest what is needed to effect a cure – with the use of a main character, a theatrical device which, as Bond recognises, carries with it the attendant danger of seeming to place too much weight on the historical and social role of distinct and favoured individuals: 'I think it's natural to provide the audience with certain figures, just as people in their daily life want to know one or two people and not everyone they see in the street. There are advantages in the theatre in concentrating a lot of the experience in one or two characters. But I don't want to resort to the idea of a central *heroic* character . . .'. With *The Woman*, there will always be a danger that an audience will respond to the main characters but fail to see, or ignore, the social analysis which Bond is presenting. In the next play, there is no room for doubt or evasion; *The Bundle* can only be understood as a study of a whole community.

11

The Bundle *or* New Narrow Road to the Deep North

During a discussion on his work at the Young People's Theatre Festival at the Royal Court theatre in July 1977, Bond emphasised the way in which *The Woman*, which he had finished writing the previous month, marked the end of a second cycle of plays: 'I decided that I would write a series of three plays which dealt specifically with this problem of culture, with the problem of the burden of the past which makes change so difficult: these plays were *Bingo, The Fool* and *The Woman*. I'm now going on to a series of plays which I will call "answer plays", in which I would like to say: I have stated the problems as clearly as I can – now let's try and look at what answers are applicable.' In a statement written shortly after the Royal Court discussion, Bond described his overall intention more explicitly and at the same time pointed to the continuity of purpose linking his previous work with the plays he now had in mind to write: 'My purpose hasn't changed at all, and I don't think I've written much, if anything, I want to disown. Nevertheless I feel I must deal with problems always more and more from a social point of view . . . When I wrote my first plays, I was, naturally, conscious of the weight of the problems. Now I've become more conscious of the strength of human beings to provide answers. The answers aren't always light, easy, or even straightforward, but the purpose – a socialist society – is clear.'[1]

The Bundle, the first of Bond's 'answer plays', was written two months later, in September 1977; it opened in January 1978 at the Royal Shakespeare Company's Warehouse theatre, directed by Howard Davies, who had previously directed *Early Morning* and *Narrow Road to the Deep North* at Bristol, and whose production of *Bingo* at The Other Place, Stratford, the previous year had contained a number of actors who also appeared in *The Bundle*. Although a number of reviewers remarked on how the play represented a new departure for Bond, their comments centred largely on the radical nature of the play's statement – that it might be necessary to use political violence or revolution in order to create a free and just society. This idea was in fact hardly a new one in Bond's work: it was already implicit in the last scene of *Stone*, it had been developed in *The Woman* to a point where it assumed a central importance, and Bond had explored the idea on a theoretical level in the 'Author's Note: On Violence' which he wrote as an Introduction to *Plays: One*.

What distinguishes *The Bundle* from any of the plays in the two earlier series is its last scene. In scene ten we see the peasant community after the revolution, living and working in a new, rational society, free of repressive and coercive structures. Where in earlier plays, such as *Early Morning* or *Lear* or *The Woman*, Bond had shown characters who couldn't accept an irrational and unjustly ordered society and so attempted to bring about change, he now shows change not just as a possibility to be striven after but as a practical reality.

The relaxed, communal society of this last scene is not presented as an easily achieved Utopian ideal. In the remainder of the play Bond concentrates on showing the difficulty of effecting such a change and the cost involved in terms of human suffering. In his introduction to the printed play, Bond discusses how changes in human consciousness must inevitably precede changes in social institutions and social structures; in the play itself, he shows how the characters must first reject the conditioned responses and the accepted moral code which contribute towards their subjection: 'One of the things I've tried to do in *The Bundle* is to demystify the use of moral argument so that we can't be morally blackmailed any more. In order to change society structurally, you may find yourself doing what is, in quotes, wrong.'[2]

The Bundle takes as its starting point the same incident from

Matsuo Bashō's 'The Records of a Weather-Exposed Skeleton' which provided Bond with the opening of *Narrow Road to the Deep North*. The setting has now changed from 'Japan about the seventeenth, eighteenth or nineteenth centuries' to Asia, this century – although in the printed text Bond gives no indication at all of place or period. As he subsequently explained: '*The Bundle* is set in a primitive Asian community . . . I chose the Asian setting because it enabled me to abstract certain social forces and show their effect in a direct and simple way.'[3]

In both *The Bundle* and *Narrow Road to the Deep North* the opening scenes function almost as a prologue, as a formal statement of the issues with which the plays deal. In *Narrow Road* the first scene is actually labelled 'Introduction' and the formality of the dramatic method is immediately apparent: Basho's opening speech is addressed directly to the audience, and his discovery of the baby lying in rags by the riverbank prompts him to ask the question which must immediately be in the audience's mind: 'Why did its parents do that to it?'. The sequence which follows, between The Peasant and his Wife, answers Basho's question, illustrating the way in which natural human feelings are hardened and brutalised by economic necessity. The actors' task is to demonstrate the reality of this situation. The audience must understand not the characters' inner psychology but the social and economic pressures which have caused them to abandon their child. The scene is not about the relationship between the Peasant and his Wife, nor about their relationship to Basho. Each of the characters in the scene is defined by the attitude they take towards the child. The scene only makes sense if the lines are delivered as statements made in relation to the bundle of rags which represents the child.

Scene one of *The Bundle* also illustrates the importance of not forcing onto the characters a kind of relationship which Bond does not intend and which is not to be found in the script. The play opens not with a direct address to the audience, but with a dialogue between Basho and the Ferryman who is taking him across the river at the start of his journey to seek enlightenment. The style of language the Ferryman uses immediately gives a certain formality to the scene: 'I ask why the reverend sir sets out so early in the morning. He is not a soldier or a tax collector.' The deferential tone instantly establishes the social relationship between

Basho and the Ferryman, just as the reference to tax collectors and soldiers at once suggests the harsh reality of the Ferryman's world. There is no *interaction* between the two characters – the Ferryman's polite questions prompt from Basho an account of his reasons for leaving to seek enlightenment. Howard Davies's production emphasised the formality of this opening by positioning the characters so that Basho was facing away from the Ferryman and out towards the audience. He looked at the Ferryman for the first time as he was being helped out of the boat.

Davies has described how in the sequence following Basho's discovery of the child the actors had to learn not to play the situation in a naturalistic way: 'When Basho and the Ferryman step out of the boat, the actors for a long while felt that there was an argument between Basho and the Ferryman. I had to say that there was a third silent figure in the scene, which was the baby on the floor – by the river. The triangle is like a balance. It's a perfect form, a system of box-girder bridges, and the dialogue is between those three . . . Just as in staging terms, I had to remind the actor playing the Ferryman not to look at Basho, as it had nothing to do with Basho at that point. He was not commenting on Basho's immoral attitude. He was just talking about the child. They were both defining the child in terms of themselves. He was one side of the world and Basho was the other. By inference they define themselves.'[4] The lesson, as we have seen before, is that to register emotions when they are not clearly required by the lines will distort the meaning of the scene.

One graphic example of this in scene one of *The Bundle* is the Ferryman's ultimate decision, once Basho has left, to save the child. His first lines are spoken directly at the bundle. They are a clear statement of why he too must abandon it: 'In my house you'd be hungry. Wake up at night with the cold. And I'm not a good man.' It is then all too easy to read the rest of his long speech as the projection of an inner debate. The temptation for the actor is to show the Ferryman struggling vainly against his better nature and natural instinct to save the baby by playing his speech as a kind of agonised soliloquy. The reality Bond wants to show is much tougher. The Ferryman would like to save the baby, but it is out of the question. As he gets back in his boat and starts to pole back across the river, he simply states the facts about his life. He explains very clearly the reasons why he cannot help – life is too hard to allow the luxury of an act of kindness. At this stage it seems the decision is already made. The actor needs to show the Ferryman's determination to get away.

Yet in the end the Ferryman's natural humanity causes him to relent. Bond wants the audience to understand the tension between the man's humanity and the dictates of his economic situation, but in order to avoid sentimentalizing the character he shows this struggle without stating it explicitly in the lines: '. . . I had to find a way of suggesting the human values of the Ferryman and that's why I used the sounds, the bell and the curlew, which are almost like feelings, I suppose.'[5] The first curlew call occurs after the Ferryman's line advising the child on how to cope with the world: 'The poet was right: patience.' The sound is like a punctuation mark in the middle of the speech: his conditioned stoicism and his counsel of passive acceptance are subverted by his natural desire to help the child. His next line is: 'There'd be no harm in making sure you're properly wrapped.' What he says is a compromise – he wants to do much more than that. The curlew call represents this feeling he is trying to suppress.

He goes back to the child and looks at it again, but still refuses to give in to his feelings, rationalising his decision by saying that many other people will be more than ready to help. For a second time, he starts to move away across the river. His lines are all short ones: 'We have no children. Heaven was kind. It knew we couldn't feed them.' They suggest the rhythm of his poling as he pushes himself away from temptation. Only on the second curlew call does his resolve break; the change is made explicit in the line: 'We must be hard to live. Yet at any moment a curlew can call and we are lost.' It is a crucial moment for the Ferryman, but the lines state the ideas, not his emotions. Even when he returns to the bank and picks up the bundle to take with him, the moral dilemma he is in is held steadily before us. As he says, in taking the child home and feeding it he is killing his wife: 'This is a bad thing. Not a wise one.' The whole of the Ferryman's speech and his actions in relation to the child is a formal demonstration of the problem which Bond answers in *The Bundle* – in an unjust society, individual acts of kindness, however commendable, are insufficient: 'Giving way always to that immediate gesture of sympathy is not necessarily what is valuable for society . . . It is necessary to remove the causes of evil rather than to deal with any particular evil that crops up.'[6] Bond deliberately takes an emotive situation and then lays bare the issues it contains. Although the Ferryman is engaged in an agonising struggle and this must be reflected in the performance, the nature of that struggle can only be expressed by the actor conveying the ideas, as opposed to playing the speech and the situation for its emotional potential.

The Ferryman is only one of many characters in *The Bundle* who are shown struggling with this kind of acute moral problem, caused by the conflict between a natural humanity and the need for survival. The effectiveness of the play derives from Bond's ability to involve the audience in the process which the characters have to go through in order to resolve these problems, while at the same time keeping the issues crystal clear. The structure of the play and the dramatic techniques used are designed to take the audience through the process of learning which the characters undergo; as Bond has commented: '*The Bundle* doesn't tell a story in the usual way but follows out an argument, an analysis about moral judgements – how you define or judge right or wrong actions.'

Many of the techniques in *The Bundle* are already familiar from earlier plays. The characters are shown in their social roles – that is to say, their behaviour is not motivated by individual and psychological factors. Instead, we are shown the social and political character of human behaviour. In this respect, Bond's intentions and his dramatic method are virtually identical with those of Brecht, and indeed there are obvious correspondences between the opening of *The Bundle* and Brecht's *The Caucasian Chalk Circle*, most notably in the similarity between the Ferryman's moral decision about the baby and the servant-girl Grusha's grudging humanity when she saves the Emperor's child in Brecht's play.

One fundamental characteristic of Bond's plays, as we saw in particular with *The Fool*, is the use of juxtaposition, counterpoint and contrast, often involving two or more points of focus on the stage, to create a dialectic through which the issues in any one scene are presented. Both these features of Bond's dramatic method are vital to the effect of the opening scene in *The Bundle* – the Ferryman and Basho are both characterised through their reactions to the discovery of the bundle, and their different reactions are conditioned by the difference in the nature of their lives and their positions in society. Basho's apparent lack of humanity comes from his obsession with his personal quest for enlightenment. His reasons for abandoning the child have a different ring to them when compared with the reasons the Ferryman gives: 'Would the sky alter by one tear if I took you with me? Does the ant on the mountain ask the pines why they sigh? One can take nothing into the mirror of eternity but the vision of oneself.' As Bond has remarked:

> One feels immediately that no matter how eloquently Basho talks he is missing the point. In the end the cleverness of his language is almost manipulating him. What he is talking about is not a true interpretation of experience but an excuse for his particular situation. When he is setting out on his journey and he sees the child, he is able to refer to the child as being like an organ-grinder's monkey. He's not really thinking about the child at all.[7]

Through the attitudes the two characters take, Bond shows two different ways of looking at the world, two different sets of values.

The transition from scene one to scene two involves yet another characteristic technique, namely the manipulation of time 'to serve the argument and not the story.'[8] The action of the play spans a period of twenty-five years or more and the gaps in time between the scenes vary considerably; however large or small the period of time which elapses may be, the relationship of one scene to another becomes part of the analysis of the action:

> One wants very sharp contrasts in time. In the first scene of *The Bundle* I use time rather slowly because I want to show the struggle in the Ferryman and that it takes him time. At another place I want to show what are the consequences of certain actions and in the theatre the consequences can be shown immediately, even if they are ten years later. In the second scene of *The Bundle*, it's fourteen years later. There are probably some people in the audience who won't realise that the boy is the baby in the bundle until the Ferryman says to Basho: "This is the boy." I wanted the audience to go through that experience of asking: "Who is he?" and then suddenly or slowly realising, so that they would be prepared for what Basho would go through.[9]

In scene two, Wang begins to ask the Ferryman questions about the way they have to behave in order to live; the Ferryman tries to provide constructive answers, but his explanations fail to hold together. When Basho appears, still travelling in search of enlightenment, Wang twice asks him to explain what it is he is seeking. He is ignored. Basho cannot even remember the incident of the bundle fourteen years earlier. His self-centredness and obsession with his personal salvation are as strong as ever. Basho has not changed one iota; the Ferryman is still trying to strike a rational compromise with the absurd injustices to which he is subjected. The fact that we are fourteen years further on is of incidental importance; it is necessary for the purposes of the narrative. But the point of the scene lies in the contrast between the three attitudes, together with the change (or the lack of any change) in the characters since we last saw them.

Bond has described his purpose in selecting the particular situations and actions which he puts before us as follows: 'My theatre is based on trying to define ideas, critical ideas about society and about human activity; trying to define those as precisely as possible, not necessarily in verbal terms but in pictures.'[10] In scene three, Wang and the Ferryman are placed in a situation which confronts each of them with an impossible moral decision. The river has flooded and a group of peasants, among them Wang, the Ferryman and the Ferryman's Wife, have taken refuge on the village burial hills. They are starving and close to exhaustion. The group of seven huddled characters serves as a microcosm of the village, while cries of distress offstage remind us that we are watching the sufferings of a whole section of the community:

> VOICES (*off, crying*). Help. Help. Quick. The woman's giving birth. The hill's slipping into the mud. The gravestones are falling over.
>
> *The* WOMAN *is heard in labour. Slowly during the scene the shouting, moaning, and sobbing increase to a climax and then fade into the hum, whimpering and stray cries of a desperate crowd.*

The landowner, we learn, is sitting safely within his compound on the hill; the villagers are at the mercy of the river each time it floods. When two of the landowner's keepers arrive in a boat, they want payment, in money or goods, from everyone they ferry to safety. Since the Ferryman and his family have nothing to offer, the keepers suggest they take Wang as payment. The Ferryman is asked to sell his son into slavery for ten years in order to save himself and his wife, who is ill and dying: 'A proper indenture. Drawn up in a lawyer's office. A form of a loan. You get him back.' He tries to bargain with the keepers about the period of indenture; when they refuse to compromise, he resolves to stay with his family on the hill. The floodwater is rising and the pressure is on Wang to do something to save his parents. He has twice insisted that he is not a slave but, as the boat leaves, he capitulates:

WANG (*stands stiffly, rooted to the spot. Yells*). Buy me! Buy me! Buy me!

The FERRYMAN *embraces his wife with one hand, reaches with the other towards* WANG *and then reaches it up as if holding off the sky. He cries. His wife embraces him.*

FERRYMAN. We're going to be saved! Saved!

These actions of Wang and the Ferryman are used in exactly the same way as Heros's challenge to all-comers to race against him round the island or the Son's orgasmic cry when offered power in Bond's production of *The Woman* at the National theatre. They are all images which summarise a character's reactions to an extreme situation, and each of them shows a moment of decision. In this case, there is a tension between the words and the actions: Wang yells his surrender, standing stiffly as he does so; the Ferryman shouts his relief that Wang has saved all three of them, but his gesture shows how much the situation weighs on him, and how much Wang's decision costs him.

In *The Woman*, the actions by Heros and the Son were found by the actors in rehearsal; in *The Bundle*, the actions of Wang and the Ferryman are described in the stage directions. It is an indication of how consciously Bond has developed this technique which, more than any other, characterises his dramatic method in *The Bundle*. Theatrically, these actions are made all the more powerful by their placement at the end of the scene, but neither is intended as a self-contained dramatic effect. They express the tensions that have mounted on the characters in the course of the scene; since the scene is designed to show the operation of harsh economic and social forces, each action sums up in a dramatic image the effects of these pressures. Bond himself is keenly aware of the danger that their emotional impact on the audience might be counter-productive and has described how carefully he has tried to use and contain them: 'I tend to avoid ending a scene on a high dramatic point, because there is something melodramatic about it. But when a scene is clearly based on an intellectual analysis, like scene three of *The Bundle*, then I think one is justified in ending the scene in that way. And Wang's scream of "Buy me!" is immediately followed by Basho's line at the beginning of scene four, about how quiet it is by the river.'

Bond uses the device again at the end of the next scene, and once again Wang is involved. The decision he makes on this occasion is the turning-point of the play – and not only in terms of the narrative. His action is yet another summing-up moment, this time showing an action which, although apparently inhuman, is necessary if Wang is to do anything to remove the causes of the suffering we witnessed in scene three. His period of indenture has just ended; he has been working as an assistant to Basho, who is now a judge and even more firmly identified with the established order. Basho embodies the belief that the evils of society stem from a decline in morality and the inherent viciousness of human nature: 'Such acts of human nature are so bestial, the times so dark, that it is not possible to see what we can do to help ourselves change the times.'

Wang, his values shaped by his reactions to years of watching Basho dispense 'justice', no longer just asks questions – he cautions Basho of the need to examine the validity of his own philosophy:

> I've waited behind you in court and heard the innocent and the guilty plead. Living women with fingers twisting like ghosts, old men staring like lost children, murderers who laughed over corpses. I marvelled at them as they talked . . . But you talk of the way as if it was laid down in an iron map. You must leave the road from time to time – to ask if it's the right road you're on.

If Bond were to develop the scene along conventional lines, the opposition between their views would result in mounting conflict between Wang and Basho. Instead, Bond makes the antithesis between the two characters the base from which he builds a dramatic illustration of how Wang must counter Basho's negative assumptions about the impossibility of change. Once more, we need to remind ourselves that Bond is concerned with presenting a dialectic as well as a narrative. The development within a scene is determined by the need to present the issues and the ideas in a way which involves the audience on a dramatic level and also 'teaches the audience their freedom in interpreting the play'.[11]

First, Wang's view of his society is explained in the dialogue with Basho – he is now convinced that the existing order should be challenged. Then Bond has Wang face the logical consequence of these views, together with the moral complexities of radical change. The focus of the second part of the scene is another child abandoned by the river. Echoes of scene one are carefully cultivated so that the contrast between Wang's action now and the Ferryman's earlier will clarify the reason for Wang's decision. Basho's reaction when he sees the bundle is subtly modified from the one he took before; he is no more concerned about this child than he was about the other one, but he seizes the opportunity to try to persuade Wang to stay on in his service: 'Heaven has done this. You take the child. Live with it in my house.' Wang refuses to compromise his newly-won freedom, so the moral dilemma of what to do about the child remains. His first approach to it is similar to the Ferryman's in scene one: he treats it with sympathy but also with fear, steeling himself to reject the claims it makes on his feelings.

At this point, Bond introduces a new element, which he had used in the Introduction of *Narrow Road to the Deep North*. The mother comes on to see what has happened to her child. The situation is far more dramatic than when Basho encounters the Peasant and his Wife in the earlier play – Wang is first confronted with his own past and asked to confirm the wisdom of the Ferryman's decision to give him life by taking the same action himself, then comes face to face with the Woman, who could just as well be the mother who had once abandoned him. Bond, however, is concerned with Wang's private psychology only insofar as it has bearing on the moral problem he wants the audience to analyse. Wang is allowed one brief expression of rage: 'Bitch! (*Hits her face.*) It could have died!' He is thinking as much about himself as about the child he is holding; having tried to persuade her to take the child off his hands before he even realised she was its mother, he is now resorting to moral self-righteousness.

The Woman's answer is an important indication of her position in the scene: 'You hit me! Will that make me take it? My husband hit me harder to get rid of it! It was torn from me! You think – one hit and you change the world?'. She questions and challenges Wang's evasions and pushes him into facing reality: he would like to save the child, but he cannot do so without selling himself to Basho; he wishes circumstances were different, but he cannot see how to change them.

In one essential, the Woman's attitude is the same as Basho's – she cannot envisage the conditions of life ever changing – although hopelessness in her case is the product of harsh experience, not the detached observation of a judge and poet indulging in the luxury of intellectual despair from the security of his privileged position in society. Both attitudes, however, show the dead weight of passive compliance with the existing order that Wang will have to shift. At the end of his first draft of this scene Bond wrote: 'There has to be more cold and darkness to give Wang's action a sufficient cause. General miasma of poverty and superstition must be spread like grease over everything.' At the same time, Bond guards against the audience taking an over-critical view of the Woman for abandoning her child – he gives her a speech in which she describes the pressures which forced the decision upon her. The stage directions are as important as the lines, because the way the speech is delivered will condition our response not only to her but to the rest of the scene:

> WOMAN (*sits wearily: speaks flatly, almost calmly and reasonably*). More anger . . . What is the use? You see how we live. I thought I'd jump in the river. Drown with it. But my husband – my children – I've done what I can. What more? You tell me what more there is. (*Slight pause. Still calm.*) I came back to give him water. Stupid. When I saw you holding him I was jealous. I wanted to shout 'My child!' and take him away. I was glad. You were clean and fed. The child had been lucky at last. He'll serve in a good house . . .

What strikes us is the accuracy and objectivity of her account. The speech is a series of independent, though connected, statements, each one delivered with thoughtfulness and deliberation. We see the Woman's exhaustion and resignation, but we also see how clearly she understands her position. There is nothing abject or self-pitying about her. She describes her condition – and that of the other villagers – precisely and dispassionately.

We are invited neither to judge the woman nor to identify with her, but to examine the conditions of her life, just as at the end of the scene we are asked to examine and assess the action Wang takes.

The Woman leaves and Wang is left alone on stage still holding the bundle. The speech which follows, like the Ferryman's long speech to the child in scene one, is in effect a soliloquy, but of a distinct kind. The tension and emotion Wang is experiencing are self-evident, but he formulates the issues very clearly, because he is no longer able to avoid making a decision. Mike Gwilym, who played Wang in the Warehouse production, describes the process the character goes through in this way: 'The steps he works through are very simple – he doesn't take any great philosophical jumps. He doesn't really discover anything he didn't know, but he works it out for once – for once, he's been given such a big problem that he has to come up with a clear-cut answer. He makes a big journey in this speech, but he makes it very quietly. Despite the emotion he feels, he is also looking at himself hard as he speaks – there are lines like "Why should I pick you up? Why do I hold you?".' He goes on to explain what this meant for him as an actor: 'I remember I once heard Edward [Bond] give a note to another member of the cast about a similar speech to this one. He suggested that she try to deliver it as if she were standing about six feet behind herself, looking at herself as she was saying it. That sort of technique does often apply in performing a play by Bond. I have found that the scenes which haven't worked in some performances of *The Bundle* were those when I was pushing at the emotion rather than playing the rationality and logic of the lines.'

Like the Ferryman before him, Wang instructs the child in why he cannot save him, though his tone is less apologetic, more aggressive than the Ferryman's had once been towards him: 'You're as big as a mountain. My back's broken. I live in his house so that you have a house? Give you the things I run away from? Nine years! I planned – no, schemed, plotted, dreamt! And now you're drowning me in the river?'. The internal struggle between human instinct and hard logic, represented in scene one by the movements of the Ferryman backwards and forwards across the river, is again shown physically, through Wang's actions in relation to the bundle. In a series of four stage directions, Bond indicates that he first puts the child down, then shortly afterwards snatches it from the ground and holds it up high to show it the river. The actions are repeated – again, he puts it down and then snatches it up. As Mike Gwilym describes it: 'Each time he talks to it, having picked it up, he's a little harder towards it and blames it a little more.' The fifth stage direction breaks the pattern and resolves the conflict: '*As he hurls the child far out into the river he holds a corner of the white sheet in his hand and it unravels, catches the wind and falls to hang from his hand.*'

Bond wants this action to shock and stun the audience, as Mike Gwilym emphasises: 'Wang's decision isn't made until the very last word – "No!". Bond doesn't want the audience to suspect at any point what Wang will do at the end of the speech.' Yet, in another sense, the whole speech, indeed the whole scene, has prepared the audience for this moment, by describing the conditions and laying out the issues which make Wang's action understandable. It is a hard lesson and Bond makes no attempt to cushion it. Wang has already stated the reason earlier in the speech: 'Is this all? – one little gush of sweetness and I pick up a child? Who picks up the rest? How can I hold my arms wide enough to hold them all?'. Isolated gestures of sympathy, like the Ferryman's in scene one, are insufficient; individual actions will not change the nature of society. The hurling of the baby into the river challenges our ability to follow through the implications of Wang's statement. It is like a slap in the face, followed by a short, sharp question, directly challenging the conventional judgement that Wang's action is 'wrong': 'The world is shivering – there! Who will speak?'.

Bond dramatizes Wang's moral dilemma, and his solution to it, in an extreme form, though effects broadly similar to this are to be found in many of Bond's earlier plays: one immediately thinks of scenes such as the baby-stoning in *Saved* or the shooting of Fred in *The Swing*, which have the same emotional impact and present in the starkest imaginable way the problem Bond is exploring in the play. The difference in *The Bundle* is that at the end of scene four Bond, having previously involved the audience in the problem, now involves them in the answer to it. The standpoint of each of the characters in the scene is first made clear, then the situation is brought to a point of crisis, culminating in a violent action. The action is in itself an enactment of the necessary first step towards a solution of the problem. Bond makes the audience commit themselves emotionally before asking them to examine their response to what is happening on the stage.

It is a fundamental break with the Brechtian tradition of epic theatre, with which Bond's dramatic method has sometimes been compared. Like Brecht, Bond wants the audience to react analytically to the incidents he shows, but instead of seeking to distance the audience from the events by interrupting the action, Bond talks of the need to involve the audience by surprising and shocking them with images which are part of the continuing action: 'Alienation is vulnerable to the audience's decision about it. Sometimes it is necessary to emotionally commit the audience – which is why I have aggro-effects.'[12]

When we next see Wang he is close to despair:

WANG *sits on the ground, doubles over, and cries.*

WANG. I ran through swamps, crying for seven days. I saw the rich prey on the poor. The poor prey on themselves. An old woman. She wore knitted mittens. Her hands were like a squirrel's paws – holding an empty bowl. She knelt by the pilgrims' path and said: 'Give – heaven will bless you.' What heaven would bless such pilgrims when it hadn't blessed her?

As Howard Davies remarks: 'There always comes a point in Bond's plays when the main character has to face a vision of horror – that the world we live in is a hell. Wang has this vision in the swamp. The development in Part One [the first five scenes], which it is important to show through the production, is that the play starts at a particular point and the situation gets worse and worse, at least until the point when Wang leaves Basho.'

In scene five, Wang takes the first positive step towards changing his world. His alliance with the bandits who trick and capture him in the swamp is as decisive in its effect as Hecuba's alliance with the Dark Man in *The Woman*. Despite his understanding of the need for change, Wang is insufficient in himself; he cannot act alone. The bandits and their leader, Tiger, already constitute one form of opposition to the established order, however crude and undirected, as Howard Davies explains: '. . . the bandits are the lowest of the low; they have nothing, like everybody else in that society. Yet Part One ends with the fact that they at least "live" and have the energy to fight. No-one else has the energy to do anything. The bandits actually spend energy on fighting and robbing and thieving and stealing and all the rest of it. They are the complete social outcasts and yet they are the most vital thing in the whole of Part One. And Wang goes and joins them.'[13]

Bond had originally conceived of Tiger as a smaller part, merely one among a number of bandits, but he has described how the character 'became far more and more prominent in my mind as I wrote the play, forcing himself into my consciousness'. His energy is expressed not only in violent action but through the rhythm of his speeches, which Bond chops into short sentences, often consisting of no more than a single word: 'So – I enter. Kowtow. Rise. Left hand shuts his mouth. Right hand: on throat. Squeeze. Like a bag of beans. (*He holds his stump up.*) Dead. Then walk down street. Still hold. One hand: throat. Lift him up. One hand. Show.' This story of Tiger's about how he lost his hand is a fine display of unbridled individualism and contempt for the kind of justice which Basho no doubt deals out, but his limitations are plain to see: 'Tiger really only has actions and a form of opportunism . . . There is very little he can do. He doesn't have concepts that interpret his experience in the way that Wang has, and in order to show this I cut off his hand.'[14]

The short mime play Wang persuades the bandits to enact, with Wang taking the part of the landowner, is the start of the process through which he overturns the landowner's power in the real world. Wang demonstrates to them, in terms they understand, the control which the landowner and Basho exercise over all their lives: 'I was the servant of a great thief. He covered his floors, walls, ceilings with loot. It filled his attics and cellars. It grew in his garden. There was so much loot he built store-houses.' It is not Tiger but Kaka, one of the other bandits, who begins to work out for himself the logical answer to the social and economic situation they have acted out: '. . . Why don't . . . the people . . . build a wall round the river? . . . Then they don't need your protection.' Bond offers a paradigm of the first prerequisite for changing society: the education of its members in a critical awareness of the nature of their oppression.

The Bundle is not a play about political tactics. Although Wang leads a successful revolution in Part Two, we are told little about the practical details of how it is achieved. In the first three scenes in

Part Two (six, seven and eight), the key incidents are those which show the difficulty Wang has in breaking through the set responses of others in the community towards their society – their acceptance of what they know and their fear of change. Wang is the agent of change, but it is the other characters in Part Two who carry the weight of Bond's argument. The smaller parts in *The Bundle* make a larger contribution towards developing this argument than in any other of his plays. In Part Two the focus detectably shifts away from Wang.

In scene five, the Ferryman and his Wife are presented with a moral dilemma which arises directly from Wang's revolutionary activities. Wang, who is now being hunted by the authorities, goes back to the Ferryman's hut with Tiger to ask his father to ferry rifles for them across the river. For a large part of the scene, the situation is played out between Wang and the Ferryman, who resists the idea on the grounds that, if he were caught, nobody would be left to nurse and care for his wife. All Wang's logical arguments fail to move him. In frustration, Wang lashes out against the blindness and ineffectiveness of his father's morality. His attack is based on the lesson he learned for himself at the end of scene four: the Ferryman made his moral gesture in picking Wang up from the river-bank, but what about the tenth child, or the hundredth? Not only has his action had no effect on the social conditions which led to Wang being abandoned, it has hastened his wife's death. The Ferryman still backs away from the logical inference that individual acts of humanity will only maintain injustice, not help to remove it. It is left to the Ferryman's Wife to break the deadlock by telling him to do what Wang asks. At the same time, she points out to Wang how much he owes to his father. As Howard Davies says:

> Bond doesn't come down totally on the side of Wang though, for he allows the Mother to say: "Allright, you're right; but remember you wouldn't be here if your father hadn't picked you up." She says that she could see that it was necessary for Wang to suppress his humane resources in order to achieve larger ends but that he was to remember that they were absolutely vital.'[15]

The Ferryman agrees, but even now he compromises with his conscience by rationalising what he is doing: 'I'll take the rifles. I've loved and hated. The river kept me alive and almost killed me. Now it will carry the rifles. I shall be careful. Your mother will be safe.'

The crux for the Ferryman and then for the Ferryman's Wife comes in scene eight. Basho confronts the Ferryman with his complicity in the rebellion. The soldiers prepare to search for Wang. Tiger, his tongue and remaining hand cut off by the soldiers, stands in front of him. The hub of the scene is the Ferryman's request to give Tiger a bowl of water:

> FERRYMAN (*to the* FIRST SOLDIER, *points to* TIGER). Some water . . . ?
> FIRST SOLDIER. Why bother? Too late.

The soldier's remark introduces into our minds the suspicion that the Ferryman is about to indulge in yet another humane gesture which will unfortunately do nothing to change Tiger's situation, or Wang's, or his own. Instead, the bowl is the focus of the Ferryman's decision to resist Basho and to save Wang. Bob Peck, who played the part in the Warehouse production, explains, step by step, the stages that the Ferryman's thoughts go through: 'He feels that, since there's a man suffering, he might as well do something about it while they are waiting. The difficulty Tiger has in drinking is a great shock. Then it comes as no surprise when Tiger is hauled out, but there is another shock when he sees that the bowl is full of blood. By then, he has had time to think, while going to fetch the water. As a result of coming into contact with this mutilated, tongueless man, and knowing that Wang is next in line unless he does something about it, he decides the only useful thing he can do is to save Wang.'

What is particularly interesting about this description of the Ferryman's thought processes is that much of it is an account of the subtext which the actor has created on the basis of the lines and actions the character is given. Bond does not show all of these steps in the way they are described here. However essential this understanding of the character may be for an actor playing the part, he cannot play the subtext because the lines give him no scope to do so. The Ferryman's decision is shown to the audience in this way:

> FERRYMAN (*simply and calmly, as if he no longer had to struggle with his thoughts but knew what to say. He holds the water in front of him. Close to his chest*). Why are our lives wasted? We have minds to see how we suffer. Why don't we use them to change the world? . . .

At the end of the speech there is the following stage direction: '*Noiselessly, carefully he puts down the bowl.*' Bob Peck describes how the bowl is used as the focus of the speech: 'I have learned that the Ferryman's first question has to be pushed out directly to the audience. Doing that integrates it with the bowl image. If the audience isn't included directly in that first question, the effect is lost when I put the bowl down at the end of the speech. If I have included them, when the bowl finally goes down it's as if it is offering it to them and saying: "Look – this is what we are doing." The image is integrated into the speech.'

In the previous scene (scene seven), Wang and Tiger, disguised as priests, sit passively by and watch a Woman being punished for stealing cabbage leaves by having to support a heavy stone which is tied to her neck. The situation is analogous to that in *Narrow Road to the Deep North* where Kiro and Shogo are escaping from the city disguised as beggar priests. Shogo, like Tiger in this scene, urges that they should take on the soldiers and fight them. In the earlier play, this situation is simply part of the narrative. Here, Wang's inaction represents another step in the dialogue Bond is conducting with the audience:

> Normally people would say that the man is being cold, pathological, diseased. What I wanted to show was the effort it cost him to make that decision, which was a very human effort . . . He is human and he wants to go and help that woman but he knows that that would be ineffectual; simply that it would not alter the conditions that have put her in that situation. So, how does one show that? One shows him talking calmly, quietly because that is what one has to do. One has to think of these situations. And then one has to find some way of physically showing on the stage the passion that he is controlling.[16]

As Wang sits there, drawing the moral for Tiger that action at the wrong time is not the answer, '*there is a sudden fall of blood from*

WANG'S *mouth. As he talks it runs down his chin.'* The shock effect not only ensures that one is aware of how much Wang's inaction costs him, it also startles one into listening even more attentively to what the character is saying. The news that the landowner is running from the district, on the pretence of visiting the capital for a few weeks, at last gives Wang his opportunity. He breaks the stone on the Woman's neck. The Watersellers, and the Woman herself, react with fear and amazement to the removal of authority and repression from their lives. Slowly, the Watersellers absorb the implications of this new situation. They give the Woman food and water.

The revolution Wang achieves is not shown through scenes of violence. Scene nine, which is set at the height of the rebellion, opens with two isolated shots in the distance – this is all we hear or see of it. It is shown instead through every detail of the behaviour of the Watersellers towards the Woman. As Bond explained at rehearsals: 'A lot of it has to do with the way you handle the cup and the bottle, and even the cork. It's as if you were laying down a new set of laws for yourself. The moment Tiger and Wang remove that authority from over your lives, there is a new possibility. It could go bad. But it doesn't. You have to learn to move and act and think in a new way.'

While the peasant characters show their strength and begin to learn to use their freedom, Basho becomes more vicious. Bond summarised it in a note in his first draft, referring to Wang's refusal to stay on in Basho's service: 'Later Basho turns sour, like all those people who spend a little emotion and expect a regular dividend back – this bitterness comes out in his relationship with the Ferryman later on. We must see how an unprincipled goodness becomes self-serving and destructive.' We have already noted Bond's concern for the design of an interior scene in the case of the prison scene in *The Fool*. When Basho condemns the Ferryman to death, Bond uses the set to provide a visual image which will express the relationship between the characters on stage:

> What I wanted to do with the window as the scene went on was to show it being pulled apart by the soldiers. At the end I wanted it to be very clear that the people – Basho, the Commanding Officer and the soldiers – were not actually related in any dignified human sense . . . They were, in fact, all isolated, seeking their own ends in that particu-

lar set-up. I wanted to show how Basho gets himself into a totally dehumanised situation because he is talking about haiku to somebody he doesn't even look at and he uses it to sentence him to death. I wanted him to be looking in one direction, the soldiers to be looking in another and the Ferryman to whom they were speaking to be completely off, and for a wall with a hole in it to stand between the man giving the order and the man receiving it.[17]

Scene nine also shows the isolation of the oppressors, as Basho and the merchant Kung Tu cower in a room in Basho's house, each preoccupied with what the success of Wang's revolution would involve. The last scene, in contrast, opens out into a sense of spaciousness and ease. It is a scene of communal relaxation after the revolution.

Wang, three of the bandits and some peasants are resting from building a bank to prevent the river flooding. The situation is similar in almost every respect to that in the final scene of Bond's 'Text for a Ballet'. It is centred not on Wang but on the death of one of the workers in the river, an incident which Bond offsets against the utopian image of the peasants at the beginning of the scene – tragedy exists even in this post-revolutionary world.

Bond compares this genuine tragedy with the broken and reduced state that Basho has been brought to – a state which, as we see him stumble on, is appalling to watch, but should not elicit any moral sympathy. His despairing assault on the corpse and his cries as he gropes his way among the audience, still in search of enlightenment, are juxtaposed with Wang's parable of the man who carried a dead king on his back and his final address to the audience: 'We live in a time of great change. It is easy to find monsters – and as easy to find heroes. To judge rightly what is good – to choose between good and evil – that is all that it is to be human.' It is a simple and direct statement of philosophy, and its truth has been tried and tested in the course of the play, as Mike Gwilym attests: 'Actors are always worried about patronising an audience or lecturing to them. But the real criterion is whether the play has earned the right to say such a thing. All the actor should try to do is to share with the audience the point which the character has got to. Bond's other constant theme in *The Bundle* is: "What has it cost?" – and if it has cost enough, you earn the right to say it.'

Bond does not offer readymade solutions to the social and political problems he describes. The plays explore and investigate the nature of human behaviour in societies which, like our own, inhibit and destroy natural human responses and turn people against each other. At the same time Bond's main argument, even in the least optimistic plays, is that change is both necessary and possible. In a recent interview, Bond talked of the need 'to make the analysis of politics part of the aesthetic experience'. His theatre can only properly be understood in the light of that statement. Its implications, for those who work on the plays and for those who see them in the theatre, are only now being fully grasped.

Notes

Notes to Introduction

1. Richard Wherrett, programme note for a production of *The Sea*, Nimrod Theatre, Australia, May 1979.
2. *T.Q.* 5, p. 5.
3. *Guardian*, 24 November 1976.
4. *Plays and Players*, December 1975.
5. *Theatre Papers*, p. 2.
6. *New Statesman*, 24 March 1956.
7. *The Stage*, 28 July 1955.
8. Quoted by T. Browne, *Playwrights' Theatre* (Pitman, 1975), p. 9.
9. *T.Q.* 5, p. 7.
10. An account of the Writers' Group by Ann Jellicoe is in *Ambit* 68 (1976), pp. 61–4.
11. Peter Gill, letter to Tony Coult, 17 May 1971; letter to R. Scharine, 12 August 1971. Gill names one of the two plays as 'He Jumped but the Bridge was Burning' but no such title exists in the drafts.
12. M. Hay and P. Roberts, 'Edward Bond: Stages in a Life', *Observer Magazine*, 6 August 1978.
13. *Theatre Papers*, p. 25.
14. Letter to U. Innig, 18 March 1977.
15. *Theatre Papers*, p. 8.

Notes to Chapter 1

1. *T.Q.* 5, p. 13.
2. T. Browne, *Playwrights' Theatre* (Pitman, 1975), pp. 37–9.
3. A year later, Devine was cautious about Bond's work and others': 'There are quite a number of what I call second-string or even third-string dramatists who've been around this place for ages. People like Edward Bond, Keith Johnstone and so on. I can't give them the

opportunities I should be able to give them' (interview with Irving Wardle, 12 December 1963. We are grateful to Mr. Wardle for this reference).

4. In view of its reception, and of course as an indication of the very small number of people who saw the performance, it is a pity that the play to date has received only six professional productions since 1962, in Hamburg (1971), Exeter (1973, and subsequently at the Bush theatre, London), Birmingham (1973), Frankfurt (1975), Vienna (1975) and Bochum (1975).
5. *T.Q.* 5, p. 7.
6. *Scharine*, p. 34.
7. *Ibid.*
8. *Gambit* 17, p. 28.
9. *Loney*, p. 45.
10. *T.Q.* 5, p. 7.
11. *Stoll*, p. 419.
12. 'Conversation with Philip Roberts', British Council Tape Series, recorded 31 March 1977.
13. *Loney*, p. 44.
14. 'Exercises for Young Writers', 28 March 1977; *Companion*, pp. 48–50. Cf. Brecht's 'Short Description of a New Technique of Acting which Produces an Alienation Effect' (1940): 'everything to do with the emotions has to be externalized; that is to say, it must be developed into a gesture. The actor has to find a sensibly perceptible outward expression for his character's emotions, preferably some action that gives away what is going on inside him'; J. Willett, *Brecht on Theatre* (Methuen, 1965), p. 139.
15. Of *The Outing*, 9 February 1960.
16. 'Plays', undated typescript, probably written shortly after *Saved*.
17. *Ibid.*
18. *Op. cit.*, n. 12.
19. *Op. cit.*, n. 16.
20. *Loney*, p. 44.

Notes to Chapter 2

1. Letter to R. Scharine, 19 March 1971.
2. See the account in T. Browne, *Playwrights' Theatre* (Pitman, 1975), chapter 4.
3. A list of reviews may be found in the *Companion*, pp. 79–80.
4. They are detailed in the *Companion*, pp. 80–2.
5. *T.Q.* 5, pp. 7–8.
6. *Loney*, p. 44.

7. *T.Q.* 5, p. 11.
8. *Listener*, 13 February 1969.
9. Letter to *The Observer*, 21 November 1965.
10. *The Theban Plays*, translated E. F. Watling (Penguin, 1949), p. 68.
11. Letter to Tony Coult, 28 July 1977; *Companion*, p. 74.
12. T. E. Kalem, *Time*, 9 November 1970 (of Schneider's New York production).
13. Letter to R. Scharine, 2 October 1974. The published version (*Scharine*, p. 73) changes the quotation.
14. *Gambit* 17, p. 16.
15. *Ibid.*, p. 23.
16. *T.Q.* 5, p. 11.
17. 'Stage Design for the Epic Theatre' (1951); J. Willett, *Brecht on Theatre* (Methuen, 1965), pp. 230–33.
18. *Gambit* 17, pp. 40–1.
19. *Plays and Players*, December 1975.
20. M. Mindlin, *Forum World Features*, week of 27 November 1965.
21. Ms. transcript of the teach-in.
22. *Gambit* 17, p. 29. Cf. Brecht's note to *Man equals Man*, where the epic actor 'has to be able to show his character's coherence despite, or rather by means of, interruptions and jumps. Since everything depends on the development, on the flow, the various phases must be able to be clearly seen, and therefore separated . . .'; *Willett, op. cit.*, p. 55. Elsewhere, Brecht, somewhat sarcastically, alludes to actors who 'fall on whatever is "inexpressible", between the lines, because it calls for their gifts' (note to *The Mother, Willett, op. cit.*, p. 59).
23. Ms. transcript of the teach-in.
24. *T.Q.* 21, pp. 22–3 (Mick Ford, Roderick Smith and David Troughton).
25. *Stoll*, p. 415.
26. 'On Brecht: a Letter to Peter Holland', *T.Q.* 30, pp. 34–5.
27. 'Brecht in Newcastle', *Arena*, B.B.C.2, 8 December 1976.
28. *Op. cit.*, n. 26.
29. *Op. cit.*, n. 26.
30. *Willett, op. cit.*, pp. 270–1.

Notes to Chapter 3

1. *Gambit* 17, p. 15.
2. *Ibid.*, p. 17.
3. *Ibid.*, p. 14.
4. Letter to R. Scharine, 2 October 1974.

5. Bond, letter to M. Whitaker, 6 November 1969. When Bond prepared the play for *Plays: One*, he reverted to his original script. The only speech left of the revisions is that of Len at the end of the eighth scene. Bond feels that the changes 'took away the "journey" element in the play (which I think is important), on the well-made-play principle that the hero has to dominate throughout' (letter to the authors, 22 April 1979).
6. Letter to Tony Coult, 27 May 1971.
7. Letter to R. Scharine, 2 October 1974.
8. *Gambit* 17, p. 14.
9. Programme note for *Narrow Road to the Deep North*, Belgrade Theatre, Coventry, June 1968.
10. *New York Times*, 2 January 1972. The reference could well be to Aeschylus's trilogy, *The Oresteia*, in which Orestes inherits the curse upon the house of Atreus for Tantalus's crime in feasting the gods upon his son's flesh and Thyestes's curse upon Atreus for feeding Thyestes with his children at a banquet. Atreus and his sons 'are cursed, their lives are an inherited disease, a miasma that threatens the health of their community and forces them, relentlessly, to commit their fathers' crimes. It is as if crime were contagious ... the dead pursued the living for revenge, and revenge could only breed more guilt' (*The Oresteia* ed. R. Fagles and W. B. Stanford (Penguin, 1977), pp. 16–17). Orestes is finally released from the blood guilt by the intervention of Athena and returns to Argos to begin again. Bond, like Aeschylus, places salvation not 'in the city of god. It is in the city of man, where paradise must be earned with every passing day ... If Aeschylus celebrates progress, it is not as a limp myth of perfectibility but as a march, a never-ending effort' (*Ibid.*, p. 93).

Notes to Chapter 4

1. 'The Lively Arts', B.B.C. Radio 4, 26 March 1969. Bond repeats the opinion in *Gambit* 17, pp. 31–2.
2. *The Narrow Road to the Deep North and Other Travel Sketches*. Translated and introduced by N. Yuasa (Penguin, 1966; reprinted 1975). It was this translation which Bond read.
3. *Op. cit.*, n. 1.
4. *Loney*, p. 43.
5. *Gambit* 17, p. 32.
6. *Op. cit.*, n. 1.
7. Gaskill to R. Scharine, 19 March 1971. The Belgrade, Coventry, production was the first of three productions of the play by Jane

Howell. After Coventry, the play transferred to the Royal Court (February 1969), was part of the English Stage Company's

7. (Cont'd.) European tour (together with *Saved*, September-October 1969) and, on her appointment as Artistic Director of the Northcott Theatre, Exeter, she opened her season with the play (April 1971), using it, as she recalls 'to train a group of actors and [as] a statement of policy'. The Coventry production was her first collaboration with the then resident designer of the Belgrade, Hayden Griffin, who subsequently went to the Northcott.
8. 26 February 1969; 28 November 1969 (of the Boston production); 31 October 1969 (Boston); *The Boston Globe*, 3 November 1969. Other critics were more accurate: A. Friedman, *Educational Theatre Journal*, 22, no. 1, March 1970; B. Dukore, *Ibid.*, 24, no. 2, May 1972; H. Clurman, *The Nation*, 24 January 1972 and D. A. N. Jones, *Listener*, 6 March 1969.
9. Bond, 'Conversation with Philip Roberts', British Council Tape Series, recorded 31 March 1977.
10. *Gambit* 17, p. 28.
11. *Plays and Players*, October 1968.
12. *Op. cit.*, n. 9.
13. To Howard Davies; *Companion*, p. 59.
14. In the first two drafts, the man goes across to Kiro and realises that he is dead. In the third draft, the man, with his back to Kiro, ignores him and dries himself.
15. *Gambit* 17, p. 35.
16. 'On Brecht: a Letter to Peter Holland', *T.Q.* 30, p. 34.
17. *Plays and Players*, October 1968.
18. Bond, 'Letter to Irene', 7 January 1970; *Companion*, p. 43.
19. Peter Holland, 'Brecht, Bond, Gaskill, and the Practice of Political Theatre', *T.Q.* 30, p. 30.
20. *Gambit* 17, p. 10.
21. *Op. cit.*, n. 18.
22. *Op. cit.*, n. 16, p. 35.
23. 'From the Mother Courage Model'. In J. Willett, *Brecht on Theatre* (Methuen, 1965), p. 221. See also 'Conversation about being forced into Empathy', *Ibid.*, pp. 270–71.

Notes to Chapter 5

1. To Geoffrey Strachan, 1 November 1971.
2. Quoted *Scharine*, p. 166. Bond sent a version of the Brecht play to Gaskill, asking if it could be put on at the Royal Court (21 July 1970).

3. *Gambit* 17, pp. 43–5. The essay was originally a letter of 19 November 1969 to Hack who was directing *Measure for Measure* in Cambridge.
4. *The King with Golden Eyes* is published with *The Pope's Wedding* (Eyre Methuen, 1971), as is 'Play for Sharpeville 70' (*Black Mass*). The other items are unpublished, although some of the poems are in *Theatre Poems and Songs* (Eyre Methuen, 1978).
5. *Times*, 13 December 1968; *Telegraph and Argus*, 27 September 1969.
6. *Gambit* 17, p. 24 (22 January 1970).
7. Amongst the books Bond read and used during this stage were: M. F. Ashley Montagu, *Man and Aggression* (OUP, 1963); C. H. Southwick, *Animal Aggression* (Van Nostrand Reinhold Co., New York, 1970); C. and W. M. A. Russell, *Violence, Monkeys and Men* (Macmillan, 1968) and G. Hardin (ed.), *Science, Conflict and Society: Readings from Scientific American* (W. H. Freeman, San Francisco, 1969). Much of this section finds its way into the opening parts of the 'Author's Preface' to *Lear*.
8. Within these details about blindness, there is a note on 9 December: 'A general retires'. The alliance of blindness and a military commander provided the basis of *We Come to the River*, which Bond began to write in the autumn of 1972.
9. Both references are from: 'Conversation with Philip Roberts,' British Council Tape Series, recorded 31 March 1977.
10. The 'fountain of blood' derives from the fact that around this time Bond put water into a dry well in his garden. The water turned red from the minerals in the soil.
11. Bond has said that the image of the Gravedigger's Boy began the play (*T.Q.* 5, p. 8).
12. The wall image derives from the remains of Devil's Dyke, near to Bond's home. In conversation with the authors, Bond pointed out the peculiarity of the Dyke and the unnatural silence which exists at the base of the ancient earthworks.
13. In *Theatre Poems and Songs* (Eyre Methuen, 1978), p. 7.
14. G. Dark. 'Edward Bond's "Lear" at the Royal Court', *T.Q.* 5, pp. 20–31. The following analysis of the play draws on Gregory Dark's account in *T.Q.*, and from his unpublished log of Bond's own production of *Lear*, which opened at the Burgtheater, Vienna, on 27 January 1973. Where the quotation has a page number, it comes from *T.Q.*. Where not, unless otherwise stated, the quotation is from Bond's copy of the Vienna Log.
15. *The Messingkauf Dialogues*, translated by J. Willett (Methuen, 1965), pp. 42–3.
16. *Ibid.*, p. 30.

17. *Ibid.*, p. 103.
18. *Ibid.*, pp. 103–4.
19. From the typescript of the *T.Q.* Log, but not published. Dated 12 August.
20. 'Scan', B.B.C. Radio 4, 30 September 1971.
21. *Guardian*, 29 September 1971.
    Writing to the authors in April 1979, Bond comments on his views of 1971: 'I would now want to explain this. Lenin entered a situation of violence – and could revolutionary violence have seemed too extreme faced with the war-violence of the great powers? Lenin would say that he would use (and couldn't avoid the use of it) violence for constructive purposes and not the destructive ones of the great powers. I think that Lenin had no alternative to doing what he did – except to do nothing'.
22. *Stoll*, p. 420.
23. From the typescript of the *T.Q.* Log, but not published. Dated 11 August.
24. Bond, letter to C. Meyerson, 28 March 1977.
25. Bond, letter to H. Uwer, 28 August 1978.
26. *Op. cit.*, n. 9.
27. *Op. cit.*, n. 21.

Notes to Chapter 6

1. 'Conversation with Philip Roberts,' British Council Tape Series, recorded 31 March 1977.
2. First notes on *The Sea*, April-June 1971.
3. As quoted by W. Woodman, interviewed by R. Dettmer, *Chicago Tribune*, 17 November 1974.
4. As quoted by W. Woodman in a letter to his assistant director, 21 July 1974; *Companion*, p. 56.
5. *Op. cit.*, n. 2.
6. Bond, letter to Tom H. Wild, 16 January 1977; *Companion*, p. 57.
7. *Op. cit.*, n. 4.
8. Interviewed by R. Hayman, *Times*, 22 May 1973.
9. *Op. cit.*, n. 4.
10. *Op. cit.*, n. 2.
11. *Op. cit.*, n. 6.
12. *Op. cit.*, n. 2.
13. S. Trussler, *Tribune*, 8 June 1973.
14. *Scharine*, p. 232.
15. *Op. cit.*, n. 4.
16. *Op. cit.*, n. 6.

17. *T.Q.* 5, p. 14.
18. *Loney*, p. 38.
19. *Op. cit.*, n. 6.
20. I. Wardle, *Times*, 24 May 1973.
21. *Loney*, p. 38.
22. *Op. cit.*, n. 6.
23. *Ibid.*
24. *Loney*, pp. 44–5.

Notes to Chapter 7

1. P. Heyworth, *Observer*, 18 July 1976.
2. 'Author's Preface' to *Lear*; *Plays: Two*, p. 12.
3. Henze, interviewed by R. Blackford, *Music and Musicians*, July 1976.
4. Henze, *Instructions for Production*, B. Schott's Söhne: Mainz.
5. *Ibid.*
6. *Ibid.*
7. Henze, *Time Out*, 16–22 July 1976.
8. Quoted in German by Hans-Klaus Jungheinrich, 'Zwei Autoren nähern sich einem Stoff', *Akzente* 2, April 1977.

Notes to Chapter 8

1. Letter to Tony Coult, 28 July 1977; *Companion*, p. 74.
2. Letter to T. H. Wild, 16 January 1977; *Companion*, p. 57.
3. *Plays and Players*, December 1975.
4. Letter to Les Waters, 13 June 1974; *Companion*, pp. 54–5.
5. *Ibid.*
6. S. Schoenbaum, *Times Literary Supplement*, 30 August 1974, p. 920.
7. Letter to U. Innig, 18 March 1977.
8. *Western Morning News*, 9 November 1973.
9. *Stoll*, p. 422.
10. See, for example, Albert Hunt, 'A Writer's Theatre', *New Society*, 11 December 1975.
11. Notes for *The Sea*, 30 April 1971. Bond explained the phrase from Leonardo as being 'very appropriate for someone like Shakespeare who has been the most influential dramatist since the Greeks' (Conversation with Howard Davies, *Companion*, p. 59). Leonardo's own words are to be found in *The Notebooks of Leonardo da Vinci*, Arranged, Rendered into English and Introduced by E.

MacCurdy, 2 vols. (London, Cape, 1938), II, pp. 522, 527, 529 etc.

12. Letter to Geoffrey Strachan, 21 October 1973. It would appear that the play had in fact been offered to the Royal Court initially. According to *Plays and Players* (March 1974) there were difficulties over casting the main part, as a result of which the play was given to the Northcott. After its subsequent success at the Royal Court (August 1974), it was to have transferred to the National theatre with John Gielgud playing Prospero in *The Tempest*, and Shakespeare, but the plan never materialised, principally because of the Court's very long financial negotiations, which 'prevented us from selling *Bingo* to the National' (Margaret Ramsay to R. Kidd and N. Wright, 31 January 1975). The play was thus performed for the first time by a company, including director and designer, which had stayed together for nearly three years. Hayden Griffin recalls that it was a great advantage to have a company intimately aware of the nature of the large Northcott stage. The play was designed for one theatre and, when it transferred to the smaller dimensions of the Royal Court (August 1974), neither director nor designer were pleased with the result, although the London showing broke all previous box-office records for the Court. Griffin remembers that 'the dates had been fixed rather quickly and, in the end, we had a very short time ... we took the wrong decision in trying to recreate, on that little stage, the space we had in Exeter' (*Plays and Players*, June 1976).
13. To Howard Davies; *Companion*, p. 60.
14. Letter to Tony Coult, 24 March 1977.
15. Letter to Philip Roberts, 24 October 1976.
16. To Howard Davies; *Companion*, pp. 61–2.
17. *Ibid.*, p. 62.
18. To M. Ferrand, 6 November 1973; *Theatre Papers*, p. 6.
19. *Sunday Times*, 25 November 1973.
20. *New Haven Register*, 25 January 1976.
21. *Stoll*, p. 420.
22. Bond, *Sunday Times*, 25 November 1973.
23. First notes on *The Fool*, March 1974.
24. Bond, interviewed by Tony Coult, *Plays and Players*, December 1975.
25. Letter to Louis Scheeder, 27 September 1976; *Companion*, p. 63.
26. *Op. cit.*, n. 23.
27. *Op. cit.*, n. 25, pp. 64–5.
28. *Op. cit.*, n. 23.
29. *Op. cit.*, n. 24.
30. *T.Q.* 21, p. 44.
31. *Op. cit.*, n. 23.

32. *Ibid.*
33. *T.Q.* 21, p. 29.
34. *Ibid.*, p. 16.
35. *Op. cit.*, n. 23.
36. *Op. cit.*, n. 25, p. 65.
37. *Ibid.*, pp. 65–6.
38. *Ibid.*, p. 66.
39. 'Clare Poems', *The Fool*, p. 76.
40. *Sunday Times*, 23 November 1975.
41. *Op. cit.*, n. 23.
42. *Op. cit.*, n. 25, p. 66.
43. Letter to Ruth Leeson, 14 January 1977; *Companion*, p. 67.

Notes to Chapter 9

1. From Bond's unpublished adaptation. Quotations in this chapter from 'The Palace of Varieties' and 'Text for a Ballet' are also taken from the unpublished scripts.
2. Letter to Geoffrey Strachan, 14 May 1976. Bond has also commented: '*Grandma Faust* is meant to be a forerunner to *The Swing* – and, I hope, eventually to a short final play set in the present decade: so you will then see three stages of racial conflict' letter to Malcolm Hay and Philip Roberts, 22 April 1979).
3. Notes on *Grandma Faust*, January 1976.
4. Bond, letter to Philip Roberts, 24 October 1976.
5. *Op. cit.*, n. 3.
6. Letter to Tony Coult, early 1977.
7. 'Do I carry a burden?
   All people in an unfree society carry a burden.
   Is homosexuality a burden?
   No. Why should it be? But you may be made to feel it's a burden.
   So it is not a burden?
   No, all people in an unfree society carry the *same* burden.
   What is that burden?
   Stone . . . Stone . . .'
   These lines do not appear in the text of the play published by Eyre Methuen, which had already been printed to coincide with the opening.
8. *Gay News* 97, 17–30 June 1976.
9. Bertolt Brecht, 'The Exception and the Rule', translated by Ralph Manheim, in *The Measures Taken and other Lehrstücke* (Eyre Methuen, 1977), p. 37.
10. Bond, letter to Angela Praesent, 25 January 1977; *Companion*, p. 73.

11. *Ibid.*
12. *Ibid.*
13. Nine of these songs appear in *Edward Bond: Theatre Poems and Songs*, edited by Malcolm Hay and Philip Roberts, Eyre Methuen, 1978.

Notes to Chapter 10

1. As quoted by Malcolm Hay and Philip Roberts, 'Edward Bond: Stages in a Life', *Observer*, 6 August 1978.
2. Unpublished interview with Tony Coult, August 1978.
3. Bond, draft of article for *Socialist Challenge*, August 1978.
4. Notes on *The Woman*, April 1975.
5. 'Us, Our Drama and the National Theatre', *Plays and Players*, October 1978.
6. *Op. cit.*, n. 3.
7. *Ibid.*
8. From 'On the Red Floor Covering', one of a group of poems Bond wrote for inclusion in the programme for the National theatre production; printed in *The Woman*, pp. 115–6.
9. *Op. cit.*, n. 5.
10. From 'On the Olivier', written July 1978.
11. *Op. cit.*, n. 5.
12. *Op. cit.*, n. 2.
13. Notes on *The Woman*, September 1976.
14. *Ibid.*
15. *Ibid.*
16. *Op. cit.*, n. 4.
17. *Op. cit.*, n. 2.
18. *Op. cit.*, n. 3.
19. *Op. cit.*, n. 4.
20. 'Creating what is normal', *Plays and Players*, December 1975.
21. Bond, 'Notes on acting *The Woman*', July 1978; written for the cast of the National theatre production.
22. *Op. cit.*, n. 5.
23. In *The Woman*, pp. 129–30.
24. *Op. cit.*, n. 4.
25. *Ibid.*
26. *Op. cit.*, n. 2.
27. *Ibid.*
28. *Ibid.*
29. *Op. cit.*, n. 2.

30. *Ibid.*
31. *Op. cit.*, n. 13.
32. Notes on *The Woman*, January 1977.
33. *Op. cit.*, n. 4.
34. *Op. cit.*, n. 5.

Notes to Chapter 11

1. Letter to Tony Coult, 28 July 1977; *Companion*, pp. 74–5.
2. Bond, interviewed by Tony Coult, *Time Out*, 13–19 January 1978.
3. 'Work in Hand', *Guardian*, 13 January 1978.
4. *Theatre Papers*, p. 11.
5. *Ibid.*, p. 19.
6. *Ibid.*, p. 20.
7. *Ibid.*, p. 19.
8. Bond, 'On Brecht: A Letter to Peter Holland'; *T.Q.* 30, p. 34.
9. *Op. cit.*, n. 4, pp. 24–5.
10. *Op. cit.*, n. 4, pp. 4–5.
11. Bond, 'A Note on Dramatic Method'; *The Bundle*, p. xix.
12. *Op. cit.*, n. 8.
13. *Op. cit.*, n. 4, p. 15.
14. *Ibid.*, p. 22.
15. *Op. cit.*, n. 4, p. 14.
16. *Ibid.*, pp. 20–1.
17. *Ibid.*, p. 24.

Bibliography

What follows lists all primary and secondary sources used in the preparation of this book. A comprehensive bibliography about Edward Bond, together with details of all professional productions from 1962–1978, may be found in the authors' *Edward Bond: A Companion to the Plays* (Theatre Quarterly Publications, 1978).

PRIMARY SOURCES

1. *Plays* (unperformed)

1. 'The Tragedy', radio play.
2. 'A Woman Weeping'.
3. 'The Asses of Kish', for the *Observer* Play Competition (1956–57).
4. 'Too Late Now', radio play.
5. 'Sylo's New Ruins', radio play.
6. 'The Performance', radio play.
7. 'The Best Laid Schemes', radio play.
8. 'The Roller Coaster'.
9. 'The Broken Shepherdess', television play.
10. 'Klaxon in Atreus' Place', submitted to the Royal Court Theatre, 1958.
11. 'The Fiery Tree', submitted to the Royal Court Theatre, 1958.
12. 'I Don't Want to Be Nice' (sketch for 'Stars in Our Eyes'), written for the Writers' Group, Royal Court Theatre, 1959.
13. 'The Golden Age', written for the Writers' Group, Royal Court Theatre, October 1959.
14. 'The Outing', written for the Writers' Group, Royal Court Theatre, December 1959 – March 1960.
15. 'Kissing the Beast', television play, 1960.
16. 'The Palace of Varieties in the Sand', written December 1975 – January 1976.
17. A further work, 'Text for a Ballet: for Dancers, Chorus and Orchestra' (written January–February 1977) awaits its first performance.)

Note: Nos. 1–16 are not available for performance, scrutiny or publication.

2. *Plays* (performed)

Unless stated otherwise place of publication is London; and the mss. are in the possession of Edward Bond.

1. *The Pope's Wedding*. Mss. A–D. Written January 1961–early 1962. Eyre Methuen, 1971. Revised for *Plays: One*. Eyre Methuen, 1977.
2. *Saved*. Mss. A–H. Written March–September 1964 (Mss. deposited in the Lilly Library, Indiana University). Eyre Methuen, 1966 (with 'Author's Preface'); second edition, 1969, reprinted 1971, 1973, 1976. Revised with a new note 'On Violence' for *Plays: One*. Eyre Methuen, 1977.
3. *Early Morning*. Mss. A-L. Written January 1965–7. Calder and Boyars, 1968; reprinted 1971, 1977. Revised for *Plays: One*. Eyre Methuen, 1977.
4. *Narrow Road to the Deep North. A Comedy*. Mss. A–D. Written February–April 1968. Eyre Methuen, 1968; reprinted 1973, 1976. Revised for *Plays: Two*. Eyre Methuen, 1978.
5. *Black Mass*. Mss. A–B. Written early 1970. Published in no. 1 and in *Plays: Two*. Eyre Methuen, 1978.
6. *Passion. A Play for C.N.D.* Mss. A–C. Written early 1971. Published in no. 9 and in *Plays: Two*. Eyre Methuen, 1978.
7. *Lear*. Mss. A–G. Written October 1969–early 1971. Eyre Methuen, 1972 (with 'Author's Preface'); reprinted 1975, 1976. Revised for *Plays: Two*. Eyre Methuen, 1978.
8. *The Sea. A Comedy*. Mss. A–H. Written April 1971–mid-1972. Eyre Methuen, 1973; reprinted 1975 (with 'Author's Note for Programmes'). Revised for *Plays: Two*. Eyre Methuen, 1978.
9. *Bingo. Scenes of Money and Death*. Mss. A–N. Written April 1973–late 1973. Eyre Methuen, 1974 (with 'Introduction'); reprinted 1975.
10. *The Fool. Scenes of Bread and Love*. Mss. A–R. Written March–October 1974. Eyre Methuen, 1976 (with 'Introduction' and 'Clare Poems').
11. *Stone. A Short Play*. Mss. A–G. Written February–May 1976. Published in no. 13 (with 'Author's Note').
12. *We Come to the River. Actions for Music in Two Parts and Eleven Scenes*. Mss. A–L. Written Autumn 1972–October 1974. Published in no. 10. *We Come to the River: libretto*. B. Schott's Söhne (Mainz, 1976).
13. *A-A-America!* (*Grandma Faust. A Burlesque* and *The Swing. A Documentary*). *Grandma Faust*. Mss. A-E. Written January-February 1976. *The Swing*. Mss. A–F. Written April–May 1976. Eyre Methuen, 1976.
14. *The Bundle or New Narrow Road to the Deep North*. Mss. A-E.

Written September 1977. Eyre Methuen, 1978 (with 'The Bundle Poems' and 'A Note on Dramatic Method').

15. *The Woman. Scenes of War and Freedom.* Mss. A–I. Written March 1974–April 1977. Eyre Methuen, 1979.
16. *The Worlds.* Eyre Methuen, 1980 (with 'The Activists Papers').
17. *Orpheus.* Unpublished.

Translations and Adaptations

18. *A Chaste Maid in Cheapside.* Adapted from the play by Middleton. Written November 1965. Unpublished.
19. *Three Sisters.* Translation of the play by Chekhov, with the assistance of Richard Cottrell. Written Autumn 1966. Published only in the programme of the original Royal Court production, April 1967.
20. *Spring Awakening.* Translation of the play by Wedekind. Written early 1974. Eyre Methuen, 1980 (with 'Introduction'). A version of the introduction appears as 'The Murder of Children', *Fireweed* 2, Summer 1975.
21. *The Master Builder.* Adapted from the play by Ibsen for American television. Written late 1974–early 1975. Unpublished.
22. *The White Devil.* An 'acting edition' of the play by Webster. Written May 1976. Unpublished.

Collected Works

Plays: One. Eyre Methuen, 1977 (*Saved, Early Morning, The Pope's Wedding*).

Plays: Two. Eyre Methuen, 1978 (*Lear, The Sea, Narrow Road to the Deep North, Black Mass, Passion*).

Theatre Poems and Songs, selected and edited by Malcolm Hay and Philip Roberts. Eyre Methuen, 1978.

3. *Other Works*

(a) *Prose* (unpublished, given in chronological order).

Ms. Sketchbook, 6 December 1959 to 10 March 1961.

'Workmen In', film synopsis, 1963.

'Plays', *c.* 1966.

'The Kite', short story, 29 March 1970.

'Exercises for Young Writers', 28 March 1977 (partly published, *Companion*, pp. 48–50).

(b) *Prose* (published, given in chronological order).

Letter to *Guardian*, 12 November 1965 (*Saved*).

Letter to *Evening Standard*, 21 November 1965 (*Saved*).

Letter to *Evening Standard*, 23 November 1965 (*Saved*).

'The Greatest Hack', *Guardian*, 13 January 1966 (on Thomas Middleton)
'Millstones round the Playwright's Neck', *Plays and Players*, April 1966.
'Censor in Mind', *Censorship*, Autumn 1966.
'Critics Reviewed', *The Critic*, 1 March 1968.
Mr. Dog (written 1968). *Gambit* 17, 45–7.
The King with Golden Eyes, written 8 December 1969. In *The Pope's Wedding*. Eyre Methuen, 1971.
Christ Wanders and Waits, written February–March 1970. In *Gambit* 17, 56–8 and *The Pope's Wedding*. Eyre Methuen, 1971.
'The Duke in Measure for Measure', *Gambit* 17, October 1970 (originally a letter to Keith Hack, 19 November 1969, for his Cambridge production and subsequently printed, in part, in the programme of the same director's production of the play for the Royal Shakespeare Company, 4 September 1974).
The Writer's Theatre (written February 1971). Issued with programme of *Lear*, Royal Court Theatre, 29 September 1971. In *Companion*, 43–4.
Reply to Roger Manvell's review of *Lear* (January 1972). *Humanist*, February 1972.
'Letter to Arthur Arnold', *Theatre Quarterly*, 2, 6, April–June 1972.
'Beating Barbarism', *Sunday Times*, 25 November 1973.
'Why I Back the Cultural Boycott', *Anti-Apartheid News*, April 1974 (partly reprinted in *Index on Censorship*, 4, 1, Spring 1975).
Programme note for *The Sea*, Manchester University Department of Drama, July 1974. In *Companion*, 54–5.
'Note by Edward Bond', for Elisabeth Bond-Pablé's translation of Kroetz's *Homeworker*, Half Moon Theatre, 21 November 1974. In *Companion*, 47–8.
'The Murder of Children', *Fireweed*, 2, Summer 1975 (extract from the Introduction to Bond's translation of *Spring Awakening*).
Service, written 1975. In *Fireweed*, 3, Autumn 1975; *New Writing and Writers*, 14 (Calder, 1977).
Programme note for *Lear*, Everyman Theatre, Liverpool, 9 October 1975. In *Companion*, 51–4.
Birthday tribute to Hans Werner Henze, B.B.C. Radio 3, 1 July 1976 (transcript available from B.B.C. Script Library).
Programme Note for *We Come to the River* (with Hans Werner Henze), Royal Opera House, Covent Garden, 12 July 1976. In *Companion*, 67–70.
'Work in hand', *Guardian*, 13 January 1978.
'On Brecht: a Letter to Peter Holland'. *Theatre Quarterly*, 8, 30, Summer 1978, 34–5.
'Us, Our Drama and the National Theatre', *Plays and Players*, October 1978.

4. *Interviews/Discussions* (given in chronological order).

Transcript of the 'Teach-In' on *Saved*, Royal Court, 14 November 1965. Unpublished.

Plays and Players, November 1965, with R. Cushman.

Isis, February 1966, with R. Jones.

Guardian, 11 April 1966, with D. Malcolm.

Town, May 1966, with J. Wilson.

Transatlantic Review, 22, 1966, 7–15, with G. Gordon; reprinted in *Behind the Scenes: Theatre and Film Interviews from the Transatlantic Review* (Pitman, 1971), 125–36.

'Thoughts on Contemporary Theatre' (edited transcript of a discussion at the Cheltenham Festival of Literature between John Willett, Ronald Bryden, Frank Marcus, Edward Bond, and David Storey), *New Theatre Magazine*, 7, 2, Spring 1967, 6–13.

Sunday Times, 31 March 1968, with A. Brien.

Evening News, 7 February 1969, with J. Green.

Observer, 9 February 1969, with R. Bryden.

Hornsey Journal, 14 February 1969.

'The Lively Arts', B.B.C. Third Programme, 26 March 1969, with E. Rhode (transcript available from B.B.C. Script Library).

Harpers Bazaar, March 1969, with S. Beauman.

Peace News, 10 April 1969, with A. Arnold.

Politika, 17 September 1969, with I. Besevic.

Telegraph and Argus, 27 September 1969, with C. Russell.

Weltwoche, 3 October 1969, with O. Trilling.

Vogue, October 1969, with M. Warner.

Theater Heute, November 1969, with W.D. Asmus.

Akzente, 16, December 1969, 578–83, with R. Taëni.

Broadsheet, 3 February 1970, with M. Cutler.

Transcript of 'Theatres outside London' Conference, Nottingham Playhouse, May 1970. In *Gambit* 17, 69–74.

A Discussion with Edward Bond (with Harold Hobson, Irving Wardle, Jane Howell, and John Calder), 22 January 1970. *Gambit*, 17, October 1970, 5–38.

Spektrum, March 1971.

Die Zeit, 16 April 1971, with R. Taëni.

Guardian, 29 September 1971, with J. Hall.

'Scan', B.B.C. Radio 4, 30 September 1971, with J. Mitchell (transcript available from B.B.C. Script Library).

New York Times, 2 January 1972, with C. Marowitz.

Theatre Quarterly, 2, 5, January–March 1972, 4–14, with the editors.

Die Presse, 8 May 1972, with G. Bohm.

Frankfurter Allgemeine Ztg, 29 September 1972, with G. Rühle.

Sipario, October 1972, 53–4, with R. de Baggis.

Kurier, 6 January 1973.
Wochenpresse, 10 January 1973.
Scena, Zeitschrift fur Theaterkunst, January – February 1973.
Vorarlberger Tageszeitung, 7 February 1973.
Times, 22 May 1973, with R. Hayman.
Neue Rundschau, 3, 1973, 571–6, with R. Taëni.
Baron Samedi, 2(1974), with M. Ferrand. In *Dartington Theatre Papers* (Second Series) 1978, no. 1, 1–8.
Observer, 11 August 1974, with H. Dawson.
Guardian, 15 August 1974, with H. Hebert.
Dagens Nyheter, 18 September 1974, with B. Hähnel.
Concourse, 25 October 1974, with P.S.
Chicago Tribune, 17 November 1974, with R. Dettmer.
De Tijd, 29 November 1974, with H. Tromp.
Spectaculum, 22, 1975, 271–5, with T. Thieringer.
Süddeutsche Zeitung, 11 August 1975, with T. Thieringer.
Liverpool Echo, 2 October 1975, with J. Riley.
Sunday Times, 2 November 1975, with P. Oakes.
'Kaleidoscope', B.B.C. Radio 4, 19 November 1975 (transcript available from B.B.C. Script Library).
Plays and Players, December 1975, with T. Coult.
New Haven Register, 25 January 1976, with M. Leech.
Time Out, 11–17 June 1976, with R. Krupp.
Gay News, 17–30 June 1976, with K. Howes.
Observer Magazine, 18 July 1976, with J. Walker.
Performing Arts Journal, 1, 2, Fall 1976, 37–45, with G. Loney.
Guardian, 24 November 1976, with N. de Jongh (objections in a letter by P. Roberts, *ibid.*, 30 November 1976.)
Twentieth Century Literature, 22, 4, December 1976, 411–22, with K.-H. Stoll.
Basler Zeitung, 18 February 1977, with O. Trilling.
Brückenbauer, 8, 25 February 1977, with S. Knecht.
British Council Tape Series, recorded 31 March 1977, with P. Roberts.
Time Out, 13–19 January 1978, with T. Coult.
Observer, 15 January 1978, with V. Radin.
Radio Times, 4–10 March 1978, with J. Emery.
Dartington Theatre Papers (Second Series, no. 1), 29 April 1978, with P. Hulton.
Morning Star, 18 August 1978, with C. Chambers.

5. *Correspondence*

Edward Bond to: The authors, 22 April 1979. Robert Brustein, 9 August 1972; 17 August 1972; 24 August 1972. N.J. Calarco, 16 June 1978.

Toby Cole, 4 December 1967; 8 April 1968; 25 November 1969; 6 April 1970; 15 September 1971; 25 January 1972; 6 July 1972. Tony Coult, 22 March 1971; 11 May 1971; 27 May 1971; 24 March 1975; 11 December 1975; 8 April 1976; 24 March 1977; 28 July 1977; 17 January 1978. Jane Dale, 6 January 1978. William Gaskill, 21 July 1970; 8 May 1971; 14 May 1971; 18 May 1971. Keith Hack, 19 November 1969. Malcolm Hay, 7 November 1978. Nicholas Hern, 25 May 1976; 6 June 1976; 6 November 1976; 1 February 1978. Mr. Hutchins, 14 April 1972. Ulric Innig, 18 March 1977. Irene –, 7 January 1970. Ruth Leeson, 14 January 1977. Christine Meyerson, 28 March 1977. Angela Praesent, 25 January 1977. Mr. Quinn, 25 May 1977. Margaret Ramsay, 10 April 1968; 7 August 1968; 31 November 1972; 6 March 1975. Robert –, 19 December 1977. Philip Roberts, 24 October 1976; 1 December 1976; 8 January 1977; 30 September 1977. Richard Scharine, 21 May 1971; 2 October 1974. Louis W. Scheeder, 27 September 1976. Geoffrey Strachan, 1 August 1966; 15 August 1967; 20 October 1969; 10 June 1970; 5 April 1971; 7 July 1971; 20 July 1971; 29 September 1971; 1 November 1971; 3 November 1971; 21 October 1973; 22 June 1975; 14 May 1976; 17 January 1978. H. Uwer, 28 August 1978. Les Waters, 18 June 1974. Michael Whitaker, 6 November 1969. Tom H. Wild, 16 January 1977.

——Robert Brustein to Bond, 14 July 1972; to Margaret Ramsay, 9 August 1972.

——Bill Bryden to Richard Scharine, 11 August 1971; to Tony Coult, 2 December 1971.

——George Devine to Bond, 17 April 1962; 13 December 1962; Memo to William Gaskill, 28 April 1965.

——Christian Enzensberger to the authors, 26 October 1976.

——Suzanne Findlay to Bond, 30 April 1963.

——Lawrence W. Fineberg to Bond, 19 January 1970.

——William Gaskill to Bond, 23 April 1965; to Richard Scharine, 19 March 1971; to Margaret Ramsay, 25 May 1973.

——Michael Geliot to Bond, 22 December 1958.

——Peter Gill to Tony Coult, 13 May 1971; to Richard Scharine, 12 August 1971.

——Keith Hack to Richard Scharine, 21 September 1971.

——Harold Hobson to Margaret Ramsay, 26 November 1975.

——Jane Howell to Richard Scharine, 6 July 1971.

——Peter James to Tony Coult, 27 May 1971.

——David Jones to Tony Coult, 16 September 1971; to Robert Brustein, 3 February 1972.

——Oscar Lewenstein to Margaret Ramsay, 21 January 1974.

——Margaret Ramsay to Toby Cole, 28 February 1969; to Bond, 20 July 1972; to Robert Brustein, 20 July 1972 and 18 August 1972; to William

Gaskill, 17 May 1973 and 25 May 1973; to J. Clarke, 15 October 1973; to R. Kidd and N. Wright, 31 January 1975; to Anne Jenkins, 20 February 1975; to Harold Hobson, 25 November 1975.
——Richard Scharine to Bond, 11 May 1971.
——Louis W. Scheeder to Bond, 22 September 1976; 27 September 1976.
——Alan Schneider to Margaret Ramsay, 3 November 1970; 4 December 1970.
——Geoffrey Strachan to Bond, 3 November 1971.
——Canon Verney to Tony Coult, 16 November 1970.
——William Woodman to his assistant director, 21 July 1974.

6. *Tape Recordings*

The following lists taped interviews used in the preparation of this book. Unless otherwise stated, the interviews are by the authors and took place in London.

Melvin Bernhardt (Director, *Early Morning*, New York, November, 1970). 16 October 1976. New York. Tape 13.
Jonathan Bolt (Director, *Bingo*, Cleveland, October 1975). 3 October 1976. New York. Tapes 12, 22.
Edward Bond
9 January 1975: 3 and 6 September 1975. Cambridge (Tony Coult). Tapes 1–3.
1 May 1975. Cambridge (S. McRoberts). Tape 4.
31 March 1977. Cambridge. Tape 55.
10 August 1977 (K. Worth). Tape 71.
21 December 1977 (Tony Coult). Tape 76.
1 May 1978. Lancaster. Tape 91.
13 June 1978. Tape 92.
17 August 1978 (Tony Coult). Tape 96.
15 September 1978. Cambridge. Tapes 97–9.
David Carson (Director, *Saved*, Leeds, May 1973; The *Sea*, Canterbury, July 1975). 23 March 1977. Canterbury. Tapes 48, 49.
Gerald Chapman (Director, *Saved*, Leicester, January 1974; *Stone*, London, June 1976). 19 June; 5 July 1976; 26 July 1977. Tapes 29, 30, 32, 70. Members of the *Stone* company, 16, 19, 22, 25 June 1976. Tapes 29, 30, 31.
Deirdre Clancy (Designer, *Early Morning*, London, March 1968 and March 1969; *Lear*, London, September 1971 (costume); *Lear*, Munich, January 1973 (costume); *The Sea*, London, May 1973; *Spring Awakening*, London, May 1974 (costume); *The White Devil*, London, July 1976 (costume). 12 July 1977. Tape 56.
Louis Criss (Director, *Narrow Road . . .*, Boston, October 1969). 22 November 1976. New Haven. Tape 14.

Ron Daniels (Director, *Bingo*, New Haven, January 1976). 21 January 1977. Tapes 43, 44.

Howard Davies (Director, *Narrow Road . . .*, Bristol, May 1971; *Early Morning*, Bristol, May 1973; *Bingo*, Stratford, November 1976; *The Bundle*, London, January 1978). 22 December 1976. Stratford; 25 July 1977; 21 December 1977 (Tony Coult); 13 January 1978. Tapes 36–7, 67–8, 76–7. Members of the company of *The Bundle*. Tapes 79, 80, 81.

John Dillon (Director, *The Sea*, Sarasota, May 1975). 19 November 1976. New York. Tapes 18–19.

William Dudley (Designer, *The Fool*, London, November 1975). 19 July 1977. Tapes 62, 81.

Christopher Dyer (Designer, *Early Morning*, Bristol, May 1973; *Bingo*, Stratford, November 1976; *The Bundle*, London, January 1978). 25 July 1977; 13 January 1978. Tapes 67–8, 77, 78.

Jack Emery (Director, *A-A-America!*, London, October – November 1976). 19 July 1977. Tapes 63–4. Members of the company, 29 October 1976. Tape 34.

David Giles (Director, *Lear*, New Haven, April 1973). 18 July 1977. Tape 60.

William Gaskill (Director, *Saved*, London, November 1965 and February 1969; *A Chaste Maid in Cheapside*, London, January 1966; *Three Sisters*, London April 1967; *Early Morning*, London, March 1968 and March 1969; *Lear*, London, September 1971 and Munich, January 1973; *The Sea*, London, May 1973). 22 March 1977 and 15 July 1977. Tapes 47, 57–8.

Peter Gill (Director, *The Fool*, London, November 1975). 29 March 1977. Tape 52.

Richard Gregson (Assistant Producer, *We Come to the River*, London, July 1976). 14 April 1978. Tapes 87–8.

Hayden Griffin (Designer, *Narrow Road . . .*, Coventry, June 1968; London, February 1969; Exeter, April 1971; *Three Sisters*, Exeter, September 1971; *Lear*, Vienna, January 1973; *Bingo*, Exeter, November 1973; *The Woman*, London, August 1978; *The Worlds*, Newcastle, March 1979). 29 March 1978. Tapes 81, 86.

John Gunter, (Designer, *Saved*, London, November 1965 and February 1969; *The Sea*, Vienna, May 1974; *The White Devil*, London, July 1976; *We Come to the River*, Cologne, May 1977). 29 March 1977. Tapes 53–4.

Giles Havergal (Director, *Early Morning*, Glasgow, February 1971). 16 July 1977. Tape 69.

Hans Werner Henze (Composer, *We Come to the River*, London, July 1976). 7 January 1978; 14 April 1978. Tape 75.

Jane Howell (Director, *Narrow Road . . .*, Coventry, June 1968;

London, February 1969; Exeter, April 1971; *The Sea*, B.B.C. T.V., March 1978; *Bingo*, Exeter, November 1973; *Three Sisters*, Exeter, September 1971). 26 July 1977; 18 November 1977. Tapes 69, 74.

Marvin Kahan (Director, *Saved*, New York, October 1976). 20 November 1976. New York. Tapes 11–12.

Jonathan Marks (literary manager, Yale rep.). 22 November 1976. New Haven. Tape 17.

Christopher Martin (Director, *Bingo*, New York, October 1976). 16 October 1976. New York. Tapes 11–12. Members of the company. Tape 17.

Bob Peck (Actor, *Bingo*, Exeter, November 1973; *The Bundle*, London, January 1978). 19 January 1978. Tape 79.

Philip Prowse (Designer, *Saved*, Glasgow, March 1972; *Early Morning*, Glasgow, February 1971; director, *Early Morning*, Glasgow, May 1974). 18 July 1977. Tape 61.

Roland Rees (Director, *Black Mass*, London, December 1970). 21 January 1977. Tape 38.

Louis Scheeder (Director, *The Fool*, Washington, October 1976). 30 October 1976. Washington. Tapes 24–6. Members of the company. Tapes 27–8.

Alan Schneider (Director, *Saved*, New York, October 1970). 1 November 1976. New York. Tape 9.

Jack Shepherd (Actor, *Early Morning*, London, March 1969; *Narrow Road* . . ., London, February 1969). 31 August 1977. Tapes 72–3.

Patrick Stewart (Actor, *Bingo*, Stratford, November 1976; *The Bundle*, London, January 1978). 19 January 1978. Tape 79.

Secondary Sources (*a selected list*)

M. Anderson, 'On the Side of Life', *Plays and Players*, March 1973 (Jane Howell at the Northcott Theatre, Exeter).

P. Ansorge, 'Directors in Interview, No.2: Jane Howell', *Plays and Players*, October 1968 (interview with the director of *Narrow Road* at the Belgrade, Coventry, and Royal Court).

P. Ansorge, 'Glittering in the Gorbals', *Plays and Players*, April 1974 (comments by Philip Prowse on his designs for *Saved* at the Citizens' Theatre, Glasgow).

P. Ansorge, *Disrupting the Spectacle* (Pitman, 1975), *passim*.

A. Arnold, 'Private Lusts and Public Nightmares', *Peace News*, 28 March 1969 (critique of *Saved, Early Morning, Narrow Road*).

A. Arnold, 'Lines of Development in Bond's Plays', *Theatre Quarterly*, 2, 5, January-March 1972, 15–19 (for Bond's reply to this article, see 3(b), above).

A. Baiwir, 'Le Théâtre d'Edward Bond', *Revue de l'université de*

Bruxelles, February–March 1971, 192–211 (analysis of the plays from *Pope's Wedding* to *Narrow Road*).

A.K.H. Barth, 'The Aggressive "Theatrum Mundi" of Edward Bond: *Narrow Road to the Deep North*', *Modern Drama*, 18, 2, June 1975, 189–200 (attempts to relate the play to 'the European tradition of tragic and religious drama').

J.R. Brown, 'Edward Bond', Programme for Royal Opera House, Covent Garden production of *We Come To The River*, first published in *About the House* (the magazine of The Friends of Covent Garden), Spring 1976 (brief consideration of a number of the plays).

T. Browne, *Playwrights' Theatre: The English Stage Company at the Royal Court* (Pitman, 1975), *passim*. (a history of the English Stage Company, incorporating numerous references to Bond and tables of figures on productions).

R. Bryden, *The Unfinished Hero* (Faber, 1969; Bryden's *New Statesman* reviews of *Saved*).

D. Clancy, 'Drawings for Lear', *Ambit*, 68 (1976), 93–5 (sketches of designs for *Lear* at the Royal Court).

R. Cohn, *Modern Shakespeare Offshoots* (Princeton University Press, 1976), 254–66 (study of *Lear* in relation to Shakespeare's *King Lear*).

T. Coult, *The Plays of Edward Bond* (Eyre Methuen, 1978).

M. Coveney, 'Space Odyssey', *Plays and Players*, June 1976 (interview with John Napier, Hayden Griffin, and William Dudley, with references to the designs for *Lear, Bingo* and *The Fool*).

I. van Dijk-van Lieshout, 'A Theatrical Approach to an Analysis of Edward Bond's *The Sea*', unpublished thesis, University of Utrecht, September 1976.

J.E. Duncan, 'The Child and the Old Man in the Plays of Edward Bond', *Modern Drama*, 19, 1, March 1976, 1–10 (on the recurrence of these figures in the plays).

E. Durbach, 'Herod in the Welfare State: *Kindermord* in the Plays of Edward Bond', *Educational Theatre Journal*, 27, 4, December 1975, 480–7 (an attempt to demonstrate that 'the metaphor of child-murder' in *Saved* and *Narrow Road* represents a tragic vision).

J. Elsom, *London Magazine*, May 1969 (on the Royal Court Season, 1969).

M. Esslin, *Brief Chronicles* (Temple Smith, 1970).

M. Esslin, ed., *The New Theatre in Europe* (New York: Dell, 1970; introduction to *Saved*, also discussing German dialect translations of the play).

M. Esslin, 'The Theatre of Edward Bond', *Times Educational Supplement*, 24 September 1971 (mainly on 'realism' and Bond's plays).

R. Fagles and W.B. Stanford (eds.), *The Oresteia* (Penguin, 1977).

R. Fricker, *Das moderne englische Drama* (Göttingen: Vandenhoeck and Ruprecht, 1974), 197–202 (discussion of the plays up to *The Sea*).
H. Gamper, 'Der Dramatiker Edward Bond', *Volksbühnen-Spiegel*, 718, 70, 22–3 (sympathetic analysis of the plays to *Narrow Road*).
W. Gaskill, 'William Gaskill on *Saved*', *Royal Court Theatre Programme*, 2 December 1965 – January 1966.
S. Gooch, 'Gaskill in Germany', *Plays and Players*, April 1973.
G. Gow, 'Putting on the Style', *Plays and Players*, August 1973 (comments by Deirdre Clancy on her designs for *The Sea* at the Royal Court).
K. Gross, 'Darstellungsprinzipien im Drama Edward Bonds', *Die neuren Sprachen*, June 1973, 313–24 (analysis of language and structure in *Lear, Early Morning, Narrow Road*).
V. Hagnell, *Entré*, 1, 1977 (interview with Jack Emery, director of *A-A-America!*).
G. Hardin (ed.), *Science, Conflict and Society: Readings from Scientific American* (San Francisco, W. H. Freeman, 1969).
M. Hay and P. Roberts, 'Edward Bond: Stages in a Life', *Observer*, 6 August 1978.
H. Hobson, 'British Theatre: Matters of Fact and Violence', *Christian Science Monitor*, 24 January 1969 (references to *Saved, Early Morning* and *Narrow Road*).
P. Holland, 'Brecht, Bond, Gaskill, and the Practice of Political Theatre', *Theatre Quarterly*, 8, 30, Summer 1978, 24–34.
P. Hulton, 'An Interview with Howard Davies', *Dartington Theatre Papers* (Second Series), no. 1, 1978, 9–17.
A. Hunt, 'A Writer's Theatre', *New Society*, 11 December 1975, 606–7 (claims that Bond's preoccupation with 'a writer's theatre' is self-indulgent and has prevented the acceptance of his plays).
C. Hunt, 'Henze and Bond Break Down Barriers', *Opera*, July 1976, 602–5 (description of the structure and range of *We Come To The River*).
P. Iden, 'Was müssen wir uns antun um zu überleben?', *Frankfurter Rundschau*, 1 December 1973 (general analysis of Bond's ideas in plays up to *The Sea*).
P. Iden, 'Uns verändernd: über Ionescos, Müllers, Bonds Stück nach Shakespeare', *Theater Heute*, Jahressonderheft, 1972, 32–9 (comparative analysis of three adaptations of Shakespeare, including Bond's *Lear*).
P. Iden, *Edward Bond* (Velber bei Hanover: Friedrich, 1973; short book of basic information about the plays).
A. Jellicoe, 'Royal Court Theatre Writers' Group', *Ambit*, 68 (1976), 61–4 (account of the formation and work of the group, including

Bond's part in it).
D. A. N. Jones, 'British Playwrights', *The Listener*, 8 August 1968, 161–3.
D. A. N. Jones, 'A Unique Style of Theatre', *Nova*, July 1969, 39–42 (Bond's style of theatre as represented by *Saved, Early Morning* and *Narrow Road*).
H.–K. Jungheinrich, 'Zwei Autoren nähern sich einem Stoff', *Akzente*, April 1977, 168–76 (Henze and Bond's collaboration on *We Come To The River*).
E. King, 'Violence in *Lear* Defended', *New Haven Register*, April 1973 (interview with David Giles, director of Yale Repertory Company's *Lear*).
G. Klotz, 'Erbezitat und Zeitlose Gewalt', *Weimarer Beiträge*, 19, 10, 1973, 54–65 (criticizing Bond's élitist position, especially in *Lear*).
Lear: tape of Royal Court production (September 1971), British Institute of Recorded Sound.
E. MacCurdy (transl.), *The Notebooks of Leonardo da Vinci*, 2 vols. (Cape, 1938).
G. Mander, 'Die Goya Welt des Edward Bond', *Theater Heute*, May 1976, 37–8 (*Saved, Early Morning* and *Narrow Road* seen in the English literary tradition).
G. Mander, 'Geschichten die ein Idiot erzählt', *Theater Heute*, January 1976, 25–7 (*Bingo* and *The Fool* discussed together).
C. Marowitz, *Confessions of a Counterfeit Critic* (Eyre Methuen, 1973; reprints his reviews of *Early Morning, Lear*, and *Three Sisters*, with introductory comments).
U. H. Mehlin, 'Die Behandlung von Liebe und Aggression in Shakespeare's *Romeo and Juliet* und in Edward Bond's *Saved*', *Jahrbuch der Deutschen Shakespeare – Gesellschaft West*, 1970, 132–59 (analysis of the themes of love and aggression in the two plays).
S. Melchinger, 'Veränderer: Ionesco, Bond, Müller und Shakespeare – kein Vergleich', *Theater Heute*, Jahressonderheft, 1972, 30–2 (comparative analysis of three adaptations of Shakespeare's plays, including Bond's *Lear*).
M. Mindlin, *Forum World Features*, week of 27 November 1965 (on *Saved*).
M. F. A. Montagu, *Man and Agression* (OUP, 1968).
A. Muller, 'Über die Fortschrittlichkeit des Grässlichen', *Kurbiskern*, 2, 1973, 354–61; and as 'Über die linken Greuel', *Theater der Zeit*, 4, 1973, 31–3 (criticism of Bond's political views as shown in *Lear*).
I. Nagel, 'Die bösen Märchen des Edward Bond', *Theater Heute*, November 1969, 38–9 (on *Saved, Early Morning*, and *Narrow Road*).
B. Nightingale, 'Irrational Hostilities', *New Statesman*, 21 March 1969 (on *Saved, Early Morning*, and *Narrow Road*).

H. Oppel and S. Christenson, *Edward Bond's Lear and Shakespeare's King Lear* (Mainz: Akademie der Wissenschaften und der Literatur, 1974; consists of two articles: H. Oppel, 'Success and Failure of Bond's Approach to Shakespeare's Tragedy', and S. Christenson, 'The Common Man in Bond's *Lear* and Shakespeare's *King Lear*').

E. Pablé, *Die Presse*, 9 April 1969 (on the Bond season at the Royal Court).

M.–C. Pasquier, 'La Place d'Edward Bond dans le Nouveau Théâtre Anglais', *Cahiers de la Compagnie Madeleine Renaud et Jean-Louis Barrault*, 74, 1970, 21–35 (general discussion of the staging of Bond's plays up to 1969, in the context of the post-war British theatre).

M.–C. Pasquier, 'Coherence Naissante d'une Oeuvre', *ibid.*, 36–57 (short study of *The Pope's Wedding, Saved, Early Morning,* and *Narrow Road*).

M.–C. Pasquier, *Bref* 144, December 1971, and 145, January 1972 (Théâtre National Populaire programme pieces on *Saved*).

J. Peter, 'Edward Bond, Violence and Poetry', *Drama*, Autumn 1975, 28–32 (a discussion of *Bingo* in the context of the earlier plays).

G. Restivo, *La Nuova Scena Inglese: Edward Bond* (Turin: Einaudi 1977).

H. Rischbieter, 'Der vage Web der Anarchie', *Theater Heute*, November 1969, 30–2 (on *Narrow Road* and *Early Morning*).

P. Roberts, 'Political Metaphors: The Plays of Edward Bond', *New Edinburgh Review*, 30, August 1975, 34–5.

R. Scharine, *The Plays of Edward Bond* (Lewisburg: Bucknell University Press; Associated University Presses, 1976).

C. H. Southwick, *Animal Aggression* (New York: Van Nostrand Reinhold Co., 1970).

K.–H. Stoll, *The New British Drama* (Bern: Lang, 1975; a bibliography with particular reference to Arden, Bond, Osborne, Pinter and Wesker).

G. Stratmann, 'Lear 1971', *Das zeitgenössische englische Drama* (Athenäum, Fischer, 1975), 274–98 (detailed analysis of *Lear* seen in terms of Bond's social and political views).

B. Strauss, 'Weltflucht und Mord', *Theater Heute*, Jahresband 1970, 88–9 (study of *Pope's Wedding*, stressing links with *Saved*).

R. Taëni, 'Der Dramatiker Edward Bond', *Akzente*, 16, 12, 1969, 564–77 (development of Bond's themes from *Saved* to *Narrow Road*).

J.R. Taylor, *The Second Wave* (Eyre Methuen, 1971), 77–93 (consideration of the plays up to *Passion*).

Theatre Quarterly, 2, 5, January-March 1972, 20–31: G. Dark, 'Production Casebook No. 5: Edward Bond's "Lear" at the Royal Court' (rehearsal log by William Gaskill's assistant director).

Theatre Quarterly, 6, 21, Spring 1976, 12–44: W. Donohue, 'Production Casebook No. 21: Edward Bond's "The Fool" at the Royal Court Theatre' (a collage of the responses of the actors to working on the play); P. Gill, 'Coming Fresh to the Fool' (an interview with the director); Edward Bond, 'An Introduction to "The Fool" (first publication; M. Esslin, 'Nor Yet a "Fool" to Fame . . .' (survey of the critical response to the Royal Court production).

Toneelgroep Centrum, 16 February 1968 (issue of the theatre's newspaper on forthcoming production of *Saved*; includes interviews with the director and actors).

L. Truchlar, 'Edward Bond', in H. W. Drescher, ed., *Englische Literatur der Gegenwart* (Stuttgart, Kronër, 1970), 476–92 (general interpretation of Bond's ideas as contained in the plays up to *Narrow Road*).

L. Truchlar, '*Lear*, oder die Pornographie der Gewalt', *Revue des Langues Vivantes*, 41, 1975, 133–8 (general article on political theatre with reference to *Lear*).

S. Trussler, *Edward Bond* (Harlow: Longman, 1976; a short detailed study of the plays up to *Bingo*).

I. Wardle, 'Dramatic Criticism Today', *Listener*, 21 April 1966 (on confusions in theatre criticism, using *Saved* as an example).

I. Wardle, 'Interview with William Gaskill', *Gambit*, 17, October 1970, 38–43 (on Bond's work at the Royal Court, from the Writers' Group onwards, and Gaskill's productions of *Saved* and *Early Morning*).

I. Wardle, 'The British Sixties', *Performance*, 1, 1, December 1971, 174–81 (on Bond's vision of society).

I. Wardle, 'Le Théâtre d'Edward Bond', *Travail Théâtral*, Autumn 1972, 143–8.

E. F. Watling (transl.), *The Theban Plays*, Penguin, 1949.

E. Wendt, *Moderne Dramaturgie* (Frankfurt: Suhrkamp, 1973), 19–37 (Bond's plays up to *Lear*, discussed together with Genet's).

J. Willett, *The Theatre of Bertolt Brecht* (Methuen, 1959), revised edition (Eyre Methuen, 1977).

J. Willett (ed.), *Brecht on Theatre* (Methuen, 1964), reprinted 1965.

K. Worth, *Revolutions in Modern English Drama* (Bell, 1972), 168–87 (study of the plays up to *Lear*).

J. Worthen, 'Endings and Beginnings: Edward Bond and the Shock of Recognition', *Educational Theatre Journal*, 27, 4, December 1975, 466–79 (good account of the positive intention and effects of Bond's plays up to *Bingo*).

N. Yuasa (transl. and ed.), *The Narrow Road to the Deep North and Other Travel Sketches*, Penguin, 1966, reprinted 1975.

Index